D1201580

QUINTESSENCE

Basic Readings from the Philosophy of

W. V. Quine

Edited by Roger F. Gibson, Jr.

The Belknap Press of Harvard University Press

Cambridge, Massachusetts

London, England

2004

Copyright © 2004 by the President and Fellows of Harvard College
All rights reserved
Printed in the United States of America

Library of Congress Cataloging-in-Publication Data

Quine, W. V. (Willard Van Orman)
[Selections. 2004]
Quintessence : basic readings from the philosophy of
W. V. Quine / edited by Roger F. Gibson, Jr.
p. cm.
Includes bibliographical references and index.
ISBN 0-674-01048-5 (alk. paper)
1. Philosophy.   I. Gibson, Roger F.   II. Title.
B945.Q51G53 2004   2003067682
·   191—dc22

QUINTESSENCE

PREFACE

When W. V. Quine gave the first of his three Paul Carus Lectures at a meeting of the American Philosophical Association in New York in December 1971, his Harvard colleague and good friend, Nelson Goodman, was on hand to introduce him. There are two memorable aspects of Goodman's introduction. First, it is strewn with hilarious plays on words and insider jokes—exactly Quine's brand of humor. Here is a sample:

> The title of Professor Quine's best-known philosophy book is *Word and Object*. From the title of these lectures ["The Roots of Reference"], I gather he is going to discuss an important relation of words to objects—or better, of words to other objects, some of which are not words—or even better, of objects some of which are words to objects some of which are not words. . . .
>
> In Professor Quine's many encounters with reference he has always insisted on such sterling principles as: "Don't refer to what isn't"; "Don't suppose that merely by talking you are saying anything about anything"; but on the other hand, "If you do say something about something, don't think you can escape the consequences by saying you were only talking."
>
> I have no idea what the roots of reference are, but I suppose that whatever has powers, as reference does, also has roots. But here I am probably guilty, in the language of *Methods of Logic*, of making, in the full sweep of a fell swoop, what amounts to a full swap or even a foul swipe.[1]

1. This and the following quotation are taken from the introduction to Quine's *The Roots of Reference* (La Salle, Ill.: Open Court, 1974), pp. xi–xii.

Second, in a more serious vein, Goodman noted that "it is high time for a meta-anthology drawn from the anthologies of his own works already published." Goodman, we now see, was a visionary as well as a humorist, ahead of his time by some thirty-three years.

All of the selections in this volume have been previously published, although not all of them are taken from Quine's anthologies; some are drawn from book chapters and some from journals. During the selection process I worked with three very knowledgeable outside readers engaged by Harvard University Press. One of the considerations affecting the contents was our desire to produce a book which would be useful to the Quine specialist and yet accessible to the Quine novice. Toward that end, we included both classic essays and expository essays. For example, we included Quine's classic "Two Dogmas of Empiricism" and his expository "Two Dogmas in Retrospect." Another consideration affecting the contents was convenience: the availability of these essays in a single volume will, we hope, prove convenient for the expert and the novice alike. Finally, in the same vein we decided not to include any of Quine's technical writings on logic.

Readers should note that Chapters 6, 7, and 12 were originally part of longer essays, and therefore they contain cross-references to sections that are not part of the present volume. For the convenience of readers who may want to consult the original work, we have left all these cross-references in place. The publication history of each essay is given in the Credits section at the back of the book.

Quine's writings of the 1930s and the 1940s were primarily about technical matters of logic. However, the publication in 1953 of his anthology *From a Logical Point of View: Nine Logico-Philosophical Essays* indicated that he had begun to widen his philosophical horizon: Quine the logician was also Quine the philosopher. He continued to publish in both fields throughout his career.

Quine's discursive philosophy includes discussions on the following topics, among others: analyticity, synonymy, indeterminacy of translation of theoretical sentences, propositions, indeterminacy of reference (or inscrutability of reference, or ontological relativity), underdetermination of physical theory, holism, naturalism, empiricism, behaviorism, extensionalism, and so on. It is important to see, however, that Quine's philosophy is systematic. He once remarked that the bulk of his philosophy consists of corollaries to his commitments to naturalism (see

"Epistemology Naturalized") and extensionalism (see "Confessions of a Confirmed Extensionalist").

The secondary literature on Quine is burgeoning. For example, there are a number of book-length introductions to Quine's philosophy, including my *The Philosophy of W. V. Quine: An Expository Essay* (Tampa: University Presses of Florida, 1982) and *Enlightened Empiricism: An Examination of W. V. Quine's Theory of Knowledge* (Tampa: University Presses of Florida, 1988); Christopher Hookway's *Quine: Language, Experience, and Reality* (Stanford, Calif.: Stanford University Press, 1988); and Alex Orenstein's *W. V. Quine* (Princeton, N.J.: Princeton University Press, 2002).

Important anthologies on Quine's philosophy include *Words and Objections: Essays on the Work of W. V. Quine,* ed. D. Davidson and J. Hintikka (Dordrecht: D. Reidel, 1969); *The Philosophy of W. V. Quine,* ed. L. Hahn and P. Schilpp (La Salle, Ill.: Open Court, 1986); *Perspectives on Quine,* ed. R. Barrett and R. Gibson (Oxford: Blackwell, 1990); *On Quine: New Essays,* ed. P. Leonardi and M. Santambrogio (Cambridge: Cambridge University Press, 1995); *Knowledge, Language, and Logic: Questions for Quine,* ed. P. Kotatko and A. Orenstein (Dordrecht: Kluwer, 2000).

Of special interest is Quine's *The Time of My Life: An Autobiography* (Cambridge, Mass.: MIT Press, 1985).

Finally, there is an invaluable, award-winning Web site maintained by Quine's son, Dr. Douglas Quine, at *http://wvquine.org.*

Roger F. Gibson, Jr.
St. Louis, October 2003

CONTENTS

I

ANALYTICITY AND REDUCTIONISM

II

INDETERMINACY AND INSCRUTABILITY

III

ONTOLOGY

IV

EPISTEMOLOGY AND PHILOSOPHY OF MIND

V

EXTENSIONALISM

QUINTESSENCE

I

ANALYTICITY AND REDUCTIONISM

1

TRUTH BY CONVENTION

The less a science has advanced, the more its terminology tends to rest on an uncritical assumption of mutual understanding. With increase of rigor this basis is replaced piecemeal by the introduction of definitions. The interrelationships recruited for these definitions gain the status of analytic principles; what was once regarded as a theory about the world becomes reconstrued as a convention of language. Thus it is that some flow from the theoretical to the conventional is an adjunct of progress in the logical foundations of any science. The concept of simultaneity at a distance affords a stock example of such development: in supplanting the uncritical use of this phrase by a definition, Einstein so chose the definitive relationship as to verify conventionally the previously paradoxical principle of the absoluteness of the speed of light. But whereas the physical sciences are generally recognized as capable only of incomplete evolution in this direction, and as destined to retain always a nonconventional kernel of doctrine, developments of the past few decades have led to a widespread conviction that logic and mathematics are purely analytic or conventional. It is less the purpose of the present inquiry to question the validity of this contrast than to question its sense.

I

A definition, strictly, is a convention of notational abbreviation.[1] A *simple* definition introduces some specific expression, e.g., 'kilometer,' or '*e*,' called the *definiendum*, as arbitrary shorthand for some complex expres-

1. See Bertrand Russell, *Principles of Mathematics* (Cambridge: Cambridge University Press, 1903), p. 429.

sion, e.g., 'a thousand meters' or ' $\lim\limits_{n\to\infty}\left(1+\dfrac{1}{n}\right)^{n}$ ', called the *definiens*. A *contextual* definition sets up indefinitely many mutually analogous pairs of definienda and definientia according to some general scheme; an example is the definition whereby expressions of the form $\dfrac{\text{'sin}---\text{'}}{\cos---}$ are abbreviated as 'tan – – –.' From a formal standpoint the signs thus introduced are wholly arbitrary; all that is required of a definition is that it be theoretically immaterial, i.e., that the shorthand which it introduces admit in every case of unambiguous elimination in favor of the antecedent longhand.[2]

Functionally a definition is not a premise to theory, but a license for rewriting theory by putting definiens for definiendum or vice versa. By allowing such replacements a definition transmits truth: it allows true statements to be translated into new statements which are true by the same token. Given the truth of the statement 'The altitude of Kibo exceeds six thousand meters,' the definition of 'kilometer' makes for the truth of the statement 'The altitude of Kibo exceeds six kilometers'; given the truth of the statement $\dfrac{\text{'sin}\,\pi}{\cos\pi}=\dfrac{\sin\pi\text{'}}{\cos\pi}$, of which logic assures us in its earliest pages, the contextual definition cited above makes for the truth of the statement 'tan $\pi = \dfrac{\sin\pi}{\cos\pi}$'. In each case the statement inferred through the definition is true only because it is shorthand for another statement which was true independently of the definition. Considered in isolation from all doctrine, including logic, a definition is incapable of grounding the most trivial statement; even 'tan $\pi = \dfrac{\sin\pi}{\cos\pi}$' is a definitional transformation of an antecedent self-identity, rather than a spontaneous consequence of the definition.

What is loosely called a logical consequence of definitions is therefore

---

2. From the present point of view a contextual definition may be recursive, but can then count among its definienda only those expressions in which the argument of recursion has a constant value, since otherwise the requirement of eliminability is violated. Such considerations are of little consequence, however, since any recursive definition can be turned into a direct one by purely logical methods. See Rudolf Carnap, *Logische Syntax der Sprache* (Vienna: Springer, 1934), pp. 23, 79. Translation with additions: *The Logical Syntax of Language* (New York: Harcourt, Brace; and London: Kegan Paul, 1937).

more exactly describable as a logical truth definitionally abbreviated: a statement which becomes a truth of logic when definienda are replaced by definientia. In this sense '$\tan \pi = \dfrac{\sin \pi}{\cos \pi}$' is a logical consequence of the contextual definition of the tangent.

Whatever may be agreed upon as the exact scope of logic, we may expect definitional abbreviations of logical truths to be reckoned as logical rather than extra-logical truths. This being the case, the preceding conclusion shows logical consequences of definitions to be themselves truths of logic. To claim that mathematical truths are conventional in the sense of following logically from definitions is therefore to claim that mathematics is part of logic. The latter claim does not represent an arbitrary extension of the term 'logic' to include mathematics; agreement as to what belongs to logic and what belongs to mathematics is supposed at the outset, and it is then claimed that definitions of mathematical expressions can so be framed on the basis of logical ones that all mathematical truths become abbreviations of logical ones.

Although signs introduced by definition are formally arbitrary, more than such arbitrary notational convention is involved in questions of definability; otherwise any expression might be said to be definable on the basis of any expressions whatever. When we speak of definability, or of finding a definition for a given sign, we have in mind some traditional usage of the sign antecedent to the definition in question. To be satisfactory in this sense a definition of the sign not only must fulfill the formal requirement of unambiguous eliminability, but must also conform to the traditional usage in question. For such conformity it is necessary and sufficient that every context of the sign which was true and every context which was false under traditional usage be construed by the definition as an abbreviation of some other statement which is correspondingly true or false under the established meanings of its signs. Thus when definitions of mathematical expressions on the basis of logical ones are said to have been framed, what is meant is that definitions have been set up whereby every statement which so involves those mathematical expressions as to be recognized traditionally as true, or as false, is construed as an abbreviation of another correspondingly true or false statement which lacks those mathematical expressions and exhibits only logical expressions in their stead.[3]

3. Note that an expression is said to be defined, in terms, e.g., of logic, not only when it is a single sign whose elimination from a context in favor of logical expres-

An expression will be said to occur *vacuously* in a given statement if its replacement therein by any and every other grammatically admissible expression leaves the truth or falsehood of the statement unchanged. Thus for any statement containing some expressions vacuously there is a class of statements, describable as *vacuous variants* of the given statement, which are like it in point of truth or falsehood, like it also in point of a certain skeleton of symbolic make-up, but diverse in exhibiting all grammatically possible variations upon the vacuous constituents of the given statement. An expression will be said to occur *essentially* in a statement if it occurs in all the vacuous variants of the statement, i.e., if it forms part of the aforementioned skeleton. (Note that though an expression occur non-vacuously in a statement it may fail of essential occurrence because some of its parts occur vacuously in the statement.)

Now let S be a truth, let the expressions E_i occur vacuously in S, and let the statements S_j be the vacuous variants of S. Thus the S_j will likewise be true. On the sole basis of the expressions belonging to a certain class α, let us frame a definition for one of the expressions F occurring in S outside the E_i. S and the S_i thereby become abbreviations of certain statements S' and S'_i which exhibit only members of α instead of those occurrences of F, but which remain so related that the S'_i are all the results of replacing the E_i in S' by any other grammatically admissible expressions. Now since our definition of F is supposed to conform to usage, S' and the S'_i will, like S and the S_i, be uniformly true; hence the S'_i will be vacuous variants of S', and the occurrences of the E_i in S' will be vacuous. The definition thus makes S an abbreviation of a truth S' which, like S, involves the E_i vacuously, but which differs from S in exhibiting only members of α instead of the occurrences of F outside the E_i. Now it is obvious that an expression cannot occur essentially in a statement if it occurs only within expressions which occur vacuously in the statement; consequently F, occurring in S' as it does only within the E_i if at all, does not occur essentially in S'; members of α occur essentially in its stead. Thus if we take F as any nonmember of α occurring essentially in S, and repeat the above reasoning for each such expression, we see that, through definitions of all such expressions in terms of members of α, S becomes an abbreviation of a truth S'' involving only members of α essentially.

Thus if in particular we take α as the class of all logical expressions,

---

sions is accomplished by a single application of one definition, but also when it is a complex expression whose elimination calls for successive application of many definitions.

the above tells us that if logical definitions be framed for all non-logical expressions occurring essentially in the true statement S, S becomes an abbreviation of a truth S'' involving only logical expressions essentially. But if S'' involves only logical expressions essentially, and hence remains true when everything except that skeleton of logical expressions is changed in all grammatically possible ways, then S'' depends for its truth upon those logical constituents alone, and is thus a truth of logic. It is therefore established that if all non-logical expressions occurring essentially in a true statement S be given definitions on the basis solely of logic, then S becomes an abbreviation of a truth S'' of logic. In particular, then, if all mathematical expressions be defined in terms of logic, all truths involving only mathematical and logical expressions essentially become definitional abbreviations of truths of logic.

Now a mathematical truth, for example, 'Smith's age plus Brown's equals Brown's age plus Smith's,' may contain non-logical, non-mathematical expressions. Still any such mathematical truth, or another whereof it is a definitional abbreviation, will consist of a skeleton of mathematical or logical expressions filled in with non-logical, non-mathematical expressions all of which occur vacuously. Every mathematical truth either is a truth in which only mathematical and logical expressions occur essentially, or is a definitional abbreviation of such a truth. Hence, granted definitions of all mathematical expressions in terms of logic, the preceding conclusion shows that all mathematical truths become definitional abbreviations of truths of logic—therefore truths of logic in turn. For the thesis that mathematics is logic it is thus sufficient that all mathematical notation be defined on the basis of logical notation.

If on the other hand some mathematical expressions resist definition on the basis of logical ones, then every mathematical truth containing such recalcitrant expressions must contain them only inessentially, or be a definitional abbreviation of a truth containing such expressions only inessentially, if all mathematics is to be logic: for though a logical truth may involve non-logical expressions, it or some other logical truth whereof it is an abbreviation must involve only logical expressions essentially. It is of this alternative that those[4] avail themselves who regard mathematical truths, insofar as they depend upon non-logical notions, as elliptical for hypothetical statements containing as tacit hypotheses all the postulates of the branch of mathematics in question. Thus, suppose

---

4. For example, Russell, *Principles,* pp. 429–430; Heinrich Behmann, *Mathematik und Logik* (Leipzig, 1927), pp. 8–10.

the geometrical terms 'sphere' and 'includes' to be undefined on the basis of logical expressions, and suppose all further geometrical expressions defined on the basis of logical expressions together with 'sphere' and 'includes,' as with Huntington. Let Huntington's postulates for (Euclidean) geometry, and all the theorems, be expanded by thoroughgoing replacement of definienda by definientia, so that they come to contain only logical expressions and 'sphere' and 'includes,' and let the conjunction of the thus expanded postulates be represented as 'Hunt (sphere, includes).' Then, where 'Φ (sphere, includes)' is any of the theorems, similarly expanded into primitive terms, the point of view under consideration is that 'Φ (sphere, includes),' insofar as it is conceived as a mathematical truth, is to be construed as an ellipsis for "If Hunt (sphere, includes) then Φ (sphere, includes).' Since 'Φ (sphere, includes)' is a logical consequence of Huntington's postulates, the above hypothetical statement is a truth of logic; it involves the expressions 'sphere' and 'includes' inessentially, in fact vacuously, since the logical deducibility of the theorems from the postulates is independent of the meanings of 'sphere' and 'includes' and survives the replacement of those expressions by any other grammatically admissible expressions whatever. Since, granted the fitness of Huntington's postulates, all and only those geometrical statements are truths of geometry which are logical consequences in this fashion of 'Hunt (sphere, includes),' all geometry becomes logic when interpreted in the above manner as a conventional ellipsis for a body of hypothetical statements.

But if, as a truth of mathematics, 'Φ (sphere, includes)' is short for 'If Hunt (sphere, includes) then Φ (sphere, includes),' still there remains, as part of this expanded statement, the original statement 'Φ (sphere, includes)'; this remains as a presumably true statement within some body of doctrine, say for the moment "non-mathematical geometry," even if the title of mathematical truth be restricted to the entire hypothetical statement in question. The body of all such hypothetical statements, describable as the "theory of deduction of non-mathematical geometry," is of course a part of logic; but the same is true of any "theory of deduction of sociology," "theory of deduction of Greek mythology," etc., which we might construct in parallel fashion with the aid of any set of postulates suited to sociology or to Greek mythology. The point of view toward geometry which is under consideration thus reduces merely to an exclusion of geometry from mathematics, a relegation of geometry to the status of sociology or Greek mythology; the labeling of the "theory of deduction of non-mathematical geometry" as "mathematical geometry" is a verbal *tour de force* which is equally applicable in the case of sociology or Greek mythology. To incorporate mathematics into logic by regarding all recalcitrant mathematical truths as elliptical hypothetical statements is thus in effect merely to restrict the term 'mathematics' to exclude those recalcitrant branches. But we are not interested in renaming. Those disciplines, geometry and the rest, which have traditionally been grouped under mathematics are the objects of the present discussion, and it is with the doctrine that mathematics in this sense is logic that we are here concerned.[5]

Discarding this alternative and returning, then, we see that if some mathematical expressions resist definition on the basis of logical ones, mathematics will reduce to logic only if, under a literal reading and without the gratuitous annexation of hypotheses, every mathematical truth contains (or is an abbreviation of one which contains) such recalcitrant expressions only inessentially if at all. But a mathematical expression sufficiently troublesome to have resisted trivial contextual definition in terms of logic can hardly be expected to occur thus idly in all its mathematical contexts. It would thus appear that for the tenability of the thesis that mathematics is logic it is not only sufficient but also necessary that all mathematical expressions be capable of definition on the basis solely of logical ones.

Though in framing logical definitions of mathematical expressions the ultimate objective be to make all mathematical truths logical truths, attention is not to be confined to mathematical and logical truths in testing the conformity of the definitions to usage. Mathematical expressions belong to the general language, and they are to be so defined that all statements containing them, whether mathematical truths, historical truths, or falsehoods under traditional usage, come to be construed as abbreviations of other statements which are correspondingly true or false. The definition introducing 'plus' must be such that the mathematical truth 'Smith's age plus Brown's equals Brown's age plus Smith's' becomes an abbreviation of a logical truth, as observed earlier; but it must also be such that 'Smith's age plus Brown's age equals Jones' age' becomes an abbreviation of a statement which is empirically true or false in conformity with the county records and the traditional usage of 'plus.' A defini-

---

5. Obviously the foregoing discussion has no bearing upon postulate method as such, nor upon Huntington's work.

tion which fails in this latter respect is no less Pickwickian than one which fails in the former; in either case nothing is achieved beyond the transient pleasure of a verbal recreation.

But for these considerations, contextual definitions of any mathematical expressions whatever could be framed immediately in purely logical terms, on the basis of any set of postulates adequate to the branch of mathematics in question. Thus, consider again Huntington's systematization of geometry. It was remarked that, granted the fitness of Huntington's postulates, a statement will be a truth of geometry if and only if it is logically deducible from 'Hunt (sphere, includes)' without regard to the meanings of 'sphere' and 'includes.' Thus 'Φ (sphere, includes)' will be a truth of geometry if and only if the following is a truth of logic: 'If α is any class and R any relation such that Hunt (α, R), then $\Phi (\alpha, R)$.' For 'sphere' and 'includes' we might then adopt the following contextual definition: Where '– – –' is any statement containing 'α' or 'R' or both, let the statement 'If α is any class and R any relation such that Hunt (α, R), then – – –' be abbreviated as that expression which is got from '– – –' by putting 'sphere' for 'α' and 'includes' for 'R' throughout. (In the case of a compound statement involving 'sphere' and 'includes,' this definition does not specify whether it is the entire statement or each of its constituent statements that is to be accounted as shorthand in the described fashion; but this ambiguity can be eliminated by stipulating that the convention apply only to whole contexts.) 'Sphere' and 'includes' thus receive contextual definition in terms exclusively of logic, for any statement containing one or both of those expressions is construed by the definition as an abbreviation of a statement containing only logical expressions (plus whatever expressions the original statement may have contained other than 'sphere' and 'includes'). The definition satisfies past usage of 'sphere' and 'includes' to the extent of verifying all truths and falsifying all falsehoods of geometry; all those statements of geometry which are true, and only those, become abbreviations of truths of logic.

The same procedure could be followed in any other branch of mathematics, with the help of a satisfactory set of postulates for the branch. Thus nothing further would appear to be wanting for the thesis that mathematics is logic. And the royal road runs beyond that thesis, for the described method of logicizing a mathematical discipline can be applied likewise to any non-mathematical theory. But the whole procedure rests on failure to conform the definitions to usage; what is logicized is not the intended subject matter. It is readily seen, e.g., that the suggested contextual definition of 'sphere' and 'includes,' though transforming purely geometrical truths and falsehoods respectively into logical truths and falsehoods, transforms certain empirical truths into falsehoods and vice versa. Consider, e.g., the true statement 'A baseball is roughly a sphere,' more rigorously 'The whole of a baseball, except for a certain very thin, irregular peripheral layer, constitutes a sphere.' According to the contextual definition, this statement is an abbreviation for the following: 'If α is any class and R any relation such that Hunt (α, R), then the whole of a baseball, except for a thin peripheral layer, constitutes an [a member of] α.' This tells us that the whole of a baseball, except for a thin peripheral layer, belongs to every class α for which a relation R can be found such that Huntington's postulates are true of α and R. Now it happens that 'Hunt $(\alpha, $ includes$)$' is true not only when α is taken as the class of all spheres, but also when α is restricted to the class of spheres a foot or more in diameter;[6] yet the whole of a baseball, except for a thin peripheral layer, can hardly be said to constitute a sphere a foot or more in diameter. The statement is therefore false, whereas the preceding statement, supposedly an abbreviation of this one, was true under ordinary usage of words. The thus logicized rendering of any other discipline can be shown in analogous fashion to yield the sort of discrepancy observed just now for geometry, provided only that the postulates of the discipline admit, like those of geometry, of alternative applications; and such multiple applicability is to be expected of any postulate set.[7]

Definition of mathematical notions on the basis of logical ones is thus a more arduous undertaking than would appear from a consideration solely of the truths and falsehoods of pure mathematics. Viewed *in vacuo,* mathematics is trivially reducible to logic through erection of postulate systems into contextual definitions; but *"cette science n'a pas uniquement pour objet de contempler éternellement son propre nombril."*[8] When mathematics is recognized as capable of use, and as forming an integral part of general language, the definition of mathematical notions in terms of logic becomes a task whose completion, if theoretically possible at all, calls for mathematical genius of a high order. It was primarily to this task that Whitehead and Russell addressed themselves

6. See E. V. Huntington, "A Set of Postulates for Abstract Geometry," *Mathematische Annalen* 73 (1913), p. 540.

7. Note that a postulate set is superfluous if it *demonstrably* admits of one and only one application: for it then embodies an adequate defining property for each of its constituent primitive terms. See Alfred Tarski, "Einige methodologische Untersuchungen uber die Definierbarkeit der Begriffe," *Erkenntnis* 5 (1934), Satz 2.

8. Henri Poincaré, *Science et méthode* (Paris: Flammarion, 1908), p. 199.

in their *Principia Mathematica*. They adopt a meager logical language as primitive, and on its basis alone they undertake to endow mathematical expressions with definitions which conform to usage in the full sense described above: definitions which not only reduce mathematical truths and falsehoods to logical ones, but reduce *all* statements, containing the mathematical expressions in question, to equivalent statements involving logical expressions instead of the mathematical ones. Within *Principia* the program has been advanced to such a point as to suggest that no fundamental difficulties stand in the way of completing the process. The foundations of arithmetic are developed in *Principia*, and therewith those branches of mathematics are accommodated which, like analysis and theory of number, spring from arithmetic. Abstract algebra proceeds readily from the relation theory of *Principia*. Only geometry remains untouched, and this field can be brought into line simply by identifying n-dimensional figures with those n-adic arithmetical relations ("equations in n variables") with which they are correlated through analytic geometry.[9] Some question Whitehead and Russell's reduction of mathematics to logic,[10] on grounds for whose exposition and criticism there is not space; the thesis that all mathematics reduces to logic is, however, substantiated by *Principia* to a degree satisfactory to most of us. There is no need here to adopt a final stand in the matter.

If for the moment we grant that all mathematics is thus definitionally constructible from logic, then mathematics becomes true by convention in a relative sense: mathematical truths become conventional transcriptions of logical truths. Perhaps this is all that many of us mean to assert when we assert that mathematics is true by convention; at least, an *analytic* statement is commonly explained merely as one which proceeds from logic and definitions, or as one which, on replacement of definienda by definientia, becomes a truth of logic.[11] But in strictness we can-

9. Eduard Study, *Die realistische Weltansicht und die Lehre vom Räume* (Brunswick, 1914), pp. 86–92.

10. See, e.g., Walter Dubislav, "Über das Verhältnis der Logik zur Mathematik," *Annalen der Philosophie* 5 (1925), pp. 198–208; also Hilbert, "Die Grundlagen der Mathematik," *Abhandlungen aus dem mathematischen Seminar der Hamburgischen Universität* 6 (1928), pp. 73, 82.

11. See Gottlob Frege, *Grundlagen der Arithmetik* (Breslau: W. Koebner, 1884), p. 4. Reprinted with English translation as *Foundations of Arithmetic* (New York: Philosophical Library; Oxford: Blackwell's, 1950). See Behmann, "Sind die mathematischen Urteile analytisch oder synthetisch?" *Erkenntnis* 4 (1934), p. 5. Carnap

not regard mathematics as true purely by convention unless all those logical principles to which mathematics is supposed to reduce are likewise
true by convention. And the doctrine that mathematics is *analytic* accomplishes a less fundamental simplification for philosophy than would
at first appear, if it asserts only that mathematics is a conventional transcription of logic and not that logic is convention in turn: for if in the end
we are to countenance any a priori principles at all which are independent of convention, we should not scruple to admit a few more, nor attribute crucial importance to conventions which serve only to diminish
the number of such principles by reducing some to others.

But if we are to construe logic also as true by convention, we must rest
logic ultimately upon some manner of convention other than definition:
for it was noted earlier that definitions are available only for transforming truths, not for founding them. The same applies to any truths of
mathematics which, contrary to the supposition of a moment ago, may
resist definitional reduction to logic; if such truths are to proceed from
convention, without merely being reduced to antecedent truths, they
must proceed from conventions other than definitions. Such a second
sort of convention, generating truths rather than merely transforming
them, has long been recognized in the use of postulates.[12] Application of
this method to logic will occupy the next section; customary ways of rendering postulates and rules of inference will be departed from, however,
in favor of giving the whole scheme the explicit form of linguistic convention.

II

Let us suppose an approximate maximum of definition to have been accomplished for logic, so that we are left with about as meager as possible
an array of primitive notational devices. There are indefinitely many
ways of framing the definitions, all conforming to the same usage of the
expressions in question; apart from the objective of defining much in
terms of little, choice among these ways is guided by convenience or
chance. Different choices involve different sets of primitives. Let us sup-

uses the term in *Logische Syntax* in essentially the same sense, but subject to more
subtle and rigorous treatment.

12. The function of postulates as conventions seems to have been first recognized
by J. D. Gergonne. His designation of them as "implicit definitions," which has had
some following in the literature, is avoided here.

pose our procedure to be such as to reckon among the primitive devices the *not*-idiom, the *if*-idiom ('if . . . then . . .'), the *every*-idiom ('No matter what x may be, $- - - x - - -$'), and one or two more as required. On the basis of this much, then, all further logical notation is to be supposed defined; all statements involving any further logical notation become construed as abbreviations of statements whose logical constituents are limited to those primitives.

'Or,' as a connective joining statements to form new statements, is amenable to the following contextual definition in terms of the *not*-idiom and the *if*-idiom: A pair of statements with 'or' between is an abbreviation of the statement made up successively of these ingredients: first, 'If'; second, the first statement of the pair, with 'not' inserted to govern the main verb (or, with 'it is false that' prefixed); third, 'then'; fourth, the second statement of the pair. The convention becomes clearer if we use the prefix '~' as an artificial notation of denial, thus writing '~ ice is hot' instead of 'Ice is not hot' or 'It is false that ice is hot.' Where '$- - -$' and '$-\!-$' are any statements, our definition then introduces '$- - -$ or $-\!-$' as an abbreviation of 'If ~$- - -$ then $-\!-$.' Again 'and,' as a connective joining statements, can be defined contextually by construing '$- - -$ and $-\!-$' as an abbreviation for '~ if $- - -$ then ~$-\!-$.' Every such idiom is what is known as a *truth function,* and is characterized by the fact that the truth or falsehood of the complex statement which it generates is uniquely determined by the truth or falsehood of the several statements which it combines. All truth functions are known to be constructible in terms of the *not-* and *if*-idioms as in the above examples.[13] On the basis of the truth functions, then, together with our further primitives—the *every*-idiom *et al.*—all further logical devices are supposed defined.

A word may, through historical or other accidents, evoke a train of ideas bearing no relevance to the truth or falsehood of its context; in point of *meaning,* however, as distinct from connotation, a word may be said to be determined to whatever extent the truth or falsehood of its contexts is determined. Such determination of truth or falsehood may be outright, and to that extent the meaning of the word is absolutely determined; or it may be relative to the truth or falsehood of statements containing other words, and to that extent the meaning of the word is deter-

13. H. M. Sheffer has shown ways of constructing these two, in turn, in terms of one; strictly, therefore, such a one should supplant the two in our ostensibly minimal set of logical primitives. Exposition will be facilitated, however, by retaining the redundancy.

mined relatively to those other words. A definition endows a word with completely determinacy of meaning relative to other words. But the alternative is open to us, on introducing a new word, of determining its meaning *absolutely* to whatever extent we like by specifying contexts which are to be true and contexts which are to be false. In fact, we need specify only the former: for falsehood may be regarded as a derivative property depending on the word '∼,' in such wise that falsehood of '– – –' means simply truth of '∼– – –.' Since all contexts of our new word are meaningless to begin with, neither true nor false, we are free to run through the list of such contexts and pick out as true such ones as we like; those selected become true by fiat, by linguistic convention. For those who would question them we have always the same answer, "You use the word differently." The reader may protest that our arbitrary selection of contexts as true is subject to restrictions imposed by the requirement of *consistency*—e.g., that we must not select both '– – –' and '∼– – –'; but this consideration, which will receive a clearer status a few pages hence, will be passed over for the moment.

Now suppose in particular that we abstract from existing usage of the locutions 'if-then,' 'not' (or '∼'), and the rest of our logical primitives, so that for the time being these become meaningless marks, and the erstwhile statements containing them lose their status as statements and become likewise meaningless, neither true nor false; and suppose we run through all those erstwhile statements, or as many of them as we like, segregating various of them arbitrarily as true. To whatever extent we carry this process, we to that extent determine meaning for the initially meaningless marks 'if,' 'then,' '∼,' and the rest. Such contexts as we render true are true by convention.

We saw earlier that if all expressions occurring essentially in a true statement S and not belonging to a class α are given definitions in terms solely of members of α, then S becomes a definitional abbreviation of a truth S'' involving only members of α essentially. Now let α comprise just our logical primitives, and let S be a statement which, under ordinary usage, is true and involves only logical expressions essentially. Since all logical expressions other than the primitives are defined in terms of the primitives, it then follows that S is an abbreviation of a truth S'' involving only the primitives essentially. But if one statement S is a definitional abbreviation of another S'', the truth of S proceeds wholly from linguistic convention if the truth of S'' does so. Hence if, in the above process of arbitrarily segregating statements as true by way of endowing our logical primitives with meaning, *we assign truth to those statements which, according to ordinary usage, are true and involve only our primitives essentially,* then not only will the latter statements be true by convention, but so will all statements which are true under ordinary usage and involve only logical expressions essentially. Since, as remarked earlier, every logical truth involves (or is an abbreviation of another which involves) only logical expressions essentially, the described scheme of assigning truth makes all logic true by convention.

Not only does such assignment of truth suffice to make all those statements true by convention which are true under ordinary usage and involve only logical expressions essentially, but it serves also to make all those statements false by convention which are false under ordinary usage and involve only logical expressions essentially. This follows from our explanation of the falsehood of '– – –' as the truth of '~– – –,' since '– – –' will be false under ordinary usage if and only if '~– – –' is true under ordinary usage. The described assignment of truth thus goes far toward fixing all logical expressions in point of meaning, and fixing them in conformity with usage. Still many statements containing logical expressions remain undecided by the described assignments: all those statements which, from the standpoint of ordinary usage, involve some non-logical expressions essentially. There is hence room for supplementary conventions of one sort or another, over and above the described truth assignments, by way of completely fixing the meanings of our primitives—and fixing them, it is to be hoped, in conformity with ordinary usage. Such supplementation need not concern us now; the described truth assignments provide partial determinations which, as far as they go, conform to usage, and which go far enough to make all logic true by convention.

But we must not be deceived by schematism. It would appear that we sit down to a list of expressions and check off as arbitrarily true all those which, under ordinary usage, are true statements involving only our logical primitives essentially; but this picture wanes when we reflect that the number of such statements is infinite. If the convention whereby those statements are singled out as true is to be formulated in finite terms, we must avail ourselves of conditions finite in length which determine infinite classes of expressions.[14]

Such conditions are ready at hand. One, determining an infinite class

14. Such a condition is all that constitutes a *formal system.* Usually we assign such meanings to the signs as to construe the expressions of the class as statements, specifically true statements, theorems; but this is neither intrinsic to the system nor necessary in all cases for a useful application of the system.

of expressions all of which, under ordinary usage, are true statements involving only our primitive *if*-idiom essentially, is the condition of being obtainable from:

(1)   If if p then q then if if q then r then if p then r

by putting a statement for 'p,' a statement for 'q,' and a statement for 'r.' In more customary language the form (1) would be expanded, for clarity, in some such fashion as this: 'If it is the case that if p then q, then, if it is the case further that if q then r, then, if p, r.' The form (1) is thus seen to be the principle of the syllogism. Obviously it is true under ordinary usage for all substitutions of statements for 'p,' 'q,' and 'r'; hence such results of substitution are, under ordinary usage, true statements involving only the *if*-idiom essentially. One infinite part of our program of assigning truth to all expressions which, under ordinary usage, are true statements involving only our logical primitives essentially, is thus accomplished by the following convention:

(I) *Let all results of putting a statement for 'p,' a statement for 'q,' and a statement for 'r' in* (1) *be true.*

Another infinite part of the program is disposed of by adding this convention:

(II) *Let any expression be true which yields a truth when put for 'q' in the result of putting a truth for 'p' in 'If p then q.'*

Given truths '– – –' and 'If – – – then ——,' (II) yields the truth of '——.' That (II) conforms to usage, i.e., that from statements which are true under ordinary usage (II) leads only to statements which are likewise true under ordinary usage, is seen from the fact that under ordinary usage a statement '——' is always true if statements '– – –' and 'If – – – then ——' are true. Given all the truths yielded by (I), (II) yields another infinity of truths which, like the former, are under ordinary usage truths involving only the *if*-idiom essentially. How this comes about is seen roughly as follows. The truths yielded by (I), being of the form of (1), are complex statements of the form 'If – – – then ——.' The statement '– – –' here may in particular be of the form (1) in turn, and hence likewise be true according to (I). Then, by (II), '——' becomes true. In general '——' will not be of the form (1), hence would not have been obtainable by (I) alone. Still '——' will in every such case be a statement which, under ordinary usage, is true and involves only the *if*-idiom essentially; this follows from the observed conformity of (I) and (II) to usage, together with the fact that the above derivation if '——' demands nothing of '——' beyond proper structure in terms of 'if-then.'

Now our stock of truths embraces not only those yielded by (I) alone, i.e., those having the form (1), but also all those thence derivable by (II) in the manner in which '——' has just now been supposed derived.[15] From this increased stock we can derive yet further ones by (II), and these likewise will, under ordinary usage, be true and involve only the *if*-idiom essentially. The generation proceeds in this fashion ad infinitum.

When provided only with (I) as an auxiliary source of truth, (II) thus yields only truths which under ordinary usage are truths involving only the *if*-idiom essentially. When provided with further auxiliary sources of truths, however, e.g., the convention (III) which is to follow, (II) yields truths involving further locutions essentially. Indeed, the effect of (II) is not even confined to statements which, under ordinary usage, involve only logical locutions essentially; (II) also legislates regarding other statements, to the extent of specifying that no two statements '– – –' and 'If – – – then ——' can both be true unless '——' is true. But this overflow need not disturb us, since it also conforms to ordinary usage. In fact, it was remarked earlier that room remained for supplementary conventions, over and above the described truth assignments, by way of further determining the meanings of our primitives. This overflow accomplishes just that for the *if*-idiom; it provides, with regard even to a statement 'If – – – then ——' which from the standpoint of ordinary usage involves non-logical expressions essentially, that the statement is not to be true if '– – –' is true and '——' not.

But present concern is with statements which, under ordinary usage, involve only our logical primitives essentially; by (I) and (II) we have provided for the truth of an infinite number of such statements, but by no means all. The following convention provides for the truth of another infinite set of such statements; these, in contrast to the preceding, involve not only the *if*-idiom but also the *not*-idiom essentially (under ordinary usage).

(III) *Let all results of putting a statement for 'p' and a statement for 'q,' in 'If p then if ~ p then q' or 'If if ~ p then p then p,' be true.*[16]

---

15. The latter in fact comprise all and only those statements which have the form 'If if if if *q* then *r* then if *p* then *r* then *s* then if if *p* then *q* then *s*.'

16. (1) and the two formulas in (III) are Lukasiewicz's three postulates for the propositional calculus.

Statements generated thus by substitution in 'If p then if $\sim p$ then q' are statements of hypothetical form in which two mutually contradictory statements occur as premises; obviously such statements are trivially true, under ordinary usage, no matter what may figure as conclusion. Statements generated by substitution in 'If [it is the case that] if $\sim p$ then p, then p' are likewise true under ordinary usage, for one reason as follows: Grant the hypothesis, viz., that if $\sim p$ then p; then we must admit the conclusion, viz., that p, since even denying it we admit it. Thus all the results of substitution referred to in (III) are true under ordinary usage no matter what the substituted statements may be; hence such results of substitution are, under ordinary usage, true statements involving nothing essentially beyond the *if*-idiom and the *not*-idiom ('$\sim$').

From the infinity of truths adopted in (III), together with those already at hand from (I) and (II), infinitely more truths are generated by (II). It happens, curiously enough, that (III) adds even to our stock of statements which involve only the *if*-idiom essentially (under ordinary usage); there are truths of that description which, though lacking the *not*-idiom, are reached by (I)–(III) and not by (I) and (II). This is true, e.g., of any instance of the principle of identity, say:

(2)   If time is money then time is money.

It will be instructive to derive (2) from (I)–(III), as an illustration of the general manner in which truths are generated by those conventions. (III), to begin with, directs that we adopt these statements as true:

(3)   If time is money then if time is not money then time is money.

(4)   If if time is not money then time is money then time is money.

(I) directs that we adopt this as true:

(5)   If if time is money then if time is not money then time is money then if if if time is not money then time is money then time is money then if time is money then time is money.

(II) tells us that, in view of the truth of (5) and (3), this is true:

(6)   If if if time is not money then time is money then time is money then if time is money then time is money.

Finally (II) tells us that, in view of the truth of (6) and (4), (2) is true.

If a statement S is generated by (I)–(III), obviously only the structure of S in terms of 'if-then' and '$\sim$' was relevant to the generation; hence all those variants S_i of S which are obtainable by any grammatically admissible substitutions upon constituents of S not containing 'if,' 'then,' or '$\sim$,' are likewise generated by (I)–(III). Now it has been observed that (I)–(III) conform to usage, i.e., generate only statements which are true under ordinary usage; hence S and all the S_i are uniformly true under ordinary usage, the S_i are therefore vacuous variants of S, and hence only 'if,' 'then,' and '$\sim$' occur essentially in S. Thus (I)–(III) generate only statements which under ordinary usage are truths involving only the *if*-idiom and the *not*-idiom essentially.

It can be shown also that (I)–(III) generate *all* such statements.[17] Consequently (I)–(III), aided by our definitions of logical locutions in terms of our primitives, are adequate to the generation of all statements which under ordinary usage are truths which involve any of the so-called truth functions but nothing else essentially: for it has been remarked that all the truth functions are definable on the basis of the *if*-idiom and the *not*-idiom. All such truths thus become true by convention. They comprise all those statements which are instances of any of the principles of the so-called propositional calculus.

To (I)–(III) we may now add a further convention or two to cover another of our logical primitives—say the *every*-idiom. A little more in this direction, by way of providing for our remaining primitives, and the program is completed; all statements which under ordinary usage are truths involving only our logical primitives essentially become true by convention. Therewith, as observed earlier, all logic becomes true by convention. The conventions with which (I)–(III) are thus to be supplemented will be more complex than (I)–(III), and considerable space would be needed to present them. But there is no need to do so, for (I)–(III) provide adequate illustration of the method; the complete set of conventions

17. The proof rests essentially upon Lukasiewicz's proof that his three postulates for the propositional calculus, viz., (1) and the formulas in (III), are *complete*. Adaptation of his result to present purposes depends upon the fact, readily established, that any formula generable by his two rules of inference (the so-called rule of substitution and a rule answering to (II)) can be generated by applying the rules in such order that all applications of the rule of substitution precede all applications of the other rule. This fact is relevant because of the manner in which the rule of substitution has been absorbed, here, into (1) and (III). The adaptation involves also two further steps, which however present no difficulty: we must make connection between Lukasiewicz's *formula*, containing variables 'p', 'q', etc., and the concrete *statements* which constitute the present subject matter; also between *completeness*, in the sense (Post's) in which Lukasiewicz uses the term, and the generability of all statements which under ordinary usage are truths involving only the *if*-idiom or the *not*-idiom essentially.

would be an adaptation of one of various existing systematizations of general logistic, in the same way in which (I)–(III) are an adaptation of a systematization of the propositional calculus.

The systematization chosen must indeed leave some logical statements undecided, by Gödel's theorem, if we set generous bounds to the logical vocabulary. But logic still becomes true by convention insofar as it gets reckoned as true on any account.

Let us now consider the protest which the reader raised earlier, viz. that our freedom in assigning truth by convention is subject to restrictions imposed by the requirement of consistency.[18] Under the fiction, implicit in an earlier stage of our discussion, that we check off our truths one by one in an exhaustive list of expressions, consistency in the assignment of truth is nothing more than a special case of conformity to usage. If we make a mark in the margin opposite an expression '– – –,' and another opposite '∼– – –,' we sin only against the established usage of '∼' as a denial sign. Under the latter usage '– – –' and '∼– – –' are not both true; in taking them both by convention as true we merely endow the sign '∼,' roughly speaking, with a meaning other than denial. Indeed, we might so conduct our assignments of truth as to allow no sign of our language to behave analogously to the denial locution of ordinary usage; perhaps the resulting language would be inconvenient, but conventions are often inconvenient. It is only the objective of ending up with our mother tongue that dissuades us from marking both '– – –' and '∼– – –,' and this objective would dissuade us also from marking 'It is always cold on Thursday.'

The requirement of consistency still retains the above status when we assign truth wholesale through general conventions such as (I)–(III). Each such convention assigns truth to an infinite sheaf of the entries in our fictive list, and in this function the conventions cannot conflict; by overlapping in their effects they reinforce one another, by not overlapping they remain indifferent to one another. If some of the conventions specified entries to which truth was *not* to be assigned, genuine conflict might be apprehended; such negative conventions, however, have not been suggested. (II) was, indeed, described earlier as specifying that 'If – – – then ——' is not to be true if '– – –' is true and '——' not; but within the framework of the conventions of truth assignment this apparent proscription is ineffectual without antecedent proscription of '——.'

18. So, e.g., Poincaré, *Science et méthode*, pp. 162ff.; Moritz Schlick, *Allgemeine Erkenntnislehre* (Berlin, 1925), pp. 36, 327.

Thus any inconsistency among the general conventions will be of the sort previously considered, viz. the arbitrary adoption of both '– – –' and '~– – –' as true; and the adoption of these was seen merely to impose some meaning other than denial upon the sign '~.' As theoretical restrictions upon our freedom in the conventional assignment of truth, requirements of consistency thus disappear. Preconceived usage may lead us to stack the cards, but does not enter the rules of the game.

III

Circumscription of our logical primitives in point of meaning, through conventional assignment of truth to various of their contexts, has been seen to render all logic true by convention. Then if we grant the thesis that mathematics is logic, i.e., that all mathematical truths are definitional abbreviations of logical truths, it follows that mathematics is true by convention.

If on the other hand, contrary to the thesis that mathematics is logic, some mathematical expressions resist definition in terms of logical ones, we can extend the foregoing method into the domain of these recalcitrant expressions: we can circumscribe the latter through conventional assignment of truth to various of their contexts, and thus render mathematics conventionally true in the same fashion in which logic has been rendered so. Thus, suppose some mathematical expressions to resist logical definition, and suppose them to be reduced to as meager as possible a set of mathematical primitives. In terms of these and our logical primitives, then, all further mathematical devices are supposed defined; all statements containing the latter become abbreviations of statements containing by way of mathematical notation only the primitives. Here, as remarked earlier in the case of logic, there are alternative courses of definition and therewith alternative sets of primitives; but suppose our procedure to be such as to count 'sphere' and 'includes' among the mathematical primitives. So far we have a set of conventions, (I)–(III) and a few more, let us call them (IV)–(VII), which together circumscribe our logical primitives and yield all logic. By way of circumscribing the further primitives 'sphere' and 'includes,' let us now add this convention to the set:

(VIII) *Let 'Hunt (sphere, includes)' be true.*

Now we saw earlier that where 'Φ (sphere, includes)' is any theorem of geometry, supposed expanded into primitive terms, the statement:

(7)   If Hunt (sphere, includes) then Φ (sphere, includes)

is a truth of logic. Hence (7) is one of the expressions to which truth is assigned by the conventions (I)–(VII). Now (II) instructs us, in view of convention (VIII) and the truth of (7), to adopt 'Φ (sphere, includes)' as true. In this way each theorem of geometry is seen to be present among the statements to which truth is assigned by the conventions (I)–(VII).

We have considered four ways of construing geometry. One way consisted of straightforward definition of geometrical expressions in terms of logical ones, within the direction of development represented by *Principia Mathematica;* this way, presumably, would depend upon identification of geometry with algebra through the correlations of analytic geometry, and definition of algebraic expressions on the basis of logical ones as in *Principia Mathematica*. By way of concession to those who have fault to find with certain technical points in *Principia,* this possibility was allowed to retain a tentative status. The other three ways all made use of Huntington's postulates, but are sharply to be distinguished from one another. The first was to include geometry in logic by construing geometrical truths as elliptical for hypothetical statements bearing 'Hunt (sphere, includes)' as hypothesis; this was seen to be a mere evasion, tantamount, under its verbal disguise, to the concession that geometry is not logic after all. The next procedure was to define 'sphere' and 'includes' contextually in terms of logical expressions by construing 'Φ (sphere, includes)' in every case as an abbreviation of 'If α is any class and R any relation such that Hunt (α, R), then Φ (α, R).' This definition was condemned on the grounds that it fails to yield the intended usage of the defined terms. The last procedure finally, just now presented, renders geometry true by convention without making it part of logic. Here 'Hunt (sphere, includes)' is made true by fiat, by way of conventionally delimiting the meanings of 'sphere' and 'includes.' The theorems of geometry then emerge not as truths of logic, but in parallel fashion to the truths of logic.

This last method of accommodating geometry is available also for any other branch of mathematics which may resist definitional reduction to logic. In each case we merely set up a conjunction of postulates for that branch as true by fiat, as a conventional circumscription of the meanings of the constituent primitives, and all the theorems of the branch thereby become true by convention: the convention thus newly adopted together with the conventions (I)–(VII). In this way mathematics becomes conventionally true, not by becoming a definitional transcription of logic, but by proceeding from linguistic convention in the same way as does logic.

But the method can even be carried beyond mathematics, into the so-called empirical sciences. Having framed a maximum of definitions in the latter realm, we can circumscribe as many of our "empirical" primitives as we like by adding further conventions to the set adopted for logic and mathematics; a corresponding portion of "empirical" science then becomes conventionally true in precisely the manner observed above for geometry.

The impossibility of defining any of the "empirical" expressions in terms exclusively of logical and mathematical ones may be recognized at the outset: for if any proved to be so definable, there can be no question but that it would thenceforward be recognized as belonging to pure mathematics. On the other hand, vast numbers of "empirical" expressions are of course definable on the basis of logical and mathematical ones together with other "empirical" ones. Thus 'momentum' is defined as 'mass times velocity'; 'event' may be defined as 'referent of the *later*-relation,' i.e., 'whatever is later than something'; 'instant' may be defined as 'maximal class of events no one of which is later than any other event of the class';[19] 'time' may be defined as 'the class of all instants'; and so on. In these examples 'momentum' is defined on the basis of mathematical expressions together with the further expressions 'mass' and 'velocity'; 'event,' 'instant,' and 'time' are all defined on the basis ultimately of logical expressions together with the one further expression 'later than.'

Now suppose definition to have been performed to the utmost among such non-logical, non-mathematical expressions, so that the latter are reduced to as few "empirical" primitives as possible.[20] *All* statements then become abbreviations of statements containing nothing beyond the logical and mathematical primitives and these "empirical" ones. Here, as before, there are alternatives of definition and therewith alternative sets of primitives; but suppose our primitives to be such as to include 'later than,' and consider the totality of the known truths which under ordi-

19. Bertrand Russell, *Our Knowledge of the External World* (Chicago and London: Open Court, 1914), p. 126.

20. In *Der Logische Aufbau der Welt* (Berlin: Weltkreis Verlag, 1928), Rudolf Carnap has pursued this program with such amazing success as to provide grounds for expecting all the expressions to be definable ultimately in terms of logic and mathematics plus just one "empirical" primitive, representing a certain dyadic relation described as *recollection of resemblance*. But for the present cursory considerations, no such spectacular reducibility need be proposed.

nary usage are truths involving only 'later than' and mathematical or logical expressions essentially. Examples of such statements are 'Nothing is later than itself'; 'If Pompey died later than Brutus and Brutus died later than Caesar then Pompey died later than Caesar.' All such statements will be either very general principles, like the first example, or else instances of such principles, like the second example. Now it is a simple matter to frame a small set of general statements from which all and only the statements under consideration can be derived by means of logic and mathematics. The conjunction of these few general statements can then be adopted as true by fiat, as 'Hunt (sphere, includes)' was adopted in (VIII); their adoption is a conventional circumscription of the meaning of the primitive 'later than.' Adoption of this convention renders all the known truths conventionally true which under ordinary usage are truths essentially involving any logical or mathematical expressions, or 'later than,' or any of the expressions which, like 'event,' 'instant,' and 'time,' are defined on the basis of the foregoing, and inessentially involving anything else.

Now we can pick another of our "empirical" primitives, perhaps 'body' or 'mass' or 'energy,' and repeat the process. We can continue in this fashion to any desired point, circumscribing one primitive after another by convention, and rendering conventionally true all known truths which under ordinary usage are truths essentially involving only the locutions treated up to that point. If in disposing successively of our "empirical" primitives in the above fashion we take them up in an order roughly describable as leading from the general to the special, then as we progress we may expect to have to deal more and more with statements which are true under ordinary usage only with reservations, only with a probability recognized as short of certainty. But such reservations need not deter us from rendering a statement true by convention; so long as under ordinary usage the presumption is rather for than against the statement, our convention conforms to usage in verifying it. In thus elevating the statement from putative to conventional truth, we still retain the right to falsify the statement tomorrow if those events should be observed which would have occasioned its repudiation while it was still putative: for conventions are commonly revised when new observations show the revision to be convenient.

If in describing logic and mathematics as true by convention what is meant is that the primitives *can* be conventionally circumscribed in such fashion as to generate all and only the accepted truths of logic and mathematics, the characterization is empty; our last considerations show that the same might be said of any other body of doctrine as well. If on the other hand it is meant merely that the speaker adopts such conventions for those fields but not for others, the characterization is uninteresting; while if it is meant that it is a general practice to adopt such conventions explicitly for those fields but not for others, the first part of the characterization is false.

Still, there is the apparent contrast between logico-mathematical truths and others that the former are a priori, the latter a posteriori; the former have "the character of an inward necessity," in Kant's phrase, the latter do not. Viewed behavioristically and without reference to a metaphysical system, this contrast retains reality as a contrast between more and less firmly accepted statements; and it obtains antecedently to any *post facto* fashioning of conventions. There are statements which we choose to surrender last, if at all, in the course of revamping our sciences in the face of new discoveries; and among these there are some which we will not surrender at all, so basic are they to our whole conceptual scheme. Among the latter are to be counted the so-called truths of logic and mathematics, regardless of what further we may have to say of their status in the course of a subsequent sophisticated philosophy. Now since these statements are destined to be maintained independently of our observations of the world, we may as well make use here of our technique of conventional truth assignment and thereby forestall awkward metaphysical questions as to our a priori insight into necessary truths. On the other hand this purpose would not motivate extension of the truth-assignment process into the realm of erstwhile contingent statements. On such grounds, then, logic and mathematics may be held to be conventional while other fields are not; it may be held that it is philosophically important to circumscribe the logical and mathematical primitives by conventions of truth assignment but that it is idle elaboration to carry the process further. Such a characterization of logic and mathematics is perhaps neither empty nor uninteresting nor false.

In the adoption of the very conventions (I)–(III), etc., whereby logic itself is set up, however, a difficulty remains to be faced. Each of these conventions is general, announcing the truth of every one of an infinity of statements conforming to a certain description; derivation of the truth of any sufficient statement from the general convention thus requires a logical inference, and this involves us in an infinite regress. E.g., in deriving (6) from (3) and (5) on the authority of (II) we *infer,* from the general announcement (II) and the specific premise that (3) and (5) are true statements, the conclusion that

(7)   (6) is to be true.

An examination of this inference will reveal the regress. For present purposes it will be simpler to rewrite (II) thus:

(II′) *No matter what x may be, no matter what y may be, no matter what z may be, if x and z are true [statements] and z is the result of putting x for 'p' and y for 'q' in 'If p then q' then y is to be true.*

We are to take (II′) as a premise, then, and in addition the premise that (3) and (5) are true. We may also grant it as known that (5) is the result of putting (3) for 'p' and (6) for 'q' in 'If p then q.' Our second premise may thus be rendered compositely as follows:

(8)   (3) and (5) are true and (5) is the result of putting (3) for 'p' and (6) for 'q' in 'If p then q.'

From these two premises we propose to infer (7). This inference is obviously sound logic; as logic, however, it involves use of (II′) and others of the conventions from which logic is supposed to spring. Let us try to perform the inference on the basis of those conventions. Suppose that our convention (IV), passed over earlier, is such as to enable us to infer specific instances from statements which, like (II′), involve the *every*-idiom; i.e., suppose that (IV) entitles us in general to drop the prefix 'No matter what x [or y, etc.] may be' and simultaneously to introduce a concrete designation instead of 'x' [or 'y,' etc.] in the sequel. By invoking (IV) three times, then, we can infer the following from (II′):

(9)   If (3) and (5) are true and (5) is the result of putting (3) for 'p' and (6) for 'q' in 'If p then q' then (6) is to be true.

It remains to infer (7) from (8) and (9). But this is an inference of the kind for which (II′) is needed; from the fact that

(10)   (8) and (9) are true and (9) is the result of putting (8) for 'p' and (7) for 'q' in 'If p then q'

we are to infer (7) with help of (II′). But the task of getting (7) from (10) and (II′) is exactly analogous to our original task of getting (6) from (8) and (II′); the regress is thus under way.[21] (Incidentally the derivation of (9) from (II′) by (IV), granted just now for the sake of argument, would

21. See Lewis Carroll, "What the Tortoise Said to Achilles," *Mind* 4 (1895), pp. 278–280.

encounter a similar obstacle; so also the various unanalyzed steps in the derivation of (8).)

In a word, the difficulty is that if logic is to proceed *mediately* from conventions, logic is needed for inferring logic from the conventions. Alternatively, the difficulty which appears thus as a self-presupposition of doctrine can be framed as turning upon a self-presupposition of primitives. It is supposed that the *if*-idiom, the *not*-idiom, the *every*-idiom, and so on, mean nothing to us initially, and that we adopt the conventions (I)–(VII) by way of circumscribing their meaning; and the difficulty is that communication of (I)–(VII) themselves depends upon free use of those very idioms which we are attempting to circumscribe, and can succeed only if we are already conversant with the idioms. This becomes clear as soon as (I)–(VII) are rephrased in rudimentary language, after the manner of (II').[22] It is important to note that this difficulty besets only the method of wholesale truth assignment, not that of definition. It is true, e.g., that the contextual definition of 'or' presented at the beginning of the second section was communicated with the help of logical and other expressions which cannot be expected to have been endowed with meaning at the stage where logical expressions are first being introduced. But a definition has the peculiarity of being theoretically dispensable; it introduces a scheme of abbreviation, and we are free, if we like, to forego the brevity which it affords until enough primitives have been endowed with meaning, through the method of truth assignment or otherwise, to accommodate full exposition of the definition. On the other hand the conventions of truth assignment cannot be thus withheld until preparations are complete, because they are needed in the preparations.

If the truth assignments were made one by one, rather than an infinite number at a time, the above difficulty would disappear; truths of logic such as (2) would simply be asserted severally by fiat, and the problem of

---

22. Incidentally, the conventions presuppose also some further locutions, e.g., 'true' ('a true statement'), 'the result of putting . . . for . . . in . . . ,' and various nouns formed by displaying expressions in quotation marks. The linguistic presuppositions can of course be reduced to a minimum by careful rephrasing; (II'), e.g., can be improved to the following extent:

(II″) *No matter what x may be, no matter what y may be, no matter what z may be, if x is true then if z is true then if z is the result of putting x for 'p' in the result of putting y for 'q' in 'If p then q' then y is true.*

This involves just the *every*-idiom, the *if*-idiom, 'is,' and the further locutions mentioned above.

inferring them from more general conventions would not arise. This course was seen to be closed to us, however, by the infinitude of the truths of logic.

It may still be held that the conventions (I)–(VIII), etc., are *observed* from the start, and that logic and mathematics thereby become conventional. It may be held that we can adopt conventions through behavior, without first announcing them in words; and that we can return and formulate our conventions verbally afterward, if we choose, when a full language is at our disposal. It may be held that the verbal formulation of conventions is no more a prerequisite of the adoption of the conventions than the writing of a grammar is a prerequisite of speech; that explicit exposition of conventions is merely one of many important uses of a completed language. So conceived, the conventions no longer involve us in vicious regress. Inference from general conventions is no longer demanded initially, but remains to the subsequent sophisticated stage where we frame general statements of the conventions and show how various specific conventional truths, used all along, fit into the general conventions as thus formulated.

It must be conceded that this account accords well with what we actually do. We discourse without first phrasing the conventions; afterwards, in writings such as this, we formulate them to fit our behavior. On the other hand it is not clear wherein an adoption of the conventions, antecedently to their formulation, consists; such behavior is difficult to distinguish from that in which conventions are disregarded. When we first agree to understand 'Cambridge' as referring to Cambridge in England, failing a suffix to the contrary, and then discourse accordingly, the role of linguistic convention is intelligible; but when a convention is incapable of being communicated until after its adoption, its role is not so clear. In dropping the attributes of deliberateness and explicitness from the notion of linguistic convention we risk depriving the latter of any explanatory force and reducing it to an idle label. We may wonder what one adds to the bare statement that the truths of logic and mathematics are a priori, or to the still barer behavioristic statement that they are firmly accepted, when he characterizes them as true by convention in such a sense.

The more restricted thesis discussed in the first section, viz., that mathematics is a conventional transcription of logic, is far from trivial; its demonstration is a highly technical undertaking and an important one, irrespectively of what its relevance may be to fundamental principles of philosophy. It is valuable to show the reducibility of any principle to another through definition of erstwhile primitives, for every such achievement reduces the number of our presuppositions and simplifies and integrates the structure of our theories. But as to the larger thesis that mathematics and logic proceed wholly from linguistic conventions, only further clarification can assure us that this asserts anything at all.

2

TWO DOGMAS OF EMPIRICISM

Modern empiricism has been conditioned in large part by two dogmas. One is a belief in some fundamental cleavage between truths which are *analytic,* or grounded in meanings independently of matters of fact, and truths which are *synthetic,* or grounded in fact. The other dogma is *reductionism*: the belief that each meaningful statement is equivalent to some logical construct upon terms which refer to immediate experience. Both dogmas, I shall argue, are ill-founded. One effect of abandoning them is, as we shall see, a blurring of the supposed boundary between speculative metaphysics and natural science. Another effect is a shift toward pragmatism.

1. Background for Analyticity

Kant's cleavage between analytic and synthetic truths was foreshadowed in Hume's distinction between relations of ideas and matters of fact, and in Leibniz's distinction between truths of reason and truths of fact. Leibniz spoke of the truths of reason as true in all possible worlds. Picturesqueness aside, this is to say that the truths of reason are those which could not possibly be false. In the same vein we hear analytic statements defined as statements whose denials are self-contradictory. But this definition has small explanatory value; for the notion of self-contradictoriness, in the quite broad sense needed for this definition of analyticity, stands in exactly the same need of clarification as does the notion of analyticity itself. The two notions are the two sides of a single dubious coin.

Kant conceived of an analytic statement as one that attributes to its subject no more than is already conceptually contained in the subject.

This formulation has two shortcomings: it limits itself to statements of subject-predicate form, and it appeals to a notion of containment which is left at a metaphorical level. But Kant's intent, evident more from the use he makes of the notion of analyticity than from his definition of it, can be restated thus: a statement is analytic when it is true by virtue of meanings and independently of fact. Pursuing this line, let us examine the concept of *meaning* which is presupposed.

Meaning, let us remember, is not to be identified with naming.[1] Frege's example of 'Evening Star' and 'Morning Star,' and Russell's of 'Scott' and 'the author of *Waverley*,' illustrate that terms can name the same thing but differ in meaning. The distinction between meaning and naming is no less important at the level of abstract terms. The terms '9' and 'the number of the planets' name one and the same abstract entity but presumably must be regarded as unlike in meaning; for astronomical observation was needed, and not mere reflection on meanings, to determine the sameness of the entity in question.

The above examples consist of singular terms, concrete and abstract. With general terms, or predicates, the situation is somewhat different but parallel. Whereas a singular term purports to name an entity, abstract or concrete, a general term does not; but a general term is *true of* an entity, or of each of many, or of none.[2] The class of all entities of which a general term is true is called the *extension* of the term. Now paralleling the contrast between the meaning of a singular term and the entity named, we must distinguish equally between the meaning of a general term and its extension. The general terms 'creature with a heart' and 'creature with kidneys,' for example, are perhaps alike in extension but unlike in meaning.

Confusion of meaning with extension, in the case of general terms, is less common than confusion of meaning with naming in the case of singular terms. It is indeed a commonplace in philosophy to oppose intension (or meaning) to extension, or, in a variant vocabulary, connotation to denotation.

The Aristotelian notion of essence was the forerunner, no doubt, of the modern notion of intension or meaning. For Aristotle it was essential in men to be rational, accidental to be two-legged. But there is an impor-

---

1. See below [Chapter 9 of the present volume].

2. See below [Chapter 9] and W. V. Quine, *From a Logical Point of View* (Cambridge, Mass.: Harvard University Press, 1953, 1961, 1980), pp. 107–115.

tant difference between this attitude and the doctrine of meaning. From the latter point of view it may indeed be conceded (if only for the sake of argument) that rationality is involved in the meaning of the word 'man' while two-leggedness is not; but two-leggedness may at the same time be viewed as involved in the meaning of 'biped' while rationality is not. Thus from the point of view of the doctrine of meaning it makes no sense to say of the actual individual, who is at once a man and a biped, that his rationality is essential and his two-leggedness accidental or vice versa. Things had essences, for Aristotle, but only linguistic forms have meanings. Meaning is what essence becomes when it is divorced from the object of reference and wedded to the word.

For the theory of meaning a conspicuous question is the nature of its objects: what sort of things are meanings? A felt need for meant entities may derive from an earlier failure to appreciate that meaning and reference are distinct. Once the theory of meaning is sharply separated from the theory of reference, it is a short step to recognizing as the primary business of the theory of meaning simply the synonymy of linguistic forms and the analyticity of statements; meanings themselves, as obscure intermediary entities, may well be abandoned.[3]

The problem of analyticity then confronts us anew. Statements which are analytic by general philosophical acclaim are not, indeed, far to seek. They fall into two classes. Those of the first class, which may be called *logically true*, are typified by:

(1)   No unmarried man is married.

The relevant feature of this example is that it not merely is true as it stands, but remains true under any and all reinterpretations of 'man' and 'married.' If we suppose a prior inventory of *logical* particles, comprising 'no,' 'un-,' 'not,' 'if,' 'then,' 'and,' etc., then in general a logical truth is a statement which is true and remains true under all reinterpretations of its components other than the logical particles.

But there is also a second class of analytic statements, typified by:

(2)   No bachelor is married.

The characteristic of such a statement is that it can be turned into a logical truth by putting synonyms for synonyms; thus (2) can be turned into (1) by putting 'unmarried man' for its synonym 'bachelor.' We still lack a

3. See below [Chapter 9] and Quine, *From a Logical Point of View*, pp. 48–49.

proper characterization of this second class of analytic statements, and therewith of analyticity generally, inasmuch as we have had in the above description to lean on a notion of "synonymy" which is no less in need of clarification than analyticity itself.

In recent years Carnap has tended to explain analyticity by appeal to what he calls state-descriptions.[4] A state-description is any exhaustive assignment of truth values to the atomic, or noncompound, statements of the language. All other statements of the language are, Carnap assumes, built up of their component clauses by means of the familiar logical devices, in such a way that the truth value of any complex statement is fixed for each state-description by specifiable logical laws. A statement is then explained as analytic when it comes out true under every state description. This account is an adaptation of Leibniz's "true in all possible worlds." But note that this version of analyticity serves its purpose only if the atomic statements of the language are, unlike 'John is a bachelor' and 'John is married,' mutually independent. Otherwise there would be a state-description which assigned truth to 'John is a bachelor' and to 'John is married,' and consequently 'No bachelors are married' would turn out synthetic rather than analytic under the proposed criterion. Thus the criterion of analyticity in terms of state-descriptions serves only for languages devoid of extra-logical synonym-pairs, such as 'bachelor' and 'unmarried man'—synonym-pairs of the type which give rise to the "second class" of analytic statements. The criterion in terms of state-descriptions is a reconstruction at best of logical truth, not of analyticity.

I do not mean to suggest that Carnap is under any illusions on this point. His simplified model language with its state-descriptions is aimed primarily not at the general problem of analyticity but at another purpose, the clarification of probability and induction. Our problem, however, is analyticity; and here the major difficulty lies not in the first class of analytic statements, the logical truths, but rather in the second class, which depends on the notion of synonymy.

2. Definition

There are those who find it soothing to say that the analytic statements of the second class reduce to those of the first class, the logical truths, by

4. Rudolf Carnap, *Meaning and Necessity* (Chicago: University of Chicago Press, 1947), pp. 9ff.; Rudolf Carnap, *Logical Foundations of Probability* (Chicago: University of Chicago Press, 1950), pp. 70ff.

definition; 'bachelor,' for example, is *defined* as 'unmarried man.' But how do we find that 'bachelor' is defined as 'unmarried man?' Who defined it thus, and when? Are we to appeal to the nearest dictionary, and accept the lexicographer's formulation as law? Clearly this would be to put the cart before the horse. The lexicographer is an empirical scientist, whose business is the recording of antecedent facts; and if he glosses 'bachelor' as 'unmarried man' it is because of his belief that there is a relation of synonymy between those forms, implicit in general or preferred usage prior to his own work. The notion of synonymy presupposed here has still to be clarified, presumably in terms relating to linguistic behavior. Certainly the "definition" which is the lexicographer's report of an observed synonymy cannot be taken as the ground of the synonymy.

Definition is not, indeed, an activity exclusively of philologists. Philosophers and scientists frequently have occasion to "define" a recondite term by paraphrasing it into terms of a more familiar vocabulary. But ordinarily such a definition, like the philologist's, is pure lexicography, affirming a relation of synonymy antecedent to the exposition in hand.

Just what it means to affirm synonymy, just what the interconnections may be which are necessary and sufficient in order that two linguistic forms be properly describable as synonymous, is far from clear; but, whatever these interconnections may be, ordinarily they are grounded in usage. Definitions reporting selected instances of synonymy come then as reports upon usage.

There is also, however, a variant type of definitional activity which does not limit itself to the reporting of pre-existing synonymies. I have in mind what Carnap calls *explication*—an activity to which philosophers are given, and scientists also in their more philosophical moments. In explication the purpose is not merely to paraphrase the definiendum into an outright synonym, but actually to improve upon the definiendum by refining or supplementing its meaning. But even explication, though not merely reporting a pre-existing synonymy between definiendum and definiens, does rest nevertheless on *other* pre-existing synonymies. The matter may be viewed as follows. Any word worth explicating has some contexts which, as wholes, are clear and precise enough to be useful; and the purpose of explication is to preserve the usage of these favored contexts while sharpening the usage of other contexts. In order that a given definition be suitable for purposes of explication, therefore, what is required is not that the definiendum in its antecedent usage be synonymous with the definiens, but just that each of these favored contexts of the definiendum, taken as a whole in its antecedent usage, be synonymous with the corresponding context of the definiens.

Two alternative definientia may be equally appropriate for the purposes of a given task of explication and yet not be synonymous with each other; for they may serve interchangeably within the favored contexts but diverge elsewhere. By cleaving to one of these definientia rather than the other, a definition of explicative kind generates, by fiat, a relation of synonymy between definiendum and definiens which did not hold before. But such a definition still owes its explicative function, as seen, to pre-existing synonymies.

There does, however, remain still an extreme sort of definition which does not hark back to prior synonymies at all: namely, the explicitly conventional introduction of novel notations for purposes of sheer abbreviation. Here the definiendum becomes synonymous with the definiens simply because it has been created expressly for the purpose of being synonymous with the definiens. Here we have a really transparent case of synonymy created by definition; would that all species of synonymy were as intelligible. For the rest, definition rests on synonymy rather than explaining it.

The word 'definition' has come to have a dangerously reassuring sound, owing no doubt to its frequent occurrence in logical and mathematical writings. We shall do well to digress now into a brief appraisal of the role of definition in formal work.

In logical and mathematical systems either of two mutually antagonistic types of economy may be striven for, and each has its peculiar practical utility. On the one hand we may seek economy of practical expression—ease and brevity in the statement of multifarious relations. This sort of economy calls usually for distinctive concise notations for a wealth of concepts. Second, however, and oppositely, we may seek economy in grammar and vocabulary; we may try to find a minimum of basic concepts such that, once a distinctive notation has been appropriated to each of them, it becomes possible to express any desired further concept by mere combination and iteration of our basic notations. This second sort of economy is impractical in one way, since a poverty in basic idioms tends to a necessary lengthening of discourse. But it is practical in another way: it greatly simplifies theoretical discourse *about* the language, through minimizing the terms and the forms of construction wherein the language consists.

Both sorts of economy, though prima facie incompatible, are valuable in their separate ways. The custom has consequently arisen of combining both sorts of economy by forging in effect two languages, the one a part of the other. The inclusive language, though redundant in grammar and vocabulary, is economical in message lengths, while the part, called primitive notation, is economical in grammar and vocabulary. Whole and part are correlated by rules of translation whereby each idiom not in primitive notation is equated to some complex built up of primitive notation. These rules of translation are the so-called *definitions* which appear in formalized systems. They are best viewed not as adjuncts to one language but as correlations between two languages, the one a part of the other.

But these correlations are not arbitrary. They are supposed to show how the primitive notations can accomplish all purposes, save brevity and convenience, of the redundant language. Hence the definiendum and its definiens may be expected, in each case, to be related in one or another of the three ways lately noted. The definiens may be a faithful paraphrase of the definiendum into the narrower notation, preserving a direct synonymy[5] as of antecedent usage; or the definiens may, in the spirit of explication, improve upon the antecedent usage of the definiendum; or finally, the definiendum may be a newly created notation, newly endowed with meaning here and now.

In formal and informal work alike, thus, we find that definition—except in the extreme case of the explicitly conventional introduction of new notations—hinges on prior relations of synonymy. Recognizing then that the notion of definition does not hold the key to synonymy and analyticity, let us look further into synonymy and say no more of definition.

3. Interchangeability

A natural suggestion, deserving close examination, is that the synonymy of two linguistic forms consists simply in their interchangeability in all contexts without change of truth value—interchangeability, in Leibniz's phrase, *salva veritate*.[6] Note that synonyms so conceived need not even be free from vagueness, as long as the vaguenesses match.

But it is not quite true that the synonyms 'bachelor' and 'unmarried

5. According to an important variant sense of 'definition,' the relation preserved may be the weaker relation of mere agreement in reference; see Quine, *From a Logical Point of View,* p. 132. But definition in this sense is better ignored in the present connection, being irrelevant to the question of synonymy.

6. See C. I. Lewis, *A Survey of Symbolic Logic* (Berkeley, 1918), p. 373.

man' are everywhere interchangeable *salva veritate*. Truths which become false under substitution of 'unmarried man' for 'bachelor' are easily constructed with the help of 'bachelor of arts' or 'bachelor's buttons'; also with the help of quotation, thus:

'Bachelor' has less than ten letters.

Such counterinstances can, however, perhaps be set aside by treating the phrases 'bachelor of arts' and 'bachelor's buttons' and the quotation "bachelor" each as a single indivisible word and then stipulating that the interchangeability *salva veritate* which is to be the touchstone of synonymy is not supposed to apply to fragmentary occurrences inside of a word. This account of synonymy, supposing it acceptable on other counts, has indeed the drawback of appealing to a prior conception of "word" which can be counted on to present difficulties of formulation in its turn. Nevertheless some progress might be claimed in having reduced the problem of synonymy to a problem of wordhood. Let us pursue this line a bit, taking "word" for granted.

The question remains whether interchangeability *salva veritate* (apparent from occurrences within words) is a strong enough condition for synonymy, or whether, on the contrary, some heteronymous expressions might be thus interchangeable. Now let us be clear that we are not concerned here with synonymy in the sense of complete identity in psychological associations or poetic quality; indeed no two expressions are synonymous in such a sense. We are concerned only with what may be called *cognitive* synonymy. Just what this is cannot be said without successfully finishing the present study; but we know something about it from the need which arose for it in connection with analyticity in §1. The sort of synonymy needed there was merely such that any analytic statement could be turned into a logical truth by putting synonyms for synonyms. Turning the tables and assuming analyticity, indeed, we could explain cognitive synonymy of terms as follows (keeping to the familiar example): to say that 'bachelor' and 'unmarried man' are cognitively synonymous is to say no more nor less than that the statement:

(3)   All and only bachelors are unmarried men

is analytic.[7]

7. This is cognitive synonymy in a primary, broad sense. Carnap and Lewis (Carnap, *Meaning and Necessity*, pp. 56ff.; C. I. Lewis, *An Analysis of Knowledge and Valuation* (LaSalle, Ill.: Open Court, 1946), pp. 83ff.) have suggested how, once

What we need is an account of cognitive synonymy not presupposing analyticity—if we are to explain analyticity conversely with help of cognitive synonymy as undertaken in §1. And indeed such an independent account of cognitive synonymy is at present up for consideration, namely, interchangeability *salva veritate* everywhere except within words. The question before us, to resume the thread at last, is whether such interchangeability is a sufficient condition for cognitive synonymy. We can quickly assure ourselves that it is, by examples of the following sort. The statement:

(4)   Necessarily all and only bachelors are bachelors

is evidently true, even supposing 'necessarily' so narrowly construed as to be truly applicable only to analytic statements. Then, if 'bachelor' and 'unmarried man' are interchangeable *salva veritate,* the result:

(5)   Necessarily all and only bachelors are unmarried men

of putting 'unmarried man' for an occurrence of 'bachelor' in (4) must, like (4), be true. But to say that (5) is true is to say that (3) is analytic, and hence that 'bachelor' and 'unmarried man' are cognitively synonymous.

Let us see what there is about the above argument that gives it its air of hocus-pocus. The condition of interchangeability *salva veritate* varies in its force with variations in the richness of the language at hand. The above argument supposes we are working with a language rich enough to contain the adverb 'necessarily,' this adverb being so construed as to yield truth when and only when applied to an analytic statement. But can we condone a language which contains such an adverb? Does the adverb really make sense? To suppose that it does is to suppose that we have already made satisfactory sense of 'analytic.' Then what are we so hard at work on right now?

Our argument is not flatly circular, but something like it. It has the form, figuratively speaking, of a closed curve in space.

Interchangeability *salva veritate* is meaningless until relativized to a language whose extent is specified in relevant respects. Suppose now we consider a language containing just the following materials. There is an

---

this notion is at hand, a narrower sense of cognitive synonymy which is preferable for some purposes can in turn be derived. But this special ramification of concept-building lies aside from the present purposes and must not be confused with the broad sort of cognitive synonymy here concerned.

indefinitely large stock of one-place predicates (for example, '*F*' where '*Fx*' means that *x* is a man) and many-place predicates (for example, '*G*' where '*Gxy*' means that *x* loves *y*), mostly having to do with extralogical subject matter. The rest of the language is logical. The atomic sentences consist each of a predicate followed by one or more variables '*x*,' '*y*,' etc.; and the complex sentences are built up of the atomic ones by truth functions ('not,' 'and,' 'or,' etc.) and quantification.[8] In effect such a language enjoys the benefits also of descriptions and indeed singular terms generally, these being contextually definable in known ways.[9] Even abstract singular terms naming classes, classes of classes, etc., are contextually definable in case the assumed stock of predicates includes the two-place predicate of class membership.[10] Such a language can be adequate to classical mathematics and indeed to scientific discourse generally, except in so far as the latter involves debatable devices such as contrary-to-fact conditionals or modal adverbs like 'necessarily.'[11] Now a language of this type is extensional, in this sense: any two predicates which agree extensionally (that is, are true of the same objects) are interchangeable *salva veritate*.[12]

In an extensional language, therefore, interchangeability *salva veritate* is no assurance of cognitive synonymy of the desired type. That 'bachelor' and 'unmarried man' are interchangeable *salva veritate* in an extensional language assures us of no more than that (3) is true. There is no assurance here that the extensional agreement of 'bachelor' and 'unmarried man' rests on meaning rather than merely on accidental matters of fact, as does the extensional agreement of 'creature with a heart' and 'creature with kidneys.'

For most purposes extensional agreement is the nearest approximation to synonymy we need care about. But the fact remains that extensional agreement falls far short of cognitive synonymy of the type

8. Quine, *From a Logical Point of View*, pp. 81ff. contains a description of just such a language, except that there happens to be just one predicate, the two-place predicate 'ε'.

9. See below [Chapter 9]; also Quine, *From a Logical Point of View*, pp. 85–86, 166–167.

10. See Quine, *From a Logical Point of View*, p. 87.

11. On such devices see Essay 8 [Chapter 24], Quine, *From a Logical Point of View*, pp. 139–159.

12. This is the substance of W. V. Quine, *Mathematical Logic* (New York: Norton, 1940; Cambridge, Mass.: Harvard University Press, 1947; rev. ed., Cambridge, Mass.: Harvard University Press, 1951), *121.

required for explaining analyticity in the manner of §1. The type of cognitive synonymy required there is such as to equate the synonymy of 'bachelor' and 'unmarried man' with the analyticity of (3), not merely with the truth of (3).

So we must recognize that interchangeability *salva veritate,* if construed in relation to an extensional language, is not a sufficient condition of cognitive synonymy in the sense needed for deriving analyticity in the manner of §1. If a language contains an intensional adverb 'necessarily' in the sense lately noted, or other particles to the same effect, then interchangeability *salva veritate* in such a language does afford a sufficient condition of cognitive synonymy; but such a language is intelligible only in so far as the notion of analyticity is already understood in advance.

The effort to explain cognitive synonymy first, for the sake of deriving analyticity from it afterward as in §1, is perhaps the wrong approach. Instead we might try explaining analyticity somehow without appeal to cognitive synonymy. Afterward we could doubtless derive cognitive synonymy from analyticity satisfactorily enough if desired. We have seen that cognitive synonymy of 'bachelor' and 'unmarried man' can be explained as analyticity of (3). The same explanation works for any pair of one-place predicates, of course, and it can be extended in obvious fashion to many-place predicates. Other syntactical categories can also be accommodated in fairly parallel fashion. Singular terms may be said to be cognitively synonymous when the statement of identity formed by putting '=' between them is analytic. Statements may be said simply to be cognitively synonymous when their biconditional (the result of joining them by 'if and only if') is analytic.[13] If we care to lump all categories into a single formulation, at the expense of assuming again the notion of "word" which was appealed to early in this section, we can describe any two linguistic forms as cognitively synonymous when the two forms are interchangeable (apart from occurrences within "words") *salva* (no longer *veritate* but) *analyticitate.* Certain technical questions arise, indeed, over cases of ambiguity or homonymy; let us not pause for them, however, for we are already digressing. Let us rather turn our backs on the problem of synonymy and address ourselves anew to that of analyticity.

13. The 'if and only if' itself is intended in the truth functional sense. See Carnap, *Meaning and Necessity,* p. 14.

4. Semantical Rules

Analyticity at first seemed most naturally definable by appeal to a realm of meanings. On refinement, the appeal to meanings gave way to an appeal to synonymy or definition. But definition turned out to be a will-o'-the-wisp, and synonymy turned out to be best understood only by dint of a prior appeal to analyticity itself. So we are back at the problem of analyticity.

I do not know whether the statement 'Everything green is extended' is analytic. Now does my indecision over this example really betray an incomplete understanding, an incomplete grasp of the "meanings," of 'green' and 'extended?' I think not. The trouble is not with 'green' or 'extended,' but with 'analytic.'

It is often hinted that the difficulty in separating analytic statements from synthetic ones in ordinary language is due to the vagueness of ordinary language and that the distinction is clear when we have a precise artificial language with explicit "semantical rules." This, however, as I shall now attempt to show, is a confusion.

The notion of analyticity about which we are worrying is a purported relation between statements and languages: a statement S is said to be *analytic for* a language L, and the problem is to make sense of this relation generally, that is, for variable 'S' and 'L.' The gravity of this problem is not perceptibly less for artificial languages than for natural ones. The problem of making sense of the idiom 'S is analytic for L,' with variable 'S' and 'L,' retains its stubbornness even if we limit the range of the variable 'L' to artificial languages. Let me now try to make this point evident.

For artificial languages and semantical rules we look naturally to the writings of Carnap. His semantical rules take various forms, and to make my point I shall have to distinguish certain of the forms. Let us suppose, to begin with, an artificial language L_0 whose semantical rules have the form explicitly of a specification, by recursion or otherwise, of all the analytic statements of L_0. The rules tell us that such and such statements, and only those, are the analytic statements of L_0. Now here the difficulty is simply that the rules contain the word 'analytic,' which we do not understand! We understand what expressions the rules attribute analyticity to, but we do not understand what the rules attribute to those expressions. In short, before we can understand a rule which begins 'A statement S is analytic for language L_0 if and only if . . .,' we must understand the general relative term 'analytic for'; we must understand 'S is analytic for L' where 'S' and 'L' are variables.

Alternatively we may, indeed, view the so-called rule as a conventional definition of a new simple symbol 'analytic-for-L_0,' which might better be written untendentiously as 'K' so as not to seem to throw light on the interesting word 'analytic.' Obviously any number of classes K, M, N, etc. of statements of L_0 can be specified for various purposes or for no purpose; what does it mean to say that K, as against M, N, etc., is the class of the "analytic" statements of L_0?

By saying what statements are analytic for L_0 we explain 'analytic-for-L_0' but not 'analytic,' not 'analytic for.' We do not begin to explain the idiom 'S is analytic for L' with variable 'S' and 'L,' even if we are content to limit the range of 'L' to the realm of artificial languages.

Actually we do know enough about the intended significance of 'analytic' to know that analytic statements are supposed to be true. Let us then turn to a second form of semantical rule, which says not that such and such statements are analytic but simply that such and such statements are included among the truths. Such a rule is not subject to the criticism of containing the un-understood word 'analytic'; and we may grant for the sake of argument that there is no difficulty over the broader term 'true.' A semantical rule of this second type, a rule of truth, is not supposed to specify all the truths of the language; it merely stipulates, recursively or otherwise, a certain multitude of statements which, along with others unspecified, are to count as true. Such a rule may be conceded to be quite clear. Derivatively, afterward, analyticity can be demarcated thus: a statement is analytic if it is (not merely true but) true according to the semantical rule.

Still there is really no progress. Instead of appealing to an unexplained word 'analytic,' we are now appealing to an unexplained phrase 'semantical rule.' Not every true statement which says that the statements of some class are true can count as a semantical rule—otherwise *all* truths would be "analytic" in the sense of being true according to semantical rules. Semantical rules are distinguishable, apparently, only by the fact of appearing on a page under the heading 'Semantical Rules'; and this heading is itself then meaningless.

We can say indeed that a statement is *analytic-for-L_0* if and only if it is true according to such and such specifically appended "semantical rules," but then we find ourselves back at essentially the same case which was originally discussed: 'S is analytic-for-L_0 if and only if . . .' Once we seek to explain '*S* is analytic for *L*' generally for variable '*L*' (even allowing limitation of '*L*' to artificial languages), the explanation 'true according to the semantical rules of *L*' is unavailing; for the relative term 'semantical rule of' is as much in need of clarification, at least, as 'analytic for.'

It may be instructive to compare the notion of semantical rule with that of postulate. Relative to a given set of postulates, it is easy to say what a postulate is: it is a member of the set. Relative to a given set of semantical rules, it is equally easy to say what a semantical rule is. But given simply a notation, mathematical or otherwise, and indeed as thoroughly understood a notation as you please in point of the translations or truth conditions of its statements, who can say which of its true statements rank as postulates? Obviously the question is meaningless—as meaningless as asking which points in Ohio are starting points. Any finite (or effectively specifiable infinite) selection of statements (preferably true ones, perhaps) is as much *a* set of postulates as any other. The word 'postulate' is significant only relative to an act of inquiry; we apply the word to a set of statements just in so far as we happen, for the year or the moment, to be thinking of those statements in relation to the statements which can be reached from them by some set of transformations to which we have seen fit to direct our attention. Now the notion of semantical rule is as sensible and meaningful as that of postulate, if conceived in a similarly relative spirit—relative, this time, to one or another particular enterprise of schooling unconversant persons in sufficient conditions for truth of statements of some natural or artificial language *L*. But from this point of view no one signalization of a subclass of the truths of *L* is intrinsically more a semantical rule than another; and, if 'analytic' means 'true by semantical rules,' no one truth of *L* is analytic to the exclusion of another.[14]

It might conceivably be protested that an artificial language *L* (unlike a natural one) is a language in the ordinary sense *plus* a set of explicit semantical rules—the whole constituting, let us say, an ordered pair; and that the semantical rules of *L* then are specifiable simply as the second component of the pair *L*. But, by the same token and more simply, we might construe an artificial language *L* outright as an ordered pair whose second component is the class of its analytic statements; and then the analytic statements of *L* become specifiable simply as the statements

14. The foregoing paragraph was not part of the present essay as originally published. It was prompted by R. M. Martin, "On 'Analytic,'" *Philosophical Studies* 3 (1952), pp. 42–47, as was the end of Essay 7 (W. V. Quine, "Notes on the Theory of Reference," *From a Logical Point of View*, pp. 130–138).

in the second component of *L*. Or better still, we might just stop tugging at our bootstraps altogether.

Not all the explanations of analyticity known to Carnap and his readers have been covered explicitly in the above considerations, but the extension to other forms is not hard to see. Just one additional factor should be mentioned which sometimes enters: sometimes the semantical rules are in effect rules of translation into ordinary language, in which case the analytic statements of the artificial language are in effect recognized as such from the analyticity of their specified translations in ordinary language. Here certainly there can be no thought of an illumination of the problem of analyticity from the side of the artificial language.

From the point of view of the problem of analyticity the notion of an artificial language with semantical rules is a *feu follet par excellence*. Semantical rules determining the analytic statements of an artificial language are of interest only in so far as we already understand the notion of analyticity; they are of no help in gaining this understanding.

Appeal to hypothetical languages of an artificially simple kind could conceivably be useful in clarifying analyticity, if the mental or behavioral or cultural factors relevant to analyticity—whatever they may be—were somehow sketched into the simplified model. But a model which takes analyticity merely as an irreducible character is unlikely to throw light on the problem of explicating analyticity.

It is obvious that truth is general depends on both language and extra-linguistic fact. The statement 'Brutus killed Caesar' would be false if the world had been different in certain ways, but it would also be false if the word 'killed' happened rather to have the sense of 'begat.' Thus one is tempted to suppose in general that the truth of a statement is somehow analyzable into a linguistic component and a factual component. Given this supposition, it next seems reasonable that in some statements the factual component should be null; and these are the analytic statements. But, for all its a priori reasonableness, a boundary between analytic and synthetic statements simply has not been drawn. That there is such a distinction to be drawn at all is an unempirical dogma of empiricists, a metaphysical article of faith.

5. The Verification Theory and Reductionism

In the course of these somber reflections we have taken a dim view first of the notion of meaning, then of the notion of cognitive synonymy, and finally of the notion of analyticity. But what, it may be asked, of the verification theory of meaning? This phrase has established itself so firmly as a catchword of empiricism that we should be very unscientific indeed not to look beneath it for a possible key to the problem of meaning and the associated problems.

The verification theory of meaning, which has been conspicuous in the literature from Peirce onward, is that the meaning of a statement is the method of empirically confirming or infirming it. An analytic statement is that limiting case which is confirmed no matter what.

As urged in §1, we can as well pass over the question of meanings as entities and move straight to sameness of meaning, or synonymy. Then what the verification theory says is that statements are synonymous if and only if they are alike in point of method of empirical confirmation or infirmation.

This is an account of cognitive synonymy not of linguistic forms generally, but of statements.[15] However, from the concept of synonymy of statements we could derive the concept of synonymy for other linguistic forms, by considerations somewhat similar to those at the end of §3. Assuming the notion of "word," indeed, we could explain any two forms as synonymous when the putting of the one form for an occurrence of the other in any statement (apart from occurrences within "words") yields a synonymous statement. Finally, given the concept of synonymy thus for linguistic forms generally, we could define analyticity in terms of synonymy and logical truth as in §1. For that matter, we could define analyticity more simply in terms of just synonymy of statements together with logical truth; it is not necessary to appeal to synonymy of linguistic forms other than statements. For a statement may be described as analytic simply when it is synonymous with a logically true statement.

So, if the verification theory can be accepted as an adequate account of statement synonymy, the notion of analyticity is saved after all. However, let us reflect. Statement synonymy is said to be likeness of method

15. The doctrine can indeed be formulated with terms rather than statements as the units. Thus Lewis describes the meaning of a term as "*a criterion in mind,* by reference to which one is able to apply or refuse to apply the expression in question in the case of presented, or imagined, things or situations" (C. I. Lewis, *An Analysis of Knowledge,* p. 133).

For an instructive account of the vicissitudes of the verification theory of meaning, centered however on the question of meaning*fulness* rather than synonymy and analyticity, see C. G. Hempel, "Problems and Changes in the Empiricist Criterion of Meaning," *Revue Internationale de Philosophie* 4 (1950), pp. 41–63.

of empirical confirmation or infirmation. Just what are these methods which are to be compared for likeness? What, in other words, is the nature of the relation between a statement and the experiences which contribute to or detract from its confirmation?

The most naïve view of the relation is that it is one of direct report. This is *radical reductionism*. Every meaningful statement is held to be translatable into a statement (true or false) about immediate experience. Radical reductionism, in one form or another, well antedates the verification theory of meaning explicitly so called. Thus Locke and Hume held that every idea must either originate directly in sense experience or else be compounded of ideas thus originating; and taking a hint from Tooke we might rephrase this doctrine in semantical jargon by saying that a term, to be significant at all, must be either a name of a sense datum or a compound of such names or an abbreviation of such a compound. So stated, the doctrine remains ambiguous as between sense data as sensory events and sense data as sensory qualities; and it remains vague as to the admissible ways of compounding. Moreover, the doctrine is unnecessarily and intolerably restrictive in the term-by-term critique which it imposes. More reasonably, and without yet exceeding the limits of what I have called radical reductionism, we may take full statements as our significant units—thus demanding that our statements as wholes be translatable into sense-datum language, but not that they be translatable term by term.

This emendation would unquestionably have been welcome to Locke and Hume and Tooke, but historically it had to await an important reorientation in semantics—the reorientation whereby the primary vehicle of meaning came to be seen no longer in the term but in the statement. This reorientation, seen in Bentham and Frege, underlies Russell's concept of incomplete symbols defined in use;[16] also it is implicit in the verification theory of meaning, since the objects of verification are statements.

Radical reductionism, conceived now with statements as units, set itself the task of specifying a sense-datum language and showing how to translate the rest of significant discourse, statement by statement, into it. Carnap embarked on this project in the *Aufbau*.

The language which Carnap adopted as his starting point was not a sense-datum language in the narrowest conceivable sense, for it included

16. See below [Chapter 9].

also the notations of logic, up through higher set theory. In effect it included the whole language of pure mathematics. The ontology implicit in it (that is, the range of values of its variables) embraced not only sensory events but classes, classes of classes, and so on. Empiricists there are who would boggle at such prodigality. Carnap's starting point is very parsimonious, however, in its extralogical or sensory part. In a series of constructions in which he exploits the resources of modern logic with much ingenuity, Carnap succeeds in defining a wide array of important additional sensory concepts which, but for his constructions, one would not have dreamed were definable on so slender a basis. He was the first empiricist who, not content with asserting the reducibility of science to terms of immediate experience, took serious steps toward carrying out the reduction.

If Carnap's starting point is satisfactory, still his constructions were, as he himself stressed, only a fragment of the full program. The construction of even the simplest statements about the physical world was left in a sketchy state. Carnap's suggestions on this subject were, despite their sketchiness, very suggestive. He explained spatio-temporal point-instants as quadruples of real numbers and envisaged assignment of sense qualities to point-instants according to certain canons. Roughly summarized, the plan was that qualities should be assigned to point-instants in such a way as to achieve the laziest world compatible with our experience. The principle of least action was to be our guide in constructing a world from experience.

Carnap did not seem to recognize, however, that his treatment of physical objects fell short of reduction not merely through sketchiness, but in principle. Statements of the form 'Quality q is at point-instant $x;y;z;t$' were, according to his canons, to be apportioned truth values in such a way as to maximize and minimize certain over-all features, and with growth of experience the truth values were to be progressively revised in the same spirit. I think this is a good schematization (deliberately oversimplified, to be sure) of what science really does; but it provides no indication, not even the sketchiest, of how a statement of the form 'Quality q is at $x;y;z;t$' could ever be translated into Carnap's initial language of sense data and logic. The connective 'is at' remains an added undefined connective; the canons counsel us in its use but not in its elimination.

Carnap seems to have appreciated this point afterward; for in his later writings he abandoned all notion of the translatability of statements about the physical world into statements about immediate experience. Reductionism in its radical form has long since ceased to figure in Carnap's philosophy.

But the dogma of reductionism has, in a subtler and more tenuous form, continued to influence the thought of empiricists. The notion lingers that to each statement, or each synthetic statement, there is associated a unique range of possible sensory events such that the occurrence of any of them would add to the likelihood of truth of the statement, and that there is associated also another unique range of possible sensory events whose occurrence would detract from that likelihood. This notion is of course implicit in the verification theory of meaning.

The dogma of reductionism survives in the supposition that each statement, taken in isolation from its fellows, can admit of confirmation or infirmation at all. My countersuggestion, issuing essentially from Carnap's doctrine of the physical world in the *Aufbau,* is that our statements about the external world face the tribunal of sense experience not individually but only as a corporate body.[17]

The dogma of reductionism, even in its attenuated form, is intimately connected with the other dogma—that there is a cleavage between the analytic and the synthetic. We have found ourselves led, indeed, from the latter problem to the former through the verification theory of meaning. More directly, the one dogma clearly supports the other in this way: as long as it is taken to be significant in general to speak of the confirmation and infirmation of a statement, it seems significant to speak also of a limiting kind of statement which is vacuously confirmed, *ipso facto,* come what may; and such a statement is analytic.

The two dogmas are, indeed, at root identical. We lately reflected that in general the truth of statements does obviously depend both upon language and upon extralinguistic fact; and we noted that this obvious circumstance carries in its train, not logically but all too naturally, a feeling that the truth of a statement is somehow analyzable into a linguistic component and a factual component. The factual component must, if we are empiricists, boil down to a range of confirmatory experiences. In the extreme case where the linguistic component is all that matters, a true statement is analytic. But I hope we are now impressed with how stub-

17. This doctrine was well argued by Pierre Duhem, *La Théorie physique: son objet et sa structure* (Paris, 1906), pp. 303–328. Or see Armand Lowinger, *The Methodology of Pierre Duhem* (New York: Columbia University Press, 1941), pp. 132–140.

bornly the distinction between analytic and synthetic has resisted any straightforward drawing. I am impressed also, apart from prefabricated examples of black and white balls in an urn, with how baffling the problem has always been of arriving at any explicit theory of the empirical confirmation of a synthetic statement. My present suggestion is that it is nonsense, and the root of much nonsense, to speak of a linguistic component and a factual component in the truth of any individual statement. Taken collectively, science has its double dependence upon language and experience; but this duality is not significantly traceable into the statements of science taken one by one.

The idea of defining a symbol in use was, as remarked, an advance over the impossible term-by-term empiricism of Locke and Hume. The statement, rather than the term, came with Bentham to be recognized as the unit accountable to an empiricist critique. But what I am now urging is that even in taking the statement as unit we have drawn our grid too finely. The unit of empirical significance is the whole of science.

6. Empiricism without the Dogmas

The totality of our so-called knowledge or beliefs, from the most casual matters of geography and history to the profoundest laws of atomic physics or even of pure mathematics and logic, is a man-made fabric which impinges on experience only along the edges. Or, to change the figure, total science is like a field of force whose boundary conditions are experience. A conflict with experience at the periphery occasions readjustments in the interior of the field. Truth values have to be redistributed over some of our statements. Reëvaluation of some statements entails reëvaluation of others, because of their logical interconnections— the logical laws being in turn simply certain further statements of the system, certain further elements of the field. Having reëvaluated one statement we must reëvaluate some others, which may be statements logically connected with the first or may be the statements of logical connections themselves. But the total field is so underdetermined by its boundary conditions, experience, that there is much latitude of choice as to what statements to reëvaluate in the light of any single contrary experience. No particular experiences are linked with any particular statements in the interior of the field, except indirectly through considerations of equilibrium affecting the field as a whole.

If this view is right, it is misleading to speak of the empirical content of an individual statement—especially if it is a statement at all remote from the experiential periphery of the field. Furthermore it becomes folly to seek a boundary between synthetic statements, which hold contingently on experience, and analytic statements, which hold come what may. Any statement can be held true come what may, if we make drastic enough adjustments elsewhere in the system. Even a statement very close to the periphery can be held true in the face of recalcitrant experience by pleading hallucination or by amending certain statements of the kind called logical laws. Conversely, by the same token, no statement is immune to revision. Revision even of the logical law of the excluded middle has been proposed as a means of simplifying quantum mechanics; and what difference is there in principle between such a shift and the shift whereby Kepler superseded Ptolemy, or Einstein Newton, or Darwin Aristotle?

For vividness I have been speaking in terms of varying distances from a sensory periphery. Let me try now to clarify this notion without metaphor. Certain statements, though *about* physical objects and not sense experience, seem peculiarly germane to sense experience—and in a selective way: some statements to some experiences, others to others. Such statements, especially germane to particular experiences, I picture as near the periphery. But in this relation of "germaneness" I envisage nothing more than a loose association reflecting the relative likelihood, in practice, of our choosing one statement rather than another for revision in the event of recalcitrant experience. For example, we can imagine recalcitrant experiences to which we would surely be inclined to accommodate our system by reëvaluating just the statement that there are brick houses on Elm Street, together with related statements on the same topic. We can imagine other recalcitrant experiences to which we would be inclined to accommodate our system by reëvaluating just the statement that there are no centaurs, along with kindred statements. A recalcitrant experience can, I have urged, be accommodated by any of various alternative reëvaluations in various alternative quarters of the total system; but, in the cases which we are now imagining, our natural tendency to disturb the total system as little as possible would lead us to focus our revisions upon these specific statements concerning brick houses or centaurs. These statements are felt, therefore, to have a sharper empirical reference than highly theoretical statements of physics or logic or ontology. The latter statements may be thought of as relatively centrally located within the total network, meaning merely that little preferential connection with any particular sense data obtrudes itself.

As an empiricist I continue to think of the conceptual scheme of science as a tool, ultimately, for predicting future experience in the light of past experience. Physical objects are conceptually imported into the situation as convenient intermediaries—not by definition in terms of experience, but simply as irreducible posits[18] comparable, epistemologically, to the gods of Homer. For my part I do, qua lay physicist, believe in physical objects and not in Homer's gods; and I consider it a scientific error to believe otherwise. But in point of epistemological footing the physical objects and the gods differ only in degree and not in kind. Both sorts of entities enter our conception only as cultural posits. The myth of physical objects is epistemologically superior to most in that it has proved more efficacious than other myths as a device for working a manageable structure into the flux of experience.

Positing does not stop with macroscopic physical objects. Objects at the atomic level are posited to make the laws of macroscopic objects, and ultimately the laws of experience, simpler and more manageable; and we need not expect or demand full definition of atomic and subatomic entities in terms of macroscopic ones, any more than definition of macroscopic things in terms of sense data. Science is a continuation of common sense, and it continues the common-sense expedient of swelling ontology to simplify theory.

Physical objects, small and large, are not the only posits. Forces are another example; and indeed we are told nowadays that the boundary between energy and matter is obsolete. Moreover, the abstract entities which are the substance of mathematics—ultimately classes and classes of classes and so on up—are another posit in the same spirit. Epistemologically these are myths on the same footing with physical objects and gods, neither better nor worse except for differences in the degree to which they expedite our dealings with sense experiences.

The over-all algebra of rational and irrational numbers is underdetermined by the algebra of rational numbers, but is smoother and more convenient; and it includes the algebra of rational numbers as a jagged or gerrymandered part.[19] Total science, mathematical and natural and human, is similarly but more extremely underdetermined by experience. The edge of the system must be kept squared with experience; the rest, with all its elaborate myths or fictions, has as its objective the simplicity of laws.

Ontological questions, under this view, are on a par with questions of

18. See below [Chapter 9].
19. See below [Chapter 9].

natural science.[20] Consider the question whether to countenance classes as entities. This, as I have argued elsewhere,[21] is the question whether to quantify with respect to variables which take classes as values. Now Carnap has maintained that this is a question not of matters of fact but of choosing a convenient language form, a convenient conceptual scheme or framework for science.[22] With this I agree, but only on the proviso that the same be conceded regarding scientific hypotheses generally. Carnap has recognized that he is able to preserve a double standard for ontological questions and scientific hypotheses only by assuming an absolute distinction between the analytic and the synthetic; and I need not say again that this is a distinction which I reject.[23]

The issue over there being classes seems more a question of convenient conceptual scheme; the issue over there being centaurs, or brick houses on Elm Street, seems more a question of fact. But I have been urging that this difference is only one of degree, and that it turns upon our vaguely pragmatic inclination to adjust one strand of the fabric of science rather than another in accommodating some particular recalcitrant experience. Conservatism figures in such choices, and so does the quest for simplicity.

Carnap, Lewis, and others take a pragmatic stand on the question of choosing between language forms, scientific frameworks; but their pragmatism leaves off at the imagined boundary between the analytic and the synthetic. In repudiating such a boundary I espouse a more thorough pragmatism. Each man is given a scientific heritage plus a continuing barrage of sensory stimulation; and the considerations which guide him in warping his scientific heritage to fit his continuing sensory promptings are, where rational, pragmatic.

20. "L'ontologie fait corps avec la science elle-même et ne peut en être séparée." Emile Meyerson, *Identité et réalité* (Paris, 1908; 4th ed., 1932), p. 439.

21. See below [Chapter 9]; Quine, *From a Logical Point of View,* pp. 102ff.

22. Carnap, "Empiricism, Semantics, and Ontology," *Revue Internationale de Philosophie* 4 (1950), pp. 20–40.

23. For an effective expression of further misgivings over this distinction, see Morton White, "The Analytic and the Synthetic: An Untenable Dualism," in Sidney Hook (ed.), *John Dewey: Philosopher of Science and Freedom* (New York: Dial Press, 1950), pp. 316–330. Reprinted in Leonard Linsky (ed.), *Semantics and the Philosophy of Language* (Urbana: University of Illinois Press, 1952).

3

TWO DOGMAS IN RETROSPECT

In restrospecting "Two Dogmas" I find myself overshooting the mark by twenty years. I think back to college days, 61 years ago. I majored in mathematics and was doing my honors reading in mathematical logic, a subject that had not yet penetrated the Oberlin curriculum. My new love, in the platonic sense, was Whitehead and Russell's *Principia Mathematica.*

I was taken with the clear, clean incisiveness of its formulas. But this was not true of its long introduction to volume 1, nor of some of the explanatory patches of prose that were interspersed through the three volumes. In those pages and passages the distinction between sign and object, or use and mention, was badly blurred. Partly in consequence, there was vague recourse to intensional properties, or ideas, under the disarmingly technical name of propositional functions. These ill-conceived mentalistic notions paraded as the philosophical foundation for the clean-cut classes, truth functions, and quantification that would have been a far better starting point in their own right.

The distrust of mentalistic semantics that found expression in "Two Dogmas" is thus detectable as far back as my senior year in college. Even earlier I had taken kindly to John B. Watson's *Psychology from the Standpoint of a Behaviorist,* which Raymond Stetson had assigned to us in his psychology class. Nor do I recall that it shocked any preconceptions. It chimed in with my predilections.

In 1931, my second year out of college, I was writing my PhD thesis

This is a revised version of a paper I presented at the University of Toronto in December 1990 in memory of my presentation of "Two Dogmas of Empiricism" there in December 1950.

under Whitehead's sponsorship at Harvard. It is my first and latest book: first because I wrote it before the others, and latest because it was published only a few months ago. Garland Publishing Company included it in their recently conceived series of twentieth-century Harvard PhD theses in philosophy. They did a surprisingly tidy job of my painfully wrought typescript, replete with logical symbols. I'm tickled. But this is not a commercial. The book is expensive, and I can offer better ones.

The relevance of my PhD thesis to our present topic is that in it I reworked the foundations of *Principia Mathematica* in strictly extensional terms, and propositional functions to the winds. The term 'propositional function' carried over, but to denote strictly classes, as I would now phrase it.

I was not abetted in my extensionalism by the Harvard professors of that time. Whitehead, C. I. Lewis, H. M. Sheffer, and E. V. Huntington all were soft on intensions and introspective meanings. But a postdoctoral fellowship the next year took me to a kindred spirit in Czechoslovakia: the great Carnap. He was just finishing his *Logische Syntax der Sprache,* and I read it and discussed it with him as it issued from his wife's typewriter. He was setting his face steadfastly against modal logic and mentalistic talk of meanings. His little logic text *Abriss der Logistik* had likewise been impeccably extensional, as was his impressive application of mathematical logic to epistemology in *Der logische Aufbau der Welt.*

True, in *Logische Syntax* we find him making capital of a purported distinction between analytic and synthetic truths. He didn't see this as a reinstatement of mentalistic meanings. He saw it as a matter of truth by linguistic convention. I expressed misgivings already in our discussions there in Prague, March 1933. Neil Tennant has uncovered, in the Carnap archives in Pittsburgh, this entry in Carnap's unpublished jottings of the time. I translate Carnap's somewhat telegraphic German:

Quine, 31.3.33
He says after some reading of my "Syntax" MS:
1. *Is there a difference in principle between logical axioms and empirical sentences?* He thinks not. Perhaps I seek a distinction just for its utility, but it seems he is right: gradual difference: they are the sentences we want to hold fast.

Evidently Carnap allayed my misgivings for a while. Three expository lectures on Carnap that I gave at Harvard in 1934 were abjectly sequacious. But my misgivings surfaced again in 1935, when I wrote "Truth by Convention." I quote the end of the first paragraph:

> [D]evelopments of the past few decades have led to a widespread conviction that logic and mathematics are purely analytic or conventional. It is less the purpose of the present inquiry to question the validity of this contrast than to question its sense.

Carnap wrote to me in 1936 expressing "very much interest" in "Truth by Convention," and added that he was "very keen of discussing it when we meet in April." So I have no record of his reaction, not remembering the discussion. There may have been frequent discussions, for he was around Harvard all that summer.

I was diverging from Carnap because his aloofness from intensions and mentalism, which had so appealed to me, had proved to be insufficiently austere. Ironically, in those same years Carnap came to welcome intensions increasingly. The trend began when Tarski persuaded him that his "Thesis of Syntax" was untenable: the thesis that "philosophy is the syntax of the language of science." *Semantics* was wanted, not just syntax. Tarski was right, in his own austere sense of semantics, namely model theory and his theory of truth. But Carnap went further, even embroiling himself in modal logic. I learned of this in 1938 from Hempel, and wrote to Carnap in dismay. He duly pondered my sermon, so he wrote in reply, and he went on to defend himself as follows:

> Although we do not ordinarily like to apply intensional languages, nevertheless I think we cannot help analyzing them. What would you think of an entomologist who refuses to investigate flees [*sic*] and lice because he dislikes them?

Well, the fleas and lice proved addictive. By 1946 he was championing modal logic.

Carnap was again at Harvard in the fall and winter term of 1940–41, along with Tarski and Russell. Glorious days. Tarksi and I argued persistently with Carnap over his appeal to analyticity in the opening pages of his work in progress, *Introduction to Semantics*.

You don't write when you can meet and talk. I find nothing on analyticity and meaning in my correspondence with Carnap until 1943, when I was in Washington as a naval officer. I wrote him a long letter about his *Introduction to Semantics*. One issue was analyticity and another was my criterion of ontological commitment as applied to abstract objects.

The two issues were linked, for Carnap viewed his appeal to abstract objects as empty convention, and their quasi-existence analytic.

I had not thought to look on my strictures over analyticity as the stuff of revolution. It was mere criticism, a negative point with no suggestion of a bright replacement. I had not felt moved to follow "Truth by Convention" with more of the same. But word got around. Nelson Goodman had joined in some of the discussions of 1940–41 with Carnap, Tarski and me. In June and July of 1947 a triangular correspondence on the issue developed among Goodman, Morton White, and me. In 1950 I was invited by the program committee of the American Philosophical Association to present a paper on the subject at the December meeting here in Toronto. Hence "Two Dogmas." It is remarkable that my most contested and anthologized paper was an assignment. The response was quick and startling. The paper appeared in *Philosophical Review* a few weeks after the Toronto meeting, and four months later there were symposia on it in Boston and at Stanford.

Looking back on it, one thing I regret is my needlessly strong statement of holism.

> The unit of empirical significance is the whole of science. . . . Any statement can be held true come what may, if we make drastic enough adjustments. . . . Conversely . . . no statement is immune to revision.

This is true enough in a legalistic sort of way, but it diverts attention from what is more to the point: the varying degrees of proximity to observation, the example of the brick houses in Elm Street. In later writings I have invoked not the whole of science but chunks of it, clusters of sentences just inclusive enough to have critical semantic mass. By this I mean a cluster sufficient to imply an observable effect of an observable experimental condition.

I formulate the matter nowadays in terms of what I call *observation categoricals*. An observation categorical is a generalization of the form 'Whenever this, that' where 'this' and 'that' are observation sentences. I'll say more about observation sentences later. Now a cluster of sentences has critical semantic mass if it implies an observation categorical; and the experimental check of the cluster of sentences consists in testing the implied categorical by arranging for fulfillment of its observable protasis and seeing whether the apodasis is realized.

This is meant as a schematic caricature of the experimental method. In practice many sentences of the cluster are tacit and some are probabilistic or dependent on unspecified things being equal. But I think it catches the essence of experimental testing, and therewith of empirical content.

I have appealed here to *implication:* the cluster of sentences implies the observation categorical. In so doing I give logic a special status: logical implication is the link between theory and experiment. However, we remain free here to adjust and to vary the limits of what to count as logic.

Thus consider the law of excluded middle, which I cited in "Two Dogmas" to illustrate my claim that 'no statement is immune to revision.' If the prospect of simplification and clarification at the level of quantum physics were to prove so overwhelming as to induce us to abrogate the law of excluded middle, we could still do so. It would just mean setting the limits of what to count as logic very narrowly and reckoning the law of excluded middle to the clusters of defeasible hypotheses that do the implying.

In a footnote to "Two Dogmas" I noted Duhem's priority in stressing holism. As a matter of curiosity, however, I might mention that when I wrote and presented "Two Dogmas" here forty years ago, and published it in the *Philosophical Review,* I didn't know about Duhem. Both Hempel and Philipp Frank subsequently brought Duhem to my attention, so I inserted the footnote when "Two Dogmas" was reprinted in *From a Logical Point of View.* Another insert was page 35 on postulates, which was prompted by a paper by Richard Martin in defense of Carnap on analyticity. But that was explained in a footnote.

I think Carnap's tenacity to analyticity was due largely to his philosophy of mathematics. One problem for him was the lack of empirical content: how could an empiricist accept mathematics as meaningful? Another problem was the *necessity* of mathematical truth. Analyticity was his answer to both.

I answer both with my moderate holism. Take the first problem: lack of content. Insofar as mathematics gets applied in natural sciences, I see it as sharing empirical content. Sentences of pure arithmetic and differential calculus contribute indispensably to the critical semantic mass of various clusters of scientific hypotheses, and so partake of the empirical content imbibed from the implied observation categoricals.

As for inapplicable parts of mathematics, say higher set theory, I sympathize with the empiricist in questioning their meaningfulness. We do keep their sentences as meaningful, but only because they are built of the same lexicon and grammatical constructions that are needed in applicable mathematics. It would be an intolerably pedantic *tour de force* to gerrymander our grammar in such a way as to account the inapplicable flights ungrammatical while preserving the applicable part.

This does put it to us to ponder truth and falsity for the inapplicable sentences. In doing so we can get some guidance from a maxim that is already serving the natural scientist, namely Occam's razor: where choice is otherwise undetermined, opt for economy. This attitude is in keeping with my inclination to minimize the cleavage between mathematics and natural science. That tendency is abetted already by my point about shared empirical content, and also by my questioning the analytic/synthetic distinction.

What then about the other problem, that of the necessary of mathematical truth? This again is nicely cleared up by moderate holism, without the help of analyticity. For let us recall that when a cluster of sentences with critical semantic mass is refuted by an experiment, the crisis can be resolved by revoking one *or* another sentence of the cluster. We hope to choose in such a way as to optimize future progress. If one of the sentences is purely mathematical, we will not choose to revoke it; such a move would reverberate excessively through the rest of science. We are restrained by a maxim of minimum mutilation. It is simply in this, I hold, that the necessity of mathematics lies: our determination to make revisions elsewhere instead. I make no deeper sense of necessity anywhere. Metaphysical necessity has no place in my naturalistic view of things, and analyticity hasn't much.

Analyticity undeniably has a place at a common-sense level, and this has made readers regard my reservations as unreasonable. My threadbare bachelor example is one of many undebatable cases. It is intelligible and often useful in discussion to point out that some disagreement is purely a matter of words rather than of fact. The point can commonly be sustained and acted upon by a paraphrase that circumvents a troublesome word. Often in talking with a foreigner we recognize some *impasse* as due to his having mislearned an English word rather than to his having a bizarre view of the subject matter. This is a bit of practical psychology at which we are all adept.

In *Roots of Reference* I proposed a rough theoretical definition of analyticity to fit these familiar sorts of cases. A sentence is analytic for a native speaker, I suggested, if he learned the truth of the sentence by learning the use of one or more of its words. This obviously works for 'No bachelor is married' and the like, and it also works for the basic laws of logic. Anyone who goes counter to modus ponens, or who affirms a conjunction and denies one of its components, is simply flouting what he learned in learning to use 'if' and 'and.' (I limit this to native speakers, because a foreigner can have learned our words indirectly by translation.)

I also recommended improving this rough definition by providing for deductive closure, so that truths deducible from analytic ones by analytic steps would count as analytic in turn. All logical truths in my narrow sense—that is, the logic of truth functions, quantification, and identity—would then perhaps qualify as analytic, in view of Gödel's completeness proof.

If the logical truths are analytic—hence true by meanings of words—then what are we to say of revisions, such as imagined in the case of the law of excluded middle? Do we thereby change our theory or just change the subject, change the meaning of our words? This has been a recurrent challenge, and my answer is that in elementary logic a change of theory *is* a change of meaning. Repudiation of the law of excluded middle would be a change of meaning, and no less a change of theory for that.

You could also have a change of meaning in elementary logic without change of theory. That would be if the word 'and' were merely put to use in place of 'or' and vice versa: no change of theory. But in abandoning the law of excluded middle we would not be preserving the law in *any* notation.

For the past five minutes I have been expressing a generous attitude toward analyticity that may seem out of character. In fact my reservations over analyticity are the same as ever, and they concern the tracing of any demarcation, even a vague and approximate one, across the domain of sentences in general. The crude criterion in *Roots of Reference*, based on word learning, is no help; we don't in *general* know how we learned a word, nor what truths were learned in the process. Nor do we have any reason to expect uniformity in this regard from speaker to speaker, and there is no reason to care. Elementary logic and the bachelor example *are* clear enough cases, but there is no going on from there.

It is the wrong kind of question. When in relativity theory momentum is found to be not quite proportional to velocity, despite its original definition as mass times velocity, there is no flurry over redefinition or contradiction in terms, and I don't think there should be. The definition served its purpose in introducing a word for subsequent use, and the word was thereafter ours to use in the evolving theory, with no lingering commitments. Definition is episodic. Mostly in natural science we are not even favored with definitions, much less bound by them. New terms are just introduced by partial descriptions: electrons, neutrinos, quarks.

In short, I recognize the notion of analyticity in its obvious and useful but epistemologically insignificant applications. The needs that Carnap felt for the notion in connection with mathematical truth are better met through holism. Beyond its manifest cases I find analyticity less help than hindrance. It begets an uncritical notion of meaning, or synonymy, that can induce a false sense of understanding. For it is clear that analyticity and synonymy are interdefinable.

Well, domestically interdefinable. Two expressions are synonymous iff their biconditional or equation is analytic. But I should mention that synonymy and therefore meaning are even worse off than analyticity when we transcend a single language. For if the two expressions to be equated belong to different languages, their biconditional or equation is far from analytic; it is incoherent, belonging to no language.

I mentioned my letter of 1943, where I took issue with Carnap both on analyticity and on ontological commitment to abstract objects, the two issues being linked. This same pairing of the two issues recurs in the antepenultimate paragraph of "Two Dogmas." Carnap's separation of questions of existence into questions of fact and questions of framework was a separation of the synthetic and the analytic. Collapse this epistemological duality and you collapse the ontological duality. Sticks, stones, sets, and numbers all become, for me, denizens of the world on an equal footing. Values of variables.

So also for the contrast noted in the remaining two paragraphs of "Two Dogmas": the contrast supposed by Carnap and C. I. Lewis between the factual and the pragmatic. "In repudiating such a boundary," I wrote, "I espouse a more thorough pragmatism." This passage had unforeseen consequences. I suspect it is responsible for my being widely classified as a pragmatist. I don't object, except that I am not clear on what it takes to qualify as a pragmatist. I was merely taking the word from Carnap and handing it back: in whatever sense the framework for science is pragmatic, so is the rest of science.

Let us now stand off, look at the two dogmas, and consider what the point is in repudiating each of them. Repudiation of the first dogma, analyticity, is insistence on empirical criteria for semantic concepts: for synonymy, meaning. Language is learned and taught by observing and correcting verbal behavior in observable circumstances. There is nothing in linguistic meaning that is not thus determined. John Dewey made this point long ago. What I did, not in "Two Dogmas" but in *Word and Object,* was to press that point for its negative implications regarding the notion of meaning.

As for the second dogma, reductionism, its repudiation is holism, seconding Duhem. The reductionism that is properly at stake here is moderate reductionism. Extreme reductionism, the notion that every scientific sentence should have a full translation in sense-datum language, is by now a straw man. Moderate reductionism was the lingering dogma, the notion that each scientific sentence has its own separate empirical content. Moderate *holism* is its denial. Its says that a scientific sentence cannot in general be expected to imply empirical consequences by itself. A bigger cluster is usually needed.

"Two Dogmas" is occasionally quoted for my depiction of

[t]he totality of our so-called knowledge or beliefs . . . [as] a man-made fabric which impinges on experience only along its edges.

Maybe this sparked Joe Ullian's title for the little manual that he and I coauthored twenty years later: *The Web of Belief*. Clearly my metaphor needed unpacking, and that was largely my concern in the ten years between "Two Dogmas" and *Word and Object*.

Becoming more consciously and explicitly naturalistic, I stiffened up my flabby reference to 'experience' by turning to our physical interface with the external world: the physical impacts of rays and molecules upon our sensory surfaces.

For purposes of a systematic account, I needed to marshal these scattered impacts as unit aggregates of some sort. Exteroceptors offered a neat solution. Impacts of rays and particles are irrelevant except as they trigger receptors, and happily it is only a question of triggering, with no question of more or less. So I identified one's input from the external world, on any given occasion, with one's global *neural input* on that occasion: hence with the temporally ordered set of all one's triggered exteroceptors during that brief moment.

Intricate brain processes, which neurologists are illuminating bit by bit, intervene between this neural input and perception. Exciting though that physiological research is, I was able to bypass it for my purposes by leaping to the resulting relation of *perceptual similarity* between global neural inputs. Inputs that are grossly dissimilar intrinsically—that is, in respect of what receptors are triggered—can issue in similar perceptual effects after the brain's swift and unconscious work of selecting and correlating. Perceptual similarity comes in degrees, and admits of a coarse behavioral criterion in the reinforcement and extinction of responses.

The grouping of global neural inputs by this relation of perceptual similarity affords a sufficient theoretical basis, I have argued, for distinguishing the sensory modalities and the various sensory qualities and *Gestalten*. A striking parallel emerges with Carnap's *Logischer Aufban der Welt*, in his derivations from similarities of global experiences.

I should say that in this sketch I am somewhat updating *Word and Object* in the light of later writings.

The sentences near the periphery of the fabric—in the metaphor of "Two Dogmas"—came in *Word and Object* to be called observation sentences. Their connection with experience was explained as association with ranges of perceptually similar neural inputs. Primitively the association was by conditioning. Further associations are forged in the fullness of time by retroaction from one's developing theory of the world.

The connections *into* the fabric, between observation sentences and theoretical sentences, are forged by shared vocabulary. For the observation sentences are couched, not in sense-datum language, but directly in the thing language, as Carnap called it. Thing words are among the words earliest learned, though learned at first only as one-word observation sentences or as segments of monolithic observation sentences. They are there awaiting gradual reification of their designata and incorporation into theoretical contexts.

Thanks to this sharing of vocabulary by observation sentences and theoretical sentences, logical relations hold between them. The pertinent logical relation, we saw, is logical implication of observation categoricals by clusters of theoretical sentences. This is, of course, the merest caricature of scientific method. It invites analysis of actual chunks of serious science, to see just what some of the typical chunks with critical semantic mass might be, and how the chains of logical implication from them to observation categoricals might run.

All this still leaves the heuristics of hypothesis untouched: that is, the technology of framing hypotheses worth testing. This is the domain of the maxim of minimum mutilation, and of Occam's razor. It is the domain also of standard deviation, probable error, and whatever else goes into sophisticated statistical method.

Deeper insights into the nature of scientific inference and explanation may some day be gained in neurology, coupled perhaps with computer simulation, as hinted by the new developments in so-called connectionist models; I think of Paul Churchland. The nature and nurture of science remains a fertile field of inquiry, varied and inviting.

4

CARNAP AND LOGICAL TRUTH

I

Kant's question "How are synthetic judgments a priori possible?" precipitated the *Critique of Pure Reason*. Question and answer notwithstanding, Mill and others persisted in doubting that such judgments were possible at all. At length some of Kant's own clearest purported instances, drawn from arithmetic, were sweepingly disqualified (or so it seemed; but see §II) by Frege's reduction of arithmetic to logic. Attention was thus forced upon the less tendentious and indeed logically prior question, "How is logical certainty possible?" It was largely this latter question thát precipitated the form of empiricism which we associate with between-war Vienna—a movement which began with Wittgenstein's *Tractatus* and reached its maturity in the work of Carnap.

Mill's position on the second question had been that logic and mathematics were based on empirical generalizations, despite their superficial appearance to the contrary. This doctrine may well have been felt to do less than justice to the palpable surface differences between the deductive sciences of logic and mathematics, on the one hand, and the empirical sciences ordinarily so-called on the other. Worse, the doctrine derogated from the certainty of logic and mathematics; but Mill may not have been one to be excessively disturbed by such a consequence. Perhaps classical mathematics did lie closer to experience then than now; at any rate the infinitistic reaches of set theory, which are so fraught with speculation and so remote from any possible experience, were unexplored in his day. And it is against just these latter-day mathematical extravagances that empiricists outside the Vienna Circle have since been known to inveigh,[1]

---

1. See P. W. Bridgman, "A Physicist's Second Reaction to Mengenlehre," *Scripta Mathematica* 2 (1933–1934), pp. 101–117, 224–234.

in much the spirit in which the empiricists of Vienna and elsewhere have inveighed against metaphysics.

What now of the empiricist who would grant certainty to logic, and to the whole of mathematics, and yet would make a clean sweep of other non-empirical theories under the name of metaphysics? The Viennese solution of this nice problem was predicated on language. Metaphysics was meaningless through misuse of language; logic was certain through tautologous use of language.

As an answer to the question "How is logical certainty possible?" this linguistic doctrine of logical truth has its attractions. For there can be no doubt that sheer verbal usage is in general a major determinant of truth. Even so factual a sentence as 'Brutus killed Caesar' owes its truth not only to the killing but equally to our using the component words as we do. Why then should a logically true sentence on the same topic, e.g., 'Brutus killed Caesar or did not kill Caesar,' not be said to owe its truth *purely* to the fact that we use our words (in this case 'or' and 'not') as we do?—for it depends not at all for its truth upon the killing.

The suggestion is not, of course, that the logically true sentence is a contingent truth about verbal usage; but rather that it is a sentence which, given the language, automatically becomes true, whereas 'Brutus killed Caesar,' given the language, becomes true only contingently on the alleged killing.

Further plausibility accrues to the linguistic doctrine of logical truth when we reflect on the question of alternative logics. Suppose someone puts forward and uses a consistent logic the principles of which are contrary to our own. We are then clearly free to say that he is merely using the familiar particles 'and,' 'all,' or whatever, in other than the familiar senses, and hence that no real contrariety is present after all. There may of course still be an important failure of intertranslatability, in that the behavior of certain of our logical particles is incapable of being duplicated by paraphrases in his system or vice versa. If the translation in this sense is possible, from his system into ours, then we are pretty sure to protest that he was wantonly using the familiar particles 'and' and 'all' (say) where we might unmisleadingly have used such-and-such other familiar phrasing. This reflection goes to support the view that the truths of logic have no content over and above the meanings they confer on the logical vocabulary.

Much the same point can be brought out by a caricature of a doctrine of Lévy-Bruhl, according to which there are pre-logical peoples who accept certain simple self-contradictions as true. Oversimplifying, no doubt, let us suppose it claimed that these natives accept as true a certain sentence of the form '*p* and not *p*.' Or—not to oversimplify too much—that they accept as true a certain heathen sentence of the form '*q* ka bu *q*' the English translation of which has the form '*p* and not *p*.' But now just how good a translation is this, and what may the lexicographer's method have been? If any evidence can count against a lexicographer's adoption of 'and' and 'not' as translations of 'ka' and 'bu,' certainly the natives' acceptance of '*q* ka bu *q*' as true counts overwhelmingly. We are left with the meaninglessness of the doctrine of there being pre-logical peoples; pre-logicality is a trait injected by bad translators. This is one more illustration of the inseparability of the truths of logic from the meanings of the logical vocabulary.

We thus see that there is something to be said for the naturalness of the linguistic doctrine of logical truth. But before we can get much further we shall have to become more explicit concerning our subject matter.

II

Without thought of any epistemological doctrine, either the linguistic doctrine or another, we may mark out the intended scope of the term 'logical truth,' within that of the broader term 'truth,' in the following way. First we suppose indicated, by enumeration if not otherwise, what words are to be called logical words; typical ones are 'or,' 'not,' 'if,' 'then,' 'and,' 'all,' 'every,' 'only,' 'some.' The logical truths, then, are those true sentences which involve only logical words *essentially*. What this means is that any other words, though they may also occur in a logical truth (as witness 'Brutus,' 'kill,' and 'Caesar' in 'Brutus killed or did not kill Caesar'), can be varied at will without engendering falsity.[2]

Though formulated with reference to language, the above clarification

2. Substantially this formulation is traced back a century and a quarter, by Bar-Hillel, to Bolzano. But note that the formulation fails of its purpose unless the phrase "can be varied at will," above, is understood to provide for varying the words not only singly but also two or more at a time. For example, the sentence 'If some men are angels some animals are angels' can be turned into a falsehood by simultaneous substitution for 'men' and 'angels,' but not by any substitution for 'angels' alone, nor for 'men,' nor for 'animals' (granted the non-existence of angels). For this observation and illustration I am indebted to John R. Myhill, who expresses some indebtedness in turn to Benson Mates.

—I added most of this footnote in May 1955, a year after the rest of the essay left my hands.

does not of itself hint that logical truths owe their truth to language. What we have thus far is only a delimitation of the class, *per accidens* if you please. Afterward the linguistic doctrine of logical truth, which is an epistemological doctrine, goes on to say that logical truths are true by virtue purely of the intended meanings, or intended usage, of the logical words. Obviously if logical truths *are* true by virtue purely of language, the logical words are the only part of the language that can be concerned in the matter; for these are the only ones that occur essentially.

Elementary logic, as commonly systematized nowadays, comprises truth-function theory, quantification theory, and identity theory. The logical vocabulary for this part, as commonly rendered for technical purposes, consists of truth-function signs (corresponding to 'or,' 'and,' 'not,' etc.), quantifiers and their variables, and '=.'

The further part of logic is set theory, which requires there to be classes among the values of its variables of quantification. The one sign needed in set theory, beyond those appropriate to elementary logic, is the connective 'ϵ' of membership. Additional signs, though commonly used for convenience, can be eliminated in well-known ways.

In this dichotomy I leave metatheory, or logical syntax, out of account. For, either it treats of special objects of an extralogical kind, viz., notational expressions, or else, if these are made to give way to numbers by arithmetization, it is reducible via number theory to set theory.

I will not here review the important contrasts between elementary logic and set theory, except for the following one. Every truth of elementary logic is obvious (whatever this really means), or can be made so by some series of individually obvious steps. Set theory, in its present state anyway, is otherwise. I am not alluding here to Gödel's incompleteness principle, but to something right on the surface. Set theory was straining at the leash of intuition ever since Cantor discovered the higher infinites; and with the added impetus of the paradoxes of set theory the leash was snapped. Comparative set theory has now long been the trend; for, so far as is known, no consistent set theory is both adequate to the purposes envisaged for set theory and capable of substantiation by steps of obvious reasoning from obviously true principles. What we do is develop one or another set theory by obvious reasoning, or elementary logic, from unobvious first principles which are set down, whether for good or for the time being, by something very like convention.

Altogether, the contrasts between elementary logic and set theory are so fundamental that one might well limit the word 'logic' to the former (though I shall not), and speak of set theory as mathematics in a sense exclusive of logic. To adopt this course is merely to deprive 'ϵ' of the status of a logical word. Frege's derivation of arithmetic would then cease to count as a derivation from logic; for he used set theory. At any rate we should be prepared to find that the linguistic doctrine of logical truth holds for elementary logic and fails for set theory, or vice versa. Kant's readiness to see logic as analytic and arithmetic as synthetic, in particular, is not superseded by Frege's work (as Frege supposed)[3] if 'logic' be taken as elementary logic. And for Kant logic certainly did not include set theory.

III

Where someone disagrees with us as to the truth of a sentence, it often happens that we can convince him by getting the sentence from other sentences, which he does accept, by a series of steps each of which he accepts. Disagreement which cannot be thus resolved I shall call *deductively irresoluble*. Now if we try to warp the linguistic doctrine of logical truth around into something like an experimental thesis, perhaps a first approximation will run thus: *Deductively irresoluble disagreement as to a logical truth is evidence of deviation in usage (or meanings) of words.* This is not yet experimentally phrased, since one term of the affirmed relationship, viz., 'usage' (or 'meanings'), is in dire need of an independent criterion. However, the formulation would seem to be fair enough within its limits; so let us go ahead with it, not seeking more subtlety until need arises.

Already the obviousness or potential obviousness of elementary logic can be seen to present an insuperable obstacle to our assigning any experimental meaning to the linguistic doctrine of elementary logical truth. Deductively irresoluble dissent from an elementary logical truth *would* count as evidence of deviation over meanings if anything can, but simply because dissent from a logical truism is as extreme as dissent can get.

The philosopher, like the beginner in algebra, works in danger of finding that his solution-in-progress reduces to '$0 = 0$.' Such is the threat to the linguistic theory of elementary logical truth. For, that theory now seems to imply nothing that is not already implied by the fact that elementary logic is obvious or can be resolved into obvious steps.

The considerations which were adduced in §I, to show the naturalness of the linguistic doctrine, are likewise seen to be empty when scrutinized

3. See Frege, *Foundations of Arithmetic*, §§87ff., §109.

in the present spirit. One was the circumstance that alternative logics are inseparable practically from mere change in usage of logical words. Another was that illogical cultures are indistinguishable from ill-translated ones. But both of these circumstances are adequately accounted for by mere obviousness of logical principles, without help of a linguistic doctrine of logical truth. For, there can be no stronger evidence of a change in usage than the repudiation of what had been obvious, and no stronger evidence of bad translation than that it translates earnest affirmations into obvious falsehoods.

Another point in §I was that true sentences generally depend for their truth on the traits of their language in addition to the traits of their subject matter; and that logical truths then fit neatly in as the limiting case where the dependence on traits of the subject matter is nil. Consider, however, the logical truth 'Everything is self-identical,' or '$(x)(x = x)$.' We *can* say that it depends for its truth on traits of the language (specifically on the usage of '='), and not on traits of its subject matter; but we can also say, alternatively, that it depends on an obvious trait, viz., self-identity, of its subject matter, viz., everything. The tendency of our present reflections is that there is no difference.

I have been using the vaguely psychological word "obvious" nontechnically, assigning it no explanatory value. My suggestion is merely that the linguistic doctrine of elementary logical truth likewise leaves explanation unbegun. I do not suggest that the linguistic doctrine is false and some doctrine of ultimate and inexplicable insight into the obvious traits of reality is true, but only that there is no real difference between these two pseudo-doctrines.

Turning away now from elementary logic, let us see how the linguistic doctrine of logical truth fares in application to set theory. As noted in §II, we may think of 'ϵ' as the one sign for set theory in addition to those of elementary logic. Accordingly the version of the linguistic doctrine which was italicized at the beginning of the present section becomes, in application to set theory, this: Among persons who are already in agreement on elementary logic, any deductively irresoluble disagreement as to a truth of set theory is evidence of deviation in usage (or meaning) of 'ϵ.'

This thesis is not trivial in quite the way in which the parallel thesis for elementary logic was seen to be. It is not indeed experimentally significant as it stands, simply because of the lack, noted earlier, of a separate criterion for usage or meaning. But it does seem reasonable, by the following reasoning.

Any acceptable evidence of usage or meaning of words must reside surely either in the observable circumstances under which the words are uttered (in the case of concrete terms referring to observable individuals) or in the affirmation and denial of sentences in which the words occur. Only the second alternative is relevant to 'ϵ.' Therefore any evidence of deviation in usage or meaning of 'ϵ' must reside in disagreement on sentences containing 'ϵ.' This is not, of course, to say of *every* sentence containing 'ϵ' that disagreement over it establishes deviation in usage or meaning of 'ϵ.' We have to assume in the first place that the speaker under investigation agrees with us on the meanings of words other than 'ϵ' in the sentences in question. And it might well be that, even from among the sentences containing only 'ϵ' and words on whose meanings he agrees with us, there is only a select species S which is so fundamental that he cannot dissent from them without betraying deviation in his usage or meaning of 'ϵ.' But S may be expected surely to include some (if not all) of the sentences which contain *nothing* but 'ϵ' and the elementary logical particles; for it is these sentences, insofar as true, that constitute (pure, or unapplied) set theory. But it is difficult to conceive of how to be other than democratic toward the truths of set theory. In exposition we may select some of these truths as so-called postulates and deduce others from them, but this is subjective discrimination, variable at will, expository and not set-theoretic. We do not change our meaning of 'ϵ' between the page where we show that one particular truth is deducible by elementary logic from another and the page where we show the converse. Given this democratic outlook, finally, the law of sufficient reason leads us to look upon S as including *all* the sentences which contain only 'ϵ' and the elementary logical particles. It then follows that anyone in agreement on elementary logic and in irresoluble disagreement on set theory is in deviation with respect to the usage or meaning of 'ϵ'; and this was the thesis.

The effect of our effort to inject content into the linguistic doctrine of logical truth has been, up to now, to suggest that the doctrine says nothing worth saying about elementary logical truth, but that when applied to set-theoretic truth it makes for a reasonable partial condensation of the otherwise vaporous notion of meaning as applied to 'ϵ.'

IV

The linguistic doctrine of logical truth is sometimes expressed by saying that such truths are true by linguistic convention. Now if this be so, certainly the conventions are not in general explicit. Relatively few persons, before the time of Carnap, had ever seen any convention that engendered truths of elementary logic. Nor can this circumstance be ascribed merely to the slipshod ways of our predecessors. For it is impossible in principle, even in an ideal state, to get even the most elementary part of logic exclusively by the explicit application of conventions stated in advance. The difficulty is the vicious regress, familiar from Lewis Carroll, which I have elaborated elsewhere.[4] Briefly the point is that the logical truths, being infinite in number, must be given by general conventions rather than singly; and logic is needed then to begin with, in the metatheory, in order to apply the general conventions to individual cases.

"In dropping the attributes of deliberateness and explicitness from the notion of linguistic convention," I went on to complain in the aforementioned paper, "we risk depriving the latter of any explanatory force and reducing it to an idle label." It would seem that to call elementary logic true by convention is to add nothing but a metaphor to the linguistic doctrine of logical truth which, as applied to elementary logic, has itself come to seem rather an empty figure (cf. §III).

The case of set theory, however, is different on both counts. For set theory the linguistic doctrine has seemed less empty (cf. §III); in set theory, moreover, convention in quite the ordinary sense seems to be pretty much what goes on (cf. §II). Conventionalism has a serious claim to attention in the philosophy of mathematics, if only because of set theory. Historically, though conventionalism was encouraged in the philosophy of mathematics rather by the non-Euclidean geometries and abstract algebras, with little good reason. We can contribute to subsequent purposes by surveying this situation. Further talk of set theory is deferred to §V.

In the beginning there was Euclidean geometry, a compendium of truths about form and void; and its truths were not based on convention (except as a conventionalist might, begging the present question, apply this tag to everything mathematical). Its truths were in practice presented by deduction from so-called postulates (including axioms; I shall not distinguish); and the selection of truths for this role of postulate, out of the totality of truths of Euclidean geometry, was indeed a matter of convention. But this is not *truth* by convention. The truths were there, and what was conventional was merely the separation of them into those

4. Late in the preceding essay [Chapter 1].

to be taken as staring point (for purposes of the exposition at hand) and those to be deduced from them.

The non-Euclidean geometries came of artificial deviations from Euclid's postulates, without thought (to begin with) of true interpretation. These departures were doubly conventional; for Euclid's postulates were a conventional selection from among the truths of geometry, and then the departures were arbitrarily or conventionally devised in turn. But still there was no truth by convention, because there was no truth.

Playing within a non-Euclidean geometry, one might conveniently make believe that his theorems were interpreted and true; but even such conventional make-believe is not truth by convention. For it is not really truth at all; and what is conventionally pretended is that the theorems are true by non-convention.

Non-Euclidean geometries have, in the fullness of time, received serious interpretations. This means that ways have been found of so construing the hitherto unconstrued terms as to identify the at first conventionally chosen set of non-sentences with some genuine truths, and truths presumably not by convention. The status of an interpreted non-Euclidean geometry differs in no basic way from the original status of Euclidean geometry, noted above.

Uninterpreted systems became quite the fashion after the advent of non-Euclidean geometries. This fashion helped to cause, and was in turn encouraged by, an increasingly formal approach to mathematics. Methods had to become more formal to make up for the unavailability, in uninterpreted systems, of intuition. Conversely, disinterpretation served as a crude but useful device (until Frege's syntactical approach came to be appreciated) for achieving formal rigor uncorrupted by intuition.

The tendency to look upon non-Euclidean geometries as true by convention applied to uninterpreted systems generally, and then carried over from these to mathematical systems generally. A tendency indeed developed to look upon all mathematical systems as, qua mathematical, uninterpreted. This tendency can be accounted for by the increase of formality, together with the use of disinterpretation as a heuristic aid to formalization. Finally, in an effort to make some sense of mathematics thus drained of all interpretation, recourse was had to the shocking quibble of identifying mathematics merely with the elementary logic which leads from uninterpreted postulates to uninterpreted theorems.[5]

5. See §1 of the preceding essay [Chapter 1].

What is shocking about this is that it puts arithmetic qua interpreted theory of number, and analysis qua interpreted theory of functions, and geometry qua interpreted theory of space, outside mathematics altogether.

The substantive reduction of mathematics to logic by Frege, Whitehead, and Russell is of course quite another thing. It is a reduction not to elementary logic but to set theory; and it is a reduction of genuine interpreted mathematics, from arithmetic onward.

V

Let us then put aside these confusions and get back to set theory. Set theory is pursued as interpreted mathematics, like arithmetic and analysis; indeed, it is to set theory that those further branches are reducible. In set theory we discourse about certain immaterial entities, real or erroneously alleged, viz., sets, or classes. And it is in the effort to make up our minds about genuine truth and falsity of sentences about these objects that we find ourselves engaged in something very like convention in an ordinary non-metaphorical sense of the word. We find ourselves making deliberate choices and setting them forth unaccompanied by any attempt at justification other than in terms of elegance and convenience. These adoptions, called postulates, and their logical consequences (via elementary logic), are true until further notice.

So here is a case where postulation can plausibly be looked on as constituting truth by convention. But in §IV we have seen how the philosophy of mathematics can be corrupted by supposing that postulates always play that role. Insofar as we would epistemologize and not just mathematize, we might divide postulation as follows. Uninterpreted postulates may be put aside, as no longer concerning us; and on the interpreted side we may distinguish between *legislative* and *discursive* postulation. Legislative postulation institutes truth by convention, and seems plausibly illustrated in contemporary set theory. On the other hand discursive postulation is mere selection, from a pre-existing body of truths, of certain ones for use as a basis from which to derive others, initially known or unknown. What discursive postulation fixes is not truth, but only some particular ordering of the truths, for purposes perhaps of pedagogy or perhaps of inquiry into logical relationships (logical in the sense of elementary logic). All postulation is of course conventional, but only legislative postulation properly hints of *truth* by convention.

It is well to recognize, if only for its distinctness, yet a further way in which convention can enter; viz., in the adoption of new notations for old ones, without, as one tends to say, change of theory. Truths containing the new notation are conventional transcriptions of sentences true apart from the convention in question. They depend for their truth partly on language, but then so did 'Brutus killed Caesar' (cf. §I). They come into being through the conventional adoption of a new sign, and they become true through conventional definition of that sign *together with* whatever made the corresponding sentences in the old notation true.

Definition, in a properly narrow sense of the word, is convention in a properly narrow sense of the word. But the phrase 'true by definition' must be taken cautiously; in its strictest usage it refers to a transcription, by the definition, of a truth of elementary logic. Whether such a sentence is true by convention depends on whether the logical truths themselves be reckoned as true by convention. Even an outright equation or biconditional connection of the definiens and the definiendum is a definitional transcription of a prior logical truth of the form '$x = x$' or '$p \equiv p$.'

Definition commonly so-called is not thus narrowly conceived, and must for present purposes be divided, as postulation was divided, into legislative and discursive. Legislative definition introduces a notation hitherto unused, or used only at variance with the practice proposed, or used also at variance, so that a convention is wanted to settle the ambiguity. Discursive definition, on the other hand, sets forth a pre-existing relation of interchangeability or coextensiveness between notations in already familiar usage. A frequent purpose of this activity is to show how some chosen part of language can be made to serve the purposes of a wider part. Another frequent purpose is language instruction.

It is only legislative definition, and not discursive definition or discursive postulation, that makes a conventional contribution to the truth of sentences. Legislative postulation, finally, affords truth by convention unalloyed.

Increasingly the word 'definition' connotes the formulas of definition which appear in connection with formal systems, signaled by some extra-systematic sign such as '$=_{df}$.' Such definitions are best looked upon as correlating two systems, two notations, one of which is prized for its economical lexicon and the other for its brevity or familiarity of expression.[6] Definitions so used can be either legislative or discursive in their

6. See *From a Logical Point of View*, pp. 26–27 [Chapter 2].

inception. But this distinction is in practice left unindicated, and wisely; for it is a distinction only between particular acts of definition, and not germane to the definition as an enduring channel of inter-translation.

The distinction between the legislative and the discursive refers thus to the act, and not to its enduring consequence, in the case of postulation as in the case of definition. This is because we are taking the notion of truth by convention fairly literally and simple-mindedly, for lack of an intelligible alternative. So conceived, conventionality is a passing trait, significant at the moving front of science but useless in classifying the sentences behind the lines. It is a trait of events and not of sentences.

Might we not still project a derivative trait upon the sentences themselves, thus speaking of a sentence as forever true by convention if its first adoption as true was a convention? No; this, if done seriously, involves us in the most unrewarding historical conjecture. Legislative postulation contributes truths which become integral to the corpus of truths; the artificiality of their origin does not linger as a localized quality, but suffuses the corpus. If a subsequent expositor singles out those once legislatively postulated truths again as postulates, this signifies nothing; he is engaged only in discursive postulation. He could as well choose his postulates from elsewhere in the corpus, and will if he thinks this serves his expository ends.

VI

Set theory, currently so caught up in legislative postulation, may some day gain a norm—even a strain of obviousness, perhaps—and lose all trace of the conventions in its history. A day could likewise have been when our elementary logic was itself instituted as a deliberately conventional deviation from something earlier, instead of evolving, as it did, mainly by unplanned shifts of form and emphasis coupled with casual novelties of notation.

Today indeed there are dissident logicians even at the elementary level, propounding deviations from the law of the excluded middle. These deviations, insofar as meant for serious use and not just as uninterpreted systems, are as clear cases of legislative postulation as the ones in set theory. For here we have again, quite as in set theory, the propounding of a deliberate choice unaccompanied (conceivably) by an attempt at justification other than in terms of convenience.

This example from elementary logic controverts no conclusion we have reached. According to §§I and III, the departure from the law of the excluded middle would count as evidence of revised usage of 'or' and 'not.' (This judgment was upheld in §III, though disqualified as evidence for the linguistic doctrine of logical truth.) For the deviating logician the words 'or' and 'not' are unfamiliar, or defamiliarized; and his decisions regarding truth values for their proposed contexts can then be just as genuinely a matter of deliberate convention as the decisions of the creative set theorist regarding contexts of 'ϵ.'

The two cases are indeed much alike. Not only is departure from the classical logic of 'or' and 'not' evidence of revised usage of 'or' and 'not'; likewise, as argued at length in §III, divergences between set theorists may reasonably be reckoned to revised usage of 'ϵ.' Any such revised usage is conspicuously a matter of convention, and can be declared by legislative postulation.

We have been at a loss to give substance to the linguistic doctrine, particularly of elementary logical truth, or to the doctrine that the familiar truths of logic are true by convention. We have found some sense in the notion of truth by convention, but only as attaching to a process of adoption, viz., legislative postulation, and not as a significant lingering trait of the legislatively postulated sentence. Surveying current events, we note legislative postulation in set theory and, at a more elementary level, in connection with the law of the excluded middle.

And do we not find the same continually in the theoretical hypotheses of natural science itself? What seemed to smack of convention in set theory (§V), at any rate, was "deliberate choice, set forth unaccompanied by any attempt at justification other than in terms of elegance and convenience"; and to what theoretical hypothesis of natural science might not this same character be attributed? For surely the justification of any theoretical hypothesis can, at the time of hypothesis, consist in no more than the elegance or convenience which the hypothesis brings to the containing body of laws and data. How then are we to delimit the category of legislative postulation, short of including under it every new act of scientific hypothesis?

The situation may seem to be saved, for ordinary hypotheses in natural science, by there being some indirect but eventual confrontation with empirical data. However, this confrontation can be remote; and, conversely, some such remote confrontation with experience may be claimed even for pure mathematics and elementary logic. The semblance of a difference in this respect is largely due to overemphasis of departmental boundaries. For a self-contained theory which we can check with experience includes, in point of fact, not only its various theoretical hypotheses of so-called natural science but also such portions of logic and mathematics as it makes use of. Hence I do not see how a line is to be drawn between hypotheses which confer truth by convention and hypotheses which do not, short of reckoning *all* hypotheses to the former category save perhaps those actually derivable or refutable by elementary logic from what Carnap used to call protocol sentences. But this version, besides depending to an unwelcome degree on the debatable notion of protocol sentences, is far too inclusive to suit anyone.

Evidently our tables are waxing. We had been trying to make sense of the role of convention in a priori knowledge. Now the very distinction between a priori and empirical begins to waver and dissolve, at least as a distinction between sentences. (It could of course still hold as a distinction between factors in one's adoption of a sentence, but both factors might be operative everywhere.)

VII

Whatever our difficulties over the relevant distinctions, it must be conceded that logic and mathematics do seem qualitatively different from the rest of science. Logic and mathematics hold conspicuously aloof from any express appeal, certainly, to observation and experiment. Having thus nothing external to look to, logicians and mathematicians look closely to notation and explicit notational operations: to expressions, terms, substitution, transposition, cancellation, clearing of fractions, and the like. This concern of logicians and mathematicians with syntax (as Carnap calls it) is perennial, but in modern times it has become increasingly searching and explicit, and has even prompted, as we see, a linguistic philosophy of logical and mathematical truth.

On the other hand an effect of these same formal developments in modern logic, curiously, has been to show how to divorce mathematics (other than elementary logic) from any peculiarly notational considerations not equally relevant to natural science. By this I mean that mathematics can be handled (insofar as it can be handled at all) by axiomatization, outwardly quite like any system of hypotheses elsewhere in science; and elementary logic can then be left to extract the theorems.

The consequent affinity between mathematics and systematized natural science was recognized by Carnap when he propounded his P-rules alongside his L-rules or meaning postulates. Yet he did not look upon the P-rules as engendering analytic sentences, sentences true purely by language. How to sustain this distinction has been very much our problem in these pages, and one on which we have found little encouragement.

Carnap appreciated this problem, in *Logical Syntax,* as a problem of finding a difference in kind between the P-rules (or the truths thereby specified) and the L-rules (or the L-truths, analytic sentences, thereby specified). Moreover he proposed an ingenious solution.[7] In effect he characterized the logical (including mathematical) vocabulary as the largest vocabulary such that (1) there are sentences which contain only that vocabulary and (2) all such sentences are determinable as true or false by a purely syntactical condition—i.e., by a condition which speaks only of concatenation of marks. Then he limited the L-truths in effect to those involving just the logical vocabulary essentially.[8]

Truths given by P-rules were supposedly excluded from the category of logical truth under this criterion, because, though the rules specifying them are formally stated, the vocabulary involved can also be recombined to give sentences whose truth values are not determinate under any set of rules formally formulable in advance.

At this point one can object (pending a further expedient of Carnap's, which I shall next explain) that the criterion based on (1) and (2) fails of its purpose. For, consider to begin with the totality of those sentences which are expressed purely within what Carnap (or anyone) would want to count as logical (and mathematical) vocabulary. Suppose, in conformity with (2), that the division of this totality into the true and the false is reproducible in purely syntactical terms. Now surely the adding of one general term of an extra-logical kind, say 'heavier than,' is not going to alter the situation. The truths which are expressible in terms of just 'heavier than,' together with the logical vocabulary, will be truths of only the most general kind, such as '$(\exists x)(\exists y)(x$ is heavier than $y)$,' '$(x) \sim (x$ is heavier than $x)$,' and '$(x)(y)(z)(x$ is heavier than y . y is heavier than z . $\supset$. x is heavier than $z)$.' The division of the truths from the falsehoods in this supplementary domain can probably be reproduced in syntactical

7. Carnap, *The Logical Syntax of Language,* §50.
8. See §1 above. Also, for certain reservations conveniently postponed at the moment, see §9 on "essential predication." [Chapter 1.]

terms if the division of the original totality could. But then, under the criterion based on (1) and (2), 'heavier than' qualifies for the logical vocabulary. And it is hard to see what whole collection of general terms of natural science might not qualify likewise.

The further expedient, by which Carnap met this difficulty, was his use of Cartesian co-ordinates.[9] Under this procedure, each spatio-temporal particular c becomes associated with a class K of quadruples of real numbers, viz., the class of those quadruples which are the co-ordinates of component point events of c. Further let us write $K[t]$ for the class of triples which with t appended belong to K; thus $K[t]$ is that class of triples of real numbers which is associated with the momentary state of object c at time t. Then, in order to say, e.g., that c_1 is heavier than c_2 at time t, we say '$H(K_1[t], K_2[t])$,' which might be translated as 'The momentary object associated with $K_1[t]$ is heavier than that associated with $K_2[t]$.' Now $K_1[t]$ and $K_2[t]$ are, in every particular case, purely mathematical objects; viz., classes of triples of real numbers. So let us consider all the true and false sentences of the form '$H(K_1[t], K_2[t])$' where, in place of '$K_1[t]$' and '$K_2[t]$,' we have purely logico-mathematical designations of particular classes of triples of real numbers. There is no reason to suppose that all the truths of *this* domain can be exactly segregated in purely syntactical terms. Thus inclusion of 'H' does violate (2), and therefore 'H' fails to qualify as logical vocabulary. By adhering to the method of co-ordinates and thus reconstruing all predicates of natural science in the manner here illustrated by 'H,' Carnap overcomes the objection noted in the preceding paragraph.

To sum up very roughly, this theory characterizes logic (and mathematics) as the largest part of science within which the true-false dichotomy *can* be reproduced in syntactical terms. This version may seem rather thinner than the claim that logic and mathematics are somehow true by linguistic convention, but at any rate it is more intelligible, and, if true, perhaps interesting and important. To become sure of its truth, interest, and importance, however, we must look more closely at this term 'syntax.'

As used in the passage: "The terms 'sentence' and 'direct consequence' are the two primitive terms of logical syntax,"[10] the term 'syntax' is of course irrelevant to a thesis. The relevant sense is that rather in which it

9. Carnap, *Logical Syntax*, §3, p. 15.
10. Carnap, *Philosophy and Logical Syntax* (London, 1935), p. 47.

connotes discourse about marks and their succession. But here still we must distinguish degrees of inclusiveness; two different degrees are exemplified in *Logical Syntax,* according as the object language is Carnap's highly restricted Language I or his more powerful Language II. For the former, Carnap's formulation of logical truth is narrowly syntactical in the manner of familiar formalizations of logical systems by axioms and rules of inference. But Gödel's proof of the incompletability of elementary number theory shows that no such approach can be adequate to mathematics in general, nor in particular to set theory, nor to Language II. For Language II, in consequence, Carnap's formulation of logical truth proceeded along the lines rather of Tarski's technique of truth definition.[11] The result was still a purely syntactical specification of the logical truths, but only in this more liberal sense of 'syntactical': it was couched in a vocabulary consisting (in effect) of (a) names of signs, (b) an operator expressing concatenation of expressions, and (c), by way of auxiliary machinery, the whole logical (and mathematical) vocabulary itself.

So construed, however, the thesis that logico-mathematical truth is syntactically specifiable becomes uninteresting. For, what it says is that logico-mathematical truth is specifiable in a notation consisting solely of (a), (b), *and* the whole logico-mathematical vocabulary itself. But *this* thesis would hold equally if 'logico-mathematical' were broadened (at *both* places in the thesis) to include physics, economics, and anything else under the sun; Tarski's routine of truth definition would still carry through just as well. No special trait of logic and mathematics has been singled out after all.

Strictly speaking, the position is weaker still. The mathematics appealed to in (c) must, as Tarski shows, be a yet more inclusive mathematical theory in certain respects than that for which truth is being defined. It was largely because of his increasing concern over this self-stultifying

11. See Carnap, *Logical Syntax,* especially §§34a-i, 60a-d, 71a-d. These sections had been omitted from the German edition, but only for lack of space; see p. xi of the English edition. Meanwhile they had appeared as articles: "Die Antinomien . . ." and "Ein Gültigkeitskriterium." At that time Carnap had had only partial access to Tarski's ideas (see Rudolf Carnap, "Ein Gültigkeitskriterium fur die Sätze der klassischen Mathematik," *Monatshefte für Mathematik und Physik* 41 (1934), footnote 3, the full details of which reached the non-Slavic world in 1936 in Alfred Tarski's "Der Wahrheitsbegriff in den formalisierten Sprachen," *Studia Philosophica* 1 (1936), pp. 261–405. Translated in *Logic, Semantics, Metamathematics* (Oxford: Clarendon Press, 1956).

situation that Carnap relaxed his stress on syntax, in the years following *Logical Syntax,* in favor of semantics.

VIII

Even if logical truth were specifiable in syntactical terms, this would not show that it was grounded in language. Any *finite* class of truths (to take an extreme example) is clearly reproducible by a membership condition couched in as narrowly syntactical terms as you please; yet we certainly cannot say of every finite class of truths that its members are true purely by language. Thus the ill-starred doctrine of syntactical specifiability of logical truth was always something other than the linguistic doctrine of logical truth, if this be conceived as the doctrine that logical truth is grounded in language. In any event the doctrine of syntactical specifiability, which we found pleasure in being able to make comparatively clear sense of, has unhappily had to go by the board. The linguistic doctrine of logical truth, on the other hand, goes sturdily on.

The notion of logical truth is now counted by Carnap as semantical. This of course does not of itself mean that logical truth is grounded in language; for note that the general notion of truth is also semantical, though truth in general is not grounded purely in language. But the semantical attribute of logical truth, in particular, *is* one which, according to Carnap, is grounded in language: in convention, fiat, meaning. Such support as he hints for this doctrine, aside from ground covered in §§I–VI, seems to depend on an analogy with what goes on in the propounding of artificial languages; and I shall now try to show why I think the analogy mistaken.

I may best schematize the point by considering a case, not directly concerned with logical truth, where one might typically produce an artificial language as a step in an argument. This is the imaginary case of a logical positivist, say Ixmann, who is out to defend scientists against the demands of a metaphysician. The metaphysician argues that science presupposes metaphysical principles, or raises metaphysical problems, and that the scientists should therefore show due concern. Ixmann's answer consists in showing in detail how people (on Mars, say) might speak a language quite adequate to all of our science but, unlike our language, incapable of expressing the alleged metaphysical issues. (I applaud this answer, and think it embodies the most telling component of Carnap's own anti-metaphysical representations; but here I digress.) Now how does our hypothetical Ixmann specify that doubly hypothetical language? By telling us, at least to the extent needed for his argument, what these Martians are to be imagined as uttering and what they are thereby to be understood to mean. Here is Carnap's familiar duality of formation rules and transformation rules (or meaning postulates), as rules of language. But these rules are part only of Ixmann's narrative machinery, not part of what he is portraying. He is not representing his hypothetical Martians themselves as somehow explicit on formation and transformation rules. Nor is he representing there to be any intrinsic difference between those truths which happen to be disclosed to us by his partial specifications (his transformation rules) and those further truths, hypothetically likewise known to the Martians of his parable, which he did not trouble to sketch in.

The threat of fallacy lurks in the fact that Ixmann's rules are indeed arbitrary fiats, as is his whole Martian parable. The fallacy consists in confusing levels, projecting the conventional character of the rules into the story, and so misconstruing Ixmann's parable as attributing truth legislation to his hypothetical Martians.

The case of a non-hypothetical artificial language is in principle the same. Being a new invention, the language has to be explained; and the explanation will proceed by what may certainly be called formation and transformation rules. These rules will hold by arbitrary fiat, the artifex being boss. But all we can reasonably ask of these rules is that they enable us to find corresponding to each of his sentences a sentence of like truth value in familiar ordinary language. There is no (to me) intelligible additional decree that we can demand of him as to the boundary between analytic and synthetic, logic and fact, among his truths. We may well decide to extend our word 'analytic' or 'logically true' to sentences of his language which he in his explanations has paired off fairly directly with English sentences so classified by us; but this is our decree, regarding our word 'analytic' or 'logically true.'

IX

We had in §II to form some rough idea of what logical truth was supposed to take in, before we could get on with the linguistic doctrine of logical truth. This we did, with help of the general notion of truth[12] to-

---

12. In defense of this general notion, in invidious contrast to that of analyticity, see Quine, *From a Logical Point of View,* pp. 137–138.

gether with a partial enumeration of the logical vocabulary of a particular language. In §VII we found hope of a less provincial and accidental characterization of logical vocabulary; but it failed. Still, the position is not intolerable We well know from modern logic how to devise a technical notation which is admirably suited to the business of 'or,' 'not,' 'and,' 'all,' 'only,' and such other particles as we would care to count as logical; and to enumerate the signs and constructions of that technical notation, or a theoretically adequate subset of them, is the work of a moment (cf. §II). Insofar as we are content to think of all science as fitted within that stereotyped logical framework—and there is no hardship in so doing— our notion of logical vocabulary is precise. And so, derivatively, is our notion of logical truth. But only in point of extent. There is no epistemological corollary as to the *ground* of logical truth (cf. §II).

Even this halfway tolerable situation obtains only for logical truth in a relatively narrow sense, omitting truths by "essential predication" (Aristotle) such as 'No bachelor is married.' I tend to reserve the term 'logically true' for the narrower domain, and to use the term 'analytic' for the more inclusive domain which includes truths by essential predication. Carnap on the contrary has used both terms in the broader sense. But the problems of the two subdivisions of the analytic class differ in such a way that it has been convenient up to now in this essay to treat mainly of logical truth in the narrower sense.

The truths by essential predication are sentences which can be turned into logical truths by supplanting certain simple predicates (e.g., 'bachelor') by complex synonyms (e.g., 'man not married'). This formulation is not inadequate to such further examples as 'If *A* is part of *B* and *B* is part of *C* then *A* is part of *C*'; this case can be managed by using for 'is part of' the synonym 'overlaps nothing save what overlaps.'[13] The relevant notion of synonymy is simply *analytic* co-extensiveness (however circular this might be as a definition).

To count analyticity a genus of logical truth is to grant, it may seem, the linguistic doctrine of logical truth; for the term 'analytic' directly suggests truth by language. But this suggestion can be adjusted, in parallel to what was said of 'true by definition' in §V. 'Analytic' means true by synonymy and logic, hence no doubt true by language and logic, and simply true by language *if* the linguistic doctrine of logical truth is right. Logic itself, throughout these remarks, may be taken as including or ex-

13. After Nelson Goodman, *The Structure of Appearance* (Cambridge, Mass.: Harvard University Press, 1951).

cluding set theory (and hence mathematics), depending on further details of one's position.

What has made it so difficult for us to make satisfactory sense of the linguistic doctrine is the obscurity of 'true by language.' Now 'synonymous' lies within that same central obscurity; for, about the best we can say of synonymous predicates is that they are somehow "co-extensive by language." The obscurity extends, of course, to 'analytic.'

One quickly identifies certain seemingly transparent cases of synonymy, such as 'bachelor' and 'man not married,' and senses the triviality of associated sentences such as 'No bachelor is married.' Conceivably the mechanism of such recognition, when better understood, might be made the basis of a definition of synonymy and analyticity in terms of linguistic behavior. On the other hand such an approach might make sense only of something like degrees of synonymy and analyticity. I see no reason to expect that the full-width analyticity which Carnap and others make such heavy demands upon can be fitted to such a foundation in even an approximate way. In any event, we at present lack any tenable general suggestion, either rough and practical or remotely theoretical, as to what it is to be an analytic sentence. All we have are purported illustrations, and claims that the truths of elementary logic, with or without the rest of mathematics, should be counted in. Wherever there has been a semblance of a general criterion, to my knowledge, there has been either some drastic failure such as tended to admit all or no sentences as analytic, or there has been a circularity of the kind noted three paragraphs back, or there has been a dependence on terms like 'meaning,' 'possible,' 'conceivable,' and the like, which are at least as mysterious (and in the same way) as what we want to define. I have expatiated on these troubles elsewhere,[14] as has White.

Logical truth (in my sense, excluding the additional category of essential predication) is, we saw, well enough definable (relatively to a fixed logical notation). *Elementary* logical truth can even be given a narrowly syntactical formulation, such as Carnap once envisaged for logic and mathematics as a whole (cf. §VII); for the deductive system of elementary logic is known to be complete. But when we would supplement the logical truths by the rest of the so-called analytic truths, true by essential predication, then we are no longer able even to say what we are talking about. The distinction itself, and not merely an epistemological question concerning it, is what is then in question.

14. "Two Dogmas" [Chapter 2].

What of settling the limits of the broad class of analytic truths by fixing on a standard language as we did for logical truth? No, the matter is very different. Once given the logical vocabulary, we have a means of clearly marking off the species logical truth within the genus truth. But the intermediate genus analyticity is not parallel, for it does not consist of the truths which contain just a certain vocabulary essentially (in the sense of §II). To segregate analyticity we should need rather some sort of accounting of synonymies throughout a universal or all-purpose language. No regimented universal language is at hand, however, for consideration; what Carnap has propounded in this direction have of course been only illustrative samples, fragmentary in scope. And even if there were one, it is not clear by what standards we would care to settle questions of synonymy and analyticity within it.

X

Carnap's present position[15] is that one has specified a language quite rigorously only when he has fixed, by dint of so-called meaning postulates, what sentences are to count as analytic. The proponent is supposed to distinguish between those of his declarations which count as meaning postulates, and thus engender analyticity, and those which do not. This he does, presumably, by attaching the label 'meaning postulate.'

But the sense of this label is far less clear to me than four causes of its seeming to be clear. Which of these causes has worked on Carnap, if any, I cannot say; but I have no doubt that all four have worked on his readers. One of these causes is misevaluation of the role of convention in connection with artificial language; thus note the unattributed fallacy described in §VIII. Another is misevaluation of the conventionality of postulates: failure to appreciate that postulates, though they are postulates always by fiat, are not *therefore* true by fiat (cf. §§IV–V). A third is over-estimation of the distinctive nature of postulates, and of definitions, because of conspicuous and peculiar roles which postulates and definitions have played in situations not really relevant to present concerns: postulates in uninterpreted systems (cf. §IV), and definitions in double systems of notation (cf. §V). A fourth is misevaluation of legislative postulation and legislative definition themselves, in two respects: failure to appreciate that this legislative trait is a trait of scientific hypotheses very

15. See particularly Carnap, "Meaning Postulates," *Philosophical Studies* 3 (1952), pp. 65–73.

generally (cf. §VI), and failure to appreciate that it is a trait of the passing event rather than of the truth which is thereby instituted (cf. end of §V).

Suppose a scientist introduces a new term, for a certain substance or force. He introduces it by an act either of legislative definition or of legislative postulation. Progressing, he evolves hypotheses regarding further traits of the named substance or force. Suppose now that some such eventual hypothesis, well attested, identifies this substance or force with one named by a complex term built up of other portions of his scientific vocabulary. We all know that this new identity will figure in the ensuing developments quite on a par with the identity which first came of the act of legislative definition, if any, or on a par with the law which first came of the act of legislative postulation. Revisions, in the course of further progress, can touch any of these affirmations equally. Now I urge that scientists, proceeding thus, are not thereby slurring over any meaningful distinction. Legislative acts occur again and again; on the other hand a dichotomy of the resulting truths themselves into analytic and synthetic, truths by meaning postulate and truths by force of nature, has been given no tolerably clear meaning even as a methodological ideal.

One conspicuous consequence of Carnap's belief in this dichotomy may be seen in his attitude toward philosophical issues as to what there is.[16] It is only by assuming the cleavage between analytic and synthetic truths that he is able to declare the problem of universals to be a matter not of theory but of linguistic decision. Now I am as impressed as anyone with the vastness of what language contributes to science and to one's whole view of the world; and in particular I grant that one's hypothesis as to what there is, e.g., as to there being universals, is at bottom just as arbitrary or pragmatic a matter as one's adoption of a new brand of set theory or even a new system of bookkeeping. Carnap in turn recognizes that such decisions, however conventional, "will nevertheless usually be influenced by theoretical knowledge."[17] But what impresses me more than it does Carnap is how well this whole attitude is suited also to the theoretical hypotheses of natural science itself, and how little basis there is for a distinction.

The lore of our fathers is a fabric of sentences. In our hands it develops

16. See "Implicit Definition Sustained," in W. V. Quine, *The Ways of Paradox* (Cambridge, Mass.: Harvard University Press, 1966, 1976).

17. Carnap, "Empiricism, Semantics, and Ontology," *Revue Internationale de Philosophie* 4 (1950), §2. Reprinted in Carnap, *Meaning and Necessity.*

and changes, through more or less arbitrary and deliberate revisions and additions of our own, more or less directly occasioned by the continuing stimulation of our sense organs. It is a pale gray lore, black with fact and white with convention. But I have found no substantial reasons for concluding that there are any quite black threads in it, or any white ones.

II

INDETERMINACY AND INSCRUTABILITY

5

SPEAKING OF OBJECTS

I

We are prone to talk and think of objects. Physical objects are the obvious illustration when the illustrative mood is on us, but there are also all the abstract objects, or so there purport to be: the states and qualities, numbers, attributes, classes. We persist in breaking reality down somehow into a multiplicity of identifiable and discriminable objects, to be referred to by singular and general terms. We talk so inveterately of objects that to say we do so seems almost to say nothing at all; for how else is there to talk?

It is hard to say how else there is to talk, not because our objectifying pattern is an invariable trait of human nature, but because we are bound to adapt any alien pattern to our own in the very process of understanding or translating the alien sentences.

Imagine a newly discovered tribe whose language is without known affinities. The linguist has to learn the language directly by observing what the natives say under observed circumstances, encountered or contrived. He makes a first crude beginning by compiling native terms for environing objects; but here already he is really imposing his own patterns. Let me explain what I mean. I will grant that the linguist may establish inductively, beyond reasonable doubt, that a certain heathen expression is one to which natives can be prompted to assent by the presence of a rabbit, or reasonable *facsimile,* and not otherwise. The linguist is then warranted in according the native expression the cautious translation "There's a rabbit," "There we have a rabbit," "Lo! a rabbit," "Lo! rabbithood again," insofar as the differences among these English sentences are counted irrelevant. This much translation can be objective, however exotic the tribe. It recognizes the native expression as in effect a rabbit-heralding sentence. But the linguist's bold further step, in which he imposes his own object-positing pattern without special warrant, is taken when he equates the native expression or any part of it with the *term* "rabbit."

It is easy to show that such appeal to an object category is unwarranted even though we cannot easily, in English, herald rabbits without objectification. For we can argue from indifference. Given that a native sentence says that a so-and-so is present, and given that the sentence is true when and only when a rabbit is present, it by no means follows that the so-and-so are rabbits. They might be all the various temporal segments of rabbits. They might be all the integral or undetached parts of rabbits. In order to decide among these alternatives we need to be able to ask more than whether a so-and-so is present. We need to be able to ask whether this is the same so-and-so as that, and whether one so-and-so is present or two. We need something like the apparatus of identity and quantification; hence far more than we are in a position to avail ourselves of in a language in which our high point as of even date is rabbit-announcing.

And the case is yet worse: we do not even have evidence for taking the native expression as of the form "A so-and-so is present"; it could as well be construed with an abstract singular term, as meaning that rabbithood is locally manifested. Better just "Rabbiteth," like "Raineth."

But if our linguist is going to be as cagey as all this, he will never translate more than these simple-minded announcements of observable current events. A cagey linguist is a caged linguist. What we want from the linguist as a serviceable finished product, after all, is no mere list of sentence-to-sentence equivalences, like the airline throwaways of useful Spanish phrases. We want a manual of instructions for custom-building a native sentence to roughly the purpose of any newly composed English sentence, within reason, and vice versa. The linguist has to resolve the potential infinity of native sentences into a manageably limited list of grammatical constructions and constituent linguistic forms, and then show how the business of each can be approximated in English; and vice versa. Sometimes perhaps he will translate a word or construction not directly but contextually, by systematic instructions for translating its containing sentences; but still he must make do with a limited lot of contextual definitions. Now once he has carried out this necessary job of lexicography, forwards and backwards, he has read our ontological point of view into the native language. He has decided what expressions to treat as referring to objects, and, within limits, what sorts of objects to treat them as referring to. He has had to decide, however arbitrarily, how to accommodate English idioms of identity and quantification in native translation.

The word "arbitrary" needs stressing, not because those decisions are wholly arbitrary, but because they are so much more so than one tends to suppose. For, what evidence does the linguist have? He started with what we may call native observation sentences, such as the rabbit announcement. These he can say how to translate into English, provided we impute no relevance to the differences between "Here a rabbit," "Here rabbithood," and the like. Also he can record further native sentences and settle whether various persons are prepared to affirm or deny them, though he find no rabbit movements or other currently observable events to tie them to. Among these untranslated sentences he may get an occasional hint of logical connections, by finding say that just the persons who are prepared to affirm A are prepared to affirm B and deny C. Thereafter his data leave off and his creativity sets in.

What he does in his creativity is attribute special and distinctive functions to component words, or conspicuously recurrent fragments, of the recorded sentences. The only ways one can appraise these attributions are as follows. One can see whether they add up to representing the rabbit sentence and the like as conforming to their previously detected truth conditions. One can see also how well they fit the available data on other sentences: sentences for which no truth conditions are known, but only the varying readiness of natives to affirm or deny them. Beyond this we can judge the attributions only on their simplicity and naturalness— to *us*.

Certainly the linguist will try out his theory on the natives, springing new sentences authorized by his theory, to see if they turn out right. This is a permuting of the time order: one frames the theory before all possible data are in, and then lets it guide one in the eliciting of additional data likeliest to matter. This is good scientific method, but it opens up no new kind of data. English general and singular terms, identity, quantification, and the whole bag of ontological tricks may be correlated with elements of the native language in any of various mutually incompatible ways, each compatible with all possible linguistic data, and none preferable to another save as favored by a rationalization of the *native* language that is simple and natural to *us*.

It makes no real difference that the linguist will turn bilingual and come to think as the natives do—whatever that means. For the arbitrariness of reading our objectifications into the heathen speech reflects not so much the inscrutability of the heathen mind, as that there is nothing to scrute. Even we who grew up together and learned English at the same knee, or adjacent ones, talk alike for no other reason than that society coached us alike in a pattern of verbal response to externally observable cues. We have been beaten into an outward conformity to an outward standard; and thus it is that when I correlate your sentences with mine by the simple rule of phonetic correspondence, I find that the public circumstances of your affirmations and denials agree pretty well with those of my own. If I conclude that you share my sort of conceptual scheme, I am not adding a supplementary conjecture so much as spurning unfathomable distinctions; for, what further criterion of sameness of conceptual scheme can be imagined? The case of a Frenchman, moreover, is the same except that I correlate his sentences with mine not by phonetic correspondence but according to a traditionally evolved dictionary.[1] The case of the linguist and his newly discovered heathen, finally, differs simply in that the linguist has to grope for a general sentence-to-sentence correlation that will make the public circumstances of the heathen's affirmations and denials match up tolerably with the circumstances of the linguist's own. If the linguist fails in this, or has a hard time of it, or succeeds only by dint of an ugly and complex mass of correlations, then he is entitled to say—in the only sense in which one *can* say it—that his heathens have a very different attitude toward reality from ours; and even so he cannot coherently suggest what their attitude is. Nor, in principle, is the natural bilingual any better off.

When we compare theories, doctrines, points of view, and cultures, on the score of what sorts of objects there are said to be, we are comparing them in a respect which itself makes sense only provincially. It makes sense only as far afield as our efforts to translate our domestic idioms of identity and quantification bring encouragement in the way of simple and natural-looking correspondences. If we attend to business we are unlikely to find a very alien culture with a predilection for a very outlandish universe of discourse, just because the outlandishness of it would detract from our sense of patness of our dictionary of translation. There is a notion that our provincial ways of positing objects and conceiving

1. See Richard von Mises, *Positivism* (Cambridge, Mass.: Harvard University Press, 1951), pp. 46ff.

nature may be best appreciated for what they are by standing off and seeing them against a cosmopolitan background of alien cultures; but the notion comes to nothing, for there is no πού στῶ.[2]

II

Yet, for all the difficulty of transcending our object-directed pattern of thought, we can examine it well enough from inside. Let us turn our attention from the heathen, who seemed to have a term for "rabbit," to our own child at home who seems to have just acquired his first few terms in our own language: "mama," "water," perhaps "red." To begin with, the case of the child resembles that of the heathen. For though we may fully satisfy ourselves that the child has learned the trick of using the utterances "mama" and "water" strictly in the appropriate presences, or as means of inducing the appropriate presences, still we have no right to construe these utterances in the child's mouth as terms, at first, for things or substances.

We in our maturity have come to look upon the child's mother as an integral body who, in an irregular closed orbit, revisits the child from time to time; and to look upon red in a radically different way, viz., as scattered about. Water, for us, is rather like red, but not quite; things can be red, but only stuff is water. But the mother, red, and water are for the infant all of a type: each is just a history of sporadic encounter, a scattered portion of what goes on. His first learning of the three words is uniformly a matter of learning how much of what goes on about him counts as the mother, or as red, or as water. It is not for the child to say in the first case "Hello! mama again," in the second case "Hello! another red thing," and in the third case "Hello! more water." They are all on a par: Hello! more mama, more red, more water. Even this last formula, which treats all three terms on the model of our provincial adult bulk term "water," is imperfect; for it unwarrantedly imputes an objectification of matter, even if only as stuff and not as bits.

Progressively, however, the child is seen to evolve a pattern of verbal behavior that finally comes to copy ours too closely for there to be any sense in questioning the general sameness of conceptual scheme. For per-

2. For a fuller development of the foregoing theme see my "Meaning and Translation," in Reuben Brower's anthology, *On Translation* (Cambridge, Mass.: Harvard University Press, 1959). For criticisms that have benefited the above section of the present essay and ensuing portions, I am grateful to Burton Dreben. [See Chapter 7.]

spective on our own objectifying apparatus we may consider what steps of development make the difference between the "mama"-babbling infant who cannot be said to be using terms for objects, and the older child who can.

It is only when the child has got on to the full and proper use of *individuative* terms like "apple" that he can properly be said to have taken to using terms as terms, and speaking of objects. Words like "apple," and not words like "mama" or "water" or "red," are the terms whose ontological involvement runs deep. To learn "apple" it is not sufficient to learn how much of what goes on counts as apple; we must learn how much counts as *an* apple, and how much as another. Such terms possess built-in modes of individuation.

Individuative terms are commonly made to double as bulk terms. Thus we may say "There is some apple in the salad," not meaning "some apple or other"; just as we may say "Mary had a little lamb" in either of two senses. Now we have appreciated that the child can learn the terms "mama," "red," and "water" quite well before he ever has mastered the ins and outs of our adult conceptual scheme of mobile enduring physical objects, identical from time to time and place to place; and in principle he might do the same for "apple," as a bulk term for uncut apple stuff. But he can never fully master "apple" in its individuative use, except as he gets on with the scheme of enduring and recurrent physical objects. He may come somewhat to grips with the individuative use of "apple" before quite mastering the comprehensive physical outlook, but his usage will be marred by misidentifications of distinct apples over time, or misdiscriminations of identical ones.

He has really got on to the individuative use, one is tempted to suppose, once he responds with the plural "apples" to a heap of apples. But not so. He may at that point have learned "apples" as another bulk term, applicable to just so much apple as is taken up in apple heaps. "Apples," for him, would be subordinated to "apple" as is "warm water" to "water," and "bright red" to "red."

The child might proceed to acquire "block" and "blocks," "ball" and "balls," as bulk terms in the same fashion. By the force of analogy among such pairs he might even come to apply the plural "-s" with seeming appropriateness to new words, and to drop it with seeming appropriateness from words first learned only with it. We might well not detect, for a while, his misconception: that "-s" just turns bulk terms into more specialized bulk terms connoting clumpiness.

A plausible variant misconception is this: "apple" bulkwise might cover just the apple stuff that is spaced off in lone apples, while "apples" still figures as last suggested. Then apples and apple would be mutually exclusive rather than subordinate the one to the other. This variant misconception could likewise be projected systematically to "block" and "blocks," "ball" and "balls," and long escape exposure.

How can we ever tell, then, whether the child as really got the trick of individuation? Only by engaging him in sophisticated discourse of "that apple," "not that apple," "an apple," "same apple," "another apple," "these apples." It is only at this level that a palpable difference emerges between genuinely individuative use and the conterfeits lately imagined.

Doubtless the child gets the swing of these peculiar adjectives "same," "another," "an," "that," "not that," contextually: first he becomes attuned to various longer phrases or sentences that contain them, and then gradually he develops appropriate habits in relation to the component words as common parts and residues of those longer forms. His tentative acquisition of the plural "-s," lately speculated on, is itself a first primitive step of the kind. The contextual learning of these various particles goes on simultaneously, we may suppose, so that they are gradually adjusted to one another and a coherent pattern of usage is evolved matching that of one's elders. This is a major step in acquiring the conceptual scheme that we all know so well. For it is on achieving this step, and only then, that there can be any general talk of objects as such. Only at this stage does it begin to make sense to wonder whether the apple now in one's hand is the apple noticed yesterday.

Until individuation emerges, the child can scarcely be said to have general *or* singular terms, there being no express talk of objects. The pre-individuative term "mama," and likewise "water" and "red" (for children who happen to learn "water" and "red" before mastering individuation), hark back to a primitive phase to which the distinction between singular and general is irrelevant. Once the child has pulled through the individuative crisis, though, he is prepared to reassess prior terms. "Mama," in particular, gets set up retroactively as the name of a broad and recurrent but withal individual object, and thus as a singular term *par excellence*. Occasions eliciting "mama" being just as discontinuous as those eliciting "water," the two terms had been on a par; but with the advent of individuation the mother becomes integrated into a cohesive spatiotemporal convexity, while water remains scattered even in space-time. The two terms thus part company.

The mastery of individuation seems scarcely to affect people's attitude toward "water." For "water," "sugar," and the like the category of bulk terms remains, a survival of the pre-individuative phase, ill fitting the dichotomy into general and singular. But the philosophical mind sees its way to pressing this archaic category into the dichotomy. The bulk term "water" after the copula can usually be smoothly reconstrued as a general term true of each portion of water, while in other positions it is usually more simply construed as a singular term naming that spatiotemporally diffuse object which is the totality of the world's water.

III

I have urged that we could know the necessary and sufficient stimulatory conditions of every possible act of utterance, in a foreign language, and still not know how to determine what objects the speakers of that language believe in. Now if objective reference is so inaccessible to observation, who is to say on empirical grounds that belief in objects of one or another description is right or wrong? How can there ever be empirical evidence against existential statements?

The answer is something like this. Grant that a knowledge of the appropriate stimulatory conditions of a sentence does not settle how to construe the sentence in terms of existence of objects. Still, it does tend to settle what is to count as empirical evidence for or against the truth of the sentence. If we then go on to assign the sentence some import in point of existence of objects, by arbitrary projection in the case of the heathen language or as a matter of course in the case of our own, thereupon what has already been counting as empirical evidence for or against the truth of the sentence comes to count as empirical evidence for or against the existence of the objects.

The opportunity for error in existential statements increases with one's mastery of the verbal apparatus of objective reference. In one's earliest phase of word learning, terms like "mama" and "water" were learned which may be viewed retrospectively as names each of an observed spatiotemporal object. Each such term was learned by a process of reinforcement and extinction, whereby the spatiotemporal range of application of the term was gradually perfected. The object named is assuredly an observed one, in the sense that the reinforced stimuli proceeded pretty directly from it. Granted, this talk of name and object belongs to a later phase of language learning, even as does the talk of stimulation.

The second phase, marked by the advent of individuative terms, is where a proper notion of object emerges. Here we get general terms, each true of each of many objects. But the objects still are observable spatiotemporal objects. For these individuative terms, e.g. "apple," are learned still by the old method of reinforcement and extinction; they differ from their predecessors only in the added feature of internal individuation.

Demonstrative singular terms like "this apple" usher in a third phase, characterized by the fact that a singular term seriously used can now, through error, fail to name: the thing pointed to can turn out to be the mere façade of an apple, or maybe a tomato. But even at this stage anything that we do succeed in naming is still an observable spatiotemporal object.

A fourth phase comes with the joining of one general term to another in attributive position. Now for the first time we can get general terms which are not true of anything; thus "blue apple," "square ball." But when there are things at all of which the thus formed general terms are true, they are still nothing new; they are just some among the same old observables whereof the component terms are true.

It is a fifth phase that brings a new mode of understanding, giving access to new sorts of objects. When we form compounds by applying relative terms to singular terms, we get such compounds as "smaller than that speck." Whereas the non-existence of observable blue apples is tantamount to the non-existence of blue apples, the non-existence of observable objects smaller than that speck is not taken as tantamount to the non-existence of objects smaller than that speck. The notable feature of this fifth phase is not that it enables us to form meaningful singular terms devoid of reference, for that was already achieved on occasion with "this apple"; nor that it enables us to form meaningful general terms true of nothing, for that was already achieved with "blue apple"; but that it enables us, for the first time, to form terms whose references can be admitted to be forever unobservable without yet being repudiated, like blue apples, as non-existent.

Such applying of relative terms to singular terms is the simplest method of forming terms that purport to name unobservables, but there are also more flexible devices to much the same effect: the relative clause and description.

And there comes yet a sixth phase, when we break through to posits more drastically new still than the objects smaller than the smallest visible speck. For the objects smaller than the speck differ from observable objects only in a matter of degree, whereas the sixth phase ushers in abstract entities. This phase is marked by the advent of abstract singular terms like "redness," "roundness," "mankind," purported names of qualities, attributes, classes. Let us speculate on the mechanism of this new move.

One wedge is the bulk term. Such terms can be learned at the very first phase, we saw, on a par with "mama." We saw them diverge from "mama" at the second phase, simply on the score that the woman comes then to be appreciated as an integrated spatiotemporal thing while the world's water or red stuff ordinarily does not. For the child, thus, who is not on to the sophisticated idea of the scattered single object, the bulk term already has an air of generality about it, comparable to the individuative "apple"; and still it is much like the singular "mama" in form and function, having even been learned or learnable at the first phase on a par with "mama." So the bulk term already has rather the hybrid air of the abstract singular term. "Water" might, from the very advent of individuation, even be said to name a shared *attribute* of the sundry puddles and glassfuls rather than a scattered portion of the world *composed* of those puddles and glassfuls; for the child of course adopts neither position.

Moreover, there is a tricky point about color words that especially encourages the transition to abstract reference. "Red" can be learned as a bulk term, like "water," but in particular it applies to apples whose insides are white. Before mastering the conceptual scheme of individuation and enduring physical object, the child sees the uncut red apple, like tomato juice, simply as so much red exposure in the passing show, and, having no sense of physical identity, he sees the subsequently exposed white interior of the apple as irrelevant. When eventually he does master the conceptual scheme of individuation and enduring physical object, then, he has to come to terms with a preacquired use of "red" that has suddenly gone double: there is red stuff (tomato juice) and there are red things (apples) that are mostly white stuff. "Red" both remains a bulk term of the ancient vintage of "water" and "mama," and becomes a concrete general term like "round" or "apple." Since the child will still not clearly conceive of "red" as suddenly two words, we have him somehow infusing singularity into the concrete general; and such is the recipe, however unappetizing, for the abstract singular. The analogy then spreads to other general terms, that were in no such special predicament as "red," until they all deliver abstract singulars.

Another force for abstract terms, or for the positing of abstract objects, lies in abbreviated cross-reference. E.g., after an elaborate remark regarding President Eisenhower, someone says: "The same holds for Churchill." Or, by way of supporting some botanical identification, one says: "Both plants have the following attribute in common"—and proceeds with a double-purpose description. In such cases a laborious repetition is conveniently circumvented. Now the cross-reference in such cases is just to a form of words. But we have a stubborn tendency to reify the unrepeated matter by positing an attribute, instead of just talking of words.

There is indeed an archaic precedent for confusing sign and object; the earliest conditioning of the infant's babbling is ambiguous on the point. For suppose a baby rewarded for happening to babble something like "mama" or "water" just as the mother or water is looming. The stimuli which are thus reinforced are bound to be two: there is not only the looming of the object, there is equally the word itself, heard by the child from his own lips. Confusion of sign and object is original sin, coeval with the word.

We have seen how the child might slip into the community's ontology of attributes by easy stages, from bulk terms onward. We have also seen how talk of attributes will continue to be encouraged, in the child and the community, by a certain convenience of cross-reference coupled with a confusion of sign and object. We have in these reflections some materials for speculation regarding the early beginnings of an ontology of attributes in the childhood of the race. There is room, as well, for alternative or supplementary conjectures; e.g., that the attributes are vestiges of the minor deities of some creed outworn.[3] In a general way such speculation is epistemologically relevant, as suggesting how organisms maturing and evolving in the physical environment we know might conceivably end up discoursing of abstract objects as we do. But the disreputability of origins is of itself no argument against preserving and prizing the abstract ontology. This conceptual scheme may well be, however accidental, a happy accident; just as the theory of electrons would be none the worse for having first occurred to its originator in the course of some absurd dream. At any rate the ontology of abstract objects is part of the ship which, in Neurath's figure, we are rebuilding at sea.[4] We may revise the

3. Thus Ernst Cassirer, *Language and Myth* (New York: Harper, 1946), pp. 95–96.

4. Otto Neurath, "Protokollsätze," *Erkenntnis* 3 (1932), p. 206.

scheme, but only in favor of some clearer or simpler and no less adequate overall account of what goes on in the world.

IV

By finding out roughly which non-verbal stimulations tend to prompt assent to a given existential statement, we settle, to some degree, what is to count as empirical evidence for or against the existence of the objects in question. This I urged at the beginning of III. Statements, however, existential and otherwise, vary in the directness with which they are conditioned to non-verbal stimulation. Commonly a stimulation will trigger our verdict on a statement only because the statement is a strand in the verbal network of some elaborate theory, other strands of which are more directly conditioned to that stimulation. Most of our statements respond thus to reverberations across the fabric of intralinguistic associations, even when also directly conditioned to extralinguistic stimuli to some degree. Highly theoretical statements are statements whose connection with extralinguistic stimulation consists pretty exclusively in the reverberations across the fabric. Statements of the existence of various sorts of subvisible particles tend to be theoretical, in this sense; and, even more so, statements of the existence of certain abstract objects. Commonly such statements are scarcely to be judged otherwise than by coherence, or by considerations of overall simplicity of a theory whose ultimate contacts with experience are remote as can be from the statements in question. Yet, remarkably enough, there are abstract existence statements that do succumb to such considerations. We have had the wit to posit an ontology massive enough to crumble of its own weight.

For there are the paradoxes of classes. These paradoxes are usually stated for classes because classes are a relatively simple kind of abstract object to talk about, and also because classes, being more innocent on the face of them than attributes, are more fun to discredit. In any event, as is both well known and obvious, the paradoxes of classes go through *pari passu* for attributes, and again for relations.

The moral to draw from the paradoxes is not necessarily nominalism, but certainly that we must tighten our ontological belts a few holes. The law of attributes that was implicit in our language habits or that fitted in with them most easily was that *every* statement that mentions a thing attributes an attribute to it; and this cultural heritage, however venerable, must go. Some judicious *ad hoc* excisions are required at least.

Systematic considerations can press not only for repudiating certain objects, and so declaring certain *terms* irreferential; they can also press for declaring certain *occurrences* of terms irreferential, while other occurrences continue to refer. This point is essentially Frege's,[5] and an example is provided by the sentence "Tom believes that Tully wrote the *Ars Magna*." If we assert this on the strength of Tom's confusion of Tully with Lully, and in full appreciation of Tom's appreciation that Cicero did not write the *Ars Magna*, then we are not giving the term "Tully" purely referential occurrence in our sentence "Tom believes that Tully wrote the *Ars Magna*"; our sentence is not squarely about Tully. If it were, it would have to be true of Cicero, who *is* Tully.

It was only after somehow deciding what heathen locutions to construe as identity and the like that our linguist could begin to say which heathen words serve as terms and what objects they refer to. It was only after getting the knack of identity and kindred devices that our own child could reasonably be said to be talking in terms and to be talking of objects. And it is to the demands of identity still, specifically the substitutivity of identity, that the adult speaker of our language remains answerable as long as he may be said to be using terms to refer.

We are free so to use the verb "believes" as to allow ensuing terms full referential status after all. To do so is to deny "Tom believes that Tully wrote the *Ars Magna*" in the light of Tom's knowledge of Cicero and despite his confusion of names. The fact is that we can and do use "believes" both ways: one way when we say that Tom believes that Tully wrote the *Ars Magna*, and the other way when we deny this, or when, resorting to quantification, we say just that there is *someone* whom Tom believes to have done thus and so. Parallel remarks are suited also to others of the *propositional attitudes,* as Russell calls them: thus doubting, wishing, and striving, along with believing.

Man in a state of nature is not aware of the doubleness of these usages of his, nor of the strings attached to each; just as he is not aware of the paradoxical consequences of a naïve ontology of classes or attributes. Now yet another ontological weakness that we are likewise unaware of

---

5. See Gottlob Frege, "On Sense and Reference," translated in P. T. Geach and M. Black (eds.), *Philosophical Writings of Gottlob Frege* (Oxford: Blackwell, 1952), and in H. Feigl and W. Sellars (eds.), *Readings in Philosophical Analysis* (New York: Appleton, 1949). See also Quine, *From a Logical Point of View,* Essay 8 ("Reference and Modality," pp. 139–159) [Chapter 24].

until, philosophically minded, we start looking to coherence consider-ations, has to do with the individuation of attributes.

The positing of attributes is accompanied by no clue as to the circum-stances under which attributes may be said to be the same or different. This is perverse, considering that the very use of terms and the very pos-iting of objects are unrecognizable to begin with except as keyed in with idioms of sameness and difference. What happens is that at first we learn general patterns of term-talk and thing-talk with the help of the neces-sary adjuncts of identity; afterward we project these well-learned gram-matical forms to attributes, without settling identity for them. We un-derstand the forms as referential just because they are grammatically analogous to ones that we learned earlier, for physical objects, with full dependence on the identity aspect.

The lack of a proper identity concept for attributes is a lack that phi-losophers feel impelled to supply; for, what sense is there in saying that there are attributes when there is no sense in saying when there is one at-tribute and when two? Carnap and others have proposed this principle for identifying attributes: two sentences about x attribute the *same* attri-bute to x if and only if the two sentences are not merely alike in truth value for each choice of x, but necessarily and analytically so, by same-ness of meaning.[6]

However, this formulation depends on a questionable notion, that of sameness of meaning. For let us not slip back into the fantasy of a gallery of ideas and labels. Let us remember rather our field lexicographer's pre-dicament: how arbitrary his projection of analogies from known lan-guages. Can an empiricist speak seriously of sameness of meaning of two conditions upon an object x, one stated in the heathen language and one in ours, when even the singling out of an object x as object at all for the heathen language is so hopelessly arbitrary?

We could skip the heathen language and try talking of sameness of meaning just within our own language. This would degrade the ontology of attributes; identity of attributes would be predicated on frankly pro-vincial traits of English usage, ill fitting the objectivity of true objects. Nor let it be said in extenuation that all talk of objects, physical ones in-cluded, is in a way provincial too; for the way is different. Our physics is provincial only in that there is no universal basis for translating it into

6. Rudolf Carnap, *Meaning and Necessity* (Chicago: University of Chicago Press, 1947), p. 23.

remote languages; it would still never condone defining physical identity in terms of verbal behavior. If we rest the identity of attributes on an admittedly local relation of English synonymy, then we count attributes secondary to language in a way that physical objects are not.

Shall we just let attributes be thus secondary to language in a way that physical objects are not? But our troubles do not end here; for the fact is that I see no hope of making reasonable sense of sameness of meaning even for English. The difficulty is one that I have enlarged on elsewhere.[7] English expressions are supposed to mean the same if, vaguely speaking, you can use one for the other in any situation and any English context without *relevant* difference of effect; and the essential difficulty comes in delimiting the required sense of relevant.

V

There is no denying the access of power that accrues to our conceptual scheme through the positing of abstract objects. Most of what is gained by positing attributes, however, is gained equally by positing classes. Classes are on a par with attributes on the score of abstractness or universality, and they serve the purposes of attributes so far as mathematics and certainly most of science are concerned; and they enjoy, unlike attributes, a crystal-clear identity concept. No wonder that in mathematics the murky intensionality of attributes tends to give way to the limpid extensionality of classes; and likewise in other sciences, roughly in proportion to the rigor and austerity of their systematization.

For attributes one might still claim this advantage over classes: they help in systematizing what we may call the *attributary attitudes*—hunting, wanting, fearing, lacking, and the like. For example, take hunting. Lion hunting is not, like lion catching, a transaction between men and individual lions; for it requires no lions. We analyze lion catching, rabbit catching, etc. as having a catching relation in common and varying only in the individuals caught; but what of lion hunting, rabbit hunting, etc.? If any common relation is to be recognized here, the varying objects of the relation must evidently be taken not as individuals but as kinds. Yet

7. "Two Dogmas of Empiricism." See further Quine, "Carnap e la verità logica," *Revista di Filosofia* 48 (1957), pp. 3–29, which is a translation of an essay whereof part has appeared also in the original English under the title "Logical Truth" in Sidney Hook (ed.), *American Philosophers at Work* (New York: Criterion, 1956).

not kinds in the sense of classes, for then unicorn hunting would cease to differ from griffin hunting. Kinds rather in the sense of attributes.

Some further supposed abstract objects that are like attributes, with respect to the identity problem, are the *propositions*—in the sense of entities that somehow correspond to sentences as attributes correspond to predicates. Now if attributes clamor for recognition as objects of the attributary attitudes, so do propositions as objects of the propositional attitudes: believing, wishing, and the rest.[8]

Overwhelmed by the problem of identity of attributes and of propositions, however, one may choose to make a clean sweep of the lot, and undertake to manage the attributary and propositional attitudes somehow without them. Philosophers who take this austere line will perhaps resort to actual linguistic forms, sentences, instead of propositions, as objects of the propositional attitudes; and to actual linguistic forms, predicates, instead of attributes, as objects of the attributary attitudes.

Against such resort to linguistic forms one hears the following objection, due to Church and Langford.[9] If what are believed are mere sentences, then "Edwin believes the English sentence *S*" goes correctly into German as "Edwin glaubt den englischen Satz *S*," with *S* unchanged. But it also goes correctly into German as "Edwin glaubt" followed by a German translation of *S* in indirect discourse. These two German reports, one quoting the English sentence and the other using German indirect discourse, must then be equivalent. But they are not, it is argued, since a German ignorant of English cannot equate them. Now I am not altogether satisfied with this argument. It rests on the notion of linguistic equivalence, or sameness of meaning; and this has seemed dubious as a tool of philosophical analysis. There is, however, another objection to taking linguistic forms as objects of the attributary and propositional attitudes; viz., simply that that course is discouragingly artificial. With this objection I sympathize.

Perhaps, after all, we should be more receptive to the first and least premeditated of the alternatives. We might keep attributes and propositions after all, but just not try to cope with the problem of their individuation. We might deliberately acquiesce in the old unregenerate positing

8. See my "Quantifiers and Propositional Attitudes," *Journal of Philosophy* 53 (1956), pp. 177–187. [Chapter 22.]

9. Alonzo Church, "On Carnap's Analysis of Statements of Assertion and Belief," *Analysis* 10 (1950), pp. 97–99. Reprinted in Margaret Macdonald (ed.), *Philosophy and Analysis* (Oxford and New York: Blackwell and Philosophical Library, 1954).

of attributes and propositions without hint of a standard of identity. The precept "No entity without identity" might simply be relaxed. Certainly the positing of first objects makes no sense except as keyed to identity; but those patterns of thing talk, once firmly inculcated, have in fact enabled us to talk of attributes and propositions in partial grammatical analogy, without an accompanying standard of identity for them. Why not just accept them thus, as twilight half-entities to which the identity concept is not to apply?[10] If the disreputability of their origins is undeniable, still bastardy, to the enlightened mind, is no disgrace. This liberal line accords with the Oxford philosophy of ordinary language, much though I should regret, by my sympathetic reference, to cause any twinge of sorrow to my revered predecessor in this presidential chair.

What might properly count against countenancing such half-entities, inaccessible to identity, is a certain disruption of logic. For, if we are to tolerate the half-entities without abdication of philosophical responsibility, we must adjust the logic of our conceptual scheme to receive them, and then weigh any resulting complexity against the benefits of the half-entities in connection with propositional and attributary attitudes and elsewhere.

But I am not sure that even philosophical responsibility requires settling for one all-purpose system.[11] Propositional and attributary attitudes belong to daily discourse of hopes, fears, and purposes; causal science gets on well without them. The fact that science has shunned them and fared so well could perhaps encourage a philosopher of sanguine temper to try to include that erstwhile dim domain within an overhauled universal system, science-worthy throughout. But a reasonable if less ambitious alternative would be to keep a relatively simple and austere conceptual scheme, free of half-entities, for official scientific business, and then accommodate the half-entities in a second-grade system.

In any event the idea of accommodating half-entities without identity illustrates how the individuative, object-oriented conceptual scheme so natural to us could conceivably begin to evolve away.

It seemed in our reflections on the child that the category of bulk terms was a survival of a pre-individuative phase. We were thinking onto-

10. Frege did so in *Grundgesetze der Arithmetik,* where he was at pains not to subject *Begriffe* to identity. See also Peter Geach, "Class and Concept," *Philosophical Review* 64 (1955), pp. 561–570.

11. See James B. Conant, *Modern Science and Modern Man* (New York: Columbia University Press, 1952), pp. 989ff.

genetically, but the phylogenetic parallel is plausible too: we may have in the bulk term a relic, half vestigial and half adapted, of a pre-individuative phase in the evolution of our conceptual scheme. And some day, correspondingly, something of our present individuative talk may in turn end up, half vestigial and half adapted, within a new and as yet unimagined pattern beyond individuation.

Transition to some such radically new pattern could occur either through a conscious philosophical enterprise or by slow and unreasoned development along lines of least resistance. A combination of both factors is likeliest; and anyway the two differ mainly in degree of deliberateness. Our patterns of thought or language have been evolving, under pressure of inherent inadequacies and changing needs, since the dawn of language; and, whether we help guide it or not, we may confidently look forward to more of the same.

Translation of our remote past or future discourse into the terms we now know could be about as tenuous and arbitrary a projection as translation of the heathen language was seen to be. Conversely, even to speak of that remote medium as radically different from ours is, as remarked in the case of the heathen language, to say no more than that the translations do not come smoothly. We have, to be sure, a mode of access to future stages of our own evolution that is denied us in the case of the heathen language: we can sit and evolve. But even those historical gradations, if somehow traced down the ages and used as clues to translation between widely separated evolutionary stages, would still be gradations only, and in no sense clues to fixed ideas beneath the flux of language. For the obstacle to correlating conceptual schemes is not that there is anything ineffable about language or culture, near or remote. The whole truth about the most outlandish linguistic behavior is just as accessible to us, in our current Western conceptual scheme, as are other chapters of zoology. The obstacle is only that any one intercultural correlation of words and phrases, and hence of theories, will be just one among various empirically admissible correlations, whether it is suggested by historical gradations or by unaided analogy; there is nothing for such a correlation to be uniquely right or wrong about. In saying this I philosophize from the vantage point only of our own provincial conceptual scheme and scientific epoch, true; but I know no better.

6

REFERENCE

---

9. Bodies

There were advantages, we saw (§3), in starting with observation sentences rather than terms. One advantage was that the nature and utility of reification could be deferred for consideration until an epistemological setting had been sketched in. We are now at that stage.

Incipient reification can already be sensed in the predicational observation sentences (§2). That mode of combination favors, as components, observation sentences that focus on conspicuously limited portions of the scene; for the compound expresses coincidence of such foci.

A second step of reification, and a step beyond ordinary observation sentences, was recognizable in the move to focal observation categoricals (§4). I think of the child as first mastering this construction, like the free observation categorical, simply as a generalized expression of expectation: whenever this, that. For her the difference between the two kinds of categorical would not at first obtrude. The difference is, we recall, that the focal categorical requires the two features—'Raven' and 'Black,' say—to fuse in the scene, while the free categorical does not. However, the scenes first associated with 'Raven' will show a raven at the salient focus, and those first associated with 'Black' will show black at the salient focus. Insofar, the free categorical already meets the focal demand. The difference between the free and the focal in other cases, and between conjunction and predication (§2), can gradually dawn on the child in its own time.

By virtue of its narrowed focus, however, the focal observation categorical—unlike the free one—has decidedly the air of general discourse about bodies: willows in the one example, ravens in the other. This is where I see bodies materializing, ontologically speaking: as ideal nodes at the foci of intersecting observation sentences. Here, I suggest, is the root of reification.

For the very young child, who has not got beyond observation sentences, the recurrent presentation of a body is much on a par with similarities of stimulation that clearly do not prompt reification. Recurrent confrontation of a ball is on a par at first with mere recurrent exposure to sunshine or cool air: the question whether it is the same old ball or one like it makes no more sense than whether it is the same old sunbeam, the same old breeze. Experience is in its *feature-placing* stage, in Strawson's phrase. Individuation comes only later.

True, an infant is observed to expect a steadily moving object to reappear after it passes behind a screen; but this all happens within the specious present, and reflects rather the expectation of continuity of a present feature than the reification of an intermittently absent object. Again a dog's recognition of a recurrent individual is beside the point; the dog is responding to a distinctive odor or other trait, unavailable in the case of qualitatively indistinguishable balls.

To us the question whether we are seeing the same old ball or just a similar one is meaningful even in cases where it remains unanswered. It is here that the reification of bodies is full blown. Our venerable theory of the persistence and recurrence of bodies is characteristic of the use of reification in integrating our system of the world. If I were to try to decide whether the penny now in my pocket is the one that was there last week, or just another one like it, I would have to explore quite varied aspects of my overall scheme of things, so as to reconstruct the simplest, most plausible account of my interim movements, costumes, and expenditures.

Perhaps such indirect equating and distinguishing of bodies is achieved by some other animals to some extent. Perhaps a dog seeking a ball that disappeared fairly recently in one quarter will not settle for a similar ball at an unlikely distance. However that may be, it seems clear that such reification of bodies across time is beyond the reach of observation sentences and categoricals. Substantial reification is theoretical.

10. Values of Variables

Even our sophisticated conception of enduring and recurrent bodies, so characteristic of our human ontology, is for us little more than a beginning. With our progressive systematization of science we have gone on to reify liquids and the invisible air, and we have integrated these things with bodies by reckoning them as aggregates of bodies too small to be detected. Nor have we stopped here. Abstract objects have long since proved indispensable to natural science—thus numbers, functions, classes.

At this level a question arises of what to count as reification, and what to count rather as just a useful but ontologically noncommittal turn of phrase; for the idea that seemed to mark so decisively the reification of bodies, namely persistence between exposures, makes no sense for abstract objects. I have urged elsewhere that the most decisive general marks of reification in our language and kindred ones are the pronouns, and indeed it was 'it' in (1) of §4 that signaled those early rumblings of reification in the focal observation categoricals. The theme is taken up in full by the relative pronouns and their auxiliaries.[1] When a language is regimented in the logical notation of the predicate calculus, the role of such pronouns is played by bound variables.

Observation sentences are to be taken holophrastically from the standpoint of evidence, I urged (§3), and analytically word by word from the retrospective standpoint of theory. From the latter standpoint a focal observation categorical is an outright quantification. 'Ravens are black' becomes

$$\forall x(x \text{ is a raven } \cdot \to \cdot x \text{ is black}).$$

Free observational categoricals would be construed similarly, usually by quantifying over times or places.

So I have insisted down the years that to be is to be the value of a variable. More precisely, what one takes there to be are what one admits as values of one's bound variables. The point has been recognized as obvious and trivial, but it has also been deemed unacceptable, even by readers who share my general philosophical outlook. Let me sort out some of the considerations.

The artificial notation '$\exists x$' of existential quantification is explained merely as a symbolic rendering of the words 'there is something x such that.' So, whatever more one may care to say about being or existence, what there are taken to be are assuredly just what are taken to qualify as values of 'x' in quantifications. The point is thus trivial and obvious.

1. See Quine, *Theories and Things*, pp. 5–6 [Chapter 18].

It has been objected that what there is is a question of fact and not of language. True enough. Saying or implying what there is, however, is a matter of language; and this is the place of the bound variables.

It has been objected that the logical notation of quantification is an arbitrary and parochial standard to adopt for ontological commitment. The answer is that the standard is transferable to any alternative language, insofar as we are agreed on how to translate quantification into it. For predicate-functor logic, thus, the equivalent principle is that what one takes there to be are what one takes one's monadic predicates (complements included) to be true of. For ordinary English what one takes there to be are what one takes one's relative pronouns to refer to. Ordinary discourse is indeed seldom meticulous about ontology, and consequently an assessment based on the relative pronouns of ordinary discourse is apt to bespeak a pretty untidy world; but ontological clarity and economy can be promoted by paraphrase, if one so desires, in terms still of relative clauses and pronouns rather than quantifiers and bound variables. The notation of quantification is what is most usual and familiar, currently, where one is expressly concerned with ontological niceties; hence my choice of it as paradigm.

One thinks of reference, first and foremost, as relating names and other singular terms to their objects. Yet singular terms often fail to refer to anything. Conversely, also, set theory teaches that there are bound to be individually unspecifiable objects—unspecifiable irrational numbers, notably—no matter how rich our notation and cumbersome our expressions. Variables, on the other hand, take all objects as values, irrespective of specifiability.

Once our language is regimented to fit the predicate calculus, moreover, it is easy and instructive to dispense with singular terms altogether, leaving variables as the only link to objects. The underlying principle here is the equivalence of '$\exists x \, (Fx$ and $a = x)$' to 'Fa'; for this enables us to maneuver every occurrence of 'a' into the context '$a =,$' and then to treat that context as an indissoluble predicate 'A,' absorbing the singular term. Singular terms can still be recovered afterward as a convenient shorthand, by introducing singular description in Russell's way and defining 'a' as '$(\imath x)Ax$.'[2]

If in some language we are at a loss to arrive at a satisfactory contextual translation of 'there is,' and hence of existential quantification, then

2. See Quine, *Word and Object*, pp. 176–190.

we are at a loss to assess the ontology of the speakers of that language. Some languages are perhaps so unlike ours that any translation of 'there is' or '∃x,' however cunningly contextual, would be too far-fetched and Procrustean to rest with. To entertain the notion of an ontology at all, known or unknown, for the speakers of such a language would be an unwarranted projection on our part of a parochial category appropriate only to our own linguistic circle. Thus I do recognize that the question of ontological commitment is parochial, though within a much broader parish than that of the speakers and writers of symbolic logic.

11. Utility of Reification

We detected the first hint of reification in the predicational compounding of observation sentences, as contrasted with simple conjunction. Predication is a stronger connection than conjunction; it requires immersion of the pebble in the blue (§2) and the raven in the black, while mere conjunction allows the features to go their separate ways.

At its inception, thus, we find reification contributing to the logical connections between observation and theory by tightening up on truth functions. Elsewhere I have made the point more emphatically by a four-part example:

(1)   A white cat is facing a dog and bristling.

Four simple observation sentences underlie this. One is 'Cat,' or, on the analogy of the ontologically innocent 'It's raining,' 'It's catting.' The others are 'White,' 'Dog-facing,' and 'Bristling.' But (1) cannot be rendered as a mere conjunction of these four, because the conjunction is too loose. It tells us only that the four things are going on in the same scene. We want them all in the same part of the scene, superimposed. It is this tightening that is achieved by subjecting the four-fold conjunction to existential quantification, thus:

> Something is catting and is white and is dog-facing and is bristling,

which is to say (1). An object has been posited, a cat.[3]

3. My approach here was inspired by Donald Davidson's logic of adverbs, in his *Essays on Actions and Events* (Oxford: Clarendon Press, 1980), p. 166. See my "Events and Reification," in E. Lepore and B. McLaughlin (eds.), *Actions and Events* (Oxford: Blackwell, 1985), pp. 161–171.

For all its complexity, (1) is an observation sentence. It *could* be acquired by direct conditioning to the complex situation that it reports, if this situation were to recur and be reported oftener than one is prepared to expect. But it is illustrative of an unlimited lot of equally complex and unlikely observation sentences. There is no hope of direct acquisition of each; systematic construction from elements is mandatory. Reification, we see, to the rescue.

For purposes of that context, a cat of the moment would suffice; no need of an enduring cat. To illustrate the need of an enduring cat I must go beyond observation sentences and suppose that we have somehow worked our way far enough up into scientific theory to treat of time; earlier and later. Suppose then we want to convey this thought:

(2)   If a cat eats a spoiled fish and sickens, then she will thereafter avoid fish.

We cannot treat this as a simple "if-then" compound of two self-sufficient component sentences. Like the "and" of the preceding example, the "if-then" connection is too weak. It has to be the same cat in both sentences, and hence an enduring cat. Our sentence is really a universally quantified conditional:

> Everything is such that if it is a cat and it eats a spoiled fish and it sickens then it will thereafter avoid fish.

Hilary Putnam and Charles Parsons have both remarked on ways of economizing on abstract objects by recourse to a modal operator of possibility.[4] We have just observed the other side of the same coin: the positing of objects can serve to reinforce the weak truth functions without recourse to modal operators. Where there are such trade-offs to choose between, I am for positing the objects. I posit abstract ones grudgingly on the whole, but gratefully where the alternative course would call for modal operators. (Cf. §30.)

My examples offer a crude notion of how it may be that reification and reference contribute to the elaborate structure that relates science to its sensory evidence. At its most rudimentary level, reification is a device for focusing observation sentences convergently; thus (1). Anaphora,

4. Hilary Putnam, "Mathematics without Foundations," *Journal of Philosophy* 64 (1967), pp. 5–22; Charles Parsons, *Mathematics and Philosophy* (Ithaca: Cornell University Press, 1983), pp. 44–47.

clinching of cross-reference, continues to be its business also at more sophisticated levels, as in (2). It is no coincidence that this is precisely the business also of pronouns, or bound variables. To be is to be the value of a variable.

12. Indifference of Ontology

Reference and ontology recede thus to the status of mere auxiliaries. True sentences, observational and theoretical, are the alpha and omega of the scientific enterprise. They are related by structure, and objects figure as mere nodes of the structure. What particular objects there may be is indifferent to the truth of observation sentences, indifferent to the support they lend to the theoretical sentences, indifferent to the success of the theory in its predictions.

The point can be accentuated by invoking what I have called *proxy functions*. A proxy function is any explicit one-to-one transformation, f, defined over the objects in our purported universe. By 'explicit' I mean that for any object x, specified in an acceptable notation, we can specify fx. Suppose now we shift our ontology by reinterpreting each of our predicates as true rather of the correlates fx of the objects x that it had been true of. Thus, where 'Px' originally meant that x was a P, we reinterpret 'Px' as meaning that x is f of a P. Correspondingly for two-place predicates and higher. Singular terms can be passed over in view of §10. We leave all the sentences as they were, letter for letter, merely reinterpreting. The observation sentences remain associated with the same sensory stimulations as before, and the logical interconnections remain intact. Yet the objects of the theory have been supplanted as drastically as you please.[5]

Sometimes we can waive the requirement that the proxy function be one to one. Thus consider Gödel's numbering of expressions, in the course of his proof of his famous incompleteness theorem. In one's global theory of things it would be unnatural to say that the expressions are identical with those numbers, but still there might be no call to distinguish them. In that event a proxy function might just as well treat them alike, assigning the same proxies to the expressions as to the numbers.

However, one-to-one proxy functions were all I needed for my present

5. For more see Quine, *Ontological Relativity,* pp. 55–58.

purpose, namely, to show the indifference of ontology. A more radical case for the indifference of ontology is afforded by the Löwenheim-Skolem theorem, in a strengthened form due to Hilbert and Bernays.[6] When applied to a theory that has been fitted to predicate logic, cleared of singular terms, and encompassed in a finite lot of axioms, this theorem enables us to express a truth-preserving reinterpretation of the predicates that makes the universe come to consist merely of natural numbers 0, 1, 2, ... This theorem does not, like proxy functions, carry each of the old objects into a definite new one, a particular number. This was not to be hoped for, since some infinite domains—notably that of the irrational numbers—are of too high a cardinality to be exhausted by correlation with natural numbers. Despite this limitation, however, the reinterpretations leave all observation sentences associated with the same old stimulations and all logical links undisturbed.

Once we have appropriately regimented our system of the world or part of it, we can so reinterpret it as to get by with only the slender ontology of the whole numbers; such is the strengthened Löwenheim-Skolem theorem. But we could not have arrived at our science in the first place under that interpretation, since the numbers do not correspond one by one to the reifications that were our stepping stones. Practically, heuristically, we must presumably pursue science in the old way or within the reach, at least of proxy functions.

13. Ontology Defused

We found that two ontologies, if explicitly correlated one to one, are empirically on a par; there is no empirical ground for choosing the one rather than the other. What is empirically significant in an ontology is just its contribution of neutral nodes to the structure of the theory. We could reinterpret 'Tabitha' as designating no longer the cat, but the whole cosmos minus the cat; or, again, as designating the cat's singleton, or unit class. Reinterpreting the rest of our terms for bodies in corresponding fashion, we come out with an ontology interchangeable with our familiar one. As wholes they are empirically indistinguishable. Bodies still continue, under each interpretation, to be distinct from their cosmic complements and from their singletons; they are distinguished in a

6. See Quine, *Methods of Logic*, 4th ed. (Cambridge, Mass.: Harvard University Press, 1982), pp. 209–211.

relativistic way, by their roles relative to one another and to the rest of the ontology. Hence my watchword *ontological relativity*. But see further §20.

The importance of the distinction between term and observation sentence shone forth in §§3 and 9, and it does so again here. 'There's a rabbit' remains keyed to the sensory stimulations by which we learned it, even if we reinterpret the term 'rabbit' as denoting cosmic complements or singletons of rabbits. The term does continue to conjure up visions appropriate to the observation sentence through which the term was learned, and so be it; but there is no empirical bar to the reinterpretation. The original sensory associations were indispensable genetically in generating the nodes by which we structure our theory of the world. But all that matters by way of evidence for the theory is the stimulatory basis of the observation sentences plus the structure that the neutral nodes serve to implement. The stimulation remains as rabbity as ever, but the corresponding node or object goes neutral and is up for grabs.

Bodies were our primordial reifications, rooted in innate perceptual similarities. It would be gratuitous to swap them for proxies; the point was just that one could. But our ontological preconceptions have a less tenacious grip on the deliberate refinements of sophisticated science. Physicists did first picture elementary particles and light waves in analogy to familiar things, but they have gone on to sap the analogies. The particles are less and less like bodies, and the waves seem more like pulsations of energy in the void. When we get to the positing of numbers and other abstract objects, I have conjectured in *Roots of Reference* that we are indebted to some fruitful confusions along the way. Language and science are rooted in what good scientific language eschews. In Wittgenstein's figure, we climb the ladder and kick it away.

Some findings known as the Bose-Einstein and Fermi-Dirac statistics suggest how we might be led actually to repudiate even the more traditional elementary particles as values of variables, rather than retaining them and just acquiescing provisionally in their mysterious ways. Those results seem to show that there is no difference even in principle between saying of two elementary particles of a given kind that they are in the respective places a and b and that they are oppositely placed, in b and a. It would seem then not merely that elementary particles are unlike bodies; it would seem that there are no such denizens of space-time at all, and that we should speak of places a and b merely as being in certain states, indeed the same state, rather than as being occupied by two things.

Perhaps physicists will accommodate this quandary in another way. But I prize the example as illustrating the kind of consideration that could prompt one to repudiate some hypothetical objects. The consideration is not based on positivistic misgivings over theoretical entities. It is based on tensions internal to theory.

Theories can take yet more drastic turns: such not merely as to threaten a cherished ontology of elementary particles, but to threaten the very sense of the ontological question, the question what there is. What I have been taking as the standard idiom for existential purposes, namely quantification, can serve as standard only when embedded in the standard form of regimented language that we have been picturing: one whose further apparatus consists only of truth functions and predicates. If there is any deviation in this further apparatus, then there arises a question of foreign exchange: we cannot judge what existential content may be added by these foreign intrusions until we have settled on how to translate it all into our standard form. Notoriously, in particular, quantum mechanics invites logical deviations whose reduction to the old standard is by no means evident. On one rendering these deviations take the form of probabilistic predications. On an alternative rendering they call for basic departures from the logic of truth functions. When the dust has settled, we may find that the very notion of existence, the old one, has had its day. A kindred notion may then stand forth that seems sufficiently akin to warrant application of the same word; such is the way of terminology. Whether to say at that point that we have gained new insight into existence, or that we have outgrown the notion and reapplied the term, is a question of terminology as well.

The objectivity of our knowledge of the external world remains rooted in our contact with the external world, hence in our neural intake and the observation sentences that respond to it. We begin with the monolithic sentence, not the term. A lesson of proxy functions is that our ontology, like grammar, is part of our own conceptual contribution to our theory of the world. Man proposes; the world disposes, but only by holophrastic yes-or-no verdicts on the observation sentences that embody man's predictions.

7

TRANSLATION AND MEANING

7. First Steps of Radical Translation[1]

We have been reflecting in a general way on how surface irritations generate, through language, one's knowledge of the world. One is taught so to associate words with words and other stimulations that there emerges something recognizable as talk of things, and not to be distinguished from truth about the world. The voluminous and intricately structured talk that comes out bears little evident correspondence to the past and present barrage of non-verbal stimulation; yet it is to such stimulation that we must look for whatever empirical content there may be. In this chapter we shall consider how much of language can be made sense of in terms of its stimulus conditions, and what scope this leaves for empirically unconditioned variation in one's conceptual scheme.

A first uncritical way of picturing this scope for empirically unconditioned variation is as follows: two men could be just alike in all their dispositions to verbal behavior under all possible sensory stimulations, and yet the meanings or ideas expressed in their identically triggered and identically sounded utterances could diverge radically, for the two men, in a wide range of cases. To put the matter thus invites, however, the charge of meaninglessness: one may protest that a distinction of meaning unreflected in the totality of dispositions to verbal behavior is a distinction without a difference.

Sense can be made of the point by recasting it as follows: the infinite totality of sentences of any given speaker's language can be so permuted,

1. An interim draft of Chapter II was published, with omissions, as "Meaning and Translation." Half of that essay survives verbatim here, comprising a scattered third of this essay.

or mapped onto itself, that (*a*) the totality of the speaker's dispositions to verbal behavior remains invariant, and yet (*b*) the mapping is no mere correlation of sentences with *equivalent* sentences, in any plausible sense of equivalence however loose. Sentences without number can diverge drastically from their respective correlates, yet the divergences can systematically so offset one another that the overall pattern of associations of sentences with one another and with non-verbal stimulation is preserved. The firmer the direct links of a sentence with non-verbal stimulation, of course, the less that sentence can diverge from its correlate under any such mapping.

The same point can be put less abstractly and more realistically by switching to translation. The thesis is then this: manuals for translating one language into another can be set up in divergent ways, all compatible with the totality of speech dispositions, yet incompatible with one another. In countless places they will diverge in giving, as their respective translations of a sentence of the one language, sentences of the other language which stand to each other in no plausible sort of equivalence however loose. The firmer the direct links of a sentence with non-verbal stimulation, of course, the less drastically its translations can diverge from one another from manual to manual. It is in this last form, as a principle of indeterminacy of translation, that I shall try to make the point plausible in the course of this chapter. But the chapter will run longer than it would if various of the concepts and considerations ancillary to this theme did not seem worthy of treatment also on their own account.

We are concerned here with language as the complex of present dispositions to verbal behavior, in which speakers of the same language have perforce come to resemble one another; not with the processes of acquisition, whose variations from individual to individual it is to the interests of communication to efface (cf. §2). The sentence 'That man shoots well,' said while pointing to an unarmed man, has as present stimulation the glimpse of the marksman's familiar face. The contributory past stimulation includes past observations of the man's shooting, as well as remote episodes that trained the speaker in the use of the words. The past stimulation is thus commonly reckoned in part to the acquisition of language and in part to the acquisition of collateral information; however, this subsidiary dichotomy can await some indication of what it is good for and what general clues there are for it in observable verbal behavior. (Cf. §§9, 12, 14.) Meanwhile what is before us is the going concern of verbal behavior and its currently observable correlations with stimulation. Reckon a man's current language by his current dispositions to respond verbally to current stimulation, and you automatically refer all past stimulation to the learning phase. Not but that even this way of drawing a boundary between language in acquisition and language in use has its fluctuations, inasmuch as we can consult our convenience in what bound we set to the length of stimulations counted as current. This bound, a working standard of what to count as specious present, I call the *modulus* of stimulation.

The recovery of a man's current language from his currently observed responses is the task of the linguist who, unaided by an interpreter, is out to penetrate and translate a language hitherto unknown. All the objective data he has to go on are the forces that he sees impinging on the native's surfaces and the observable behavior, vocal and otherwise, of the native. Such data evince native "meanings" only of the most objectively empirical or stimulus-linked variety. And yet the linguist apparently ends up with native "meanings" in some quite unrestricted sense; purported translations, anyway, of all possible native sentences.

Translation between kindred languages, e.g., Frisian and English, is aided by resemblance of cognate word forms. Translation between unrelated languages, e.g., Hungarian and English, may be aided by traditional equations that have evolved in step with a shared culture. What is relevant rather to our purposes is *radical* translation, i.e., translation of the language of a hitherto untouched people. The task is one that is not in practice undertaken in its extreme form, since a chain of interpreters of a sort can be recruited of marginal persons across the darkest archipelago. But the problem is the more nearly approximated the poorer the hints available from interpreters; thus attention to techniques of utterly radical translation has not been wanting.[2] I shall imagine that all help of interpreters is excluded. Incidentally I shall here ignore phonematic analysis (§18), early though it would come in our field linguist's enterprise; for it does not affect the philosophical point I want to make.

The utterances first and most surely translated in such a case are ones keyed to present events that are conspicuous to the linguist and his informant. A rabbit scurries by, the native says 'Gavagai,' and the linguist notes down the sentence 'Rabbit' (or 'Lo, a rabbit') as tentative translation, subject to testing in further cases. The linguist will at first refrain

2. See K. L. Pike, *Phonemics: A Technique for Reducing Languages to Writing* (Ann Arbor: University of Michigan, 1947).

from putting words into his informant's mouth, if only for lack of words to put. When he can, though, the linguist has to supply native sentences for his informant's approval, despite the risk of slanting the data by suggestion. Otherwise he can do little with native terms that have references in common. For, suppose the native language includes sentences S_1, S_2, and S_3, really translatable respectively as 'Animal,' 'White,' and 'Rabbit.' Stimulus situations always differ, whether relevantly or not; and, just because volunteered responses come singly, the classes of situations under which the native happens to have volunteered S_1, S_2, and S_3, are of course mutually exclusive, despite the hidden actual meanings of the words. How then is the linguist to perceive that the native would have been willing to assent to S_1 in all the situations where he happened to volunteer S_3, and in some but perhaps not all of the situations where he happened to volunteer S_2? Only by taking the initiative and querying combinations of native sentences and stimulus situations so as to narrow down his guesses to his eventual satisfaction.

So we have the linguist asking 'Gavagai?' in each of various stimulatory situations, and noting each time whether the native assents, dissents, or neither. But how is he to recognize native assent and dissent when he sees or hears them? Gestures are not to be taken at face value; the Turks' are nearly the reverse of our own. What he must do is guess from observation and then see how well his guesses work. Thus suppose that in asking 'Gavagai?' and the like, in the conspicuous presence of rabbits and the like, he has elicited the responses 'Evet' and 'Yok' often enough to surmise that they may correspond to 'Yes' and 'No,' but has no notion which is which. Then he tries the experiment of echoing the native's own volunteered pronouncements. If thereby he pretty regularly elicits 'Evet' rather than 'Yok,' he is encouraged to take 'Evet' as 'Yes.' Also he tries responding with 'Evet' and 'Yok' to the native's remarks; the one that is the more serene in its effect is the better candidate for 'Yes.' However inconclusive these methods, they generate a working hypothesis. If extraordinary difficulties attend all his subsequent steps, the linguist may decide to discard that hypothesis and guess again.[3]

Let us then suppose the linguist has settled on what to treat as native signs of assent and dissent. He is thereupon in a position to accumulate inductive evidence for translating 'Gavagai' as the sentence 'Rabbit.' The

3. See Raymond Firth, *Elements of Social Organization,* p. 23, on the analogous matter of identifying a gesture of greeting.

general law for which he is assembling instances is roughly that the native will assent to 'Gavagai?' under just those stimulations under which we, if asked, would assent to 'Rabbit?'; and correspondingly for dissent.

But we can do somewhat more justice to what the linguist is after in such a case if, instead of speaking merely of stimulations under which the native will assent or dissent to the queried sentence, we speak in a more causal vein of stimulations that will *prompt* the native to assent or dissent to the queried sentence. For suppose the queried sentence were one rather to the effect that someone is away tracking a giraffe. All day long the native will assent to it whenever asked, under all manner of irrelevant attendant stimulations; and on another day he will dissent from it under the same irrelevant stimulations. It is important to know that in the case of 'Gavagai?' the rabbit-presenting stimulations actually prompt the assent, and that the others actually prompt the dissent.

In practice the linguist will usually settle these questions of causality, however tentatively, by intuitive judgment based on details of the native's behavior: his scanning movements, his sudden look of recognition, and the like. Also there are more formal considerations which, under favorable circumstances, can assure him of the prompting relation. If, just after the native has been asked S and has assented or dissented, the linguist springs stimulation σ on him, asks S again, and gets the opposite verdict, then he may conclude that σ did the prompting.

Note that to prompt, in our sense, is not to elicit. What elicits the native's 'Evet' or 'Yok' is a combination: the prompting stimulation plus the ensuing query 'Gavagai?'.

8. Stimulation and Stimulus Meaning

It is important to think of what prompts the native's assent to 'Gavagai?' as stimulations and not rabbits. Stimulation can remain the same though the rabbit be supplanted by a counterfeit. Conversely, stimulation can vary in its power to prompt assent to 'Gavagai' because of variations in angle, lighting, and color contrast, though the rabbit remains the same. In experimentally equating the uses of 'Gavagai' and 'Rabbit' it is stimulations that must be made to match, not animals.

A visual stimulation is perhaps best identified, for present purposes, with the pattern of chromatic irradiation of the eye. To look deep into the subject's head would be inappropriate even if feasible, for we want to keep clear of his idiosyncratic neural routings or private history of habit formation. We are after his socially inculcated linguistic usage, hence his responses to conditions normally subject to social assessment. (Cf. §2.) Ocular irradiation *is* intersubjectively checked to some degree by society and linguist alike, by making allowances for the speaker's orientation and the relative disposition of objects.

In taking the visual stimulations as irradiation patterns we invest them with a fineness of detail beyond anything that our linguist can be called upon to check for. But this is all right. He can reasonably conjecture that the native would be prompted to assent to 'Gavagai' by the microscopically same irradiations that would prompt him, the linguist, to assent to 'Rabbit,' even though this conjecture rests wholly on samples where the irradiations concerned can at best be hazarded merely to be pretty much alike.

It is not, however, adequate to think of the visual stimulations as momentary static irradiation patterns. To do so would obstruct examples which, unlike 'Rabbit,' affirm movement. And it would make trouble even with examples like 'Rabbit,' on another account: too much depends on what immediately precedes and follows a momentary irradiation. A momentary lepiform image flashed by some artifice in the midst of an otherwise rabbitless sequence might not prompt assent to 'Rabbit' even though the same image would have done so if ensconced in a more favorable sequence. The difficulty would thus arise that far from hoping to match the irradiation patterns favorable to 'Gavagai' with those favorable to 'Rabbit,' we could not even say unequivocally of an irradiation pattern, of itself and without regard to those just before and after, that it is favorable to 'Rabbit' or that it is not.[4] Better, therefore, to take as the relevant stimulations not momentary irradiation patterns, but evolving irradiation patterns of all durations up to some convenient limit or *modulus*. Furthermore we may think of the ideal experimental situation as one in which the desired ocular exposure concerned is preceded and followed by a blindfold.

In general the ocular irradiation patterns are best conceived in their spatial entirety. For there are examples such as 'Fine weather' which, unlike 'Rabbit,' are not keyed to any readily segregated fragments of the scene. Also there are all those rabbit-free patterns that are wanted as prompting dissent from 'Rabbit.' And as for the patterns wanted as prompting assent to 'Rabbit,' whole scenes will still serve better than se-

---

4. This difficulty was raised by [Donald] Davidson.

lected portions might; for the difference between center and periphery, which is such an important determinant of visual attention, is then automatically allowed for. Total ocular irradiation patterns that differ in centering differ also in limits, and so are simply different patterns. One that shows the rabbit too peripherally simply will not be one that prompts assent to 'Gavagai' or 'Rabbit.'

Certain sentences of the type of 'Gavagai' are the sentences with which our jungle linguist must begin, and for these we now have before us the makings of a crude concept of empirical meaning. For meaning, supposedly, is what a sentence shares with its translation; and translation at the present stage turns solely on correlations with non-verbal stimulation.

Let us make this concept of meaning more explicit and give it a neutrally technical name. We may begin by defining the *affirmative stimulus meaning* of a sentence such as 'Gavagai,' for a given speaker, as the class of all the stimulations (hence evolving ocular irradiation patterns between properly timed blindfoldings) that would prompt his assent. More explicitly, in view of the end of §7, a stimulation σ belongs to the affirmative stimulus meaning of a sentence S for a given speaker if and only if there is a stimulation σ' such that if the speaker were given σ', then were asked S, then were given σ, and then were asked S again, he would dissent the first time and assent the second. We may define the *negative* stimulus meaning similarly with 'assent' and 'dissent' interchanged, and then define the *stimulus meaning* as the ordered pair of the two. We could refine the notion of stimulus meaning by distinguishing degrees of doubtfulness of assent and dissent, say by reaction time; but for the sake of fluent exposition let us forbear. The imagined equating of 'Gavagai' and 'Rabbit' can now be stated thus: they have the same stimulus meaning.

A stimulus meaning is the stimulus meaning of a sentence for a speaker at a date; for we must allow our speaker to change his ways. Also it varies with the modulus, or maximum duration recognized for stimulations. For, by increasing the modulus we supplement the stimulus meaning with some stimulations that were too long to count before. Fully ticketed, therefore, a stimulus meaning is the stimulus meaning *modulo n* seconds of sentence S for speaker a at time t.

The stimulations to be gathered into the stimulus meaning of a sentence have for vividness been thought of thus far as visual, unlike the queries that follow them. Actually, of course, we should bring the other senses in on a par with vision, identifying stimulations not with just ocular irradiation patterns but with these and the various barrages of other senses, separately and in all synchronous combinations. Perhaps we can pass over the detail of this.

The affirmative and negative stimulus meanings of a sentence (for a given speaker at a given time) are mutually exclusive. Granted, our subject might be prompted once by a given stimulation σ to assent to S, and later, by a recurrence of σ, to dissent from S; but then we would simply conclude that his meaning for S had changed. We would then reckon σ to his affirmative stimulus meaning of S as of the one date and to his negative stimulus meaning of S as of the other date.

Yet the affirmative and negative stimulus meanings do not determine each other; for many stimulations may be expected to belong to neither. In general, therefore, comparison of whole stimulus meanings can be a better basis for translations than comparison merely of affirmative stimulus meanings.

What now of that strong conditional, the 'would' in our definition of stimulus meaning? Its use here is no worse than its use when we explain 'x is soluble in water' as meaning that x would dissolve if it were in water. What the strong conditional defines is a disposition, in this case a disposition to assent to or dissent from S when variously stimulated. The disposition may be presumed to be some subtle structural condition, like an allergy and like solubility; like an allergy, more particularly, in not being understood. The ontological status of dispositions, or the philosophical status of talk of dispositions, is a matter which I defer to §46; but meanwhile we are familiar enough in a general way with how one sets about guessing, from judicious tests and samples and observed uniformities, whether there is a disposition of a specified sort.

The stimulus meaning of a sentence for a subject sums up his disposition to assent to or dissent from the sentence in response to present stimulation. The stimulation is what activates the disposition, as opposed to what instills it (even though the stimulation chance to contribute somehow to the instilling of some further disposition).

Yet a stimulation must be conceived for these purposes not as a dated particular event but as a universal, a repeatable event form. We are to say not that two like stimulations have occurred, but that the same stimulation has recurred. Such an attitude is implied the moment we speak of sameness of stimulus meaning for two speakers. We could indeed overrule this consideration, if we liked, by readjusting our terminology. But there would be no point, for there remains elsewhere a compelling reason for taking the stimulations as universals; viz., the strong conditional in the definition of stimulus meaning. For, consider again the affirmative stimulus meaning of a sentence S: the class Σ of all those stimulations that *would* prompt assent to S. If the stimulations were taken as events rather than event forms, then Σ would have to be a class of events which largely did not and will not happen, but which would prompt assent to S if they were to happen. Whenever Σ contained one realized or unrealized particular stimulatory event σ, it would have to contain all other unrealized duplicates of σ; and how many are there of *these*? Certainly it is hopeless nonsense to talk thus of unrealized particulars and try to assemble them into classes. Unrealized entities have to be construed as universals.

We were impressed in §3 with the interdependence of sentences. We may well have begun then to wonder whether meanings even of whole sentences (let alone shorter expressions) could reasonably be talked of at all, except relative to the other sentences of an inclusive theory. Such relativity would be awkward, since, conversely, the individual component sentences offer the only way into the theory. Now the notion of stimulus meaning partially resolves the predicament. It isolates a sort of net empirical import of each of various single sentences without regard to the containing theory, even though without loss of what the sentence owes to that containing theory. It is a device, as far as it goes, for exploring the fabric of interlocking sentences, a sentence at a time.

Between the notion of stimulus meaning and Carnap's remarks on empirical semantics[5] there are connections and differences worth noting. He suggests exploring the meaning of a term by asking the subject whether he would apply it under various imaginary circumstances, to be described to him. That approach has the virtue of preserving contrasts between such terms as 'goblin' and 'unicorn' despite the non-existence of contrasting instances in the world. Stimulus meaning has the same virtue, since there are stimulation patterns that would prompt assent to 'Unicorn?' and not to 'Goblin?'. Carnap's approach presupposes some decision as to what descriptions of imaginary circumstances are admissible; e.g., 'unicorn' would be not wanted in descriptions used in probing the meaning of 'unicorn.' He hints of appropriate restrictions for the

---

5. *Meaning and Necessity*, 2d ed., Suppl. D. See also Chisholm, *Perceiving*, pp. 175ff., and his references.

purpose, mentioning "size, shape, color"; and my notion of stimulus meaning itself amounts to a firmer definition in that same direction. There remains a significant contrast in the uses the two of us make of subjunctive conditionals: I limit them to my investigator's considered judgment of what the informant would do if stimulated; Carnap has his investigator putting such conditionals to the judgment of the informant. Certainly my investigator would in practice ask the same questions as Carnap's investigator, as a quick way of estimating stimulus meanings, if language for such questions happened to be available. But stimulus meaning can be explored also at the first stages of radical translation, where Carnap's type of questionnaire is unavailable. On this score it is important, as we shall see in §12, that my theory has to do primarily with sentences of a sort and not, like Carnap's, with terms.

9. Occasion Sentences. Intrusive Information

Occasion sentences, as against *standing* sentences, are sentences such as 'Gavagai,' 'Red,' 'It hurts,' 'His face is dirty,' which command assent or dissent only if queried after an appropriate prompting stimulation. Verdicts to standing sentences *can* be prompted too: stimulation implemented by an interferometer once prompted Michelson and Morley to dissent from the standing sentence 'There is ether drift,' and a speaker's assent can be prompted yearly to 'The crocuses are out,' daily to 'The *Times* has come.' But these standing sentences contrast with occasion sentences in that the subject may repeat his old assent or dissent unprompted by current stimulation when we ask him again on later occasions, whereas an occasion sentence commands assent or dissent only as prompted all over again by current stimulation. Standing sentences grade off toward occasion sentences as the interval between possible repromptings diminishes; and the occasion sentence is the extreme case where that interval is less than the modulus. Like the stimulus meanings themselves, the distinction between standing sentences and occasion sentences is relative to the modulus; an occasion sentence modulo n seconds can be a standing sentence modulo $n - 1$.

The stimulations belonging to neither the affirmative nor the negative stimulus meaning of an occasion sentence are just those that would inhibit a verdict on the queried sentence, whether through indecisiveness (as in the case of a poor glimpse) or through shocking the subject out of his wits. On the other hand the stimulations belonging to neither the affirmative nor the negative stimulus meaning of a standing sentence are of two sorts: besides the inhibitory ones there are the *irrelevant* ones, which neither prompt nor inhibit. Querying the sentence on the heels of such a stimulation would elicit a verdict, but always the one that the query would have elicited without the attendant stimulation; never a change of verdict.

The stimulus meaning is a full cross-section of the subject's evolving dispositions to assent to or dissent from a sentence, if the sentence is an occasion sentence; less so if it is a standing sentence. Standing sentences can differ among themselves in "meaning," by any intuitive account,[6] as freely as occasion sentences; but, the less susceptible they are to prompted assent and dissent, the fewer clues are present in stimulus meaning. The notion of stimulus meaning is thus most important for occasion sentences, and we shall limit our attention for a while to them.

Even for such favored occasion sentences as 'Gavagai' and 'Rabbit,' actually, sameness of stimulus meaning has its shortcomings as a synonymy relation. The difficulty is that an informant's assent to or dissent from 'Gavagai?' can depend excessively on prior collateral information as a supplement to the present prompting stimulus. He may assent on the occasion of nothing better than an ill-glimpsed movement in the grass, because of his earlier observation, unknown to the linguist, of rabbits near the spot. Since the linguist would not on his own information be prompted by that same poor glimpse to assent to 'Rabbit?', we have here a discrepancy between the present stimulus meaning of 'Gavagai' for the informant and that of 'Rabbit' for the linguist.

More persistent discrepancies of the same type can be imagined, affecting not one native but all, and not once but regularly. There may be a local rabbit-fly,[7] unknown to the linguist, and recognizable some way off by its long wings and erratic movements; and seeing such a fly in the neighborhood of an ill-glimpsed animal could help a native to recognize the latter as a rabbit. Ocular irradiations combining poor glimpses of rabbits with good ones of rabbit-flies would belong to the stimulus meaning of 'Gavagai' for natives generally, and not to that of 'Rabbit' for the linguist.

6. Twice I have been startled to find my use of 'intuitive' misconstrued as alluding to some special and mysterious avenue of knowledge. By an intuitive account I mean one in which terms are used in habitual ways, without reflecting on how they might be defined or what presuppositions they might conceal.

7. Here I am indebted to Davidson.

And, to be less fanciful, there are all those stimulations that incorporate verbal hints from native kibitzers. Thus suppose that the stimulation on the heels of which the informant is asked 'Gavagai?' is a composite stimulation presenting a bystander pointing to an ill-glimpsed object and saying 'Gavagai.' This composite stimulation will probably turn out to belong to the affirmative stimulus meaning of 'Gavagai' for the informant, and not to the stimulus meaning of 'Rabbit' for most English speakers, on whom the force of the bystander's verbal intervention would be lost. Such cases would not fool our linguist, but they do count against defining synonymy as sameness of stimulus meaning. For we must remember that every sufficiently brief stimulation pattern, though it be one that never gets actualized or that the linguist would never use, still by definition belongs to the stimulus meaning of 'Gavagai' for a man at a given time if it is one that *would* prompt his assent at that time.

Intuitively the ideal would be to accord to the affirmative meaning of 'Gavagai' just those stimulations that would prompt assent to 'Gavagai?' on the strength purely of an understanding of 'Gavagai,' unaided by collateral information: unaided by recent observation of rabbits near the spot, unaided by knowledge of the nature and habits of the rabbit-fly, unaided by conversance with the kibitzer's language. On the face of it there is a difficulty in excluding this third aid, considering our continuing dependence on the subject's understanding of 'Gavagai.' But also the trouble is more widespread. It is precisely that we have made no general experimental sense of a distinction between what goes into a native's learning to apply an expression and what goes into his learning supplementary matters about the objects concerned. True, the linguist can press such a distinction part way; he can filter out such idiosyncratic bits of collateral matter as the informant's recent observation of rabbits near the spot, by varying his times and his informants and so isolating a more stable and more social stimulus meaning as common denominator. But any socially shared information, such as that about the rabbit-fly or the ability to understand a bystander's remark, will continue to affect even that common denominator. There is no evident criterion whereby to strip such effects away and leave just the meaning of 'Gavagai' properly so-called—whatever meaning properly so-called may be.

Thus, to depict the difficulty in more general terms, suppose it said that a particular class Σ comprises just those stimulations each of which suffices to prompt assent to a sentence S outright, without benefit of collateral information. Suppose it said that the stimulations comprised in a further class Σ', likewise sufficient to prompt assent to S, owe their efficacy rather to certain widely disseminated collateral information, C. Now couldn't we just as well have said, instead, that on acquiring C, men have found it convenient implicitly to change the very "meaning" of S, so that the members of Σ' now suffice outright like members of Σ? I suggest that we may say either; even historical clairvoyance would reveal no distinction, though it reveal all stages in the acquisition of C, since meaning can evolve *pari passu*. The distinction is illusory: as mistaken as the notion, scouted in §4, that we can determine separately what to talk about and what to say about it. It is simply a question whether to call the transitivity shortcuts (§3) changes of meaning or condensations of proof; and in fact an unreal question. What we objectively have is just an evolving adjustment to nature, reflected in an evolving set of dispositions to be prompted by stimulations to assent to or dissent from sentences. These dispositions may be conceded to be impure in the sense of including worldly knowledge, but they contain it in a solution which there is no precipitating.

Incidentally, note that stimulus meanings as defined in §8 can even suffer some discrepancies that are intuitively attributable neither to differences of meaning nor to differences of collateral information. Thus take shocked silence. To begin with, if the speaker is already stunned at time t, all stimulus meanings for him at t will be empty. This outcome of the definition of stimulus meaning is unnatural but harmless, since we can ignore stimulus meanings for stunned persons. But in the case of a speaker alert at t there are stimulations that *would* stun him at t and so *would* preclude any assent to or dissent from the ensuing 'Gavagai?'. These, by definition, belong to neither the affirmative nor the negative stimulus meaning of 'Gavagai' for him at t. Now where a discrepancy in stimulus meanings will ensue is where a stimulation is such as would stun one speaker and not another; for it could belong say to the negative stimulus meaning of 'Gavagai' or 'Rabbit' for the latter speaker and to neither the affirmative nor the negative stimulus meaning for the former speaker. This again is a discrepancy that would not puzzle the linguist, but that exists under our definition. Also there are interferences of less drastic sorts. The native may dissent from 'Gavagai' in plain sight of the rabbit's ears, because the rabbit is in no position for shooting;[8] he has misjudged the linguist's motive for asking 'Gavagai?'.

8. Here I am indebted to Raymond Firth.

We have now seen that stimulus meaning as defined falls short in various ways of one's intuitive demands on "meaning" as undefined, and that sameness of stimulus meaning is too strict a relation to expect between a native occasion sentence and its translation—even in so benign a case as 'Gavagai' and 'Rabbit.' Yet stimulus meaning, by whatever name, may be properly looked upon still as the objective reality that the linguist has to probe when he undertakes radical translation. For the stimulus meaning of an occasion sentence is by definition the native's total battery of present dispositions to be prompted to assent to or to dissent from the sentence; and these dispositions are just what the linguist has to sample and estimate. We do best to revise not the notion of stimulus meaning, but only what we represent the linguist as doing with stimulus meanings. The fact is that he translates not by identity of stimulus meanings, but by significant approximation of stimulus meanings.

If he translates 'Gavagai' as 'Rabbit' despite the discrepancies in stimulus meaning imagined above, he does so because the stimulus meanings seem to coincide to an overwhelming degree and the discrepancies, so far as he finds them, seem best explained away or dismissed as effects of unidentified interferences. Some discrepancies he may sift out, as lately suggested, by varying his times and informants. Some, involving poor glimpses or shock or verbal intrusions, he would not even bother to bring to fulfillment by a querying of the sentence. Some, such as those involving the rabbit-fly, he will dismiss as effects of unidentified interferences if he does not encounter them often. In taking this last rather high line, clearly he is much influenced by his natural expectation that any people in rabbit country would have *some* brief expression that could in the long run be best translated simply as 'Rabbit.' He conjectures that the now-unexplained discrepancies between 'Gavagai' and 'Rabbit' are ones that may eventually be reconciled with his translation, after he has somehow got deep enough into the native language to ask sophisticated questions.

In practice, of course, the natural expectation that the natives will have a brief expression for 'Rabbit' counts overwhelmingly. The linguist hears 'Gavagai' once, in a situation where a rabbit seems to be the object of concern. He will then try 'Gavagai' for assent or dissent in a couple of situations designed perhaps to eliminate 'White' and 'Animal' as alternative translations, and will forthwith settle upon 'Rabbit' as translation without further experiment—though always in readiness to discover through some unsought experience that a revision is in order. I made the linguist preternaturally circumspect, and maximized his bad luck in respect of discrepant observations, in order to consider what theoretical bearing a native's collateral information can have upon the linguist's in fact wholly facile opening translation.

10. Observation Sentences

Some stimulus meanings are less susceptible than others to the influences of intrusive information. There is on this score a significant contrast between 'Red' and 'Rabbit' even when 'Red' is taken on a par with 'Rabbit' as announcing not a passing sense datum but an enduring objective trait of the physical object. True, there are extreme cases where we may be persuaded, by collateral information about odd lighting and juxtaposition, that something is really red that did not seem so or vice versa; but, despite such cases, there is less scope for collateral information in deciding whether a glimpsed thing is red than in deciding whether it is a rabbit. In the case of 'Red,' therefore, sameness of stimulus meaning comes unusually close to what one intuitively expects of synonymy.

Color words are notoriously ill matched between remote languages, because of differences in customary grouping of shades. But this is no present problem; it means merely that there may well be no native occasion sentence, at least no reasonably simple one, with approximately the stimulus meaning of 'Red.' Again, even if there is one, there may still be a kind of trouble in equating it to 'Red,' just because of the vagueness of color boundaries in both languages. But this again is no problem of collateral information; it is a difficulty that would remain even if a distinction between meaning and collateral information were successfully drawn. It can be coped with by a rough matching of statistical scatterings. The penumbra of vagueness of 'Red' consists of stimulations in respect of which the stimulus meanings of 'Red' tend to vary from speaker to speaker and from occasion to occasion; correspondingly for the penumbra of vagueness of the native sentence; and then 'Red' is a good translation to the extent that it resembles the native sentence umbra for umbra and penumbra for penumbra.

In terms of direct behavioral evidence, how do those fluctuations of stimulus meaning that are attributable to a penumbra of vagueness differ from those fluctuations of stimulus meaning (e.g. of 'Gavagai') that are laid to variations of collateral information from occasion to occasion? Partly in that the penumbral fluctuations increase rather smoothly as the stimulations grade off, while the fluctuations laid to collateral information are more irregular, suggesting intrusion of extraneous factors. But mainly in that each individual's assent or dissent tends to be marked by doubt and hesitation when the prompting stimulation belongs to the penumbra. If we were to complicate the notion of stimulus meaning to the extent of weighting each stimulation inversely according to reaction time (cf. §8), then discrepancies in stimulus meaning from speaker to speaker would tend to count for little where due to vagueness, and for more where not.

If 'Red' is somewhat less susceptible than 'Rabbit' to the influences of intrusive information, there are other sentences that are vastly more so. An example is 'Bachelor.' An informant's assent to it is prompted genuinely enough by the sight of a face, yet it draws mainly on stored information and none on the prompting stimulation except as needed for recognizing the bachelor friend concerned. As one says in the uncritical jargon of meaning, the trouble with 'Bachelor' is that its meaning transcends the looks of the prompting faces and concerns matters that can be known only through other channels. 'Rabbit' is a little this way, as witness papier-mâché counterfeits; 'Bachelor' much more so. The stimulus meaning of 'Bachelor' cannot be treated as its "meaning" by any stretch of the imagination, unless perhaps accompanied by a stretch of the modulus.

A mark of the intrusion of collateral information, except when the information is generally shared as in the examples of the kibitzer and the rabbit-fly (§9), was discrepancy in stimulus meaning from speaker to speaker of the same language. In a case like 'Bachelor,' therefore, we may expect the discrepancies to be overwhelming; and indeed they are. For any two speakers whose social contacts are not virtually identical, the stimulus meanings of 'Bachelor' will diverge far more than those of 'Rabbit.'

The less susceptible the stimulus meaning of an occasion sentence is to the influences of collateral information, the less absurdity there is in thinking of the stimulus meaning of the sentence as the meaning of the sentence. Occasion sentences whose stimulus meanings vary none under the influence of collateral information may naturally be called *observation sentences,* and their stimulus meanings may without fear of contradiction be said to do full justice to their meanings. These are the occasion sentences that wear their meanings on their sleeves. Or, better, we may speak of degrees of observationality; for even the stimulus meaning of

'Red' can, we noted, be made to fluctuate a little from occasion to occasion by collateral information on lighting conditions. What we have is a gradation of observationality from one extreme, at 'Red' or above, to the other extreme at 'Bachelor' or below.

In the foregoing paragraph we have wallowed most unfastidiously in the conceptual slough of meaning and collateral information. But now it is interesting to note that what we have dredged out, a notion of degree of observationality, is not beyond cleaning up and rendering respectable. For, in behavioral terms, an occasion sentence may be said to be the more observational the more nearly its stimulus meanings for different speakers tend to coincide. Granted, this definition fails to give demerit marks for the effects of generally shared information, such as that about the rabbit-fly. But, as argued in §9, I suspect that no systematic experimental sense is to be made of a distinction between usage due to meaning and usage due to generally shared collateral information.

The notion of observationality is relative to the modulus of stimulation. This is not to be wondered at, since the notion of stimulus meaning was relative to the modulus (cf. §8), and so is the very distinction between habit formation and habit formed (cf. §7). Observationality increases with the modulus, in the following way. A typical case of discrepancy between the stimulus meanings of 'Gavagai,' for two natives, is the case where one native and not the other has lately seen rabbits near the spot that they are now viewing. An ill-glimpsed movement would now prompt the one native and not the other to assent to 'Gavagai?'. But if we make the modulus long enough to include as part of the one native's present stimulation his recent observation of rabbits near the spot, then what had been a discrepancy between stimulus meanings is a mere difference of stimulations: the one stimulation is such as would prompt either native to assent, and the other neither. Increase the modulus sufficiently to take in extended periods of learning about friends and you even increase the observationality of 'Bachelor.' But let us forget moduli again for a while, thus keeping our variables down.

We have defined observationality for occasion sentences somewhat vaguely, as degree of constancy of stimulus meaning from speaker to speaker. It would not do to use this definition generally among standing sentences, since the stimulus meaning of a standing sentence can show fair constancy from speaker to speaker for the wrong reason: mere sparseness of member stimulations. Among standing sentences that are well over toward the occasion end (cf. §9), however, the notion of observationality works quite as well as among occasion sentences, and is significant in the same way; viz., the higher the observationality, the better we can get on with translation by stimulus meaning. We could hope, e.g., to translate 'The tide is out' by a rough matching of stimulus meanings; not so 'There is a famous novelist on board.'

Viewing the graded notion of observationality as the primary one, we may still speak of sentences simply as observation sentences when they are high in observationality. In a narrow sense, just 'Red' would qualify; in a wider sense, also 'Rabbit' and 'The tide is out.' It is for observation sentences in some such sense that the notion of stimulus meaning constitutes a reasonable notion of meaning.

To philosophers 'observation sentence' suggests the datum sentences of science. On this score our version is not amiss; for the observation sentences as we have identified them are just the occasion sentences on which there is pretty sure to be firm agreement on the part of well-placed observers. Thus they are just the sentences on which a scientist will tend to fall back when pressed by doubting colleagues. Moreover, the philosophical doctrine of infallibility of observation sentences is sustained under our version. For there is scope for error and dispute only insofar as the connections with experience whereby sentences are appraised are multifarious and indirect, mediated through time by theory in conflicting ways; there is none insofar as verdicts to a sentence are directly keyed to present stimulation. (This immunity to error is, however, like observationality itself, for us a matter of degree.) Our version of observation sentences departs from a philosophical tradition in allowing the sentences to be about ordinary things instead of requiring them to report sense data, but this departure has not lacked proponents.[9]

In estimating the stimulus meaning of a sentence for a speaker at a given time, the linguist is helped by varying the time and speaker. In choosing a translation, he is helped by comparing native speakers and so eliminating idiosyncrasies of stimulus meaning. Still the notion of stimulus meaning itself, as defined, depends on no multiplicity of speakers. Now the notion of observationality, in contrast, is social. The behavioral

9. For remarks on this matter and references see von Mises, *Positivism*, pp. 91–95, 379. To the main theme of this paragraph I sense harmony in Strawson, *Individuals*, p. 212: "If any facts deserve ... to be called ... atomic facts, it is the facts stated by those propositions which demonstratively indicate the incidence of a general feature." For the propositions alluded to seem, in the light of adjacent text, to correspond pretty well to what I have called occasion sentences.

definition offered for it above turns on similarities of stimulus meanings over the community.

What makes an occasion sentence low on observationality is, by definition, wide intersubjective variability of stimulus meaning. Language as a socially inculcated set of dispositions is substantially uniform over the community, but it is uniform in different ways for different sentences. If a sentence is one that (like 'Red' and 'Rabbit') is inculcated mostly by something like direct ostension, the uniformity will lie at the surface and there will be little variation in stimulus meaning; the sentence will be highly observational. If it is one that (like 'Bachelor') is inculcated through connections with other sentences, linking up thus indirectly with past stimulations of other sorts than those that serve directly to prompt present assent to the sentence, then its stimulus meaning will vary with the speakers' pasts, and the sentence will count as very unobservational. The stimulus meaning of a very unobservational occasion sentence for a speaker is a product of two factors, a fairly standard set of sentence-to-sentence connections and a random personal history; hence the largely random character of the stimulus meaning from speaker to speaker.

Now this random character has the effect not only that the stimulus meaning of the sentence for one speaker will differ from the stimulus meaning of *that* sentence for other speakers. It will differ from the stimulus meaning also of any other discoverable sentence for other speakers, in the same language or any other. Granted, a great complex English sentence can be imagined whose stimulus meaning for one man matches, by sheer exhaustion of cases, another man's stimulus meaning of 'Bachelor'; but such a sentence would never be spotted, because nobody's stimulus meaning of 'Bachelor' would ever be suitably inventoried to begin with.

For, consider again how it was with 'Gavagai.' Here the stimulations belonging to the affirmative stimulus meaning share a distinctive trait that is salient, to us as well as to the native: the containing of rabbit glimpses. The trait is salient enough so that the linguist generalizes on it from samples: he expects the next glimpse of a rabbit to prompt assent to 'Gavagai' as past ones have. His generalization is repeatedly borne out, and he concludes with his conjecture that the native's whole stimulus meaning of 'Gavagai'—never experimentally exhausted, of course—will tend to match ours of 'Rabbit.' Now a similar effort with a non-observational native occasion sentence, of the type of our 'Bachelor,' would have bogged down in its early stages. Sample stimulations belonging to the affirmative stimulus meaning of such a sentence, for the given native, would show no tempting common traits by which to conjecture further cases, or none but such as fail to hold up on further tries.

11. Intrasubjective Synonymy of Occasion Sentences

Stimulus meaning remains defined without regard to observationality. But when applied to non-observational sentences like 'Bachelor' it bears little resemblance to what might reasonably be called meaning. Translation of 'Soltero' as 'Bachelor' manifestly cannot be predicated on identity of stimulus meanings between speakers; nor can synonymy of 'Bachelor' and 'Unmarried man.'

But curiously enough the stimulus meanings of 'Bachelor' and 'Unmarried man' are, despite all this, identical for any one speaker.[10] An individual would at any one time be prompted by the same stimulations to assent to 'Bachelor' and 'Unmarried man'; and similarly for dissent. *Stimulus synonymy*, or sameness of stimulus meaning, is as good a standard of synonymy for non-observational occasion sentences as for observation sentences as long as we stick to one speaker. For each speaker, 'Bachelor' and 'Unmarried man' are stimulus-synonymous without having the same meaning in any acceptably defined sense of 'meaning' (for stimulus meaning is, in the case of 'Bachelor,' nothing of the kind). Very well; here is a case where we may welcome the synonymy and let the meaning go.

The one-speaker restriction presents no obstacle to saying that 'Bachelor' and 'Unmarried man' are stimulus-synonymous for the whole community, in the sense of being thus for each member. A practical extension even to the two-language case is not far to seek if a bilingual speaker is at hand. 'Bachelor' and 'Soltero' will be stimulus-synonymous for him. Taking him as a sample, we may treat 'Bachelor' and 'Soltero' as synonymous for the translation purposes of the two whole linguistic communities that he represents. Whether he is a good enough sample would be

10. It can be argued that this much-used example of synonymy has certain imperfections having to do with ages, divorce, and bachelors of arts. Another example much used in philosophy, 'brother' and 'male sibling,' may be held to bog down under certain church usages. An example that is perhaps unassailable is 'mother's father' and 'maternal grandfather' (poetic connotations not being here in point), or 'widower' and 'man who lost his wife.' However, with this much by way of caveat against quibbling, perhaps we can keep to our conventional example and overlook divagations.

checked by observing the fluency of his communication in both communities and by comparing other bilinguals.

Section 10 left the linguist unable to guess the trend of the stimulus meaning of a non-observational occasion sentence from sample cases. We now see a way, though costly, in which he can still accomplish radical translation of such sentences. He can settle down and learn the native language directly as an infant might. Having thus become bilingual, he can translate the non-observational occasion sentences by introspected stimulus synonymy.

This step has the notable effect of initiating clear recognition of native falsehoods. As long as the linguist does no more than correlate the native's observation sentences with his own by stimulus meaning, he cannot discount any of the native's verdicts as false—unless *ad hoc,* most restrainedly, to simplify his correlations. But once he becomes bilingual and so transcends the observation sentences, he can bicker with the native as a brother.

Even short of going bilingual there is no difficulty in comparing two non-observational native sentences to see if they are intrasubjectively stimulus-synonymous for the native. The linguist can do this without having intuitively conjectured the trend of stimulus meaning of either sentence. He need merely query the sentences in parallel under random stimulations until he either hits a stimulation that prompts assent or dissent to one sentence and not to the other, or else is satisfied at last that he is not going to. A visiting Martian who never learns under what circumstances to apply 'Bachelor,' or 'Unmarried man' either, can still find out by the above method that 'Bachelor' for one English speaker does not have the same stimulus meaning as 'Bachelor' for a different English speaker and that it has the same as 'Unmarried man' for the same speaker. He can, anyway, apart from one difficulty: there is no evident reason why it should occur to him thus blindly to try comparing 'Unmarried man' with 'Bachelor.' This difficulty makes the intrasubjective stimulus synonymy of non-observational occasion sentences less readily accessible to an alien linguist than the stimulus synonymy of observation sentences such as 'Gavagai' and 'Rabbit.' Still the linguist can examine for intrasubjective stimulus synonymy any pair of native occasion sentences that it occurs to him to wonder about; and we shall see in §15 how indirect considerations can even suggest such pairs for examination.

Between the stimulus meaning of any sentence for one man and the stimulus meaning of the same or any other sentence for another man there are almost bound to be countless discrepancies in point of verbally contaminated stimulations, as long as one man understands a language that the other does not. The argument is that of the kibitzer case in §9. The translating linguist had for this reason to discount verbally contaminated discrepancies. But intrasubjective comparisons are free of this trouble. Intrasubjectively we can even compare the occasion sentences 'Yes,' 'Uh huh,' and 'Quite' for stimulus synonymy, though the stimulations that enter into the stimulus meanings of these sentences are purely verbal in their relevant portions. A further advantage of the intrasubjective situation appears in the case of stimulations that would at a given time shock one speaker and not another into silence (cf. §9); for clearly these will constitute no discrepancies intrasubjectively. Altogether the equating of stimulus meanings works out far better intrasubjectively than between subjects: it goes beyond observation sentences, it absorbs shock, and it better accommodates verbal stimulations.

Verbal stimulations can plague even the intrasubjective comparisons when they are stimulations of "second intention"—i.e., when besides consisting of words they are about words. Second-intention examples are the bane of theoretical linguistics, also apart from synonymy studies. Thus take the linguist engaged in distinguishing between those sequences of sounds or phonemes that can occur in English speech and those that cannot: all his excluded forms can return to confound him in second-intention English, as between quotation marks. Now some second-intention stimulations that could prompt a subject to assent to one of the queries 'Bachelor?' and 'Unmarried man?' to the exclusion of the other are as follows: a stimulation presenting the spelling of 'bachelor'; a stimulation presenting the words 'rhymes with "harried man"'; a stimulation presenting a glimpse of a bachelor friend together with a plea to redefine 'bachelor.' It is not easy to find a behavioral criterion of second-intention whereby to screen such cases, especially the last.

Leaving that problem unsolved, we have still to note another and more humdrum restriction that needs to be observed in equating sentences by stimulus meanings: we should stick to short sentences. Otherwise subjects' mere incapacity to digest long questions can, under our definitions, issue in difference of stimulus meanings between long and short sentences which we should prefer to find synonymous. A stimulation may prompt assent to the short sentence and not to the long one just because of the opacity of the long one; yet we should then like to say not that the subject has shown the meaning of the long sentence to be differ-

ent, but merely that he has failed to encompass it. Still a concept of synonymy initially significant only for short sentences can be extended to
long sentences by analogy, e.g. as follows. By a *construction*, linguisti-
cally speaking, let us understand any fixed way of building a composite
expression from arbitrary components of appropriate sort, one or more
at a time. (What is fixed may include certain additive words, as well as
the way of arranging the unfixed components.) Now two sentence-form-
ing constructions may be so related that whenever applied to the same
components they yield mutually synonymous results, as long as the results are short enough to be compared for synonymy. In this event it is
natural, by extension, to count also as mutually synonymous any results
of applying those constructions to identical components however long.
But to simplify ensuing considerations let us continue to reason without
reference to this refinement where we can.

Our success with 'Bachelor' and 'Unmarried man' has been sufficient,
despite the impasse at second intention, to tempt us to overestimate
how well intrasubjective stimulus synonymy withstands collateral information. By way of corrective, consider the Himalayan explorer who
has learned to apply 'Everest' to a distant mountain seen from Tibet
and 'Gaurisanker' to one seen from Nepal. As occasion sentences these
words have mutually exclusive stimulus meanings for him until his ex-
plorations reveal, to the surprise of all concerned, that the peaks are
identical. His discovery is painfully empirical, not lexicographic; nevertheless the stimulus meanings of 'Everest' and 'Gaurisanker' coincide for
him thenceforward.[11]

Or again consider the occasion sentences 'Indian nickel' and 'Buffalo
nickel.' These have distinct stimulus meanings for a boy for his first minute or two of passive acquaintance with these coins, and when he gets to
turning them over the stimulus meanings tend to fuse.

Do they fully fuse? The question whether 'Indian nickel' and 'Buffalo
nickel' have the same stimulus meaning for a given subject is the question whether any sequence of ocular irradiations or other stimulation
(within the modulus), realized or not, *would* now prompt the subject to
assent to or dissent from 'Indian nickel' and not 'Buffalo nickel' or vice
versa. Among such stimulations are those that present, to all appearances, a coin whose obverse is like that of an Indian nickel but whose re-

11. I am indebted to Davidson for this point and Schrödinger, *What Is Life?*, for
the example.

verse bears some device other than the buffalo. Such stimulations can with a little felony even be realized. After a modulus-long examination of such a hybrid coin, a novice might conclude with surprise that there are after all two kinds of Indian nickel, while an expert, sure of his numismatics, might conclude that the coin must be fraudulent. For the expert, 'Indian nickel' and 'Buffalo nickel' are stimulus-synonymous; for the novice not.

The novice does believe and continues to believe, as the expert does, that all Indian nickels are buffalo nickels and vice versa; for the novice has not been and will not be actually subjected to the surprising stimulation described. But the mere fact that there is such a stimulation pattern and that the novice *would* now thus respond to it (whether we know it or not) is what, by definition, makes the stimulus meanings of 'Indian nickel' and 'Buffalo nickel' differ for the novice even as of now.

To keep our example pertinent we must abstract from what may be called the conniving mode of speech: the mode in which we knowingly speak of Olivier as Macbeth, of a statue of a horse as a horse, of a false nickel as a nickel. Even the expert would in practice speak of the prepared coin as "that Indian nickel with the whoozis on the back," adding that it was phony. Here we have a broader usage of 'nickel,' under which nobody would seriously maintain even that all Indian nickels are in point of fact buffalo nickels and vice versa; whereas our purpose in the example is to examine two supposedly coextensive terms for sameness of stimulus meaning. In the example, therefore, read 'Indian nickel' and 'buffalo nickel' as 'real Indian nickel,' 'real buffalo nickel.'

From the example we see that two terms can in fact be coextensive, or true of the same things, without being intrasubjectively stimulus-synonymous as occasion sentences. They can be believed coextensive without being, even for the believer, stimulus-synonymous as occasion sentences; witness 'Indian nickel' and 'Buffalo nickel' for the novice. But when as in the expert's case the belief is so firm that no pattern of stimulation (within the modulus) would suffice to dislodge it, they are stimulus-synonymous as occasion sentences.

So it is apparent that intrasubjective stimulus synonymy remains open to criticism, from intuitive preconceptions, for relating occasion sentences whose stimulus meanings coincide on account of collateral information. Now there is still a way of cutting out the effects of idiosyncratic information: we can hold out for virtual constancy over the community. In this social sense of stimulus synonymy, 'Indian nickel' and 'Buffalo nickel' would cease to count as stimulus-synonymous, because of such speakers as our novice; whereas 'Bachelors' and 'Unmarried man' might still rate as stimulus-synonymous even socially, as being intrasubjectively stimulus-synonymous for nearly everybody. There is still no screen against the effects of collateral information common to the community; but, as urged in §9, I think that at that point the ideal becomes illusory.

12. Synonymy of Terms

In starting our consideration of meaning with sentences we have hewn the line of §§3 and 4, where it was stressed that words are learned only by abstraction from their roles in learned sentences. But there are one-word sentences, such as 'Red' and 'Rabbit.' Insofar as the concept of stimulus meaning may be said to constitute in some strained sense a meaning concept for these, it would seem to constitute a meaning concept for general terms like 'red' and 'rabbit.' This, however, is a mistake. Stimulus synonymy of the occasion sentences 'Gavagai' and 'Rabbit' does not even guarantee that 'gavagai' and 'rabbit' are coextensive terms, terms true of the same things.

For, consider 'gavagai.' Who knows but what the objects to which this term applies are not rabbits after all, but mere stages, or brief temporal segments, of rabbits? In either event the stimulus situations that prompt assent to 'Gavagai' would be the same as for 'Rabbit.' Or perhaps the objects to which 'gavagai' applies are all and sundry undetached parts of rabbits; again the stimulus meaning would register no difference. When from the sameness of stimulus meanings of 'Gavagai' and 'Rabbit' the linguist leaps to the conclusion that a gavagai is a whole enduring rabbit, he is just taking for granted that the native is enough like us to have a brief general term for rabbits and no brief general term for rabbit stages or parts.

A further alternative likewise compatible with the same old stimulus meaning is to take 'gavagai' as a singular term naming the fusion, in Goodman's sense, of all rabbits: that single though discontinuous portion of the spatiotemporal world that consists of rabbits. Thus even the distinction between general and singular terms is independent of stimulus meaning. The same point can be seen by considering, conversely, the singular term 'Bernard J. Ortcutt': it differs none in stimulus meaning from a general term true of each of the good dean's temporal segments, and none from a general term true of each of his spatial parts. And a still further alternative in the case of 'gavagai' is to take it as a singular term naming a recurring universal, rabbithood. The distinction between concrete and abstract object, as well as that between general and singular term, is independent of stimulus meaning.

Commonly we can translate something (e.g. 'for the sake of') into a given language though nothing in that language corresponds to certain of the component syllables. Just so the occasion sentence 'Gavagai' is translatable as saying that a rabbit is there, even if no part of 'Gavagai' nor anything at all in the native language quite corresponds to the term 'rabbit.' Synonymy of 'Gavagai' and 'Rabbit' as sentences turns on considerations of prompted assent; not so synonymy of them as terms. We are right to write 'Rabbit,' instead of 'rabbit,' as a signal that we are considering it in relation to what is synonymous with it as a sentence and not in relation to what is synonymous with it as a term.

Does it seem that the imagined indecision between rabbits, stages of rabbits, integral parts of rabbits, the rabbit fusion, and rabbithood must be due merely to some special fault in our formulation of stimulus meaning, and that it should be resoluble by a little supplementary pointing and questioning? Consider, then, how. Point to a rabbit and you have pointed to a stage of a rabbit, to an integral part of a rabbit, to the rabbit fusion, and to where rabbithood is manifested. Point to an integral part of a rabbit and you have pointed again to the remaining four sorts of things; and so on around. Nothing not distinguished in stimulus meaning itself is to be distinguished by pointing, unless the pointing is accompanied by questions of identity and diversity: 'Is this the same gavagai as that?,' 'Do we have here one gavagai or two?'. Such questioning requires of the linguist a command of the native language far beyond anything that we have as yet seen how to account for. We cannot even say what native locutions to count as analogues of terms as we know them, much less equate them with ours term for term, except as we have also decided what native devices to view as doing in their devious ways the work of our own various auxiliaries to objective reference: our articles and pronouns, our singular and plural, our copula, our identity predicate.[12] The whole apparatus is interdependent, and the very notion of term is as pro-

12. Strawson is making this point when he writes that "feature-placing sentences do not introduce particulars into our discourse" ("Particular and General," *Proceedings of the Aristotelian Society* 54 [1954], p. 244).

vincial to our culture as are those associated devices. The native may achieve the same net effects through linguistic structures so different that any eventual construing of our devices in the native language and vice versa can prove unnatural and largely arbitrary. (Cf. §15.) Yet the net effects, the occasion sentences and not the terms, can match up in point of stimulus meanings as well as ever for all that. Occasion sentences and stimulus meaning are general coin; terms and reference are local to our conceptual scheme.[13]

It will perhaps be countered that there is no essential difficulty in spotting judgments of identity on the part of the jungle native, or even of a speechless animal. This is true enough for qualitative identity, better called resemblance. In an organism's susceptibility to the conditioning of responses we have plentiful criteria for his standards of resemblance of stimulations. (Cf. §17.) But what is relevant to the preceding reflections is numerical identity. Two pointings may be pointings to a numerically identical rabbit, to numerically distinct rabbit parts, and to numerically distinct rabbit stages; the inscrutability lies not in resemblance, but in the anatomy of sentences. We could equate a native expression with any of the disparate English terms 'rabbit,' 'rabbit stage,' 'undetached rabbit part,' etc., and still, by compensatorily juggling the translation of numerical identity and associated particles, preserve conformity to stimulus meanings of occasion sentences.

Intrasubjective stimulus synonymy, for all its advantages over the two-speaker case, is similarly powerless to equate terms. Our Martian of §11 can find as he did that 'Bachelor' and 'Unmarried man' are synonymous occasion sentences for the English speaker, but still either *term* to the exclusion of the other might, so far as he knows, apply not to men but to their stages or parts or even to a scattered concrete totality or an abstract attribute.

We saw in §11 that coextensiveness of terms, or even believed coextensiveness, is not sufficient for their stimulus synonymy as occasion sentences. We now see also that it is not necessary. Where other languages than our own are involved, coextensiveness of terms is not a manifestly clearer notion than synonymy or translation itself; it is no clearer than

13. Russell conceived of what he called "object words" as in effect occasion sentences (*An Inquiry into Meaning and Truth* [New York: Norton, 1940]; see Ch. IV), but, like Carnap (see end of §8 above), he failed to note the present point: that the use of a word as an occasion sentence, however determinate, does not fix the extension of the word as a term.

the considerations, whatever they are (§§15 and 16), that make for contextual translation of the identity predicate, the copula, and related particles.

Yet surely the main interest of the synonymy of 'Bachelor' and 'Unmarried man' as occasion sentences was the line it seemed to give on the synonymy of 'bachelor' and 'unmarried man' as terms. Now within English the situation is not beyond saving. To get synonymy of terms from synonymy of the corresponding occasion sentences we need only add a condition that will screen out such pairs as 'bachelor' and 'part of a bachelor'; and this we can do by requiring that the subject be prepared to assent to the standing sentence 'All Fs are Gs and vice versa,' thinking of 'F' and 'G' as the terms in question. The definition becomes this: 'F' and 'G' are stimulus-synonymous as terms for a speaker at t if and only if as occasion sentences they have the same stimulus meaning for him at t and he would assent to 'All Fs are Gs and vice versa' if asked at t. But we can simplify this definition, by strengthening the latter part to make it assure the former part. Instead of just saying he would assent to 'All Fs are Gs and vice versa' as things stand at t, we can say he would still assent to it, if to anything, following any stimulation that might be imposed at t. (The 'if to anything' accommodates shock.) This strengthened condition assures that 'F' and 'G' will also agree in stimulus meaning as occasion sentences; for, if each stimulation would leave the subject prepared to assent to 'All Fs are Gs and vice versa' if to anything, then none would prompt him to assent to or dissent from one of 'F' and 'G' and not the other.[14]

For reasons evident in §14, I call a sentence *stimulus-analytic* for a subject if he would assent to it, or nothing, after every stimulation (within the modulus). Our condition of stimulus synonymy of 'F' and 'G' as general terms then reduces to stimulus analyticity of 'All Fs are Gs and vice versa.' This condition has its parallel for singular terms, represented by 'a' and 'b'; viz., stimulus-analyticity of '$a = b$.' But note that our formulations apply only to English and to languages whose translations of 'all,' 'are,' and '=' are somehow settled in advance. This limitation is to be expected in notions relating to terms.

Our simplification of the definition of term synonymy extends it to all terms, regardless of whether their objects are such that we could reason-

---

14. Incoherent behavior is possible, but there is a limit to the bizarreness of exceptions worth allowing for in these behavioral formulations.

ably use the terms as occasion sentences. We must not conclude, from seeming appropriateness of the definition as applied to terms like 'rabbit,' 'bachelor,' and 'buffalo nickel,' that it is as appropriate to the wider domain. However, let us leave that question and think further about the narrower domain.

Our version of synonymy makes the terms 'Indian nickel' and 'buffalo nickel' synonymous for the expert of §11, and not for the novice. It is open to criticism, from intuitive preconceptions, for its equating of terms whose coextensiveness the subject has learned by exploration and experiment and not merely by encompassing their "meanings." Such, then, is the concept of stimulus synonymy of terms that comes out of stimulus synonymy of occasion sentences for individual speakers. We can still socialize the concept and so cut out the effects of idiosyncratic information, as we did for occasion sentences at the end of §11: we can count just those terms as socially stimulus-synonymous that come out stimulus-synonymous for each individual speaker almost without exception. Socially, 'bachelor' and 'unmarried man' remain stimulus-synonymous while 'Indian nickel' and 'buffalo nickel' do not.

We welcome this consequence of socializing our concept of stimulus synonymy because our intuitive semantics[15] rates 'bachelor' and 'unmarried man' as synonymous, and probably 'Indian nickel' and 'buffalo nickel' not. But now what can have been the cause of those intuitive ratings themselves? Not, I think any close analogue, however unconscious, of our present construction: not an implicit sociological guess that under extraordinary stimulation most people would hold 'bachelor' and 'unmarried man' coextensive while many would let 'Indian nickel' and 'buffalo nickel' diverge. A likelier place to seek the cause is in the difference between how we whose mother tongue is English learn 'bachelor' and how we learn 'Indian nickel.' We learn 'bachelor' by learning appropriate associations of words with words, and 'Indian nickel' by learning directly to associate the term with sample objects.[16] It is the difference, so central to Russell's philosophy, between description and acquaintance. It is kept before us in synchronic behavior as a difference between the nonobservational occasion sentences, with their random variation in stimulus meaning from speaker to speaker, and observation sentences with

15. See note 6 above.

16. To be precise about the example, we learn 'nickel' and 'Indian' in direct association with sample objects or likenesses, and then 'Indian nickel' is self-explanatory once we see one.

their socially uniform stimulus meanings. (Cf. §10.) One looks to 'un-married man' as semantically anchoring 'bachelor' because there is no socially constant stimulus meaning to govern the use of the word; sever its tie with 'unmarried man' and you leave it no very evident social deter-mination, hence no utility in communication.

'Brother,' in its synonymy with 'male sibling,' is essentially like 'bache-lor' in its synonymy with 'unmarried man.' We learn 'brother' (in its ac-curate adult use) only by verbal connections with sentences about child-birth, and 'sibling' by verbal connections with 'brother' and 'sister.' The occasion sentences 'Brother' and 'Sibling' are non-observational: their stimulus meanings vary over society in as random a fashion as that of 'Bachelor,' and it is only the few verbal links that give the terms the fixity needed in communication.

Many terms of systematic theoretical science are of a third sort. They are like 'bachelor' and 'brother' in having no socially constant stimulus meanings to govern their use; indeed such a term is commonly useless in the role of occasion sentence, so that there is no question of stimulus meaning. Yet they are unlike 'bachelor' and 'brother' in having a more complex network of verbal connections, so that no one tie seems cru-cial to communication. Thus it is that in theoretical science, unless as recast by semantics enthusiasts, distinctions between synonymies and "factual" equivalences are seldom sensed or claimed. Even the identity historically introduced into mechanics by defining 'momentum' as 'mass times velocity' takes its place in the network of connections on a par with the rest; if a physicist subsequently so revises mechanics that mo-mentum fails to be proportional to velocity, the change will probably be seen as a change of theory and not peculiarly of meaning.[17] Synonymy intuitions do not emerge here, just because the terms are linked to the rest of language in more ways than words like 'bachelor' are.[18]

13. Translating Logical Connectives

In §§7 through 11 we accounted for radical translation of occasion sen-tences, by approximate identification of stimulus meanings. Now there is also a decidedly different domain that lends itself directly to radical translation: that of *truth functions* such as negation, logical conjunction,

17. See the last section of my "Carnap and Logical Truth" [Chapter 4].

18. Putnam in "The Analytic and the Synthetic" has offered an illuminating ac-count of the synonymy intuition in terms of a contrast between terms that connote

and alternation. For this purpose the sentences put to the native for assent or dissent may be occasion sentences and standing sentences indifferently. Those that are occasion sentences will have to be accompanied by a prompting stimulation, if assent or dissent is to be elicited; the standing sentences, on the other hand, can be put without props. Now by reference to assent and dissent we can state semantic criteria for truth functions; i.e., criteria for determining whether a given native idiom is to be construed as expressing the truth function in question. The semantic criterion of negation is that it turns any short sentence to which one will assent into a sentence from which one will dissent, and vice versa. That of conjunction is that it produces compounds to which (so long as the component sentences are short) one is prepared to assent always and only when one is prepared to assent to each component. That of alternation is similar with assent changed twice to dissent.

The point about short components is merely, as in §11, that when they are long the subject may get mixed up. Identification of a native idiom as negation, or conjunction, or alternation, is not to be ruled out in view of a subject's deviation from our semantic criteria when the deviation is due merely to confusion. No limit is imposed on the lengths of the component sentences to which negation, conjunction, or alternation may be applied; it is just that the test cases for first spotting such constructions in a strange language are cases with short components.

When we find that a native construction fulfills one or another of these three semantic criteria, we can ask no more toward an understanding of it. Incidentally we can then translate the idiom into English as 'not,' 'and,' or 'or' as the case may be, but only subject to sundry humdrum provisos; for it is well known that these three English words do not represent negation, conjunction, and alternation exactly and unambiguously.

Any construction for compounding sentences from sentences is counted in logic as expressing a truth function if it fulfills this condition: the compound has a unique truth value (truth or falsity) for each assignment of truth values to the components. Semantic criteria can obviously be stated for all truth functions along the lines already followed for negation, conjunction, and alternation.

This approach ill accords with a doctrine of "prelogical mentality." To

---

clusters of traits and terms that do not. My account fits with his and perhaps adds to the explanation. His cases of clustering correspond to my observational terms such as 'Indian nickel' and theoretical terms such as 'momentum,' as against 'bachelor.'

take the extreme case, let us suppose that certain natives are said to accept as true certain sentences translatable in the form 'p and not p.' Now this claim is absurd under our semantic criteria. And, not to be dogmatic about them, what criteria might one prefer? Wanton translation can make natives sound as queer as one pleases. Better translation imposes our logic upon them, and would beg the question of prelogicality if there were a question to beg.[19]

Consider, for that matter, the Spaniard with his 'No hay nada.' Lovers of paradox may represent him as flouting the law of double negation. Soberer translators may reckon 'no' and 'nada,' in this context, as halves of one negative.

That fair translation preserves logical laws is implicit in practice even where, to speak paradoxically, no foreign language is involved. Thus when to our querying of an English sentence an English speaker answers 'Yes and no,' we assume that the queried sentence is meant differently in the affirmation and negation; this rather than that he would be so silly as to affirm and deny the same thing. Again, when someone espouses a logic whose laws are ostensibly contrary to our own, we are ready to speculate that he is just giving some familiar old vocables ('and,' 'or,' 'not,' 'all,' etc.) new meanings. This talk of meaning is intuitive, uncritical, and undefined, but it is a piece with translation; what it registers is our reluctance under such circumstances to "translate" the speaker's English into our English by the normal tacit method of homophonic translation.

Or consider the familiar remark that even the most audacious system-builder is bound by the law of contradiction. How is he really bound? If he were to accept contradiction, he would so readjust his logical laws as to insure distinctions of some sort; for the classical laws yield all sentences as consequences of any contradiction. But then we would proceed

19. B. Malinowski, *Coral Gardens and Their Magic* (New York: American Book Co., 1935), vol. 2, pp. 68ff., spared his islanders the imputation of prelogicality by so varying his translations of terms, from occurrence to occurrence, as to sidestep contradiction. . . . It is understandable that the further alternative of blaming the translation of conjunctions, copulas, or other logical particles is nowhere considered; for any considerable complexity on the part of the English correlates of such words would of course present the working translator with forbidding practical difficulties.

—Eventually Levy-Bruhl gave up his original doctrine of prelogical mentality; but the considerations that operated are not easy to relate to the present ones.

to reconstrue his heroically novel logic as a non-contradictory logic, perhaps even as familiar logic, in perverse notation.

The maxim of translation underlying all this is that assertions startingly false on the face of them are likely to turn on hidden differences of language. This maxim is strong enough in all of us to swerve us even from the homophonic method that is so fundamental to the very acquisition and use of one's mother tongue.

The common sense behind the maxim is that one's interlocutor's silliness, beyond a certain point, is less likely than bad translation—or, in the domestic case, linguistic divergence.[20] Another account of the matter, as it touches logical laws in the domestic case, is as follows. The logical particles 'and,' 'all,' etc. are learned only from sentential contexts. Dropping a logical law means a devastatingly widespread unfixing of truth values of contexts of the particles concerned, leaving no fixity to rely on in using those particles. In short, their meanings are gone; new ones may be supplied. What prompts a sense of meaning-involvement here is thus at bottom the same as in the case of 'bachelor' and 'unmarried man' (§12).

Let us now resume our reflections on logic under radical translation. We have settled a people's logical laws completely, so far as the truth-functional part of logic goes, once we have fixed our translations by the above semantic criteria. Truths of this part of logic are called *tautologies*: the truth-functional compounds that are true by truth-functional structure alone. There is a familiar tabular routine for determining, for sentences in which the truth functions are however immoderately iterated and superimposed, just what assignments of truth values to the ultimate component sentences will make the whole compound true; and the tautologies are the compounds that come out true under all assignments.

But the truth functions and tautologies are only the simplest of the logical functions and logical truths. Can we perhaps do better? The logical functions that most naturally next suggest themselves are the categoricals, traditionally designated A, E, I, and O, and commonly construed in English by the constructions 'all are' ('All rabbits are timid'), 'none are,' 'some are,' 'some are not.' A semantic criterion for A perhaps suggests itself as follows: the compound commands assent (from a given speaker) if and only if the affirmative stimulus meaning (for him) of the

20. Cf. Wilson's principle of charity: "We select as designatum that individual which will make the largest possible number of . . . statements true" (Wilson, "Substances without Substrata," *Review of Metaphysics* 12 [1959], pp. 521–539).

first component is a subclass of the affirmative stimulus meaning of the second component and the negative stimulus meanings are conversely related. How to vary this for E, I, and O is obvious enough, except that the whole idea is wrong in view of §12. Thus take A. All Indian nickels are buffalo nickels, and even are believed by the novice of §12 to be buffalo nickels, but still the affirmative stimulus meaning of 'Indian nickel,' for our novice anyway, has stimulus patterns in it that are not in the affirmative stimulus meaning of 'Buffalo nickel.' On this score the suggested semantic criterion is at odds with 'All Fs are Gs' in that it goes beyond extension. And it has a yet more serious failing of the opposite kind; for, whereas rabbit stages are not rabbits, we saw in §12 that in point of stimulus meaning there is no distinction.

The difficulty is fundamental. The categoricals depend for their truth on the objects, however external and however inferential, of which the component terms are true; and what those objects are is not uniquely determined by stimulus meanings. Indeed the categoricals, like plural endings and identity, are part of our own special apparatus of objective reference, whereas stimulus meaning is, to repeat §12, common coin. Of what we think of as logic, the truth-functional part is the only part the recognition of which, in a foreign language, we seem to be able to pin down to behavioral criteria.

The condition that was seen to be inadequate as a semantic condition for the A copula does still determine a copula. Let me write 'pars' for this copula. Its usage is to be such that a compound of the form '. . . pars . . . ,' formed of two occasion sentences S_1 and S_2 in that order, is a standing sentence and is to command assent of just the speakers for whom the affirmative stimulus meaning of S_1 is a subclass of that of S_2 and conversely for the negative. Thus, if we think of S_1 and S_2 as general terms— a detail of translation left open by stimulus meaning—then 'F pars G' says approximately that every F is part of the fusion (§12) of the Gs; and if we think of S_1 and S_2 as singular terms, 'a pars b' says approximately that a is part of b. The theory of the part relation, called mereology by Leśniewski and the calculus of individuals by Goodman and Leonard,[21] is thus more amenable to radical semantic criteria than is the logic of the syllogism. But we must give full weight to the word 'approximately,' twice used just now; the correspondence is rather poor, because, as re-

21. See N. Goodman, *The Structure of Appearance* (Cambridge, Mass.: Harvard University Press, 1951), pp. 42ff., and further references therein.

marked two paragraphs back, our semantic criterion makes demands beyond extension.

14. Synonymous and Analytic Sentences

By its etymology, 'synonymous' applies to names. Though in use the term is intended simply to impute sameness of meaning, an effect of its etymology is seen in a tendency to invoke some other word, 'equivalent' or 'equipollent,' for cases where both of the compared expressions are (unlike 'bachelor') verbally complex. My use of 'synonymous' is not thus restricted; I intend the word to carry the full generality of 'same in meaning,' whatever that is. Indeed I have made no essential use of a distinction between word and phrase. Even the first object of translation, say 'Gavagai,' may or may not in the end be parsed as a string of several words, depending on one's eventual choice of analytical hypotheses (§§15, 16).

Taking this minor liberalization hereafter for granted, we still must distinguish between a broad and a narrow type of synonymy, or sameness of meaning, as applied to sentences. The broad one may be formulated in intuitive terms thus: the two sentences command assent concomitantly and dissent concomitantly, and this concomitance is due strictly to word usage rather than to how things happen in the world. One usually hears the matter described in terms rather of truth values than of assent and dissent; but I warp it over to the latter terms in order to maximize chances of making sense of the relation on the basis of verbal behavior.

For some purposes a narrower sort of synonymy of sentences is wanted, such as what Carnap calls intensional isomorphism, involving certain part-by-part correspondences of the sentences concerned. (Cf. §42.) But such variant versions can be defined on the basis of the broader one. Synonymy of parts is defined by appeal to analogy of roles in synonymous wholes; then synonymy in the narrower sense is defined for the wholes by appeal to synonymy of homologous parts. So let us concentrate on the broader and more basic notion of sentence synonymy.

By talking in terms of assent and dissent here instead of in terms of truth values we introduce this difficulty: assent and dissent can be influenced by confusion due to a sentence's length and complexity. But this difficulty can be accommodated in the way sketched in §11. Also it would be automatically taken care of under the program, just now mentioned, of deriving a relation of synonymy of sentence fragments and thence constructing a reformed synonymy relation for wholes. Let us pass over these points, for there is a more basic problem.

When the sentences are occasion sentences, the envisaged notion of synonymy is pretty well realized in intrasubjective stimulus synonymy, especially as socialized. For we can argue that only verbal habit can plausibly account for concomitant variation of two occasion sentences, in point of assent and dissent, over the whole gamut of possible stimulations. There are still the unscreened effects of community-wide collateral information, but there is no evident reason not to count such information simply as a determinant of the verbal habit (§9). When the sentences are standing sentences which, like 'The *Times* has come,' closely resemble occasion sentences in the variability of assent and dissent, stimulus synonymy still does pretty well.

But the less variable the standing sentences are in point of assent and dissent, the sparser their stimulus meanings will be and hence the more poorly stimulus synonymy will approximate to synonymy of the envisaged sort. For, however sparse its stimulus meaning, a sentence retains its connections with other sentences and plays its distinctive part in theories. The sparseness of its stimulus meaning is no sparseness of meaning intuitively speaking, but has the effect that stimulus meaning fails to do the sentence much justice.

By lengthening the modulus of stimulation we can enrich the stimulus meanings and so tighten the relation of stimulus synonymy; for, the longer the stimulations the better their chance of influencing assent and dissent. However, matters get out of hand when the modulus is excessive. Thus consider stimulus synonymy modulo a month. To say that two sentences are now so related is to say that any and every pattern of month-long stimulation, if begun now and terminated next month with a querying of the two sentences, would elicit the same verdict on both. The trouble is that there is no telling what to expect under fairly fantastic stimulation sequences of such duration. The subject might revise his theories in unforeseeable ways that would be claimed to change meanings of words. There is no reason to expect the concomitances of sentences under such circumstances to reflect present sameness of meaning in any intuitively plausible sense. Lengthening the modulus enriches stimulus meanings and tightens stimulus synonymy only as it diminishes scrutability of stimulus synonyms.

Stimulus synonymy, on an optimum modulus, is an approximation to what philosophers loosely call sameness of confirming experiences and of disconfirming experiences. It is an approximation to what it might mean "to speak of two statements as standing in the same germaneness-relation to the same particular experiences."[22] Where standing sentences are of highly unoccasional type, the inadequacy of stimulus synonymy to synonymy intuitively so-called is shared by the vaguer formulations just now noted. And it is shared by the proposal of Perkins and Singer, viz., that we compare sentences for synonymy by putting them to our informant for verification and seeing whether he proceeds similarly in both cases. The trouble lies in the interconnections of sentences. If the business of a sentence can be exhausted by an account of the experiences that would confirm or disconfirm it as an isolated sentence in its own right, then the sentence is substantially an occasion sentence. The significant trait of other sentences is that experience is relevant to them largely in indirect ways, through the mediation of associated sentences. Alternatives emerge: experiences call for changing a theory, but do not indicate just where and how. Any of various systematic changes can accommodate the recalcitrant datum, and all the sentences affected by any of those possible alternative readjustments would evidently have to count as disconfirmed by that datum indiscriminately or not at all. Yet the sentences can be quite unlike with respect to content, intuitively speaking, or role in the containing theory.

Grice and Strawson try *(loc. cit.)* to meet this difficulty by defining S_1 and S_2 as synonymous when, for every assumption as to the truth values of other sentences, the same experiences confirm (and disconfirm) S_1 on that assumption as confirm (and disconfirm) S_2 on that assumption. Now instead of 'every assumption as to the truth values of other sentences' we can as well say simply 'every sentence S'; for S can be the logical conjunction of those "other sentences" in question or their negations. So S_1 and S_2 are defined to be synonymous when, for every S, the same experiences confirm (and disconfirm) S_1 on the hypothesis S as confirm (and disconfirm) S_2 on S. The notion of confirmatory and disconfirmatory experiences had a behavioral approximation in our notion of stimulus meaning; but can we relativize it thus to a hypothesis S? I think we can; for confirmation or disconfirmation of S_1 on S is presumably

22. Grice and Strawson, "In Defense of a Dogma," *Philosophical Review* 65 (1956), p. 156.

confirmation or disconfirmation of the conditional sentence consisting of S as antecedent and S_1 as consequent. Then the proposed definition of synonymy becomes: S_1 and S_2 are synonymous if for every S the conditional compound of S and S_1 and that of S and S_2 are stimulus-synonymous. But now it is apparent that the definition fails to provide a tighter relation between S_1 and S_2 than stimulus synonymy. For, if S_1 and S_2 are stimulus-synonymous than *a fortiori* the conditionals are too.

A variant suggestion would be to define S_1 and S_2 as synonymous when, for every S, the logical conjunction of S and S_1 and that of S and S_2 are stimulus-synonymous. But this is yet more readily seen not to provide a tighter relation.

If either of these ventures had succeeded, the synonymy yielded would still have been strictly intralinguistic; for the auxiliary S, belonging to one language, gets joined to both S_1 and S_2. But the language would not have to be our own. For, by §13, conjunction is translatable; and so is the conditional, if we take it in the material sense 'Not (p and not q).'

The general relation of intrasubjective sentence synonymy thus unsuccessfully sought is interdefinable with another elusive notion of intuitive philosophical semantics: that of an *analytic* sentence. Here the intuitive notion is that the sentence is true purely by meaning and independently of collateral information: thus 'No bachelor is married,' 'Pigs are pigs,' and, by some accounts, '2 + 2 = 4.'[23] The interdefinitions run thus: sentences are synonymous if and only if their biconditional (formed by joining them with 'if and only if') is analytic, and a sentence is analytic if and only if synonymous with self-conditionals ('If p then p').

As synonymy of sentences is related to analyticity, so stimulus synonymy of sentences is related to stimulus analyticity (§12).

Philosophical tradition hints of three nested categories of firm truths: the analytic, the *a priori,* and the necessary. Whether the first exhausts the second, and the second the third, are traditional matters of disagreement, though none of the three has traditionally been defined in terms of detectable features of verbal behavior. Pressed nowadays for such a

23. There is a small confusion that I should like to take this opportunity to resolve, though it lies aside from the main course of the present reflections. Those who talk confidently of analyticity have been known to disagree on the analyticity of the truths of arithmetic, but are about unanimous on that of the truths of logic. We who are less clear on the notion of analyticity may therefore seize upon the generally conceded analyticity of the truths of logic as a partial extensional clarification of analyticity; but to do this is not to embrace the analyticity of the truths of logic as an antecedently intelligible doctrine.

clarification, some who are content to take the three as identical have responded in this vein: the analytic sentences are those that we are prepared to affirm come what may. This comes to naught unless we independently circumscribe the 'what may.' Thus one may object that we would not adhere to 'No bachelor is married' if we found a married bachelor; and how are we to disallow his example without appealing to the very notion of analyticity we are trying to define? One way is to take 'come what may' as 'come what stimulation (§8) may'; and this gives virtually the definition (§12) of stimulus analyticity.[24]

We improved stimulus synonymy a bit by socializing it. We can do the same for analyticity, calling socially stimulus-analytic just the sentences that are stimulus-analytic for almost everybody. But analyticity in even this improved sense will apply as well to 'There have been black dogs' as to '2 + 2 = 4' and 'No bachelor is married.' Let us face it: our socialized stimulus synonymy and stimulus analyticity are still not behavioristic reconstructions of intuitive semantics, but only a behavioristic ersatz.

At the end of §12 we speculated on what makes for the intuition of synonymy of terms. Similar considerations apply to intuitions of sentence synonymy and analyticity. Such an intuition figures in the case of analyticity despite the technical sound of the word; sentences like 'No unmarried man is married,' 'No bachelor is married,' and '2 + 2 = 4' have a feel that everyone appreciates. Moreover the notion of "assent come what may" gives no fair hint of the intuition involved. One's reaction to denials of sentences typically felt as analytic has more in it of one's reaction to ungrasped foreign sentences.[25] Where the sentence concerned is a law of logic, something of the ground of this reaction was discerned in §13: dropping a logical law disrupts a pattern on which the communicative use of a logical particle heavily depends. Much the same applies to '2 + 2 = 4,' and even to 'The parts of the parts of a thing are parts of the thing.' The key words here have countless further contexts to anchor their usage, but somehow we feel that if our interlocutor will not agree with us on these platitudes there is no depending on him in most of the further contexts containing the terms in question.

Examples like 'No bachelor is married' rate as analytic both directly on the vague count just now conjectured and by virtue of coming from logical truths by synonymy substitution.

24. I am indebted to Davidson for the concept of stimulus analyticity, as well as for this observation concerning it.

25. Cf. Grice and Strawson, pp. 150f.

If the mechanism of analyticity intuitions is substantially as I have vaguely suggested, they will in general tend to set in where bewilderment sets in as to what the man who denies the sentence can be talking about. This effect can be gradual and also cumulative.[26] The intuitions are blameless in their way, but it would be a mistake to look to them for a sweeping epistemological dichotomy between analytic truths as by-products of language and synthetic truths as reports on the world. I suspect that the notion of such a dichotomy only encourages confused impressions of how language relates to the world.[27] Stimulus analyticity, our strictly vegetarian imitation, is of course not here in question.

15. Analytical Hypotheses

We have had our linguist observing native utterances and their circumstances passively, to begin with, and then selectively querying native sentences for assent and dissent under varying circumstances. Let us sum up the possible yield of such methods. (1) Observation sentences can be translated. There is uncertainty, but the situation is the normal inductive one. (2) Truth functions can be translated. (3) Stimulus-analytic sentences can be recognized. So can the sentences of the opposite type, the "stimulus-contradictory' sentences, which command irreversible dissent. (4) Questions of intrasubjective stimulus synonymy of native occasion sentences even of non-observational kind can be settled if raised, but the sentences cannot be translated.

And how does the linguist pass these bounds? In broad outline as follows. He segments heard utterances into conveniently short recurrent parts, and thus compiles a list of native "words." Various of these he hy-

26. Apostel and his associates have explored this matter experimentally by asking subjects to classify chosen sentences, with and without the guidance of prior headings. Their findings suggest a gradualism of intuitive analyticity.

27. The notion is often uncritically assumed in modern epistemological writing. Sometimes it has been given a semblance of foundation in terms of "semantical rules" or "meaning postulates," but these devices only assume the notion in disguised form. (See my "Two Dogmas of Empiricism" [Chapter 2] and "Carnap and Logical Truth" [Chapter 4].) My misgivings over the notion came out in a limited way in "Truth by Convention" (1936) [Chapter 1], and figured increasingly in my lectures at Harvard. Tarski and I long argued the point with Carnap there in 1939–40. Soon White was pursuing the matter with Goodman and me in triangular correspondence. The ensuing controversy has run to many articles and several books.

pothetically equates to English words and phrases, in such a way as to confirm to (1)–(4). Such are his *analytical hypotheses,* as I call them. Their conformity to (1)–(4) is ideally as follows. The sentence translations derivable from the analytical hypotheses are to include those already established under (1); they are to fit the prior translation of truth functions, as of (2); they are to carry sentences that are stimulus-analytic or stimulus-contradictory, according to (3), into English sentences that are likewise stimulus-analytic or stimulus-contradictory; and they are to carry sentence pairs that are stimulus-synonymous, according to (4), into English sentences that are likewise stimulus-synonymous.

The analytical hypotheses are begun, however tentatively, long before the work of (1)–(4) is finished, and they help guide the choice of examples for investigation under (1)–(4). This point is essential to (4), since without indirect hints through analytical hypotheses there is virtually no telling what pairs of non-observational sentences to try for intrasubjective stimulus synonymy.

Our recipe is overschematic. If the analytical hypotheses give some English platitude as translation of some native standing sentence, there would be encouragement in finding that the latter also commands general and unreflective assent among natives, even if neither is quite stimulus-analytic. Degrees of approximation to stimulus-analyticity, as well as degrees of observationality, would be allowed for in a truer account. And anyway the analytical hypotheses are not strictly required to conform to (1)–(4) with respect to quite every example; the neater the analytical hypotheses, the more tolerance.

Tolerance is bound to have been exercised if a native sentence, believed by the whole community with a firmness that no stimulus pattern of reasonable duration would suffice to shake, is translated as 'All rabbits are men reincarnate.' To translate a stimulus-analytic native sentence thus into an English sentence that is not stimulus-analytic is to invoke translator's license. I think this account gives such a translation quite the proper air: that of a bold departure, to be adopted only if its avoidance would seem to call for much more complicated analytical hypotheses. For certainly, the more absurd or exotic the beliefs imputed to a people, the more suspicious we are entitled to be of the translations; the myth of the prelogical people marks only the extreme.[28] For translation theory, banal messages are the breath of life.

28. See §13 on this myth and the principle of charity.

It may occur to the reader to try to derive from stimulus analyticity a finer analyticity concept by screening out sentences such as the native one about reincarnation, using this criterion: through indirect considerations they get translated into sentences of another language that are not stimulus-analytic. However, this criterion is illusory because of its relativity to analytical hypotheses, which, as stressed in succeeding pages, are not determinate functions of linguistic behavior.

Let us now get back to the analytical hypotheses for a more leisurely consideration of their form and content. They are not in general held to equational form. There is no need to insist that the native word be equated outright to any one English word or phrase. Certain contexts may be specified in which the word is to be translated one way and others in which the word is to be translated in another way. The equational form may be overlaid with supplementary semantical instructions *ad libitum*. Since there is no general positional correspondence between the words and phrases of one language and their translations in another, some analytical hypotheses will be needed also to explain syntactical constructions. These are usually described with help of auxiliary terms for various classes of native words and phrases. Taken together, the analytical hypotheses and auxiliary definitions constitute the linguist's jungle-to-English dictionary and grammar. The form they are given is immaterial because their purpose is not translation of words or constructions but translation of coherent discourse; single words and constructions come up for attention only as means to that end.

Nevertheless there is reason to draw particular attention to the simple form of analytical hypothesis which equates a native word or construction to a hypothetical English equivalent. For hypotheses need thinking up, and the typical case of thinking up is the case where the linguist apprehends a parallelism in function between some component fragment of a translated whole native sentence and some component word of the translation of the sentence. Only in some such way can we account for anyone's ever thinking to translate a native locution radically into English as a plural ending, or as the identity predicate '$=$,' or as a categorical copula, or as any other part of our domestic apparatus of objective reference. It is only by such outright projection of prior linguistic habits that the linguist can find general terms in the native language at all, or, having found them, match them with his own; stimulus meanings never suffice to determine even what words are terms, if any, much less what terms are coextensive.

The method of analytical hypotheses is a way of catapulting oneself into the jungle language by the momentum of the home language. It is a way of grafting exotic shoots on to the old familiar bush—to recur to the concluding metaphor of §2—until only the exotic meets the eye. From the point of view of a theory of translational meaning the most notable thing about the analytical hypotheses is that they exceed anything implicit in any native's dispositions to speech behavior. By bringing out analogies between sentences that have yielded to translation and others they extend the working limits of translation beyond where independent evidence can exist.

Not that (1)–(4) themselves cover all available evidence. For remember that we stated those only with reference to a linguist whose gathering of data proceeded by querying native sentences for assent and dissent under varying circumstances. A linguist can broaden his base, as remarked in §11, by becoming bilingual. Point (1) is thereupon extended to this: (1′) All occasion sentences can be translated. Point (4) drops as superfluous. But even our bilingual, when he brings off translations not allowed for under (1′)–(3), must do so by essentially the method of analytical hypotheses, however unconscious. Thus suppose, unrealistically to begin with, that in learning the native language he had been able to simulate the infantile situation to the extent of keeping his past knowledge of languages out of account. Then, when as a bilingual he finally turns to his project of a jungle-to-English manual, he will have to project analytical hypotheses much as if his English personality were the linguist and his jungle personality the informant; the differences are just that he can introspect his experiments instead of staging them, that he has his notable inside track on non-observational occasion sentences, and that he will tend to feel his analytical hypotheses as obvious analogies when he is aware of them at all. Now of course the truth is that he would not have strictly simulated the infantile situation in learning the native language, but would have helped himself with analytical hypotheses all along the way; thus the elements of the situation would in practice be pretty inextricably scrambled. What with this circumstance and the fugitive nature of introspective method, we have been better off theorizing about meaning from the more primitive paradigm: that of the linguist who deals observably with the native informant as live collaborator rather than first ingesting him.

Whatever the details of its expository devices of word translation and syntactical paradigm, the linguist's finished jungle-to-English manual has as its net yield an infinite *semantic correlation* of sentences: the implicit specification of an English sentence, or various roughly interchangeable English sentences, for every one of the infinitely many possible jungle sentences. Most of the semantic correlation is supported only by analytical hypotheses, in their extension beyond the zone where independent evidence for translation is possible. That those unverifiable translations proceed without mishap must not be taken as pragmatic evidence of good lexicography, for mishap is impossible.

Thus let us recall §12, where we saw that stimulus meaning was incapable of deciding among 'rabbit,' 'rabbit stage,' and various other terms as translations of 'gavagai.' If by analytical hypothesis we take 'are the same' as translation of some construction in the jungle language, we may proceed on that basis to question our informant about sameness of gavagais from occasion to occasion and so conclude that gavagais are rabbits and not stages. But if instead we take 'are stages of the same animal' as translation of that jungle construction, we will conclude from the same subsequent questioning of our informant that gavagais are rabbit stages. Both analytical hypotheses may be presumed possible. Both could doubtless be accommodated by compensatory variations in analytical hypotheses concerning other locutions, so as to conform equally to all independently discoverable translations of whole sentences and indeed all speech dispositions of all speakers concerned. And yet countless native sentences admitting no independent check, not falling under (1')–(3), may be expected to receive radically unlike and incompatible English renderings under the two systems.

There is an obstacle to offering an actual example of two such rival systems of analytical hypotheses. Known languages are known through unique systems of analytical hypotheses established in tradition or painfully arrived at by unique skilled linguists. To devise a contrasting system would require an entire duplicate enterprise of translation, unaided even by the usual hints from interpreters. Yet one has only to reflect on the nature of possible data and methods to appreciate the indeterminacy. Sentences translatable outright, translatable by independent evidence of stimulatory occasions, are sparse and must woefully under-determine the analytical hypotheses on which the translation of all further sentences depends. To project such hypotheses beyond the independently translatable sentences at all is in effect to impute our sense of linguistic analogy unverifiably to the native mind. Nor would the dictates even of our own sense of analogy tend to any intrinsic uniqueness; using what first comes to mind engenders an air of determinacy though freedom reign. There can be no doubt that rival systems of analytical hypotheses can fit the totality of speech behavior to perfection, and can fit the totality of dispositions to speech behavior as well, and still specify mutually incompatible translations of countless sentences insusceptible of independent control.

16. On Failure to Perceive the Indeterminacy

Thus the analytical hypotheses, and the grand synthetic one that they add up to, are only in an incomplete sense hypotheses. Contrast the case of translation of the occasion sentence 'Gavagai' by similarity of stimulus meaning. This is a genuine hypothesis from sample observations, though possibly wrong. 'Gavagai' and 'There's a rabbit' have stimulus meanings for the two speakers, and these are roughly the same or significantly different, whether we guess right or not. On the other hand no such sense is made of the typical analytical hypothesis. The point is not that we cannot be sure whether the analytical hypothesis is right, but that there is not even, as there was in the case of 'Gavagai,' an objective matter to be right or wrong about.

There are at least seven causes of failure to appreciate this point. One is that analytical hypotheses are confirmed in the field. Now this simply means that supplementary cases of the sorts summed up under (1)–(4) or (1')–(3) of §15 are gathered after the analytical hypotheses have been framed. The unverifiable consequences I mean are translations not covered by (1)–(4) or even (1')–(3). They can be defended only through the analytical hypotheses, now and forever.

Another of the causes of failure to appreciate the point is confusion of it with the more superficial reflection that uniqueness of grammatical systematization is not to be expected. Obviously the grammatical theories can differ in word segmentations, in parts of speech, in constructions, and perforce then in dictionaries of translation, and still have identical net outputs in the way of whole sentences and even of English sentence translations. But I am talking of difference in net output.

A third cause of failure to appreciate the point is confusion of it with the platitude that uniqueness of translation is absurd. The indeterminacy that I mean is more radical. It is that rival systems of analytical hypotheses can conform to all speech dispositions within each of the languages concerned and yet dictate, in countless cases, utterly disparate translations; not mere mutual paraphrases, but translations each of which would be excluded by the other system of translation. Two such translations might even be patently contrary in truth value, provided there is no stimulation that would encourage assent to either.

A fourth and major cause of failure to appreciate the point is a stubborn feeling that a true bilingual surely is in a position to make uniquely right correlations of sentences generally between his languages. This feeling is fostered by an uncritical mentalistic theory of ideas: each sentence and its admissible translations express an identical idea in the bilingual's mind. The feeling can also survive rejection of the ideas: one can protest still that the sentence and its translations all correspond to some identical even though unknown neural condition in the bilingual. Now let us grant that; it is only to say that the bilingual has his own private semantic correlation—in effect his private implicit system of analytical hypotheses—and that it is somehow in his nerves. My point remains; for my point is then that another bilingual could have a semantic correlation incompatible with the first bilingual's without deviating from the first bilingual in his speech dispositions within either language, except in his dispositions to translate.

A fifth cause is that linguists adhere to implicit supplementary canons that help to limit their choice of analytical hypotheses. For example, if a question were to arise over equating a short native locution to 'rabbit' and a long one to 'rabbit part' or vice versa (§12), they would favor the former course, arguing that the more conspicuously segregated wholes are likelier to bear the simpler terms. Such an implicit canon is all very well, unless mistaken for a substantive law of speech behavior.

A sixth cause is that a few early analytical hypotheses carry the linguist so far. Once he has hypotheses covering identity, the copula, and associated particles, he can translate terms by stimulus synonymy of sentences. A few further hypotheses can create a medium in which to challenge native statements and elicit argument, or even to ask about intuitive synonymy. Abundant new structural data are then forthcoming, and one fails to note the free prior decisions to which these data owe their significance.

A seventh cause is that in framing his analytical hypotheses the linguist is subject to practical constraints. For he is not, in his finitude, free to assign English sentences to the infinitude of jungle ones in just any way whatever that will fit his supporting evidence; he has to assign them in some way that is manageably systematic with respect to a manageably limited set of repeatable speech segments. Once he has cut the segments, begun his analytical hypotheses, and devised an auxiliary apparatus of word classes for his formulations, his freedom of subsequent choice is narrowed further still.

The linguist's working segmentation does yet more than narrow the possibilities of analytical hypotheses. It even contributes to setting, for him or the rest of us, the ends of translation. For a premium is put on structural parallels: on correspondence between the parts of the native sentence, as segmented, and the parts of the English translation. Other things being equal, the more literal translation is seen as more literally a translation. A tendency to literal translation is assured anyway, since the purpose of segmentation is to make long translations constructible from short correspondences; but one goes farther and makes of this tendency an objective—and an objective that even varies in detail with the practical segmentation adopted.

Complete radical translation goes on, and analytical hypotheses are indispensable. Nor are they capricious; we have seen in outline how they are supported. May we not then say that in those very ways of thinking up and supporting the analytical hypotheses a sense *is* after all given to sameness of meaning of the expressions which those hypotheses equate? No. We could claim this only if no two conflicting sets of analytical hypotheses could be tied for first place on all theoretically accessible evidence. The indefinability of synonymy by reference to the methodology of analytical hypotheses is formally the same as the indefinability of truth by reference to scientific method (§5). Also the consequences are parallel. Just as we may meaningfully speak of the truth of a sentence only within the terms of some theory or conceptual scheme (cf. §5), so on the whole we may meaningfully speak of interlinguistic synonymy only within the terms of some particular system of analytical hypotheses.

May we conclude that translational synonymy at its worst is no worse off than truth in physics? To be thus reassured is to misjudge the parallel. In being able to speak of the truth of a sentence only within a more inclusive theory, one is not much hampered; for one is always working within some comfortably inclusive theory, however tentative. Truth is even overtly relative to language, in that e.g. the form of words 'Brutus killed Caesar' could by coincidence have unrelated uses in two languages; yet this again little hampers one's talk of truth, for one works within some language. In short, the parameters of truth stay conveniently fixed most of the time. Not so the analytical hypotheses that constitute the parameter of translation. We are always ready to wonder about the meaning of a foreigner's remark without reference to any one set of analytical hypotheses, indeed even in the absence of any; yet two sets of analytical hypotheses equally compatible with all linguistic behavior can give contrary answers, unless the remark is of one of the limited sorts that can be translated without recourse to analytical hypotheses.

Something of the true situation verges on visibility when the sentences concerned are extremely theoretical. Thus who would undertake to translate 'Neutrinos lack mass' into the jungle language? If anyone does, we may expect him to coin words or distort the usage of old ones. We may expect him to plead in extenuation that the natives lack the requisite concepts; also that they know too little physics. And he is right, except for the hint of there being some free-floating, linguistically neutral meaning which we capture, in 'Neutrinos lack mass,' and the native cannot.

Containment in the Low German continuum facilitated translation of Frisian into English (§7), and containment in a continuum of cultural evolution facilitated translation of Hungarian into English. In facilitating translation these continuities encourage an illusion of subject matter: an illusion that our so readily intertranslatable sentences are diverse verbal embodiments of some intercultural proposition or meaning, when they are better seen as the merest variants of one and the same intracultural verbalism. The discontinuity of radical translation tries our meanings: really sets them over against their verbal embodiments, or, more typically, finds nothing there.

Observation sentences peel nicely; their meanings, stimulus meanings, emerge absolute and free of residual verbal taint. Similarly for occasion sentences more generally, since the linguist can go native. Theoretical sentences such as 'Neutrinos lack mass,' or the law of entropy, or the constancy of the speed of light, are at the other extreme. It is of such sentences above all that Wittgenstein's dictum holds true: "Understanding a sentence means understanding a language."[29] Such sentences, and countless ones that lie intermediate between the two extremes, lack linguistically neutral meaning.

There is no telling how much of one's success with analytical hypothe-

---

29. See L. Wittgenstein's *Blue and Brown Books,* p. 5. Perhaps the doctrine of indeterminacy of translation will have little air of paradox for readers familiar with Wittgenstein's latter-day remarks on meaning.

ses is due to real kinship of outlook on the part of the natives and our-selves, and how much of it is due to linguistic ingenuity or lucky coinci-dence. I am not sure that it even makes sense to ask. We may alternately wonder at the inscrutability of the native mind and wonder at how very much like us the native is, where in the one case we have merely muffed the best translation and in the other case we have done a more thorough job of reading our own provincial modes into the native's speech.

Thus consider, in contrast, a simple instance where cultural difference does objectively manifest itself in language without intervention of ana-lytical hypotheses. Certain islanders are said to speak of pelicans as their half-brothers. One is not of course put off by this obvious shorthand translation of a native word as 'half-brother' rather than in some such more inclusive fashion as 'half-brother or totem associate.' There re-mains an objective cultural difference apart from that, and it is linguisti-cally reflected as follows: the islanders have a short occasion sentence that commands an islander's assent indiscriminately on presentation of any of his half-brothers or any pelican, and presumably no comparably short one for the case of half-brothers exclusively, whereas English is op-positely endowed. Such contrasts, between peoples' basic or short-sen-tence partitionings of stimulations, are genuine cultural contrasts objec-tively describable by reference to stimulus meanings. Where cultural contrasts begin to be threatened with meaninglessness is rather where they depend on analytical hypotheses.

One frequently hears it urged that deep differences of language carry with them ultimate differences in the way one thinks, or looks upon the world. I would urge that what is most generally involved is indetermi-nacy of correlation. There is less basis of comparison—less sense in say-ing what is good translation and what is bad—the farther we get away from sentences with visibly direct conditioning to non-verbal stimuli and the farther we get off home ground.

Our advantage with a compatriot is that with little deviation the auto-matic or homophonic (§13) hypothesis of translation fills the bill. If we were perverse and ingenious we could scorn that hypothesis and devise other analytical hypotheses that would attribute unimagined views to our compatriot, while conforming to all his dispositions to verbal re-sponse to all possible stimulations. Thinking in terms of radical transla-tion of exotic languages has helped make factors vivid, but the main les-son to be derived concerns the empirical slack in our own beliefs. For our own views could be revised into those attributed to the compatriot in the impractical joke imagined; no conflicts with experience could ever supervene, except such as would attend our present sensible views as well. To the same degree that the radical translation of sentences is underdetermined by the totality of dispositions to verbal behavior, our own theories and beliefs in general are under-determined by the totality of possible sensory evidence time without end.

It may be protested that when two theories agree thus in point of all possible sensory determinants they are in an important sense not two but one. Certainly such theories are, as wholes, empirically equivalent. If something is affirmed in the one theory and denied in the other, one may argue that the particular form of words affirmed and denied is itself unlike in meaning in the two cases but that the containing theories as wholes have the same net meaning still. Similarly one may protest that two systems of analytical hypotheses are, as wholes, equivalent so long as no verbal behavior makes any difference between them; and, if they offer seemingly discrepant English translations, one may again argue that the apparent conflict is a conflict only of parts seen out of context. Now this account is fair enough, apart from its glibness on the topic of meaning; and it helps to make the principle of indeterminacy of translation less surprising. When two systems of analytical hypotheses fit the totality of verbal dispositions to perfection and yet conflict in their translations of certain sentences, the conflict is precisely a conflict of parts seen without the wholes. The principle of indeterminacy of translation requires notice just because translation proceeds little by little and sentences are thought of as conveying meanings severally. That it requires notice is plainly illustrated by the almost universal belief that the objective references of terms in radically different languages can be objectively compared.

The indeterminacy of translation has been less generally appreciated than its somewhat protean domestic analogue. In mentalistic philosophy there is the familiar predicament of private worlds. In speculative neurology there is the circumstance that different neural hookups can account for identical verbal behavior. In language learning there is the multiplicity of individual histories capable of issuing in identical verbal behavior. Still one is ready to say of the domestic situation in all positivistic reasonableness that if two speakers match in all dispositions to verbal behavior there is no sense in imagining semantic differences between them. It is ironic that the interlinguistic case is less noticed, for it is just here that the semantic indeterminacy makes clear empirical sense.

8

PROGRESS ON TWO FRONTS

In these pages I update my views on two epistemological matters.

1. Preestablished Harmony

Correct translation, we used to say, preserves meaning. In *Word and Object*,[1] chary of mentalism and meaning, I represented correct translation of an observation sentence as preserving what I called its *stimulus meaning*. I explained its stimulus meaning as the range of stimulations, any one of which would prompt the subject to assent to the sentence. Each stimulation, in my sense of the term, was the near-simultaneous firing of some subset of the subject's neuroceptors.

Not that I pictured the translator as neurologizing. He would just guess his translation of the native's observation sentence in the obvious way, picturing himself in the native's stance and considering what English sentence it would prompt of him. Eventually, he would build his translations of theoretic sentences upon those of observation sentences by what I called *analytical hypotheses*; still no talk of nerve endings. Talk of stimulus meaning and of analytical hypotheses was rather *my* business, my theory of the translator's activity. Stimulus meaning was what, theoretically speaking, correct translation of an observation sentence preserved.

This is uncomfortable theory, however. It calls for sameness of stimulus meaning of the native sentence for the native and the English sen-

Thanks to discussions with Burton Dreben, this paper has much improved through several drafts.
1. Cambridge, Mass.: MIT Press, 1960.

tence for the translator, and hence a sharing of stimulations by native and translator. Well, they cannot share neuroceptors, so we must settle rather for homology of receptors. Such homology is by no means to be expected, and anyway surely should not matter, as I remarked in a lecture five years later.[2] I expressed the same discomfort again in 1974,[3] citing Charles Darwin[4] on the diversity of nerve nets from individual to individual. But I saw no steps to take.

The matter surfaced again at a conference with Donald Davidson, Burton Dreben, and Dagfinn Føllesdal at Stanford in 1986. Davidson favored treating translation purely in terms of the external objects of reference, bypassing consideration of neural receptors. Such is the familiar practice also of experimental psychologists, for whom the so-called stimulus is out there, shared by subject and experimenter. I recognized the adequacy of this object-oriented line in describing the procedures of translation, having described them thus myself, and its adequacy likewise for lexicography. There remains a problem for epistemology and neuropsychology, however, when we reflect with Darwin on the intersubjective diversity of nerve nets and receptors. How does the mere sameness of the distal cause, the jointly observed object, prevail over the diversity of the proximal segments of the causal chains, inside the two observers, and still issue in agreeing response? In short, *why* can the translator and the lexicographer blithely rest with the distal stimulus, as indeed they can?

Let me pinpoint the problem. A rabbit appears, the native says 'Gavagai,' and the translator conjectures 'Rabbit.' On a later occasion they espy another rabbit, the translator says 'Gavagai,' and the native concurs. The two occasions were *perceptually similar*[5] for the native, by his subjective standards of perceptual similarity, and likewise for the translator by his independently testable subjective standards of perceptual similarity. Anatomic likeness of the native's receptors and those of the translator could have helped to account for this agreement, but that is out. What then does?

If I had thus pinpointed my uneasiness back then, I would have quickly resolved it. What we have is a preestablished *harmony* of standards of perceptual similarity, independent of intersubjective likeness of

2. "Propositional Objects" (1965), published in *Ontological Relativity;* see p. 157.
3. *Roots of Reference* (La Salle, Ill.: Open Court, 1974), pp. 23–24, 41.
4. Charles Darwin, *Origin of Species* (London: John Murray, 1859), pp. 45–46.
5. See *Roots of Reference,* pp. 16–18; *From Stimulus to Science* (Cambridge, Mass.: Harvard University Press, 1995), pp. 17–18.

receptors or sensations. Shades of G. W. Leibniz, thus, but without appeal to divine intervention. The harmony is explained by a yet deeper, but more faltering preestablished harmony between perceptual similarity and the environment. This, in turn, is accounted for by natural selection, as follows.

We have, to begin with, an *inductive* instinct: we tend to expect perceptually similar stimulations to have sequels that are similar to each other. This is the basis of expectation, habit formation, and learning. Successful expectation has always had survival value, notably in the elusion of predators and the capture of prey. Natural selection has accordingly favored innate standards of perceptual similarity which have tended to harmonize with trends in the environment. Hence the success, so much better than random, of our inductions and expectations. Derivatively, then, through our sharing of an ancestral gene pool, our innate standards of perceptual similarity harmonize also intersubjectively.

Natural selection is Darwin's solvent of metaphysics. It dissolved Aristotle's final cause, teleology, into efficient cause, and now Leibniz's preestablished harmony as well.

Harmony without interaction: that was the subtlety. We take its ubiquitous effects for granted, not thinking them through. It was only in *From Stimulus to Science* (pp. 20–21) that I got the matter into proper focus and explained it as here.

Note that the harmony was needed not only in respect of the rabbits, in my example, but also in respect of the utterance of 'Gavagai.' The sound of it was perceptually similar for the native and likewise for the translator when it was spoken by either of them. This applies equally, of course, to the child's learning of words from the mother.

The effect of the intersubjective harmony, we see, is that what the two observers agree on is the shared distal subject matter and not the unshared proximal stimulations. The latter, however, are what are related by perceptual similarity, though not intersubjectively. Might it be more straightforward to readjust the terminology and treat the external subject matter as the relata of perceptual similarity?

One reason not to is that it would put the whole vital causal structure of preestablished harmony back where it had been, out of sight and out of mind. Another reason is individuation. What is distally perceived may be an ill-defined event rather than a body, or, if a body, a body in an ill-defined range of perspectives, accommodating our two observers on the occasion in question and perhaps excluding others. I cut through all this by adhering to the subject's neural intakes as the relata of that subject's relation of perceptual similarity, which then enjoys harmony, generous but probably not complete, with that of other subjects.

Ironically, I had described this harmony of perceptual similarity standards already in *Roots of Reference,* on the very page (23) where I then proceeded to bemoan my dependence on intersubjective matching of neural intakes. I even accounted for the harmony by natural selection, shared environment, and heredity, just as in the present pages and in *From Stimulus to Science.* My account differed only in one crucial detail. Today, I have the two subjects exposed to the same external event, whereas in *Roots of Reference* I was still grudgingly according them homologous neural intakes. It made a difference of twenty years. I left myself and others hanging with this enigmatic envoi: "I shall not pause over the lesson, but there is surely one there" (*op. cit.,* p. 23).

2. Theory-Laden Observation

In his early years, the only way a child can go wrong on an observation sentence is by affirming it in a situation that would not have commanded the adult's outright assent. Second thoughts are not yet relevant; they become so only at a later stage, when scientific theory has begun to interrelate observation sentences and generate conflict. The adult may affirm 'There's a rabbit' outright, and then rescind it when a later observation suggests that it was the neighbor's cat.

In *Word and Object* (pp. 42–44) I consequently recognized degrees of observationality, and treated the intrusion of theory or collateral information as dilution of observationality. But in later writings, I held observationality as absolute, based on immediacy of assent, and then I accommodated the intrusion of theory by contrasting the *holophrastic* conditioning of the observation sentence to neural intake with the *analytic* relations of the component words to the rest of language. The sentence figures holophrastically both in the infant's first acquisition of it and in the scientist's immediate assent to it when testing a theory.

My attention was turned anew to these matters by a recent letter from Lars Bergström adumbrating an empirical theory of truth. I ended up not adopting it, but it has prompted me to reflect further on the bipolarity of the holophrastic and analytic perspectives, as against the gradualism of observationality in *Word and Object,* or, as we might say, a gradualism of theoreticity.

In conclusion, I retained the absolute notion of an observation sentence as simply an occasion sentence that commands the subject's immediate assent, however fallible and revisable. Fallibility is then accommodated in a separate dimension, *theoreticity*, which invests observation sentences in varying degrees.

As before, all observation sentences are holophrastic in their association to stimulation. Thus it is that assent to them is immediate, unless the stimulation is off in the fringe of appropriate stimuli. Also, as before, it is in the analytic or word-by-word relations of the sentence to others that theory comes in, in varying degrees. Theoreticity is at a minimum in the observation sentence 'That's blue,' and appreciable in 'That's a rabbit.' It may even be said to invest innate perceptual similarity, for theory is implicit in our innate readiness to integrate varied perspectives into an objective reality. A square on the floor, seen from various angles, projects on the retina now a square and now one and another trapezoid, but all these neural intakes are perceptually similar; we are said to "see the square."

I am thus won over to Thomas Kuhn and others who have insisted that observation is inseparable from theory. But my observation sentences stay on in their old definition and their old role as clauses in the observation categoricals that are the checkpoints of science.

This fits nicely with scientific practice. The experimenter settles for criteria that he can confidently adjudicate on the spot: confidently, not infallibly. He looks carefully, and if he is subsequently in doubt he repeats the experiment if he can. The finality of an experiment is historical, not logical.

The evidential burden borne by a highly theoretic observation sentence such as 'There was copper in it,' when it is invoked at a checkpoint, can certainly be shifted to less theoretic observation sentences by deeper analysis. The ideal of reducing all checkpoints to minimally theoretic observation sentences like 'That's blue,' however, is the old phenomenalistic reductionism of what I have long since despaired.

Observation categoricals, formed of observation sentences two by two, remain the checkpoints of scientific theory as before, and the experimental refutation of an implied categorical refutes the theory that implied it. But the refutation is not final, for the refutation of the categorical was not final; the experimenter may have misjudged the protasis of the categorical as fulfilled, or misjudged the apodasis as failed, such being the fallibility of observation. We just expect him to do the best he can.

III

ONTOLOGY

9

ON WHAT THERE IS

A curious thing about the ontological problem is its simplicity. It can be put in three Anglo-Saxon monosyllables: 'What is there?' It can be answered, moreover, in a word—'Everything'—and everyone will accept this answer as true. However, this is merely to say that there is what there is. There remains room for disagreement over cases; and so the issue has stayed alive down the centuries.

Suppose now that two philosophers, McX and I, differ over ontology. Suppose McX maintains there is something which I maintain there is not. McX can, quite consistently with his own point of view, describe our difference of opinion by saying that I refuse to recognize certain entities. I should protest, of course, that he is wrong in his formulation of our disagreement, for I maintain that there are no entities, of the kind which he alleges, for me to recognize; but my finding him wrong in his formulation of our disagreement is unimportant, for I am committed to considering him wrong in his ontology anyway.

When *I* try to formulate our difference of opinion, on the other hand, I seem to be in a predicament. I cannot admit that there are some things which McX countenances and I do not, for in admitting that there are such things I should be contradicting my own rejection of them.

It would appear, if this reasoning were sound, that in any ontological dispute the proponent of the negative side suffers the disadvantage of not being able to admit that his opponent disagrees with him.

This is the old Platonic riddle of nonbeing. Nonbeing must in some sense be, otherwise what is it that there is not? This tangled doctrine might be nicknamed *Plato's beard;* historically it has proved tough, frequently dulling the edge of Occam's razor.

It is some such line of thought that leads philosophers like McX to impute being where they might otherwise be quite content to recognize that there is nothing. Thus, take Pegasus. If Pegasus *were* not, McX argues, we should not be talking about anything when we use the word; therefore it would be nonsense to say even that Pegasus is not. Thinking to show thus that the denial of Pegasus cannot be coherently maintained, he concludes that Pegasus is.

McX cannot, indeed, quite persuade himself that any region of space-time, near or remote, contains a flying horse of flesh and blood. Pressed for further details on Pegasus, then, he says that Pegasus is an idea in men's minds. Here, however, a confusion begins to be apparent. We may for the sake of argument concede that there is an entity, and even a unique entity (though this is rather implausible), which is the mental Pegasus-idea; but this mental entity is not what people are talking about when they deny Pegasus.

McX never confuses the Parthenon with the Parthenon-idea. The Parthenon is physical; the Parthenon-idea is mental (according anyway to McX's version of ideas, and I have no better to offer). The Parthenon is visible; the Parthenon-idea is invisible. We cannot easily imagine two things more unlike, and less liable to confusion, than the Parthenon and the Parthenon-idea. But when we shift from the Parthenon to Pegasus, the confusion sets in—for no other reason than that McX would sooner be deceived by the crudest and most flagrant counterfeit than grant the nonbeing of Pegasus.

The notion that Pegasus must be, because it would otherwise be nonsense to say even that Pegasus is not, has been seen to lead McX into an elementary confusion. Subtler minds, taking the same precept as their starting point, come out with theories of Pegasus which are less patently misguided than McX's, and correspondingly more difficult to eradicate. One of these subtler minds is named, let us say, Wyman. Pegasus, Wyman maintains, has his being as an unactualized possible. When we say of Pegasus that there is no such thing, we are saying, more precisely, that Pegasus does not have the special attribute of actuality. Saying that Pegasus is not actual is on a par, logically, with saying that the Parthenon is not red; in either case we are saying something about an entity whose being is unquestioned.

Wyman, by the way, is one of those philosophers who have united in ruining the good old word 'exist.' Despite his espousal of unactualized possibles, he limits the word 'existence' to actuality—thus preserving an illusion of ontological agreement between himself and us who repudiate the rest of his bloated universe. We have all been prone to say, in our common-sense usage of 'exist,' that Pegasus does not exist, meaning simply that there is no such entity at all. If Pegasus existed he would indeed be in space and time, but only because the word 'Pegasus' has spatio-temporal connotations, and not because 'exists' has spatio-temporal connotations. If spatio-temporal reference is lacking when we affirm the existence of the cube root of 27, this is simply because a cube root is not a spatio-temporal kind of thing, and not because we are being ambiguous in our use of 'exist.'[1] However, Wyman, in an ill-conceived effort to appear agreeable, genially grants us the nonexistence of Pegasus and then, contrary to what *we* meant by nonexistence of Pegasus, insists that Pegasus *is*. Existence is one thing, he says, and subsistence is another. The only way I know of coping with this obfuscation of issues is to *give* Wyman the word 'exist.' I'll try not to use it again; I still have 'is.' So much for lexicography; let's get back to Wyman's ontology.

Wyman's overpopulated universe is in many ways unlovely. It offends the aesthetic sense of us who have a taste for desert landscapes, but this is not the worst of it. Wyman's slum of possibles is a breeding ground for disorderly elements. Take, for instance, the possible fat man in that doorway; and, again, the possible bald man in that doorway. Are they the same possible man, or two possible men? How do we decide? How many possible men are there in that doorway? Are there more possible thin ones than fat ones? How many of them are alike? Or would their being alike make them one? Are no *two* possible things alike? Is this the same as saying that it is impossible for two things to be alike? Or, finally, is the concept of identity simply inapplicable to unactualized possibles? But what sense can be found in talking of entities which cannot meaningfully be said to be identical with themselves and distinct from one another? These elements are well-nigh incorrigible. By a Fregean therapy of individual concepts,[2] some effort might be made at

---

1. The impulse to distinguish terminologically between existence applied to objects actualized somewhere in space-time and existence (or subsistence or being) as applied to other entities arises in part, perhaps, from an idea that the observation of nature is relevant only to questions of existence of the first kind. But this idea is readily refuted by counter-instances such as 'the ratio of the number of centaurs to the number of unicorns.' If there were such a ratio, it would be an abstract entity, viz., a number. Yet it is only by studying nature that we conclude that the number of centaurs and the number of unicorns are both 0 and hence there is no such ratio.
2. See below [Chapter 24].

rehabilitation; but I feel we'd do better simply to clear Wyman's slum and be done with it.

Possibility, along with the other modalities of necessity and impossibility and contingency, raises problems upon which I do not mean to imply that we should turn our backs. But we can at least limit modalities to whole statements. We may impose the adverb 'possibly' upon a statement as a whole, and we may well worry about the semantical analysis of such usage; but little real advance in such analysis is to be hoped for in expanding our universe to include so-called *possible entities*. I suspect that the main motive for this expansion is simply the old notion that Pegasus, for example, must be because otherwise it would be nonsense to say even that he is not.

Still, all the rank luxuriance of Wyman's universe of possibles would seem to come to naught when we make a slight change in the example and speak not of Pegasus but of the round square cupola on Berkeley College. If, unless Pegasus were, it would be nonsense to say that he is not, then by the same token, unless the round square cupola on Berkeley College were, it would be nonsense to say that it is not. But, unlike Pegasus, the round square cupola on Berkeley College cannot be admitted even as an unactualized *possible*. Can we drive Wyman now to admitting also a realm of unactualizable impossibles? If so, a good many embarrassing questions could be asked about them. We might hope even to trap Wyman in contradictions, by getting him to admit that certain of these entities are at once round and square. But the wily Wyman chooses the other horn of the dilemma and concedes that it is nonsense to say that the round square cupola on Berkeley College is not. He says that the phrase 'round square cupola' is meaningless.

Wyman was not the first to embrace this alternative. The doctrine of the meaninglessness of contradictions runs away back. The tradition survives, moreover, in writers who seem to share none of Wyman's motivations. Still, I wonder whether the first temptation to such a doctrine may not have been substantially the motivation which we have observed in Wyman. Certainly the doctrine has no intrinsic appeal; and it has led its devotees to such quixotic extremes as that of challenging the method of proof by *reductio ad absurdum*—a challenge in which I sense a *reductio ad absurdum* of the doctrine itself.

Moreover, the doctrine of meaninglessness of contradictions has the severe methodological drawback that it makes it impossible, in principle, ever to devise an effective test of what is meaningful and what is not.

It would be forever impossible for us to devise systematic ways of deciding whether a string of signs made sense—even to us individually, let alone other people—or not. For it follows from a discovery in mathematical logic, due to Church, that there can be no generally applicable test of contradictoriness.

I have spoken disparagingly of Plato's beard, and hinted that it is tangled. I have dwelt at length on the inconveniences of putting up with it. It is time to think about taking steps.

Russell, in his theory of so-called singular descriptions, showed clearly how we might meaningfully use seeming names without supposing that there be the entities allegedly named. The names to which Russell's theory directly applies are complex descriptive names such as 'the author of *Waverley*,' 'the present King of France,' 'the round square cupola on Berkeley College.' Russell analyzes such phrases systematically as fragments of the whole sentences in which they occur. The sentence 'The author of *Waverley* was a poet,' for example, is explained as a whole as meaning 'Someone (better: something) wrote *Waverley* and was a poet, and nothing else wrote *Waverley*.' (The point of this added clause is to affirm the uniqueness which is implicit in the word 'the,' in '*the* author of *Waverley*.') The sentence 'The round square cupola on Berkeley College is pink' is explained as 'Something is round and square and is a cupola on Berkeley College and is pink, and nothing else is round and square and a cupola on Berkeley College.'[3]

The virtue of this analysis is that the seeming name, a descriptive phrase, is paraphrased *in context* as a so-called incomplete symbol. No unified expression is offered as an analysis of the descriptive phrase, but the statement as a whole which was the context of that phrase still gets its full quota of meaning—whether true or false.

The unanalyzed statement 'The author of *Waverley* was a poet' contains a part, 'the author of *Waverley*,' which is wrongly supposed by McX and Wyman to demand objective reference in order to be meaningful at all. But in Russell's translation, 'Something wrote *Waverley* and was a poet and nothing else wrote *Waverley*,' the burden of objective reference which had been put upon the descriptive phrase is now taken over by words of the kind that logicians call bound variables, variables of quantification, namely, words like 'something,' 'nothing,' 'everything.'

3. For more on the theory of descriptions see *From a Logical Point of View*, pp. 85–86, 166–167.

These words, far from purporting to be names specifically of the author of *Waverley*, do not purport to be names at all; they refer to entities generally, with a kind of studied ambiguity peculiar to themselves.[4] These quantificational words or bound variables are, of course, a basic part of language, and their meaningfulness, at least in context, is not to be challenged. But their meaningfulness in no way presupposes there being either the author of *Waverley* or the round square cupola on Berkeley College or any other specifically preassigned objects.

Where descriptions are concerned, there is no longer any difficulty in affirming or denying being. 'There *is* the author of *Waverley*' is explained by Russell as meaning 'Someone (or, more strictly, something) wrote *Waverley* and nothing else wrote *Waverley*.' 'The author of *Waverley* is not' is explained, correspondingly, as the alternation 'Either each thing failed to write *Waverley* or two or more things wrote *Waverley*.' This alternation is false, but meaningful; and it contains no expression purporting to name the author of *Waverley*. The statement 'The round square cupola on Berkeley College is not' is analyzed in similar fashion. So the old notion that statements of nonbeing defeat themselves goes by the board. When a statement of being or nonbeing is analyzed by Russell's theory of descriptions, it ceases to contain any expression which even purports to name the alleged entity whose being is in question, so that the meaningfulness of the statement no longer can be thought to presuppose that there be such an entity.

Now what of 'Pegasus'? This being a word rather than a descriptive phrase, Russell's argument does not immediately apply to it. However, it can easily be made to apply. We have only to rephrase 'Pegasus' as a description, in any way that seems adequately to single out our idea; say, 'the winged horse that has captured by Bellerophon.' Substituting such a phrase for 'Pegasus,' we can then proceed to analyze the statement 'Pegasus is,' or 'Pegasus is not,' precisely on the analogy of Russell's analysis of 'The author of *Waverley* is' and 'The author of *Waverley* is not.'

In order thus to subsume a one-word name or alleged name such as 'Pegasus' under Russell's theory of description, we must, of course, be able first to translate the word into a description. But this is no real restriction. If the notion of Pegasus had been so obscure or so basic a one that no pat translation into a descriptive phrase had offered itself along

4. For more explicit treatment of the bound variable see *From a Logical Point of View*, pp. 82, 102–103.

familiar lines, we could still have availed ourselves of the following artificial and trivial-seeming device: we could have appealed to the *ex hy-
pothesi* unanalyzable, irreducible attribute of *being Pegasus,* adopting,
for its expression, the verb 'is-Pegasus,' or "pegasizes.' The noun 'Pegasus' itself could then be treated as derivative, and identified after all with
a description: 'the thing that is-Pegasus,' 'the thing that pegasizes.'[5]

If the importing of such a predicate as 'pegasizes' seems to commit
us to recognizing that there is a corresponding attribute, pegasizing, in
Plato's heaven or in the minds of men, well and good. Neither we nor
Wyman nor McX have been contending, thus far, about the being or
nonbeing of universals, but rather about that of Pegasus. If in terms of
pegasizing we can interpret the noun 'Pegasus' as a description subject to
Russell's theory of descriptions, then we have disposed of the old notion
that Pegasus cannot be said not to be without presupposing that in some
sense Pegasus is.

Our argument is now quite general. McX and Wyman supposed that
we could not meaningfully affirm a statement of the form 'So-and-so is
not,' with a simple or descriptive singular noun in place of 'so-and-so,'
unless so-and-so is. This supposition is now seen to be quite generally
groundless, since the singular noun in question can always be expanded
into a singular description, trivially or otherwise, and then analyzed out
à la Russell.

We commit ourselves to an ontology containing numbers when we say
there are prime numbers larger than a million; we commit ourselves to
an ontology containing centaurs when we say there are centaurs; and we
commit ourselves to an ontology containing Pegasus when we say Pegasus is. But we do not commit ourselves to an ontology containing Pegasus or the author of *Waverley* or the round square cupola on Berkeley
College when we say that Pegasus or the author of *Waverley* or the cupola in question is *not.* We need no longer labor under the delusion that
the meaningfulness of a statement containing a singular term presupposes an entity named by the term. A singular term need not name to be
significant.

An inkling of this might have dawned on Wyman and McX even without benefit of Russell if they had only noticed—as so few of us do—that
there is a gulf between *meaning* and *naming* even in the case of a singular

5. For further remarks on such assimilation of all singular terms to descriptions
see *From a Logical Point of View,* p. 167; also *Methods of Logic,* pp. 218–224.

term which is genuinely a name of an object. The following example from Frege will serve. The phrase 'Evening Star' names a certain large physical object of spherical form, which is hurtling through space some scores of millions of miles from here. The phrase 'Morning Star' names the same thing, as was probably first established by some observant Babylonian. But the two phrases cannot be regarded as having the same meaning; otherwise that Babylonian could have dispensed with his observations and contented himself with reflecting on the meanings of his words. The meanings, then, being different from one another, must be other than the named object, which is one and the same in both cases.

Confusion of meaning with naming not only made McX think he could not meaningfully repudiate Pegasus; a continuing confusion of meaning with naming no doubt helped engender his absurd notion that Pegasus is an idea, a mental entity. The structure of his confusion is as follows. He confused the alleged *named object* Pegasus with the *meaning* of the word 'Pegasus,' therefore concluding that Pegasus must be in order that the word have meaning. But what sorts of things are meanings? This is a moot point; however, one might quite plausibly explain meanings as ideas in the mind, supposing we can make clear sense in turn of the idea of ideas in the mind. Therefore Pegasus, initially confused with a meaning, ends up as an idea in the mind. It is the more remarkable that Wyman, subject to the same initial motivation as McX, should have avoided this particular blunder and wound up with unactualized possibles instead.

Now let us turn to the ontological problem of universals: the question whether there are such entities as attributes, relations, classes, numbers, functions. McX, characteristically enough, thinks there are. Speaking of attributes, he says: "There are red houses, red roses, red sunsets; this much is prephilosophical common sense in which we must all agree. These houses, roses, and sunsets, then, have something in common; and this which they have in common is all I mean by the attribute of redness." For McX, thus, there being attributes is even more obvious and trivial than the obvious and trivial fact of there being red houses, roses, and sunsets. This, I think, is characteristic of metaphysics, or at least of that part of metaphysics called ontology: one who regards a statement on this subject as true at all must regard it as trivially true. One's ontology is basic to the conceptual scheme by which he interprets all experiences, even the most commonplace ones. Judged within some particular conceptual scheme—and how else is judgment possible?—an ontological statement goes without saying, standing in need of no separate justification at all. Ontological statements follow immediately from all manner of casual statements of commonplace fact, just as—from the point of view, anyway, of McX's conceptual scheme—'There is an attribute' follows from 'There are red houses, red roses, red sunsets.'

Judged in another conceptual scheme, an ontological statement which is axiomatic to McX's mind may, with equal immediacy and triviality, be adjudged false. One may admit that there are red houses, roses, and sunsets, but deny, except as a popular and misleading manner of speaking, that they have anything in common. The words 'houses,' 'roses,' and 'sunsets' are true of sundry individual entities which are houses and roses and sunsets, and the word 'red' or 'red object' is true of each of sundry individual entities which are red houses, red roses, red sunsets; but there is not, in addition, any entity whatever, individual or otherwise, which is named by the word 'redness,' nor, for that matter, by the word 'househood,' 'rosehood,' 'sunsethood.' That the houses and roses and sunsets are all of them red may be taken as ultimate and irreducible, and it may be held that McX is no better off, in point of real explanatory power, for all the occult entities which he posits under such names as 'redness.'

One means by which McX might naturally have tried to impose his ontology of universals on us was already removed before we turned to the problem of universals. McX cannot argue that predicates such as 'red' or 'is-red,' which we all concur in using, must be regarded as names each of a single universal entity in order that they be meaningful at all. For we have seen that being a name of something is a much more special feature than being meaningful. He cannot even charge us—at least not by *that* argument—with having posited an attribute of pegasizing by our adoption of the predicate 'pegasizes.'

However, McX hits upon a different strategem. "Let us grant," he says, "this distinction between meaning and naming of which you make so much. Let us even grant that 'is red,' 'pegasizes,' etc., are not names of attributes. Still, you admit they have meanings. But these *meanings,* whether they are *named* or not, are still universals, and I venture to say that some of them might even be the very things that I call attributes, or something to much the same purpose in the end."

For McX, this is an unusually penetrating speech; and the only way I know to counter it is by refusing to admit meanings. However, I feel no reluctance toward refusing to admit meanings, for I do not thereby deny that words and statements are meaningful. McX and I may agree to the letter in our classification of linguistic forms into the meaningful and the meaningless, even though McX construes meaningfulness as the *having* (in some sense of 'having') of some abstract entity which he calls a meaning, whereas I do not. I remain free to maintain that the fact that a given linguistic utterance is meaningful (or *significant,* as I prefer to say so as not to invite hypostasis of meanings as entities) is an ultimate and irreducible matter of fact; or, I may undertake to analyze it in terms directly of what people do in the presence of the linguistic utterance in question and other utterances similar to it.

The useful ways in which people ordinarily talk or seem to talk about meanings boil down to two: the *having* of meanings, which is significance, and *sameness* of meaning, or synonymy. What is called *giving* the meaning of an utterance is simply the uttering of a synonym, couched, ordinarily, in clearer language than the original. If we are allergic to meanings as such, we can speak directly of utterances as significant or insignificant, and as synonymous or heteronymous one with another. The problem of explaining these adjectives 'significant' and 'synonymous' with some degree of clarity and rigor—preferably, as I see it, in terms of behavior—is as difficult as it important.[6] But the explanatory value of special and irreducible intermediary entities called meanings is surely illusory.

Up to now I have argued that we can use singular terms significantly in sentences without presupposing that there are the entities which those terms purport to name. I have argued further that we can use general terms, for example, predicates, without conceding them to be names of abstract entities. I have argued further that we can view utterances as significant, and as synonymous or heteronymous with one another, without countenancing a realm of entities called meanings. At this point McX begins to wonder whether there is any limit at all to our ontological immunity. Does *nothing* we may say commit us to the assumption of universals or other entities which we may find unwelcome?

I have already suggested a negative answer to this question, in speaking of bound variables, or variables of quantification, in connection with Russell's theory of descriptions. We can very easily involve ourselves in ontological commitments by saying, for example, that *there is something* (bound variable) which red houses and sunsets have in common; or that

---

6. See Essay 2 [Chapter 2] and Essay 3 (Quine, "The Problem of Meaning in Linguistics," *From a Logical Point of View,* pp. 47–64).

there is something which is a prime number larger than a million. But this is, essentially, the *only* way we can involve ourselves in ontological commitments: by our use of bound variables. The use of alleged names is no criterion, for we can repudiate their namehood at the drop of a hat unless the assumption of a corresponding entity can be spotted in the things we affirm in terms of bound variables. Names are, in fact, altogether immaterial to the ontological issue, for I have shown, in connection with 'Pegasus' and 'pegasize,' that names can be converted to descriptions, and Russell has shown that descriptions can be eliminated. Whatever we say with the help of names can be said in a language which shuns names altogether. To be assumed as an entity is, purely and simply, to be reckoned as the value of a variable. In terms of the categories of traditional grammar, this amounts roughly to saying that to be is to be in the range of reference of a pronoun. Pronouns are the basic media of reference; nouns might better have been named propronouns. The variables of quantification, 'something,' 'nothing,' 'everything,' range over our whole ontology, whatever it may be; and we are convicted of a particular ontological presupposition if, and only if, the alleged presuppositum has to be reckoned among the entities over which our variables range in order to render one of our affirmations true.

We may say, for example, that some dogs are white and not thereby commit ourselves to recognizing either doghood or whiteness as entities. 'Some dogs are white' says that some things that are dogs are white; and, in order that this statement be true, the things over which the bound variable 'something' ranges must include some white dogs, but need not include doghood or whiteness. On the other hand, when we say that some zoölogical species are cross-fertile we are committing ourselves to recognizing as entities the several species themselves, abstract though they are. We remain so committed at least until we devise some way of so paraphrasing the statement as to show that the seeming reference to species on the part of our bound variable was an avoidable manner of speaking.[7]

Classical mathematics, as the example of primes larger than a million clearly illustrates, is up to its neck in commitments to an ontology of abstract entities. Thus it is that the great mediaeval controversy over universals has flared up anew in the modern philosophy of mathematics. The issue is clearer now than of old, because we now have a more ex-

---

7. For more on this topic see Essay 6 (Quine, "Logic and the Reification of Universals," *From a Logical Point of View*, pp. 102–129).

plicit standard whereby to decide what ontology a given theory or form of discourse is committed to: a theory is committed to those and only those entities to which the bound variables of the theory must be capable of referring in order that the affirmations made in the theory be true.

Because this standard of ontological presupposition did not emerge clearly in the philosophical tradition, the modern philosophical mathematicians have not on the whole recognized that they were debating the same old problem of universals in a newly clarified form. But the fundamental cleavages among modern points of view on foundations of mathematics do come down pretty explicitly to disagreements as to the range of entities to which the bound variables should be permitted to refer.

The three main mediaeval points of view regarding universals are designated by historians as *realism, conceptualism,* and *nominalism.* Essentially these same three doctrines reappear in twentieth-century surveys of the philosophy of mathematics under the new names *logicism, intuitionism,* and *formalism.*

Realism, as the word is used in connection with the mediaeval controversy over universals, is the Platonic doctrine that universals or abstract entities have being independently of the mind; the mind may discover them but cannot create them. *Logicism,* represented by Frege, Russell, Whitehead, Church, and Carnap, condones the use of bound variables to refer to abstract entities known and unknown, specifiable and unspecifiable, indiscriminately.

Conceptualism holds that there are universals but they are mind-made. *Intuitionism,* espoused in modern times in one form or another by Poincaré, Brouwer, Weyl, and others, countenances the use of bound variables to refer to abstract entities only when those entities are capable of being cooked up individually from ingredients specified in advance. As Fraenkel has put it, logicism holds that classes are discovered while intuitionism holds that they are invented—a fair statement indeed of the old opposition between realism and conceptualism. This opposition is no mere quibble; it makes an essential difference in the amount of classical mathematics to which one is willing to subscribe. Logicists, or realists, are able on their assumptions to get Cantor's ascending orders of infinity; intuitionists are compelled to stop with the lowest order of infinity, and, as an indirect consequence, to abandon even some of the classical laws of real numbers.[8] The modern controversy between logicism and intuitionism arose, in fact, from disagreements over infinity.

8. See *From a Logical Point of View,* pp. 125ff.

Formalism, associated with the name of Hilbert, echoes intuitionism in deploring the logicist's unbridled recourse to universals. But formalism also finds intuitionism unsatisfactory. This could happen for either of two opposite reasons. The formalist might, like the logicist, object to the crippling of classical mathematics; or he might, like the *nominalists* of old, object to admitting abstract entities at all, even in the restrained sense of mind-made entities. The upshot is the same: the formalist keeps classical mathematics as a play of insignificant notations. This play of notations can still be of utility—whatever utility it has already shown itself to have as a crutch for physicists and technologists. But utility need not imply significance, in any literal linguistic sense. Nor need the marked success of mathematicians in spinning out theorems, and in finding objective bases for agreement with one another's results, imply significance. For an adequate basis for agreement among mathematicians can be found simply in the rules which govern the manipulation of the notations—these syntactical rules being, unlike the notations themselves, quite significant and intelligible.[9]

I have argued that the sort of ontology we adopt can be consequential—notably in connection with mathematics, although this is only an example. Now how are we to adjudicate among rival ontologies? Certainly the answer is not provided by the semantical formula "To be is to be the value of a variable"; this formula serves rather, conversely, in testing the conformity of a given remark or doctrine to a prior ontological standard. We look to bound variables in connection with ontology not in order to know what there is, but in order to know what a given remark or doctrine, ours or someone else's, *says* there is; and this much is quite properly a problem involving language. But what there is is another question.

In debating over what there is, there are still reasons for operating on a semantical plane. One reason is to escape from the predicament noted at the beginning of this essay: the predicament of my not being able to admit that there are things which McX countenances and I do not. So long as I adhere to my ontology, as opposed to McX's, I cannot allow my

9. See Nelson Goodman and W. V. Quine, "Steps toward a Constructive Nominalism," *Journal of Symbolic Logic* 12 (1947), pp. 105–122. For further discussion of the general matters touched on in the past two pages, see Paul Bernays, "Sur le platonism dans les mathématiques," *L'Enseignement mathématique* 34 (1935–1936), pp. 52–69; A. A. Fraenkel, "Sur la notion dans les mathématiques," *L'Enseignement mathématique* 34 (1935–1936), pp. 18–32; and Max Black, *The Nature of Mathematics* (London: Kegan Paul, 1933; New York: Harcourt Brace, 1934).

bound variables to refer to entities which belong to McX's ontology and not to mine. I can, however, consistently describe our disagreement by characterizing the statements which McX affirms. Provided merely that my ontology countenances linguistic forms, or at least concrete inscriptions and utterances, I can talk about McX's sentences.

Another reason for withdrawing to a semantical plane is to find common ground on which to argue. Disagreement in ontology involves basic disagreement in conceptual schemes; yet McX and I, despite these basic disagreements, find that our conceptual schemes converge sufficiently in their intermediate and upper ramifications to enable us to communicate successfully on such topics as politics, weather, and, in particular, language. In so far as our basic controversy over ontology can be translated upward into a semantical controversy about words and what to do with them, the collapse of the controversy into question-begging may be delayed.

It is no wonder, then, that ontological controversy should tend into controversy over language. But we must not jump to the conclusion that what there is depends on words. Translatability of a question into semantical terms is no indication that the question is linguistic. To see Naples is to bear a name which, when prefixed to the words 'sees Naples,' yields a true sentence; still there is nothing linguistic about seeing Naples.

Our acceptance of an ontology is, I think, similar in principle to our acceptance of a scientific theory, say a system of physics: we adopt, at least insofar as we are reasonable, the simplest conceptual scheme into which the disordered fragments of raw experience can be fitted and arranged. Our ontology is determined once we have fixed upon the over-all conceptual scheme which is to accommodate science in the broadest sense; and the considerations which determine a reasonable construction of any part of that conceptual scheme, for example, the biological or the physical part, are not different in kind from the considerations which determine a reasonable construction of the whole. To whatever extent the adoption of any system of scientific theory may be said to be a matter of language, the same—but no more—may be said of the adoption of an ontology.

But simplicity, as a guiding principle in constructing conceptual schemes, is not a clear and unambiguous idea; and it is quite capable of presenting a double or multiple standard. Imagine, for example, that we have devised the most economical set of concepts adequate to the play-by-play reporting of immediate experience. The entities under this scheme—the values of bound variables—are, let us suppose, individual subjective events of sensation or reflection. We should still find, no doubt, that a physicalistic conceptual scheme, purporting to talk about external objects, offers great advantages in simplifying our over-all reports. By bringing together scattered sense events and treating them as perceptions of one object, we reduce the complexity of our stream of experience to a manageable conceptual simplicity. The rule of simplicity is indeed our guiding maxim in assigning sense data to objects: we associate an earlier and a later round sensum with the same so-called penny, or with two different so-called pennies, in obedience to the demands of maximum simplicity in our total world-picture.

Here we have two competing conceptual schemes, a phenomenalistic one and a physicalistic one. Which should prevail? Each has its advantages; each has its special simplicity in its own way. Each, I suggest, deserves to be developed. Each may be said, indeed, to be the more fundamental, though in different senses: the one is epistemologically, the other physically, fundamental.

The physical conceptual scheme simplifies our account of experience because of the way myriad scattered sense events come to be associated with single so-called objects; still there is no likelihood that each sentence about physical objects can actually be translated, however deviously and complexly, into the phenomenalistic language. Physical objects are postulated entities which round out and simplify our account of the flux of experience, just as the introduction of irrational numbers simplifies laws of arithmetic. From the point of view of the conceptual scheme of the elementary arithmetic of rational numbers alone, the broader arithmetic of rational and irrational numbers would have the status of a convenient myth, simpler than the literal truth (namely, the arithmetic of rationals) and yet containing that literal truth as a scattered part. Similarly, from a phenomenalistic point of view, the conceptual scheme of physical objects is a convenient myth, simpler than the literal truth and yet containing that literal truth as a scattered part.[10]

Now what of classes or attributes of physical objects, in turn? A platonistic ontology of this sort is, from the point of view of a strictly physicalistic conceptual scheme, as much a myth as that physicalistic conceptual scheme itself is for phenomenalism. This higher myth is a good and useful one, in turn, in so far as it simplifies our account of physics. Since mathematics is an integral part of this higher myth, the

10. The arithmetical analogy is due to Philipp Frank, *Modern Science and Its Philosophy* (Cambridge, Mass.: Harvard University Press, 1949), pp. 108–109.

utility of this myth for physical science is evident enough. In speaking of it nevertheless as a myth, I echo that philosophy of mathematics to which I alluded earlier under the name of formalism. But an attitude of formalism may with equal justice be adopted toward the physical conceptual scheme, in turn, by the pure aesthete or phenomenalist.

The analogy between the myth of mathematics and the myth of physics is, in some additional and perhaps fortuitous ways, strikingly close. Consider, for example, the crisis which was precipitated in the foundations of mathematics, at the turn of the century, by the discovery of Russell's paradox and other antinomies of set theory. These contradictions had to be obviated by unintuitive, *ad hoc* devices;[11] our mathematical myth-making became deliberate and evident to all. But what of physics? An antinomy arose between the undular and the corpuscular accounts of light; and if this was not as out-and-out a contradiction as Russell's paradox, I suspect that the reason is that physics is not as out-and-out as mathematics. Again, the second great modern crisis in the foundations of mathematics—precipitated in 1931 by Gödel's proof that there are bound to be undecidable statements in arithmetic—has its companion piece in physics in Heisenberg's indeterminacy principle.

In earlier pages I undertook to show that some common arguments in favor of certain ontologies are fallacious. Further, I advanced an explicit standard whereby to decide what the ontological commitments of a theory are. But the question what ontology actually to adopt still stands open, and the obvious counsel is tolerance and an experimental spirit. Let us by all means see how much of the physicalistic conceptual scheme can be reduced to a phenomenalistic one; still, physics also naturally demands pursuing, irreducible *in toto* though it be. Let us see how, or to what degree, natural science may be rendered independent of platonistic mathematics; but let us also pursue mathematics and delve into its platonistic foundations.

From among the various conceptual schemes best suited to these various pursuits, one—the phenomenalistic—claims epistemological priority. Viewed from within the phenomenalistic conceptual scheme, the ontologies of physical objects and mathematical objects are myths. The quality of myth, however, is relative; relative, in this case, to the epistemological point of view. This point of view is one among various, corresponding to one among our various interests and purposes.

11. See *From a Logical Point of View,* pp. 90ff., 96ff., 122ff.

10

THE SCOPE AND LANGUAGE OF SCIENCE

I am a physical object sitting in a physical world. Some of the forces of this physical world impinge on my surface. Light rays strike my retinas; molecules bombard my eardrums and fingertips. I strike back, emanating concentric air waves. These waves take the form of a torrent of discourse about tables, people, molecules, light rays, retinas, air waves, prime numbers, infinite classes, joy and sorrow, good and evil.

My ability to strike back in this elaborate way consists in my having assimilated a good part of the culture of my community, and perhaps modified and elaborated it a bit on my own account. All this training consisted in turn of an impinging of physical forces, largely other people's utterances, upon my surface, and of gradual changes in my own constitution consequent upon these physical forces. All I am or ever hope to be is due to irritations of my surface, together with such latent tendencies to response as may have been present in my original germ plasm. And all the lore of the ages is due to irritation of the surfaces of a succession of persons, together, again, with the internal initial conditions of the several individuals.

Now how is it that we know that our knowledge must depend thus solely on surface irritation and internal conditions? Only because we know in a general way what the world is like, with its light rays, molecules, men, retinas, and so on. It is thus our very understanding of the physical world, fragmentary though that understanding be, that enables us to see how limited the evidence is on which that understanding is predicated. It is our understanding, such as it is, of what lies beyond our surfaces, that shows our evidence for that understanding to be limited to our surfaces. But this reflection arouses certain logical misgivings: for is not our very talk of light rays, molecules, and men then only sound and

193

fury, induced by irritation of our surfaces and signifying nothing? The world view which lent plausibility to this modest account of our knowledge is, according to this very account of our knowledge, a groundless fabrication.

To reason thus is, however, to fall into fallacy: a peculiarly philosophical fallacy, and one whereof philosophers are increasingly aware. We cannot significantly question the reality of the external world, or deny that there is evidence of external objects in the testimony of our senses; for, to do so is simply to dissociate the terms 'reality' and 'evidence' from the very applications which originally did most to invest those terms with whatever intelligibility they may have for us.

We imbibe an archaic natural philosophy with our mother's milk. In the fullness of time, what with catching up on current literature and making some supplementary observations of our own, we become clearer on things. But the process is one of growth and gradual change: we do not break with the past, nor do we attain to standards of evidence and reality different in kind from the vague standards of children and laymen. Science is not a substitute for common sense, but an extension of it. The quest for knowledge is properly an effort simply to broaden and deepen the knowledge which the man in the street already enjoys, in moderation, in relation to the commonplace things around him. To disavow the very core of common sense, to require evidence for that which both the physicist and the man in the street accept as platitudinous, is no laudable perfectionism; it is a pompous confusion, a failure to observe the nice distinction between the baby and the bath water.

Let us therefore accept physical reality, whether in the manner of unspoiled men in the street or with one or another degree of scientific sophistication. In so doing we constitute ourselves recipients and carriers of the evolving lore of the ages. Then, pursuing in detail our thus accepted theory of physical reality, we draw conclusions concerning, in particular, our own physical selves, and even concerning ourselves as lorebearers. One of these conclusions is that this very lore which we are engaged in has been induced in us by irritation of our physical surfaces and not otherwise. Here we have a little item of lore about lore. It does not, if rightly considered, tend to controvert the lore it is about. On the contrary, our initially uncritical hypothesis of a physical world gains pragmatic support from whatever it contributes towards a coherent account of lorebearing or other natural phenomena.

Once we have seen that in our knowledge of the external world we have nothing to go on but surface irritation, two questions obtrude themselves—a bad one and a good one. The bad one, lately dismissed, is the question whether there is really an external world after all. The good one is this: Whence the strength of our notion that there is an external world? Whence our persistence in representing discourse as somehow *about* a reality, and a reality beyond the irritation?

It is not as though the mere occurrence of speech itself were conceived somehow as *prima facie* evidence of there being a reality as subject matter. Much of what we say is recognized even by the man in the street as irreferential: 'Hello,' 'Thank you,' 'Ho hum,' these make no claims upon reality. These are physical responses on a par, semantically, with the patellar reflex. Whence then the idea of scientific objectivity? Whence the idea that language is occasionally descriptive in a way that other quiverings of irritable protoplasm are not?

This is a question for the natural science of the external world: in particular, for the psychology of human animals. The question has two not quite separate parts: whence the insistence on a world of reference, set over against language? and whence the insistence on a world of external objects, set over against oneself? Actually we can proceed to answer this twofold question plausibly enough, in a general sort of way, without any very elaborate psychologizing.

II

Let us suppose that one of the early words acquired by a particular child is 'red.' How does he learn it? He is treated to utterances of the word simultaneously with red presentations; further, his own babbling is applauded when it approximates to 'red' in the presence of red. At length he acquires the art of applying the word neither too narrowly nor too broadly for his mother's tastes. This learning process is familiar to us under many names: association, conditioning, training, habit formation, reinforcement and extinction, induction.

Whatever our colleagues in the laboratory may discover of the inner mechanism of that process, we may be sure of this much: the very possibility of it depends on a prior tendency on the child's part to weight qualitative differences unequally. Logically, as long as a, b, and c are three and not one, there is exactly as much difference between a and b as between a and c; just as many classes, anyway, divide a from b (i.e., contain one and not the other) as a from c. For the child, on the other hand, some differences must count for more than others if the described process of learning 'red' is to go forward at all. Whether innately or as a result of pre-linguistic learning, the child must have more tendency to associate a red ball with a red ball than with a yellow one; more tendency to associate a red ball with a red ribbon than with a blue one; and more tendency to dissociate the ball from its surroundings than to dissociate its parts from one another. Otherwise no training could mold the child's usage of the word 'red,' since no future occasion would be more strongly favored by past applications of the word than any other. A working appreciation of something like 'natural kinds,' a tendency anyway to respond in different degrees to different differences, has to be there before the word 'red' can be learned.

At the very beginning of one's learning of language, thus, words are learned in relation to such likenesses and contrasts as are already appreciated without benefit of words. No wonder we attribute those likenesses and contrasts to real stuff, and think of language as a superimposed apparatus for talking *about* the real.

The likenesses and contrasts which underlie one's first learning of language must not only be pre-verbally appreciable; they must, in addition, be intersubjective. Sensitivity to redness will avail the child nothing, in learning 'red' from the mother, except insofar as the mother is in a position to appreciate that the child is confronted with something red. Hence, perhaps, our first glimmerings of an external world. The most primitive sense of externality may well be a sense of the mother's reinforcement of likenesses and contrasts in the first phases of word learning. The real is thus felt, first and foremost, as prior to language and external to oneself. It is the stuff that mother vouches for and calls by name.

This priority of the non-linguistic to the linguistic diminishes as learning proceeds. *Scholarship* sets in; i.e., the kind of learning which depends on prior learning of words. We learn 'mauve' at an advanced age, through a verbal formula of the form 'the color of' or 'a color midway between.' And the scholarly principle takes hold early; the child will not have acquired many words before his vocabulary comes to figure as a major agency in its own increase. By the time the child is able to sustain rudimentary conversation in his narrow community, his knowledge of language and his knowledge of the world are a unitary mass.

Nevertheless, we are so overwhelmingly impressed by the initial phase of our education that we continue to think of language generally as a secondary or superimposed apparatus for talking about real things. We tend not to appreciate that most of the things, and most of the supposed traits of the so-called world, are learned through language and believed in by a projection from language. Some uncritical persons arrive thus at a copy theory of language: they look upon the elements of language as names of elements of reality, and true discourse as a map of reality. They project vagaries of language indiscriminately upon the world, stuffing the universe with ands and ors, singulars and plurals, definites and indefinites, facts and states of affairs, simply on the ground that there are parallel elements and distinctions on the linguistic side.

The general task which science sets itself is that of specifying how reality "really" is: the task of delineating the structure of reality as distinct from the structure of one or another traditional language (except, of course, when the science happens to be grammar itself). The notion of reality independent of language is carried over by the scientist from his earliest impressions, but the facile reification of linguistic features is avoided or minimized.

But how is it possible for scientists to be thus critical and discriminating about their reifications? If all discourse is mere response to surface irritation, then by what evidence may one man's projection of a world be said to be sounder than another's? If, as suggested earlier, the terms 'reality' and 'evidence' owe their intelligibility to their applications in archaic common sense, why may we not then brush aside the presumptions of science?

The reason we may not is that science is itself a continuation of common sense. The scientist is indistinguishable from the common man in his sense of evidence, except that the scientist is more careful. This increased care is not a revision of evidential standards, but only the more patient and systematic collection and use of what anyone would deem to be evidence. If the scientist sometimes overrules something which a superstitious layman might have called evidence, this may simply be because the scientist has other and contrary evidence which, if patiently presented to the layman bit by bit, would be conceded superior. Or it may be that the layman suffers from some careless chain of reasoning of his own whereby, long since, he came wrongly to reckon certain types of connection as evidential: wrongly in that a careful survey of his own ill-observed and long-forgotten steps would suffice to disabuse him. (A likely example is the "gambler's fallacy"—the notion that the oftener black pays the likelier red becomes.)

Not that the layman has an explicit standard of evidence—nor the scientist either. The scientist begins with the primitive sense of evidence which he possessed as layman, and uses it carefully and systematically. He still does not reduce it to rule, though he elaborates and uses sundry statistical methods in an effort to prevent it from getting out of hand in complex cases. By putting nature to the most embarrassing tests he can devise, the scientist makes the most of his lay flair for evidence; and at the same time he amplifies the flair itself, affixing an artificial proboscis of punch cards and quadrille paper.

Our latest question was, in brief, how science gets ahead of common sense; and the answer, in a word, is 'system.' The scientist introduces system into his quest and scrutiny of evidence. System, moreover, dictates the scientist's hypotheses themselves: those are most welcome which are seen to conduce most to simplicity in the overall theory. Predictions, once they have been deduced from hypotheses, are subject to the discipline of evidence in turn; but the hypotheses have, at the time of hypothesis, only the considerations of systematic simplicity to recommend them. Insofar, simplicity itself—in some sense of this difficult term—counts as a kind of evidence; and scientists have indeed long tended to look upon the simpler of the two hypotheses as not merely the more likable, but the more likely. Let it not be supposed, however, that we have found at last a type of evidence that is acceptable to science and foreign to common sense. On the contrary, the favoring of the seemingly simpler hypothesis is a lay habit carried over by science. The quest of systematic simplicity seems peculiarly scientific in spirit only because science is what it issues in.

III

The notion of a reality independent of language is derived from earliest impressions, if the speculations in the foregoing pages are right, and is then carried over into science as a matter of course. The stress on externality is likewise carried over into science, and with a vengeance. For the sense of externality has its roots, if our speculations are right, in the intersubjectivity which is so essential to the learning of language; and intersubjectivity is vital not only to language but equally to the further enterprise, likewise a social one, of science. All men are to qualify as witnesses to the data of science, and the truths of science are to be true no matter who pronounces them. Thus it is that science has got on rather with masses and velocities than with likes and dislikes. And thus it is that when science does confront likes and dislikes it confronts them as behavior, intersubjectively observable. Language in general is robustly extravert, but science is more so.

It would be unwarranted rationalism to suppose that we can stake out the business of science in advance of pursuing science and arriving at a certain body of scientific theory. Thus consider, for the sake of analogy, the smaller task of staking out the business of chemistry. Having got on with chemistry, we can describe it *ex post facto* as the study of the combining of atoms in molecules. But no such clean-cut delimitation of the business of chemistry was possible until that business was already in large measure done. Now the situation is similar with science generally. To describe science as the domain of cognitive judgment avails us nothing, for the definiens here is in as urgent need of clarification as the definiendum. Taking advantage of existing scientific work, however, and not scrupling to identify ourselves with a substantive scientific position, we can then delineate the scientific objective, or the cognitive domain, to some degree. It is a commonplace predicament to be unable to formulate a task until half done with it.

Thought, if of any considerable complexity, is inseparable from language—in practice surely and in principle quite probably. Science, though it seeks traits of reality independent of language, can neither get on without language nor aspire to linguistic neutrality. To some degree, nevertheless, the scientist can enhance objectivity and diminish the interference of language, by his very choice of language. And we, concerned to distill the essence of scientific discourse, can profitably purify the language of science beyond what might reasonably be urged upon the practicing scientist. To such an operation we now turn.

In a spirit thus not of practical language reform but of philosophical schematism, we may begin by banishing what are known as *indicator words* (Goodman) or *egocentric particulars* (Russell): 'I,' 'you,' 'this,' 'that,' 'here,' 'there,' 'now,' 'then,' and the like. This we clearly must do if the truths of science are literally to be true independently of author and occasion of utterance. It is only thus, indeed, that we come to be able to speak of sentences, i.e., certain linguistic forms, as true and false. As long as the indicator words are retained, it is not the sentence but only the several events of its utterance that can be said to be true or false.

Besides indicator words, a frequent source of fluctuation in point of truth and falsity is ordinary ambiguity. One and the same sentence, qua linguistic form, may be true in one occurrence and false in another because the ambiguity of a word in it is differently resolved by attendant circumstances on the two occasions. The ambiguous sentence 'Your mothers bore you' is likely to be construed in one way when it follows on the heels of a sentence of the form '*x* bore *y*,' and in another when it follows on the heels of a sentence of the form '*x* bores *y*.'

In Indo-European languages there is also yet a third conspicuous source of fluctuation in point of truth and falsity; viz., tense. Actually tense is just a variant of the phenomenon of indicator words; the tenses can be paraphrased in terms of tenseless verbs governed by the indicator word 'now,' or by 'before now,' etc.

How can we avoid indicator words? We can resort to personal names or descriptions in place of 'I' and 'you,' to dates or equivalent descriptions in place of 'now,' and to place names or equivalent descriptions in place of 'here.' It may indeed be protested that something tantamount to the use of indicator words is finally unavoidable, at least in the teaching of the terms which are to be made to supplant the indicator words. But this is no objection; all that matters is the *subsequent* avoidability of indicator words. All that matters is that it be possible in principle to couch science in a notation such that none of *its* sentences fluctuates between truth and falsity from utterance to utterance. Terms which are primitive or irreducible, from the point of view of that scientific notation, may still be intelligible to us only through explanations in an ordinary language rife with indicator words, tense, and ambiguity. Scientific language is in any event a splinter of ordinary language, not a substitute.

Granted then that we can rid science of indicator words, what would be the purpose? A kind of objectivity, to begin with, appropriate to the aims of science: truth becomes invariant with respect to speaker and occasion. At the same time a technical purpose is served: that of simplifying and facilitating a basic department of science, viz., deductive logic. For, consider, e.g., the very elementary canons of deduction which lead from '*p* and *q*' to '*p*', and from '*p*' to '*p* or *q*,' and from '*p* and if *p* then *q*' to '*q*'. The letter '*p*' standing for any sentence, turns up twice in each of these rules; and clearly the rules are unsound if the sentence which we put for '*p*' is capable of being true in one of its occurrences and false in the other. But to formulate logical laws in such a way as not to depend thus upon the assumption of fixed truth and falsity would be decidedly awkward and complicated, and wholly unrewarding.

In practice certainly one does not explicitly rid one's scientific work of indicator words, tense, and ambiguity, nor does one limit one's use of logic to sentences thus purified. In practice one merely *supposes* all such points of variation fixed for the space of one's logical argument; one does not need to resort to explicit paraphrase, except at points where local shifts of context *within* the logical argument itself threaten equivocation.

This practical procedure is often rationalized by positing abstract entities, 'propositions,' endowed with all the requisite precision and fixity which is wanting in the sentences themselves; and then saying that it is with propositions, and not their coarse sentential embodiments, that the laws of logic really have to do. But this posit achieves only obscurity. There is less mystery in imagining an idealized form of scientific language in which sentences are so fashioned as never to vacillate between truth and falsity. It is significant that scientific discourse actually does tend toward this ideal, in proportion to the degree of development of the science. Ambiguities and local and epochal biases diminish. Tense, in particular, gives way to a four-dimensional treatment of space-time.

IV

A basic form for sentences of science may be represented as '*Fa*,' where '*a*' stands in place of a singular term referring to some object, from among those which exist according to the scientific theory in question, and '*F*' stands in place of a general term or predicate. The sentence '*Fa*' is true if and only if the object fulfills the predicate. No tense is to be read into the predication '*Fa*'; any relevant dating is to be integral rather to the terms represented by '*F*' and '*a*'.

Compound sentences are built up of such predications with help of familiar logical connectives and operators: 'and,' 'not,' the universal quantifier '(x)' ('each object x is such that'), and the existential quantifier '$(\exists x)$' ('at least one object x is such that'). An example is '(x) not (Fx and not Gx),' which says that no object x is such that Fx and not Gx; briefly, every F is a G.

A given singular term and a given general term or predicate will be said to *correspond* if the general term is true of just one object, viz., the object to which the singular term refers. A general term which thus corresponds to a singular term will of course be "of singular extension," i.e., true of exactly one object; but it belongs nevertheless to the grammatical category of general terms, represented by the '*F*' rather than the '*a*' of '*Fa*.' Now the whole category of singular terms can, in the interests of economy, be swept away in favor of general terms, viz., the general terms which correspond to those singular terms. For let '*a*' represent any singular term, '*F*' any corresponding general term, and '. . . *a* . . .' any sentence we may have cared to affirm containing '*a*'. Then we may instead dispense with '*a*' and affirm '$(\exists x)(Fx$ and . . . *x* . . .).' Clearly this will be true if and only if '. . . *a* . . .' was true. If we want to go on explicitly to remark that the object fulfilling '*F*' is unique, we can easily do that too, thus:

$$(x)(y) \text{ not } [Fx \text{ and } Fy \text{ and not } (x = y)]$$

provided that the identity sign '=' is in our vocabulary.

How, it may be asked, can we be sure there will be a general term corresponding to a given singular term? The matter can be viewed thus: we merely *reparse* what had been singular terms as general terms of singular extension, and what had been reference-to as truth-of, and what had been '. . . *a* . . .' as '$(\exists x)(Fx$ and . . . *x* . . .).' If the old singular term was a proper name learned by ostension, then it is reparsed as a general term similarly learned.

The recent reference to '=' comes as a reminder that relative general terms, or polyadic predicates, must be allowed for along with the monadic ones; i.e., the atomic sentences of our regimented scientific language will comprise not only '*Fx*,' '*Fy*,' '*Gx*,' etc., but also '*Hxy*,' '*Hzx*,' '*Jyz*,' '*Kryz*,' and the like, for appropriately interpreted predicates '*F*', '*G*', '*H*', '*J*', '*K*', etc. (whereof '*H*' might in particular be interpreted as '='). The rest of the sentences are built from these atomic ones by 'and,' 'not,' '(*x*),' '(*y*),' etc. Singular terms '*a*', '*b*', etc., can, we have seen, be left out of account. So can the existential quantifiers '$(\exists x)$,' '$(\exists y)$,' etc., since '$(\exists x)$' can be paraphrased 'not (*x*) not.'

Besides simple singular terms there are operators to reckon with, such as '+', which yield complex singular terms such as '*x* + *y*.' But it is not difficult to see how these can be got rid of in favor of corresponding polyadic predicates—e.g., a predicate 'Σ' such that 'Σzxy' means that *z* is *x* + *y*.

This pattern for a scientific language is evidently rather confining. There are no names of objects. Further, no sentences occur within sentences save in contexts of conjunction, negation, and quantification. Yet it suffices very generally as a medium for scientific theory. Most or all of what is likely to be wanted in a science can be fitted into this form, by dint of constructions of varying ingenuity which are familiar to logic students. To take only the most trivial and familiar example, consider the 'if–then' idiom; it can be managed by rendering 'if p then q' as 'not (p and not q).'

It may be instructive to dwell on this example for a moment. Notoriously, 'not (p and not q)' is no translation of 'if p then q'; and it need not pretend to be. The point is merely that in the places where, at least in mathematics and other typical scientific work, we would ordinarily use the 'if–then' construction, we find we can get on perfectly well with the substitute form 'not (p and not q),' sometimes eked out with a universal quantifier. We do not ask whether our reformed idiom constitutes a genuine semantical analysis, somehow, of the old idiom; we simply find ourselves ceasing to depend on the old idiom in our technical work. Here we see, in paradigm, the contrast between linguistic analysis and theory construction.

V

The variables 'x', 'y', etc., adjuncts to the notation of quantification, bring about a widening of the notion of sentence. A sentence which contains a variable without its quantifier (e.g., 'Fx' or '$(y)Fxy$,' lacking '(x)') is not a sentence in the ordinary true-or-false sense; it is true *for* some values of its free variables, perhaps, and false for others. Called an *open* sentence, it is akin rather to a predicate: instead of having a *truth value* (truth or falsity) it may be said to have an *extension,* this being conceived as the class of those evaluations of its free variables for which it is true. For convenience one speaks also of the extension of a closed sentence, but what is then meant is simply the truth value.

A compound sentence which contains a sentence as a component clause is called an *extensional* context of that component sentence if, whenever you supplant the component by any sentence with the same extension, the compound remains unchanged in point of its own extension. In the special case where the sentences concerned are closed sentences, then, contexts are extensional if all substitutions of truths for true components and falsehoods for false components leave true contexts true and false ones false. In the case of closed sentences, in short, extensional contexts are what are commonly known as truth functions.

It is well known, and easily seen, that the conspicuously limited means

which we have lately allowed ourselves for compounding sentences—
viz., 'and,' 'not,' and quantifiers—are capable of generating only extensional contexts. It turns out, on the other hand, that they confine us no
more than that; the *only* ways of embedding sentences within sentences
which ever obtrude themselves, and resist analysis by 'and,' 'not,' and
quantifiers, prove to be contexts of other than extensional kind. It will
be instructive to survey them.

Clearly *quotation* is, by our standards, non-extensional; we cannot
freely put truths for truths and falsehoods for falsehoods within quotation, without affecting the truth value of a broader sentence whereof the
quotation forms a part. Quotation, however, is always dispensable in favor of spelling. Instead, e.g., of:

> Heraclitus said '$\pi\acute{\alpha}\nu\tau\alpha$ $\acute{\rho}\hat{\epsilon}\iota$',
> '$\pi\acute{\alpha}\nu\tau\alpha$ $\acute{\rho}\hat{\epsilon}\iota$' contains three syllables,

we can say (following Tarski):

> Heraclitus said pi-alpha-nu-tau-alpha-space-rho-epsilon-iota,

and correspondingly for the other example, thus availing ourselves of
names of letters together with a hyphen by way of concatenation sign.
Now, whereas the quotational version showed a sentence (the Greek
one) embedded within a sentence, the version based on spelling does not;
here, therefore, the question of extensionality no longer arises.

Under either version, we are talking about a certain object—a linguistic form—with help, as usual, of a singular term which refers to that object. Quotation produces one singular term for the purpose; spelling another. Quotation is a kind of picture-writing, convenient in practice; but
it is rather spelling that provides the proper analysis for purposes of the
logical theory of signs.

We saw lately that singular terms are never finally needed. The singular terms involved in spelling, in particular, can of course finally be eliminated in favor of a notation of the sort envisaged in recent pages, in
which there are just predicates, quantifiers, variables, 'and,' and 'not.'
The hyphen of concatenation then gives way to a triadic predicate analogous to the 'Σ' of §IV, and the singular terms 'pi,' 'alpha,' etc., give way
to general terms which "correspond" to them in the sense of §IV.

A more seriously non-extensional context is indirect discourse: "Her-
aclitus said that all is flux." This is not, like the case of quotation, a sen-

tence about a specific and namable linguistic form. Perhaps, contrary to the line pursued in the case of quotation, we must accept indirect discourse as involving an irreducibly non-extensional occurrence of one sentence in another. If so, then indirect discourse resists the schematism lately put forward for scientific language.

It is the more interesting, then, to reflect that indirect discourse is in any event at variance with the characteristic objectivity of science. It is a subjective idiom. Whereas quotation reports an external event of speech or writing by an objective description of the observable written shape or spoken sound, on the other hand indirect discourse reports the event in terms rather of a subjective projection of oneself into the imagined state of mind of the speaker or writer in question. Indirect discourse is quotation minus objectivity and precision. To marshal the evidence for indirect discourse is to revert to quotation.

It is significant that the latitude of paraphrase allowable in indirect discourse has never been fixed; and it is more significant that the need of fixing it is so rarely felt. To fix it would be a scientific move, and a scientifically unmotivated one in that indirect discourse tends away from the very objectivity which science seeks.

Indirect discourse, in the standard form 'says that,' is the head of a family which includes also 'believes that,' 'doubts that,' 'is surprised that,' 'wishes that,' 'strives that,' and the like. The subjectivity noted in the case of 'says that' is shared by these other idioms twice over; for what these describe in terms of a subjective projection of oneself is not even the protagonist's speech behavior, but his subjective state in turn.

Further cases of non-extensional idiom, outside the immediate family enumerated above, are 'because' and the closely related phenomenon of the contrary-to-fact conditional. Now it is an ironical but familiar fact that though the business of science is describable in unscientific language as the discovery of causes, the notion of cause itself has no firm place in science. The disappearance of causal terminology from the jargon of one branch of science and another has seemed to mark the progress in understanding of the branches concerned.

Apart from actual quotation, therefore, which we have seen how to deal with, the various familiar non-extensional idioms tend away from what best typifies the scientific spirit. Not that they should or could be generally avoided in everyday discourse, or even in science broadly so-called; but their use dwindles in proportion as the statements of science are made more explicit and objective. We begin to see how it is that the language form schematized in §IV might well, despite its narrow limitations, suffice for science at its purest.

VI

Insofar as we adhere to that idealized schematism, we think of a science as comprising those truths which are expressible in terms of 'and,' 'not,' quantifiers, variables, and certain predicates appropriate to the science in question. In this enumeration of materials we may seem to have an approximation to a possible standard of what counts as "purely cognitive." But the standard, for all its seeming strictness, is still far too flexible. To specify a science, within the described mold, we still have to say what the predicates are to be, and what the domain of objects is to be over which the variables of quantification range. Not all ways of settling these details will be congenial to scientific ideals.

Looking at actual science as a going concern, we can fix in a general way on the domain of objects. Physical objects, to begin with—denizens of space-time—clearly belong. This category embraces indiscriminately what would anciently have been distinguished as substances and as modes or states of substances. A man is a four-dimensional object, extending say eighty-three years in the time dimension. Each spatio-temporal part of the man counts as another and smaller four-dimensional object. A president-elect is one such, two months long. A fit of ague is another, if for ontological clarity we identify it, as we conveniently may, with its victim for the duration of the seizure.

Contrary to popular belief, such a physical ontology has a place also for states of mind. An inspiration or a hallucination can, like the fit of ague, be identified with its host for the duration. The feasibility of this artificial identification of any mental seizure, x, with the corresponding time slice x' of its physical host, may be seen by reflecting on the following simple maneuver. Where P is any predicate which we might want to apply to x, let us explain P' as true of x' if and only if P is true of x. Whatever may have been looked upon as evidence, cause, or consequence of P, as applied to x, counts now for P' as applied to x'. This parallelism, taken together with the extensionality of scientific language, enables us to drop the old P and x from our theory and get on with just P' and x', rechristened as P and x. Such, in effect, is the identification. It leaves our mentalistic idioms fairly intact, but reconciles them with a physical ontology.

This facile physicalization of states of mind rests in no way on a theory of parallelism between nerve impulses, say, or chemical concentrations, and the recurrence of predetermined species of mental state. It might be, now and forever, that the only way of guessing whether a man is inspired, or depressed, or deluded, or in pain, is by asking him or by observing his gross behavior; not by examining his nervous workings, albeit with instruments of undreamed-of subtlety. Discovery of the suggested parallelism would be a splendid scientific achievement, but the physicalization here talked of does not require it.

This physicalization does not, indeed, suffice to make 'inspiration,' 'hallucination,' 'pain,' and other mentalistic terms acceptable to science. Though these become concrete general terms applicable to physical objects, viz., time slices of persons, still they may, some or others of them, remain too vague for scientific utility. Disposition terms, and other predicates which do not lend themselves to immediate verification, are by no means unallowable as such; but there are better and worse among them. When a time slice of a person is to be classified under the head of inspiration or hallucination, and when not, may have been left too unsettled for any useful purpose. But what is then at stake is the acceptability of certain predicates, and not the acceptability of certain objects, values of variables of quantification.

Let us not leave the latter topic quite yet: ontology, or the values available to variables. As seen, we can go far with physical objects. They are not, however, known to suffice. Certainly, as just now argued, we do not need to add mental objects. But we do need to add *abstract* objects, if we are to accommodate science as currently constituted. Certain things we want to say in science may compel us to admit into the range of values of the variables of quantification not only physical objects but also classes and relations of them; also numbers, functions, and other objects of pure mathematics. For, mathematics—not uninterpreted mathematics, but genuine set theory, logic, number theory, algebra of real and complex numbers, differential and integral calculus, and so on—is best looked upon as an integral part of science, on a par with the physics, economics, etc., in which mathematics is said to receive its applications.

Researches in the foundations of mathematics have made it clear that all of mathematics in the above sense can be got down to logic and set theory, and that the objects needed for mathematics in this sense can be got down to a single category, that of *classes*—including classes of classes, classes of classes of classes, and so on. Our tentative ontology for science, our tentative range of values for the variables of quantification, comes therefore to this: physical objects, classes of them, classes in turn of the elements of this combined domain, and so on up.

We have reached the present stage in our characterization of the scientific framework not by reasoning a priori from the nature of science qua science, but rather by seizing upon traits of the science of our day. Special traits thus exploited include the notion of physical object, the four-dimensional concept of space-time, the classial mold of modern classical mathematics, the true–false orientation of standard logic, and indeed extensionality itself. One or another of these traits might well change as science advances. Already the notion of a physical object, as an intrinsically determinate portion of the space-time continuum, squares dubiously with modern developments in quantum mechanics. Savants there are who even suggest that the findings of quantum mechanics might best be accommodated by a revision of the true–false dichotomy itself.

To the question, finally, of admissible predicates. In general we may be sure that a predicate will lend itself to the scientific enterprise only if it is relatively free from vagueness in certain crucial respects. If the predicate is one which is mainly to be used in application to the macroscopic objects of common sense, then there is obvious utility in there being a general tendency to agreement, among observers, concerning its application to those objects; for it is in such applications that the intersubjective verifiability of the data of science resides. In the case of a predicate which is mainly applicable to scientific objects remote from observation or common sense, on the other hand, what is required is that it be free merely from such vagueness as might blur its theoretical function. But to say these things is merely to say that the predicates appropriate to science are those which expedite the purposes of intersubjective confirmation and theoretical clarity and simplicity. These same purposes govern also the ontological decision—the determination of the range of quantification; for clearly the present tentative ontology of physical objects and classes will be abandoned forthwith when we find an alternative which serves those purposes better.

In science all is tentative, all admits of revision—right down, as we have noted, to the law of the excluded middle. But ontology is, pending revision, more clearly in hand than what may be called *ideology*—the question of admissible predicates. We have found a tentative ontology in physical objects and classes, but the lexicon of predicates remains decidedly open. That the ontology should be relatively definite, pending revision, is required by the mere presence of quantifiers in the language of science; for quantifiers may be said to have been interpreted and understood only insofar as we have settled the range of their variables. And that the fund of predicates should be forever subject to supplementation is implicit in a theorem of mathematics; for it is known that for any theory, however rich, there are classes which are not the extensions (cf. §V) of any of its sentences.

11

ON SIMPLE THEORIES OF A COMPLEX WORLD

It is not to be wondered that theory makers seek simplicity. When two theories are equally defensible on other counts, certainly the simpler of the two is to be preferred on the score of both beauty and convenience. But what is remarkable is that the simpler of two theories is generally regarded not only as the more desirable but also as the more probable. If two theories conform equally to past observations, the simpler of the two is seen as standing the better chance of confirmation in future observations. Such is the maxim of the simplicity of nature. It seems to be implicitly assumed in every extrapolation and interpolation, every drawing of a smooth curve through plotted points. And the maxim of the uniformity of nature is of a piece with it, uniformity being a species of simplicity.

Simplicity is not easy to define. But it may be expected, whatever it is, to be relative to the texture of a conceptual scheme. If the basic concepts of one conceptual schema are the derivative concepts of another, and vice versa, presumably one of two hypotheses could count as simpler for the one scheme and the other for the other. This being so, how can simplicity carry any peculiar presumption of objective truth? Such is the implausibility of the maxim of the simplicity of nature.

Corresponding remarks apply directly to the maxim of the uniformity of nature, according to which, vaguely speaking, things similar in some respects tend to prove similar in others. For again similarity, whatever it is, would seem to be relative to the structure of one's conceptual scheme or quality space. Any two things, after all, are shared as members by as many classes as any other two things; degrees of similarity depend on which of those classes we weight as the more basic or natural.

Belief in the simplicity of nature, and hence in the uniformity of nature, can be partially accounted for in obvious ways. One plausible factor is wishful thinking. Another and more compelling cause of the belief is to be found in our perceptual mechanism: there is a subjective selectivity that makes us tend to see the simple and miss the complex. Thus consider streamers, as printers call them: vertical or diagonal white paths formed by a fortuitous lining up of the spaces between words. They are always straight or gently curved. The fastidious typesetter makes them vanish just by making them crooked.

This subjective selectivity is not limited to the perceptual level. It can figure even in the most deliberate devising of experimental criteria. Thus suppose we try to map out the degrees of mutual affinity of stimuli for a dog, by a series of experiments in the conditioning and extinction of his responses. Suppose further that the resulting map is challenged: suppose someone protests that what the map reflects is not some original spacing of qualities in the dog's pre-experimental psyche or original fund of dispositions, but only a history of readjustments induced successively by the very experiments of the series. Now how would we rise to this challenge? Obviously, by repeating the experiments in a different order on another dog. If we get much the same map for the second dog despite the permutation, we have evidence that the map reflects a genuinely pre-experimental pattern of dispositions. And we then have evidence also of something more: that this pattern or quality space is the same for both dogs. But now I come to the point of my example: we cannot, by this method, get evidence of pre-experimental quality spaces unlike for the two dogs. By the very nature of our criterion, in this example, we get evidence either of uniformity or of nothing. An analysis of experimental criteria in other sciences would no doubt reveal many further examples of the same sort of experimentally imposed bias in favor of uniformity, or in favor of simplicity of other sorts.

This selective bias affords not only a partial explanation of belief in the maxim of the simplicity of nature but also, in an odd way, a partial justification. For, if our way of framing criteria is such as to preclude, frequently, any confirmation of the more complex of two rival hypotheses, then we may indeed fairly say that the simpler hypothesis stands the better chance of confirmation; and such, precisely, was the maxim of the simplicity of nature. We have, insofar, justified the maxim while still avoiding the paradox that seemed to be involved in trying to reconcile the relativity of simplicity with the absoluteness of truth.

This solution, however, is too partial to rest with. The selective bias in favor of simplicity, in our perceptual mechanism and in our deliberate experimental criteria, is significant but not overwhelming. Complex hypotheses do often stand as live options, just as susceptible to experimental confirmation as their simpler alternatives; and in such cases still the maxim of simplicity continues to be applied in scientific practice, with as much intuitive plausibility as in other cases. We fit the simplest possible curve to plotted points, thinking it the likeliest curve pending new points to the contrary; we encompass data with a hypothesis involving the fewest possible parameters, thinking this hypothesis the likeliest pending new data to the contrary; and we even record a measurement as the roundest near number, pending repeated measurements to the contrary.

Now this last case, the round number, throws further light on our problem. If a measured quantity is reported first as 5.21, say, and more accurately in the light of further measurement as 5.23, the new reading supersedes the old; but if it is reported first as 5.2 and later as 5.23, the new reading may well be looked upon as confirming the old one and merely supplying some further information regarding the detail of further decimal places. Thus the "simpler hypothesis," 5.2 as against 5.21, is quite genuinely ten times likelier to be confirmed, just because ten times as much deviation is tolerated under the head of confirmation.

True, we do not customarily say "simple hypothesis" in the round-number case. We invoke here no maxim of the simplicity of nature, but only a canon of eschewing insignificant digits. Yet the same underlying principle that operates here can be detected also in cases where one does talk of simplicity of hypotheses. If we encompass a set of data with a hypothesis involving the fewest possible parameters, and then are constrained by further experiment to add another parameter, we are likely to view the emendation not as a refutation of the first result but as a confirmation plus a refinement; but if we have an extra parameter in the first hypothesis and are constrained by further experiment to alter it, we view the emendation as a refutation and revision. Here again the simpler hypothesis, the one with fewer parameters, is initially the more probable simply because a wider range of possible subsequent findings is classified as favorable to it. The case of the simplest curve through plotted points is similar: an emendation prompted by subsequent findings is the likelier to be viewed as confirmation-cum-refinement, rather than as refutation and revision, the simpler the curve.[1]

---

1. I expect that J. K. Kemeny has had all this in mind. He remarks on the kinship of the rule of significant digits to that of simplicity on p. 399 of "The Use of Simplicity in Induction," *Philosophical Review* 62 (1953), pp. 391–408.

We have noticed four causes for supposing that the simpler hypothesis stands the better chance of confirmation. There is wishful thinking. There is a perceptual bias that slants the data in favor of simple patterns. There is a bias in the experimental criteria of concepts, whereby the simpler of two hypotheses is sometimes opened to confirmation while its alternative is left inaccessible. And finally there is a preferential system of scorekeeping, which tolerates wider deviations the simpler the hypothesis. These last two of the four causes operate far more widely, I suspect, than appears on the surface. Do they operate widely enough to account in full for the crucial role that simplicity plays in scientific method?

12

ONTIC DECISION

48. Nominalism and Realism[1]

One finds or can imagine disagreement on whether there are wombats, unicorns, angels, neutrinos, classes, points, miles, propositions. Philosophy and the special sciences afford infinite scope for disagreement on what there is. One such issue that has traditionally divided philosophers is whether there are abstract objects. *Nominalists* have held that there are not; *realists* (in a special sense of the word), or *Platonists* (as they have been called to avoid the troubles of 'realist'), have held that there are.

General definition of the term 'abstract,' or 'universal,' and its opposite 'concrete,' or 'particular,' need not detain us.[2] No matter if there are things whose status under the dichotomy remains enigmatic—"abstract particulars" such as the Equator and the North Pole, for instance; for no capital will be made of the dichotomy as such. It will suffice for now to cite classes, attributes, propositions, numbers, relations, and functions as typical abstract objects, and physical objects as concrete objects *par excellence,* and to consider the ontological issue as it touches such typical cases.

That more confidence should be felt in there being physical objects than in there being classes, attributes, and the like is not to be wondered. For one thing, terms for physical objects belong to a more basic stage in

1. A penultimate draft of much of this chapter was presented under the title "The Assuming of Objects" at the University of California, Berkeley, on May 13, 1959, as the Howison Lecture in Philosophy.

2. P. F. Strawson's ingenious partial formulation of the distinction in "Particular and General," *Proceedings of the Aristotelian Society* 54 (1954), p. 257, presupposes a general notion of analyticity.

our acquisition of language than abstract terms do. Concrete reference is felt as more secure than abstract reference because it is more deeply rooted in our formative past. For another thing, terms for intersubjectively observable physical things are at the focus of the most successful of unprepared communication, as between strangers in the marketplace. Surely such rapport tends to encourage confidence, however unconsciously, that one is making no mistake about his objects. Third, our terms for physical objects are commonly learned through fairly direct conditioning to stimulatory effects of the denoted objects. The empirical evidence for such physical objects, if not immediate, is at any rate less far-fetched and so less suspect than that for objects whose terms are learned only in deep context. Note that whereas the first two causes for relative confidence in physical objects were causes only, this third one is a defensible reason.

Defensible but still contestable, on two counts: that it makes no case for physical objects of highly inferential sorts, and that it makes yet more of a case for sense data or sense qualities than for physical objects. Now the former of these two objections might be answered by appeal to continuity. If some physical objects are better attested than any abstract ones, then other and more conjectural physical objects are likewise more to be welcomed than abstract ones, because their acceptance along with those well-attested objects entails less loss of homogeneity, hence less loss of simplicity *(caeteris paribus)*, than would acceptance of the abstract objects.

The other objection, insofar as it champions sense data in the sense of concrete sensory events (as against recurrent qualities), is an objection at most to physicalism and not to nominalism. But no matter; the likely rejoinder to the objection is independent of whether the subjective sensory objects envisaged are events or qualities. It is that no sufficient purpose is served by positing subjective sensory objects. This rejoinder would need sustaining on perhaps three counts, as follows, corresponding to three real or fancied purposes of positing such objects. (*a*) It would be argued that we cannot hope to make such objects suffice to the exclusion of physical objects. This point, urged in §1, seems pretty widely acknowledged nowadays. (*b*) It would be argued (against Roderick Firth, for instance) that we do not need them in addition to physical objects, as means e.g. of reporting illusions and uncertainties. Thus one might claim that such purposes are adequately met by a propositional-attitude construction in which 'seems that' or the like is made to govern a subsidiary sentence about physical objects. One might claim that special objects of illusion are then no more called for than peculiar non-physical objects of quest or desire were called for in §32. True, this argument is threatened by our high line on propositional attitudes in §§45 and 47; but perhaps appearance deserves no better, after all, than the *demimondain* status accorded to propositional attitudes generally. (*c*) It would be argued that we also do not need sensory objects to account for our knowledge or discourse of physical objects themselves. The claim here would be that the relevance of sensory stimulation to sentences about physical objects can as well (and better) be explored and explained in terms directly of the conditioning of such sentences or their parts to physical irritations of the subject's surfaces. Intervening neural activity goes on, but the claim is that nothing is clarified, nothing but excess baggage is added, by positing intermediary subjective objects of apprehension anterior to the physical objects overtly alleged in the spoken sentences themselves. The supposed function of sense-datum reports, in contributing a component of something like certainty to the formulations of empirical knowledge, may more realistically be assigned to observation sentences in the sense of §10. These enjoy a privileged evidential position, in the directness of their correlation with non-verbal stimulation; yet they are not, typically, about sense data.

Points (*a*), (*b*), and (*c*) reflect my own general attitude. What perhaps basically distinguishes this from the attitude of sense-datum philosophers is that I favor treating cognition from within our own evolving theory of a cognized world, not fancying that firmer ground exists somehow outside all that. However, such cursory remarks as these on the philosophy of sense data can aspire at most to sort out issues and sketch a position; not to persuade.[3]

Let us now locate all this in its immediate context. What had been confronting us was the plea in behalf of sense data that if some physical objects are to be preferred to abstract ones on the score of comparative directness of association with sensory stimulation, then sense data are to be preferred *a fortiori*. The answer proposed was predicated on utility for theory: that sense data neither suffice to the exclusion of physical ob-

---

3. For further representations against sense data, and bibliographical references, see R. M. Chisholm, *Perceiving: A Philosophical Study* (Ithaca: Cornell University Press, 1957), pp. 117–125, 151–157, and Alan Pasch, *Experience and the Analytic* (Chicago: University of Chicago Press, 1958), Ch. 3. Further see §54 from my *Word and Object,* and my note "On Mental Entities," in *The Ways of Paradox* [Chapter 19].

jects nor are needed in addition. Now here we begin to witness the collision of two standards. Comparative directness of association with sensory stimulation was counted in favor of physical objects, but then we raised against the sense data themselves a second standard: utility for theory. Does one then have simply to weigh opposing considerations? No; on maturer reflection the picture changes. For let us recall the predicament in radical translation, which showed that a full knowledge of the stimulus meaning of an observation sentence is not sufficient for translating or even spotting a term. In our own language, by the same token, the stimulus meaning of an observation sentence in no way settles whether any part of the sentence should be distinguished as a term for sense data, or as a term for physical objects, or as a term at all. How directly the sentence and its words are associated with sensory stimulation, or how confidently the sentence may be affirmed on the strength of a given sensory stimulation, does not settle whether to posit objects of one sort or another for words of the sentence to denote in the capacity of terms.

We may be perceived to have posited the objects only when we have brought the contemplated terms into suitable interplay with the whole distinctively objectificatory apparatus of our language: articles and pronouns and the idioms of identity, plurality, and predication, or, in canonical notation, quantification. Even a superficially termlike occurrence is no proof of termhood, failing systematic interplay with the key idioms generally. Thus we habitually say 'for the sake of,' with 'sake' seemingly in term position, and never thereby convict ourselves of positing any such objects as sakes, for we do not bring the rest of the apparatus to bear: we never use 'sake' as antecedent of 'it,' nor do we predicate 'sake' of anything. 'Sake' figures in effect as an invariable fragment of a preposition 'for the sake of,' or 'for 's sake.'

Let a word, therefore, have occurred as a fragment of ever so many empirically well-attested sentential wholes; even as a rather termlike fragment, by superficial appearances. Still, the question whether to treat it as a term is the question whether to give it general access to positions appropriate to general terms, or perhaps to singular terms, subject to the usual laws of such contexts. Whether to do so may reasonably be decided by considerations of systematic efficacy, utility for theory.

But if nominalism and realism are to be adjudicated on such grounds, nominalism's claims dwindle. The reason for admitting numbers as objects is precisely their efficacy in organizing and expediting the sciences.

The reason for admitting classes is much the same. Examples have been noted (§43) of the access of power that comes with classes. A further example is Frege's celebrated definition of 'x is ancestor of y':

> (z)(if all parents of members of z belong to z and $y \in z$
> then $x \in z$).

Simplicity ensues, since we are spared separate, piecemeal provision for the things that classes provide. The efficacy of classes becomes yet more impressive when we find that they can be made to serve the purposes also of a great lot of further abstract objects of undeniable utility: relations, functions, numbers themselves (§§53–55).

We gain a perhaps more fundamental insight into the unifying force of the class concept when we observe how classes help us get by with quantifiers as the sole variable-binding operators. Thus think of '. . . z . . .' as some open sentence. *Concretion*[4] is the transformation that carries '$x \in \hat{z}(\ldots z \ldots)$' into '. . . x . . .'. Now let 'Φ_x' represent some variable-binding operator that builds sentences from sentences. If we suppose merely that 'Φ_x' is such that the substitutivity of concretion holds under it, we can drop 'Φ_x' in favor of a general term 'G'. For, take 'G' as true of just the classes y such that $\Phi_x(x \in y)$; then '$\Phi_x(\ldots x \ldots)$' can be rendered '$G\hat{x}(\ldots x \ldots)$.' Finally the operator of class abstraction in '$G\hat{x}(\ldots x \ldots)$' can be reduced to description, and description to quantifiers. (Cf. §§34, 38. But see also §55.)

Closeness of association with stimulation has stood up poorly as an argument for giving physical objects preferential status. But something could still perhaps be salvaged from it. For, grant that the question whether to dignify given words as terms is a question whether to admit them freely to all term positions. Then instead of what was said earlier for physical objects, viz. that terms for them are fairly directly associated with sensory stimulation, perhaps we could say this: sentences fairly directly associated with sensory stimulation exhibit terms for physical objects in all sorts of term positions, not just in rather special positions. It seems plausible that common terms for physical objects come out better by such a standard than abstract terms do.[5] But I shall not try to establish the point.

4. So called in my dissertation (Harvard, 1932), and in *A System of Logistic* (Cambridge, Mass.: Harvard University Press, 1934).

5. See W. P. Alston, "Ontological Commitment," *Philosophical Studies* 9 (1958), note 7.

The case that emerged meanwhile for classes rested on systematic efficacy. Now it is certainly a case against nominalism's negative claims, but still it is no case against a preferential status for physical objects. In a contest for sheer systematic utility to science, the notion of physical object still leads the field.[6] On this score alone, therefore, one might still put a premium on explanations that appeal to physical objects and not to abstract ones, even if abstract objects be grudgingly admitted too for their efficacy elsewhere in the theory.

Nor let us scorn those two earlier causes for confidence in physical objects—the causes that were not recognized as reasons. One was that terms for such objects are so basic to our language; the other was that they are at the focus of such successful communication. To show why certain terms are felt as comfortable termini of explanation is not, after all, to render them otherwise.

49. False Predilections, Ontic Commitment

We have considered the predilection for concrete objects and the case, despite such predilection, for admitting abstract objects. For symmetry let us now ponder the positive predilection for abstract objects; for it is not unknown.

An apparent reason for favoring physical objects was proximity to stimulation. This seemed all the more reason for favoring sensory objects of some sort, even sense qualities. Then, if attributes generally are held to be broadly analogous to sense qualities (as are the inferential particles of physics to common-sense bodies), the same appeal to continuity can be made in support of attributes as was made in support of the particles (§48). Here, I think, is one cause of the predilection that is sometimes manifested for attributes.

Not that I accept the line of reasoning. That argument for sensory objects is offset, as urged in §48, if we hold that such objects are neither adequate in lieu of physical objects nor helpful in addition to them. Moreover, to project non-sensory attributes purely on the analogy of sense qualities, hence as recurrent characters somehow of a subjective show within the mind, betrays surely a cavalier attitude toward psychological processes and a lack of curiosity about the mechanisms of behavior.

Such is one likely cause of a predilection for attributes (apart from motives of systematic utility). There is also a second. Some of us are car-

6. See P. F. Strawson, *Individuals* (London: Methuen, 1959), pp. 38–58.

ried away by the object-directed pattern of our thinking, to the point of seeking the gist of every sentence in things it is about. When a general term occurs predicatively alongside a name, the sentence thus formed will be seen by such a person as 'about' not just the named object, but the named object and an attribute symbolized by the general term.[7] He will feel therefore that any general term for physical objects, such as 'round' or 'dog,' simultaneously symbolizes an attribute. But then, he will reason, any argument for physical objects from the utility of such terms must, *ipso facto*, support attributes as well *and even better;* for the terms neatly symbolize one precise attribute apiece, while standing in no such pat correspondence to the indefinitely numerous physical objects that they purport to be true of. (Much the same argument can be used also to support classes instead of attributes, since a general term can as well be said to symbolize its extension as its intension if we appropriately shade the sense of 'symbolize.')

In this reasoning the mistake is not just the initial one of overdoing the object matter. There is a subsequent fallacy in the idea that the utility of a word counts, of itself, in favor of all associated objects. A word can prove useful in such positions as to favor the assumption of objects for it to be true of, without thereby favoring the assumption of objects related to it in other ways, e.g., as extension or intension. Let us reflect on the mechanism.

Typical of the positions proper to general terms are the post articular and the predicative. The one position is contained in singular terms; the other accompanies singular terms (which can be variables). These singular terms in turn are marked as singular terms by their occurrences as subjects of other predicatively occurring general terms, notably '=', and in variable-binding operators. And where do objects come in? The purported objects of whatever sort, concrete or abstract, are just what the

---

7. Thus for John Locke general terms were names of general ideas (*Essays concerning the Human Understanding* (1690), Bk. 2, Ch. 11, paragraph 9). Again Gustav Bergmann: "Who admits a single primitive predicate admits properties among the building stones of his world" ("Two Types of Linguistic Philosophy," *Review of Metaphysics* 5 [1952], p. 430). And see C. A. Baylis, "Universals, Communicable Knowledge, and Metaphysics," *Journal of Philosophy* 48 (1951), pp. 636–644, where he argues in effect that to understand a general term is to grasp its meaning, and hence that there are such meanings, or attributes. The fallacy of subtraction noted at the beginning of *Word and Object*, §43, has doubtless encouraged the tendency to overdo 'about.'

singular terms in their several ways name, refer to, take as values.[8] They are what count as cases when, quantifying, we say that everything, or something, is thus and so. So when on grounds of systematic efficacy we decide to allow a word—'glint,' say, to take a debatable case—full currency as general term, the effect is only that the glints, not glinthood or glintkind, are made to count as objects.

Actually, the effect is not even quite that much; for a general term in good standing can still, like 'unicorn,' be true of nothing. But what typically happens is the following. Already while we debate whether our sentences may best be so analyzed and extended as to count 'glint' a full-fledged general term, we have before us certain incompletely analyzed but useful truths of theory or observation that contain the word; and then our taking 'glint' as a general term settles the analysis of these sentences in such a way that some of them come to affirm or imply '$(\exists x)(x$ is a glint).'

So if 'round' and 'dog' have acquitted themselves to the glory of physical objects, they have done so as general terms true of physical objects and not as singular terms naming attributes or classes. The case for attributes or classes remains open as a separate question, however analogous. The general terms relevant to it are not 'round,' 'dog,' and the like, but 'trait,' 'species,' and the like; and the relevant singular terms are not such as 'Sputnik I' and 'Fido,' but such as 'roundness,' 'caninity,' 'dogkind.'

The offenders who have called forth the past few pages are those who, through a confusion that I have just now tried to clear up, take it for granted that everyone in his use of general terms talks directly of attributes (or classes), *ipso facto* and willy nilly. The offenders are not those who make a considered argument for the existence of an attribute or class for every general term. Such an argument, coming under the head of what was tolerantly viewed in §48, would be predicated on the systematic efficacy of admitting abstract general and perhaps abstract singular terms and using them in such a way as to bring attributes or classes into the universe of discourse as values, in effect, of the variables of quantification. The merits of such a course are considered further in §§43 and 55.

The offenders may be depended upon to dismiss the distinction between concrete general terms like 'round' and abstract singular terms

8. See *Word and Object,* §40, note 1.

like 'roundness' as an insignificant quirk of grammar. Now let me not seem to be making capital of any pedantic distinction in word forms. This distinction is only a convenient and dispensable way of marking an underlying difference that can be uncovered anyway in a distinction of functions, as lately outlined. But I venture to say that a failure to appreciate the underlying difference correlates nicely with the dismissal of the verbal distinction.

Along with the offenders last touched on there are others who, likewise making light of the distinction between abstract singular and concrete general terms, decide *against* abstract objects. Apparently these thinkers have appreciated, for whatever reasons, that concrete general terms carry no commitment to attributes or classes, and then have concluded the same for the corresponding abstract singular terms, by dint of drawing no distinction. This line of thought derives wishful vigor from a distaste for abstract objects coupled with a taste for their systematic efficacy. The motivation has proved sufficient to induce remarkable extremes. We find philosophers allowing themselves not only abstract terms but even pretty unmistakable quantifications over abstract objects ("There are concepts with which . . . ," ". . . some of which propositions . . . ," ". . . there is something that he doubts or believes"), and still blandly disavowing, within the paragraph, any claim that there are such objects.[9]

Pressed, they may explain that abstract objects do not exist the way physical ones do. The difference is not, they say, just a difference in two sorts of objects, one in space-time and one not, but a difference in two senses of 'there are'; so that, in the sense in which there are concrete objects, there are no abstract ones. But then there remain two difficulties, a little one and a big one. The little one is that the philosopher who would repudiate abstract objects seems to be left saying that there are such after all, in the sense of 'there are' appropriate to them. The big one is that the distinction between there being one sense of 'there are' for concrete objects and another for abstract ones, and there being just one sense of 'there are' for both, makes no sense.[10]

9. See Alonzo Church, "Ontological Commitment," *Journal of Philosophy* 55 (1958), pp. 1008–1014, for discussion of illustrative texts by A. J. Ayer and G. Ryle.

10. See *Word and Object*, §27. But the familiar vague notion that the assumption of abstract entities is somehow a purely formal expedient, as against the more factual character of the assumption of physical objects, may still not be wholly beyond making sense of; see Hilary Putnam, "Mathematics and the Existence of Abstract Entities," *Philosophical Studies* 7 (1956), pp. 81–88.

Such philosophical double talk, which would repudiate an ontology while enjoying its benefits, thrives on vagaries of ordinary language. The trouble is that at best there is no simple correlation between the outward forms of ordinary affirmations and the existences implied. Thus, granted that the construction exemplified by 'Agnes has fleas' can very often be accorded the forthrightly existential sense intended by '$(\exists x)(Fx$ and $Gx)$,' there remain abundant cases like 'Tabby eats mice' (§28) and 'Ernest hunts lions' (§32) that cannot. Reflective persons unswayed by wishful thinking can themselves now and again have cause to wonder what, if anything, they are talking about.

In our canonical notation of quantification, then, we find the restoration of law and order. Insofar as we adhere to this notation, the objects we are to be understood to admit are precisely the objects which we reckon to the universe of values over which the bound variables of quantification are to be considered to range. Such is simply the intended sense of the quantifiers '(x)' and '$(\exists x)$': 'every object x is such that,' 'there is an object x such that.' The quantifiers are encapsulations of these specially selected, unequivocally referential idioms of ordinary language. To paraphrase a sentence into the canonical notation of quantification is, first and foremost, to make its ontic content explicit, quantification being a device for talking in general of objects.

The moot or controversial part of the question of the ontic import of a sentence may of course survive in a new guise, as the question how to paraphrase the sentence into canonical notation. But the change of guise conveniently shifts the burden of claims and disavowals. Futile caviling over ontic implications gives way to an invitation to reformulate one's point in canonical notation. We cannot paraphrase our opponent's sentences into canonical notation for him and convict him of the consequences, for there is no synonymy; rather we must ask him what canonical sentences he is prepared to offer, consonantly with his own inadequately expressed purposes. If he declines to play this game, the argument terminates. To decline to explain oneself in terms of quantification, or in terms of those special idioms of ordinary language by which quantification is directly explained, is simply to decline to disclose one's referential intent. We saw in our consideration of radical translation that an alien language may well fail to share, by any universal standard, the object-positing pattern of our own; and now our supposititious opponent is simply standing, however legalistically, on his alien rights. We remain free as always to project analytical hypotheses (§§15f.) and translate his sentences into canonical notation as seems most reasonable;

but he is no more bound by our conclusions than the native by the field linguist's.[11]

50. Entia Non Grata

The resort to canonical notation as an aid to clarifying ontic commitments is of limited polemical power, as just now explained. But it does help us who are agreeable to the canonical forms to judge what we care to consider there to be. We can face the question squarely as a question what to admit to the universe of values of our variables of quantification.

Economy is a consideration, but economy of theory and not just of objects. Also some objects may be preferable to others in the way suggested for physical objects late in §48: representative sentences in which they are treated as objects may be relatively closely associated with sensory stimulation.

We have looked into the benefits of admitting physical objects and classes (§48), though there will be more to say of classes (§55). We considered also the claims and the difficulties of attributes and propositions

11. For more on quantification as avenue of ontic commitment see *From a Logical Point of View*, Essays 1 [Chapter 2] and 6. On pp. 19 [Chapter 2] and 103 thereof it is stressed that I look to variables and quantification for evidence as to what a theory says that there is, not for evidence as to what there is; but the point can be missed, as by G. P. Henderson, "Intensional Entities and Ontology," *Proceedings of the Aristotelian Society* 58 (1958), pp. 279–280.

—A more accountable misapprehension is that I am a nominalist. I must correct it; my best efforts to write clearly about reference, referential position, and ontic commitment will fail of communication to readers who, like Benson Mates ("Synonymity," *University of California Publications in Philosophy* 25 [1950], p. 213) and R. B. Braithwaite (review of *From a Logical Point of View, Cambridge Review* 75 [1954], pp. 417–418), endeavor in all good will to reconcile my words with a supposed nominalist doctrine. In all books and most papers I have appealed to classes and recognized them as abstract objects. I have indeed inveighed against making and imputing platonistic assumptions gratuitously, but equally for obscuring them. Where I have speculated on what can be got from a nominalistic basis, I have stressed the difficulties and limitations. True, my 1947 paper with Goodman opened on a nominalist declaration; readers cannot be blamed. For consistency with my general attitude early and late, that sentence needs demotion to the status of a mere statement of conditions for the construction in hand; see *From a Logical Point of View*, top of p. 174.

(§§42f.), and the weakness of the case for sense data (§§1, 48). At the extreme, finally, are the sakes and behalves. No one wants these, but the form of the argument for their exclusion is instructive. It is that 'sake' and 'behalf' have their uses only in the clichés 'for the sake of' and 'in behalf of' and their variants: hence these clichés can be left unanalyzed as simple prepositions. (From the point of view of canonical notation, prepositions in turn ordinarily get bundled off into relative terms; cf. §22.)

Units of measure turn out somewhat like sakes and behalves. 'Mile,' 'minute,' 'degree Fahrenheit,' and the like resemble 'sake' and 'behalf' in being *defective* nouns: they are normally used only in a limited selection of the usual term positions. Their defectiveness, though less extreme than that of 'sake' and 'behalf,' is easily exposed in absurd interrogation. Are miles alike? If so, how can they count as many? And if they cannot, what of the two hundred between Boston and New York?

Questions about identity of attributes or of propositions are in their turn less absurd, on the face of them, than these about identity of miles. Still the lack of a standard of identity for attributes and propositions can be viewed similarly, as a case of defectiveness on the part of 'attribute' and 'proposition.' Philosophers undertook, however unsuccessfully, to supply this defect by devising a standard of identity, because they were persuaded of the advantages, in systematic utility or whatever, of taking 'attribute' and 'proposition' as full-fledged terms and so admitting attributes and propositions to the universe of discourse. This line is debatable on its specific merits, and we have debated it. The case of 'mile,' 'degree Fahrenheit,' and the like is clearer: no purpose is served by making units of measure accessible to variables of quantification. We can adequately accommodate these nouns as parts of relative terms 'length in miles,' 'temperature in degrees Fahrenheit.'[12]

Just as the relative term 'author' is true of this and that man relative to this and that book, so 'length in miles' is to be understood as true of this and that number relative to this and that body or region. Thus instead of 'length of Manhattan = 11 miles' we would now say 'length-in-miles of Manhattan = 11' (form 'F of $b = a$') or '11 is length-in-miles-of Manhattan' (form 'Fab').

This leaves us recognizing numbers as objects. For the numeral '11' figures here as a singular term, on a par with 'Manhattan.' If we were to

12. So Rudolf Carnap, *Physikalische Begriffsbildung* (Karlsruhe, 1926).

push forward to minimum canonical notation by eliminating singular terms as in Chapter V we would find our quantifiers calling for the number and the island unmistakably enough:

$(\exists x)(\exists y)(x$ is-11 and y is-Manhattan and x is-length-in-miles-of $y)$.

And indeed we may expect numbers to be very much wanted, not only for this example, as values of our variables; they are nearly as useful as classes.

In *possible* concrete objects, unactualized possibles, we have another category of doubtful objects whose doubtfulness can be laid to defective nouns, with as good reason at least as in the case of attributes and propositions. For here again, and more glaringly than in the case of intensions, there is perplexity over identity; cf. §8. Even when a position is specified, as in 'the possible new church on that corner,' 'the possible hotel on that corner,' the identity of position does not make the possible objects identical. Happily we can cut through all this, sometimes by retreating to universals as in §8, and more usually by just absorbing the 'possible' of 'possible object' appropriately into the context and so not treating 'possible object' as a term. A sentence about possible churches can usually be paraphrased satisfactorily enough into a sentence that treats of churches and is governed, as a whole, by a modal operator of possibility. One may still ask what kind of modality is wanted, how to make sense of it, and how to cope with other problems that the modalities of one or another sort have been known to raise; but talk of possible objects would have been no better off with respect to such questions.

The notion of possible objects has been encouraged by two philosophical quandaries. One of them is raised by the verbs 'hunting,' 'wanting,' and the like, which cannot in general be looked upon as relating the agent to actual objects (cf. §§28, 32). Possible lions, possible unicorns, possible sloops suggest themselves as surrogate objects for such activities. But these matters can be handled more illuminatingly by paraphrase, as seen, into the idioms of propositional attitude. One is left with the problems of propositional attitude, but those, unlike the vagaries of unactualized possibles, are with us anyway.

The other quandary is raised by terms in want of objects: what are we talking about when we say there are no unicorns, or that there is no such thing as Pegasus? Partly this quandary comes of being carried away by the object-directed pattern of our thinking—if not to the extreme talked of in §49, at least to the point of trying to see every sentence as "about" certain objects. Actually 'unicorn' and 'Pegasus' can be perfectly good terms, well understood in that their contexts are well enough linked to sensory stimulation or to intervening theory, without there being unicorns or Pegasus. Mainly it is on singular terms like 'Pegasus' that the quandary has centered rather than general ones like 'unicorn'; for it is there that under ordinary usage the truth-value gaps set in (§37), in a philosophically uncomfortable way. However, the canonical expedient of reparsing singular terms regularizes these matters and so ends, one may hope, any temptation to venture out on the morass of unactualized possibles.[13]

The notions of possible object and proposition are two that were encouraged by philosophical quandaries. A third is that of fact. The word 'fact' is commonplace enough, but where the philosophical motivation enters is in choosing to admit facts as objects rather than fob the word off with the lower-grade sort of treatment accorded 'sake' and 'mile.'

Part of what encouraged admission of propositions was a wish for eternal truth-value vehicles independent of particular languages (§40). Part of what encourages admission of facts is perhaps a wish to defer the question what makes a sentence or proposition true: those are true that state facts. Another force that has encouraged both acceptances is, again, the tendency to be carried away by object-directed thinking: a tendency, in this case, to liken sentences to names and then posit objects for them to name. It is perhaps where this force is the dominant one that we encounter readiness, as we occasionally do, to identify facts with propositions (viz., with some or all of the true ones).

An additional connotation that often invests the word 'fact,' both in philosophy and in lay usage, is that of unvarnished objectivity plus a certain accessibility to observation. In philosophical usage this connotation is sometimes adopted and widened in such wise that facts come to be posited corresponding to all the "synthetic" truths and withheld only from the "analytic" ones. So here that same analytic-synthetic dichotomy intrudes which we have found so dubious (§14); and it intrudes in a most implausibly absolute guise, independent apparently of all choice of language. The disarmingly commonplace ring of the word 'fact' comes even to lend the dichotomy a spurious air of intelligibility: the analytic sentences (or propositions) are the true ones that lack factual content.

There is a tendency—not among those who take facts as proposi-

13. See Bertrand Russell, "On Denoting," *Mind* 14 (1905), pp. 479–493.

tions—to think of facts as concrete. This is fostered by the commonplace ring of the word and the hint of bruteness, and is of a piece, for that matter, with the basic conception that it is facts that make sentences true. Yet what can they be, and be concrete? The sentences 'Fifth Avenue is six miles long' and 'Fifth Avenue is a hundred feet wide,' if we suppose them true, presumably state different facts; yet the only concrete or at any rate physical object involved is Fifth Avenue. I resolved (§48) not to cavil over 'concrete,' but I suspect that the sense of 'concrete' in which facts are concrete is not one that need endear them to us.

Facts, moreover, are in the same difficulty over a standard of identity as propositions were seen to be. And surely they cannot be seriously supposed to help us explain truth. Our two sentences last quoted are true because of Fifth Avenue, because it is a hundred feet wide and six miles long, because it was planned and made that way, and because of the way we use our words; only indirection results from positing facts, in the image of sentences, as intermediaries. Probably no such temptation would arise if the word were not already there performing an overlapping though unphilosophical function for ordinary discourse.

In ordinary usage 'fact' often occurs where we could without loss say 'true sentence' or (if it is our way) 'true proposition.' But its main utility seems to be rather as a reinforcement of the flimsy 'that' of propositional abstraction (§34). It is wanted there merely because of the idiomatic unnaturalness, in many substantival positions, of a pure 'that'-clause. (Yet it is limited in this syntactical service to 'that'-clauses that are taken to be true; for 'fact' persists in imputing truth.) It has a further use still in abbreviated cross-reference: we often manage to avoid repeating a long previous affirmation by saying 'that fact.' Now so far as these uses go there is no call to posit facts, certainly not over and above propositions, nor any difficulty in absorbing or paraphrasing away the word. Nor have the peculiarly philosophical appeals to fact impressed us.

13

THINGS AND THEIR PLACE IN THEORIES

Our talk of external things, our very notion of things, is just a conceptual apparatus that helps us to foresee and control the triggering of our sensory receptors in the light of previous triggering of our sensory receptors. The triggering, first and last, is all we have to go on.

In saying this I too am talking of external things, namely, people and their nerve endings. Thus what I am saying applies in particular to what I am saying, and is not meant as skeptical. There is nothing we can be more confident of than external things—some of them, anyway—other people, sticks, stones. But there remains the fact—a fact of science itself—that science is a conceptual bridge of our own making, linking sensory stimulation to sensory stimulation; there is no extrasensory perception.

I should like now to consider how this bridging operation works. What does it mean to assume external objects? And what about objects of an abstract sort, such as numbers? How do objects of both sorts help us in developing systematic connections between our sensory stimulations?

The assuming of objects is a mental act, and mental acts are notoriously difficult to pin down—this one more than most. Little can be done in the way of tracking thought processes except when we can put words to them. For something objective that we can get our teeth into we must go after the words. Words accompany thought for the most part anyway, and it is only as thoughts are expressed in words that we can specify them.

If we turn our attention to the words, then what had been a question of assuming objects becomes a question of verbal *reference* to objects. To ask what the *assuming* of an object consists in is to ask what *referring* to the object consists in.

We refer by using words, and these we learn through more or less devious association with stimulations of our sensory receptors. The association is direct in cases where the word is learned by ostension. It is thus that the child learns to volunteer the word 'milk,' or to assent if the word is queried, in the conspicuous presence of milk; also to volunteer the word so as to induce the presence of milk.

The mechanism in such a case is relatively clear and simple, as psychological mechanisms go. It is the conditioning of a response. To call it objective reference, however, is premature. Learning the expression 'milk' in this way, by direct association with appropriate stimulations, is the same in principle as learning the sentence 'It's windy' or 'It's cold' or 'It's raining' by direct association with appropriate stimulations. It is we in our adult ontological sophistication that recognize the word 'milk' as referring to an object, a substance, while we are less ready to single out an object of reference for 'It's windy' or 'It's cold' or 'It's raining.' This is the contrast that we need eventually to analyze if we are to achieve a satisfactory analysis of what to count as objective reference; and it is not a contrast that obtrudes in the primitive phase of learning by ostension. The word 'milk,' when uttered in recognition or when queried and assented to, is best regarded at first as a sentence on a par with 'It's windy,' 'It's cold,' and the rest; it is as if to say 'It's milk.' It is a one-word sentence. All of these examples are *occasion* sentences, true on some occasions of utterance and false on others. We are conditioned to assent to them under appropriate stimulation. There is no call to read into them, as yet, any reference to objects.

The view of sentences as primary in semantics, and of names or other words as dependent on sentences for their meaning, is a fruitful idea that began perhaps with Jeremy Bentham's theory of fictions.[1] What Bentham observed was that you have explained any term quite adequately if you have shown how all contexts in which you propose to use it can be paraphrased into antecedently intelligible language. When this is recognized, the philosophical analysis of concepts or explication of terms comes into its own. Sentences come to be seen as the primary repository of meaning, and words are seen as imbibing their meaning through their use in sentences.

Recognition of sentences as primary has not only expedited philosophical analysis; it has also given us a better picture of how language is

1. See Essay 7 below [Chapter 18].

actually learned. First we learn short sentences, next we get a line on various words through their use in those sentences, and then on that basis we manage to grasp longer sentences in which those same words recur. Accordingly the development leading from sensory stimulation to objective reference is to be seen as beginning with the flat conditioning of simple occasion sentences to stimulatory events, and advancing through stages more forthrightly identifiable with objective reference. We have still to consider what the distinguishing traits of these further stages might be.

As long as the word 'milk' can be accounted for simply as an occasion sentence on a par with 'It's raining,' surely nothing is added by saying that it is a name of something. Nothing really is said. Similarly for 'sugar,' 'water,' 'wood.' Similarly even for 'Fido' and 'Mama.' We would be idly declaring there to be designata of the words, counterparts, shadows, one apiece: danglers, serving only as honorary designata of expressions whose use as occasion sentences would continue as before.

The outlook changes when individuative words emerge: words like 'chair' and 'dog.' These differ from the previous examples in the complexity of what has to be mastered in learning them. By way of mastery of any of those previous words, all that was called for was the ability to pass a true-false test regarding points or neighborhoods taken one at a time. It is merely a question, in the case of Fido or milk, of what visible points are on Fido or on milk and what ones are not. To master 'dog' or 'chair,' on the other hand, it is not enough to be able to judge of each visible point whether it is on a dog or chair; we have also to learn where one dog or chair leaves off and another sets in.

In the case of such words, individuative ones, the idea of objective reference seems less trivial and more substantial. The word 'dog' is taken to denote each of many things, each dog, and the word 'chair,' each chair. It is no longer an idle one-to-one duplication, a mirroring of each word in an object dreamed up for that exclusive purpose. The chairs and dogs are indefinite in number and individually, for the most part, nameless. The 'Fido'-Fido principle, as Ryle called it, has been transcended.

However, this contrast between the individuatives and the previous words does not become detectable until a further device has become available: predication. The contrast emerges only when we are in a position to compare the predication 'Fido is a dog' with the predication 'Milk is white.' Milk's being white comes down to the simple fact that whenever you point at milk you point at white. Fido's being a dog does not come down to the simple fact that whenever you point at Fido you point at a dog: it involves that and more. For whenever you point at Fido's head you point at a dog, and yet Fido's head does not qualify as a dog.

It is in this rather subtle way that predication creates a difference between individuative terms and others. Prior to predication, such words as 'dog' and 'chair' differ in no pertinent way from 'milk' and 'Fido'; they are simple occasion sentences that herald, indifferently, the presence of milk, Fido, dog, chair.

Thus reference may be felt to have emerged when we take to predicating individuative terms, as in 'Fido is a dog.' 'Dog' then comes to qualify as a general term denoting each dog, and thereupon, thanks again to the predication 'Fido is a dog,' the word 'Fido' comes at last to qualify as a singular term naming one dog. In view then of the analogy of 'Milk is white' to 'Fido is a dog,' it becomes natural to view the word 'milk' likewise as a singular term naming something, this time not a body but a substance.

In *Word and Object* and *The Roots of Reference* I have speculated on how we learn individuative terms, predication, and various further essentials of our language. I will not go further into that, but will merely remind you of what some of these further essentials are. Along with singular predication, as in 'Milk is white' and 'Fido is a dog,' we want plural predication: 'Dogs are animals.' Along with monadic general terms, moreover, such as 'dog' and 'animal,' we want dyadic ones, such as 'part of,' 'darker than,' 'bigger than,' and 'beside'; also perhaps triadic and higher. Also we want predication of these polyadic terms, at least in the singular: thus 'Mama is bigger than Fido,' 'Fido is darker than milk.' Also we want the truth functions—'not,' 'and,' 'or'—by means of which to build compound sentences.

Now a further leap forward, as momentous as predication, is the *relative clause*. It is a way of segregating what a sentence says about an object, and packaging it as a complex general term. What the sentence

> Mont Blanc is higher than the Matterhorn but the Matterhorn is steeper

says about the Matterhorn is packaged in the relative clause:

> object that is not as high as Mont Blanc but is steeper.

Predicating this of the Matterhorn carries us back in effect to the original sentence.

The grammar of relative clauses can be simplified by rewriting them in the 'such that' idiom:

object x such that Mont Blanc is higher than x but x is steeper.

This keeps the word order of the original sentence. The 'x' is just a relative pronoun written in mathematical style. We can change the letter to avoid ambiguity in case one relative clause is embedded in another.

The relative clause serves no purpose in singular predication, since such predication just carries us back to a sentence of the original form. Where it pays off is in plural predication. Without relative clauses, the use of plural predication is cramped by shortage of general terms. We could still say 'Dogs are animals' and perhaps 'Small dogs are amusing animals,' but it is only with the advent of relative clauses that we can aspire to such heights as 'Whatever is salvaged from the wreck belongs to the state.' It becomes:

Objects x such that x is salvaged from the wreck are objects x such that x belongs to the state.

In general, where 'Fx' and 'Gx' stand for any sentences that we are in a position to formulate about x, relative clauses open the way to the plural predication:

Objects x such that Fx are objects x such that Gx.

Once we have this equipment, we have the full benefit of universal and existential quantification. This is evident if we reflect that '$(x)Fx$' is equivalent to '(x)(if not Fx then Fx)' and hence to:

Objects x such that not Fx are objects x such that Fx.

I said that reference may be felt to emerge with the predicating of individuatives. However, it is better seen as emerging by degrees. Already at the start the sentences 'Fido' and 'Milk,' unlike 'It's raining,' are learned by association with distinctively salient portions of the scene. Typically the salience is induced by pointing. Here already, in the selectivity of salience, is perhaps a first step toward the eventual namehood of 'Fido' and 'Milk.' Predications such as 'Milk is white' further enhance this air of objective reference, hinging as they do on a coinciding of saliences. Thus contrast the predication 'Milk is white' with 'When night falls the lamps are lit.' 'When' here is a connective comparable to the truth functions; it just happens to deliver standing sentences rather than occasion sentences when applied to occasion sentences. 'Milk is white' likewise can be viewed as a standing sentence compounded of the occasion sentences 'Milk' and 'White,' but it says more than 'When there is milk there is white'; it says '*Where* there is milk there is white.' The concentration on a special part of the scene is thus doubly emphasized, and in this I sense further rumblings of objective reference.

Predications such as 'Milk is white' still afford, even so, little reason for imputing objective reference. As already remarked, we might as well continue to use the purported names as occasion sentences and let the objects go. A finite and listed ontology is no ontology.

Predication of individuatives, next, as in 'Fido is a dog,' heightens reference in two ways. The concentration on a special part of the scene is emphasized here more strongly still than in 'Milk is white,' since Fido is required not merely to be contained in the scattered part of the world that is made up of dog; he is required to fill one of its discrete blobs. And the more telling point, already noted, is that 'dog' transcends the 'Fido'-Fido principle; dogs are largely nameless.

Even at this stage, however, the referential apparatus and its ontology are vague. Individuation goes dim over any appreciable time interval. Thus consider the term 'dog.' We would recognize any particular dog in his recurrences if we noticed some distinctive trait in him; a dumb animal would do the same. We recognize Fido in his recurrences in learning the occasion sentence 'Fido,' just as we recognize further milk and sugar in learning 'Milk' and 'Sugar.' Even in the absence of distinctive traits we will correctly concatenate momentary canine manifestations as stages of the same dog as long as we keep watching. After any considerable lapse of observation, however, the question of identity of unspecified dogs simply does not arise—not at the rudimentary stage of language learning. It scarcely makes sense until we are in a position to say such things as that in general if *any* dog undergoes such and such then in due course that *same* dog will behave thus and so. This sort of general talk about long-term causation becomes possible only with the advent of quantification or its equivalent, the relative clause in plural predication. Such is the dependence of individuation, in the time dimension, upon relative clauses; and it is only with full individuation that reference comes fully into its own.

With the relative clause at hand, objective reference is indeed full blown. In the relative clause the channel of reference is the relative pronoun 'that' or 'which,' together with its recurrences in the guise of 'it,' 'he,' 'her,' and so on. Regimented in symbolic logic, these pronouns give way to bound variables of quantification. The variables range, as we say, over all objects; they admit all objects as values. To assume objects of some sort is to reckon objects of that sort among the values of our variables.

II

What objects, then, do we find ourselves assuming? Certainly bodies. The emergence of reference endowed the occasion sentences 'Dog' and 'Animal' with the status of general terms denoting bodies, and the occasion sentences 'Fido' and 'Mama' with the status of singular terms designating bodies.

We can see how natural it is that some of the occasion sentences ostensively learned should have been such as to foreshadow bodies, if we reflect on the social character of ostension. The child learns the occasion sentence from the mother while they view the scene from their respective vantage points, receiving somewhat unlike presentations. The mother in her childhood learned the sentence in similarly divergent circumstances. The sentence is thus bound to be versatile, applying regardless of angle. Thus it is that the aspects of a body in all their visual diversity are naturally gathered under a single occasion sentence, ultimately a single designation.

We saw how the reification of milk, wood, and other substances would follow naturally and closely on that of bodies. Bodies are our paradigmatic objects, but analogy proceeds apace; nor does it stop with substances. Grammatical analogy between general terms and singular terms encourages us to treat a general term as if it designated a single object, and thus we are apt to posit a realm of objects for the general terms to designate: a realm of properties, or sets. What with the nominalizing also of verbs and clauses, a vaguely varied and very untidy ontology grows up.

The common man's ontology is vague and untidy in two ways. It takes in many purported objects that are vaguely or inadequately defined. But also, what is more significant, it is vague in its scope; we cannot even tell in general which of these vague things to ascribe to a man's ontology at all, which things to count him as assuming. Should we regard grammar as decisive? Does every noun demand some array of denotata? Surely not; the nominalizing of verbs is often a mere stylistic variation. But where can we draw the line?

It is a wrong question; there is no line to draw. Bodies are assumed, yes; they are the things, first and foremost. Beyond them there is a succession of dwindling analogies. Various expressions come to be used in ways more or less parallel to the use of the terms for bodies, and it is felt that corresponding objects are more or less posited, *pari passu;* but there is no purpose in trying to mark an ontological limit to the dwindling parallelism.

My point is not that ordinary language is slipshod, slipshod though it be. We must recognize this grading off for what it is, and recognize that a fenced ontology is just not implicit in ordinary language. The idea of a boundary between being and nonbeing is a philosophical idea, an idea of technical science in a broad sense. Scientists and philosophers seek a comprehensive system of the world, and one that is oriented to reference even more squarely and utterly than ordinary language. Ontological concern is not a correction of a lay thought and practice; it is foreign to the lay culture, though an outgrowth of it.

We can draw explicit ontological lines when desired. We can regiment our notation, admitting only general and singular terms, singular and plural predication, truth functions, and the machinery of relative clauses; or, equivalently and more artificially, instead of plural predication and relative clauses we can admit quantification. Then it is that we can say that the objects assumed are the values of the variables, or of the pronouns. Various turns of phrase in ordinary language that seemed to invoke novel sorts of objects may disappear under such regimentation. At other points new ontic commitments may emerge. There is room for choice, and one chooses with a view to simplicity in one's overall system of the world.

More objects are wanted, certainly, than just bodies and substances. We need all sorts of parts or portions of substances. For lack of a definable stopping place, the natural course at this point is to admit as an object the material content of any portion of space-time, however irregular and discontinuous and heterogeneous. This is the generalization of the primitive and ill-defined category of bodies to what I call physical objects.

Substances themselves fall into place now as physical objects. Milk, or wood, or sugar, is the discontinuous four-dimensional physical object comprising all the world's milk, or wood, or sugar, ever.

The reasons for taking the physical objects thus spatiotemporally, and treating time on a par with space, are overwhelming and have been adequately noted in various places.[2] Let us pass over them and ponder rather the opposition to the four-dimensional view; for it is a curiosity worth looking into. Part of the opposition is obvious misinterpretation: the notion that time is stopped, change is denied, and all is frozen eternally in a fourth dimension. These are the misgivings of unduly nervous folk who overestimate the power of words. Time as a fourth dimension is still time, and differences along the fourth dimension are still changes; they are merely treated more simply and efficiently than they otherwise might be.

Opposition has proceeded also from the venerable doctrine that not all the statements about the future have truth values now, because some of them remain, as of now, causally undetermined. Properly viewed, however, determinism is beside the point. The question of future truths is a matter of verbal convenience and is as innocuous as Doris Day's tautological fatalism "Che sarà sarà."

Another question that has been similarly linked to determinism, wrongly and notoriously, is that of freedom of the will. Like Spinoza, Hume, and so many others, I count an act as free insofar as the agent's motives or drives are a link in its causal chain. Those motives or drives may themselves be as rigidly determined as you please.

It is for me an ideal of pure reason to subscribe to determinism as fully as the quantum physicists will let me. But there are well-known difficulties in the way of rigorously formulating it. When we say of some event that it is determined by present ones, shall we mean that there is a general conditional, true but perhaps unknown to us, whose antecedent is instantiated by present events and whose consequent is instantiated by the future event in question? Without some drastic limitations on complexity and vocabulary, determinism so defined is pretty sure to boil down to "Che sarà sarà" and to afford at best a great idea for a song. Yet the idea in all its vagueness retains validity as an ideal of reason. It is valid as a general injunction: look for mechanisms.

This has been quite a spray, or spree, of philosophical miscellany. Let us now return to our cabbages, which is to say, our newly generalized physical objects. One of the benefits that the generalization confers is the accommodation of events as objects. An action or transaction can be identified with the physical objects consisting of the temporal segment or

2. For example, in my *Word and Object,* pp. 170ff.

segments of the agent or agents for the duration. Misgivings about this approach to events have been expressed, on the grounds that it does not distinguish two acts that are performed simultaneously, such as walking and chewing gum. But I think that all the distinctions that need to be drawn can be drawn, still, at the level of general terms. Not all walks are gum chewings, nor vice versa, even though an occasional one may be. Some things may be said of an act on the score of its being a walk, and distinctive things may be said of it on the score of its being a chewing of gum, even though it be accounted one and the same event. There are its crural features on the one hand and its maxillary features on the other.

A reason for being particularly glad to have accommodated events is Davidson's logic of adverbs,[3] for Davidson has shown to my satisfaction that quantification over events is far and away the best way of construing adverbial constructions.

Our liberal notion of physical objects brings out an important point about identity. Some philosophers propound puzzles as to what to say about personal identity in cases of split personality or in fantasies about metempsychosis or brain transplants. These are not questions about the nature of identity. They are questions about how we might best construe the term 'person.' Again there is the stock example of the ship of Theseus, rebuilt bit by bit until no original bit remained. Whether we choose to reckon it still as the same ship is a question not of 'same' but of 'ship'; a question of how we choose to individuate that term over time.

Any coherent general term has its own principle of individuation, its own criterion of identity among its denotata. Often the principle is vague, as the principle of individuation of persons is shown to be by the science-fiction examples; and a term is as vague as its principle of individuation.

Most of our general terms individuate by continuity considerations, because continuity favors causal connections. But even useful terms, grounded in continuity, often diverge in their individuation, as witness the evolving ship of Theseus, on the one hand, and its original substance, gradually dispersed, on the other. Continuity follows both branches.

All this should have been clear without help of our liberal notion of physical object, but this notion drives the point home. It shows how empty it would be to ask, out of context, whether a certain glimpse yes-

---

3. Donald Davidson, "The Logical Form of Action Sentences," in Nicholas Rescher (ed.), *The Logic of Action and Preference* (Pittsburgh: University of Pittsburgh Press, 1967), pp. 91–95.

terday and a certain glimpse today were glimpses of the same thing. They may or may not have been glimpses of the same body, but they certainly were glimpses of *a* same thing, a same physical object; for the content of any portion of space-time, however miscellaneously scattered in space and time that portion be, counts as a physical object.

The president or presidency of the United States is one such physical object, though not a body. It is a spatially discontinuous object made up of temporal segments, each of which is a temporal stage also of a body, a human one. The whole thing has its temporal beginning in 1789, when George Washington took office, and its end only at the final takeover, quite possibly more than two centuries later. Another somewhat similar physical object is the Dalai Lama, an example that has been invigorated by a myth of successive reincarnation. But the myth is unnecessary.

A body is a special kind of physical object, one that is roughly continuous spatially and rather chunky and that contrasts abruptly with most of its surroundings and is individuated over time by continuity of displacement, distortion, and discoloration. These are vague criteria, especially so in view of molecular theory, which teaches that the boundary of a solid is ill defined and that the continuity of a solid is only apparent and properly a matter of degree.

The step of generalization from body to physical object follows naturally, we saw, on the reification of portions of stuff. It follows equally naturally on molecular theory: if even a solid is diffuse, why stop there?

We can be happy not to have to rest existence itself on the vague notions of body and substance, as we would have to do if bodies and substances were our whole ontology. Specific individuatives such as 'dog' or 'desk' continue, like 'body,' to suffer from vagueness on the score of the microphysical boundaries of their denotata, as well as vagueness on the score of marginal denotata themselves, such as makeshift desks and remote ancestors of dogs; but all this is vagueness only of classification and not of existence. All the variants qualify as physical objects.

Physical objects in this generous sense constitute a fairly lavish universe, but more is wanted—notably numbers. Measurement is useful in cookery and commerce, and in the fullness of time it rises to a nobler purpose: the formulation of quantitative laws. These are the mainstay of scientific theory,[4] and they call upon the full resources of the real numbers. Diagonals call for irrationals, circumferences call for transcenden-

---

4. See Essay 18 below (Quine, "Success and Limits of Mathematization," in *Theories and Things*, pp. 148–155).

tals. Nor can we rest with constants; we must quantify over numbers. Admitting numbers as values of variables means reifying them and recognizing numerals as names of them; and this is required for the sake of generality in our quantitative laws.

Measures have sometimes been viewed as impure numbers: nine miles, nine gallons. We do better to follow Carnap[5] in construing each scale of measurement as a polyadic general term relating physical objects to pure numbers. Thus 'gallon xy' means that the presumably fluid and perhaps scattered physical object x amounts to y gallons, and 'mile xyz' means that the physical objects x and y are z miles apart. Pure numbers, then, apparently belong in our ontology.

Classes do too, for whenever we count things we measure a class. If a statistical generality about populations quantifies over numbers of people, it has to quantify also over the classes whose numbers those are. Quantification over classes figures also in other equally inconspicuous ways, as witness Frege's familiar definition of ancestor in terms of parent: one's ancestors are the members shared by every class that contains oneself and the parents of its members.

Sometimes in natural science we are concerned explicitly with classes, or seem to be—notably in taxonomy. We read that there are over a quarter-million species of beetles. Here evidently we are concerned with a quarter-million classes and, over and above these, a class of all these classes. However, we can economize here. Instead of talking of species in this context, we can make do with a dyadic general term applicable to beetles: 'conspecific.' To say that there are over a quarter-million species is equivalent to saying that there is a class of over a quarter-million *beetles* none of which are conspecific. This still conveys impressive information, and it still requires reification of a big class, but a class only of beetles and not of classes.

This way of dodging a class of classes is not always available. It worked here because species are mutually exclusive.

Note the purely auxiliary role of classes in all three examples. In counting things we are more interested in the things counted than in their class. In the genealogical example the concern is with people, their parentage and ancestry; classes entered only in deriving the one from the other. In the example of the beetles, classes were indeed out in the open—even inordinately so, I argued. But even so, it is because of an interest still strictly in beetles, not classes, that one says there are so many

5. Carnap, *Physikalische Begriffsbildung* (Karlsruhe, 1926).

species. The statement tells us that beetles are highly discriminate in their mating. It conveys this sort of information, but more precisely, and it makes auxiliary reference to classes as a means of doing so. Limited to physical objects though our interests be, an appeal to classes can thus be instrumental in pursuing those interests. I look upon mathematics in general in the same way, in its relation to natural science. But to view classes, numbers, and the rest in this instrumental way is not to deny having reified them; it is only to explain why.

III

So we assume abstract objects over and above the physical objects. For a better grasp of what this means, let us consider a simple case: the natural numbers. The conditions we need to impose on them are simple and few: we need to assume an object as first number and an operator that yields a unique new number whenever applied to a number. In short, we need a progression. Any progression will do, for the following reasons. The fundamental use of natural numbers is in measuring classes: in saying that a class has n members. Other serious uses prove to be reducible to this use. But any progression will serve *this* purpose; for we can say that a class has n members by saying that its members are in correlation with the members of the progression up to n—not caring which progression it may be.

There are ways of defining specific progressions of classes, no end of ways. When we feel the need of natural numbers we can simply reach for members of one of these progressions instead—whichever one comes handy. On the basis of natural numbers, in turn, it is possible with the help of classes to define the ratios and the irrational numbers in well-known ways. On one such construction they turn out to be simply certain classes of natural numbers. So, when we feel the need of ratios and irrationals, we can simply reach for appropriate subclasses of one of the progressions of classes. We need never talk of numbers, though in practice it is convenient to carry over the numerical jargon.

Numbers, then, except as a manner of speaking, are by the board. We have physical objects and we have classes. Not just classes of physical objects, but classes of classes and so on up. Some of these higher levels are needed to do the work of numbers and other gear of applied mathematics, and one then assumes the whole hierarchy if only for want of a natural stopping place.

But now what are classes? Consider the bottom layer, the classes of physical objects. Every relative clause or other general term determines a class, the class of those physical objects of which the term can be truly predicated. Two terms determine the same class of physical objects just in case the terms are true of just the same physical objects. Still, compatibly with all this we could reconstrue every class systematically as its complement and then compensate for the switch by reinterpreting the dyadic general term 'member of' to mean what had been meant by 'not a member of.' The effects would cancel and one would never know.

We thus seem to see a profound difference between abstract objects and concrete ones. A physical object, one feels, can be pinned down by pointing—in many cases, anyway, and to a fair degree. But I am persuaded that this contrast is illusory.

By way of example, consider again my liberalized notion of a physical object as the material content of any place-time, any portion of space-time. This was an intuitive explanation, intending no reification of space-time itself. But we could just as well reify those portions of space-time and treat of them instead of the physical objects. Or, indeed, call them physical objects. Whatever can be said from the old point of view can be paraphrased to suit the new point of view, with no effect on the structure of scientific theory or on its links with observational evidence. Wherever we had a predication 'x is a P,' said of a physical object x, we would in effect read 'x is the place-time of a P'; actually we would just reinterpret the old 'P' as 'place-time of a P,' and rewrite nothing.

Space separately, or place anyway, is an untenable notion. If there were really places, there would be absolute rest and absolute motion; for change of place would be absolute motion. However, there is no such objection to place-times or space-time.

If we accept a redundant ontology containing both physical objects and place-times, then we can indeed declare them distinct; but even then, if we switch the physical objects with their place-times and then compensate by reinterpreting the dyadic general term 'is the material content of' to mean 'is the place-time of' and vice versa, no one can tell the difference. We could choose either interpretation indifferently if we were translating from an unrelated language.

These last examples are unnatural, for they work only if the empty place-times are repudiated and just the full ones are admitted as values of the variables. If we were seriously to reconstrue physical objects as place-times, we would surely enlarge our universe to include the empty ones and thus gain the simplicity of a continuous system of coordinates.

This change in ontology, the abandonment of physical objects in favor of pure space-time, proves to be more than a contrived example. The elementary particles have been wavering alarmingly as physics progresses. Situations arise that curiously challenge the individuality of a particle, not only over time, but even at a single time. A field theory in which states are ascribed directly to place-times may well present a better picture, and some physicists think it does.

At this point a further transfer of ontology suggests itself: we can drop the space-time regions in favor of the corresponding classes of quadruples of numbers according to an arbitrarily adopted system of coordinates. We are left with just the ontology of pure set theory, since the numbers and their quadruples can be modeled within it. There are no longer any physical objects to serve as individuals at the base of the hierarchy of classes, but there is no harm in that. It is common practice in set theory nowadays to start merely with the null class, form its unit class, and so on, thus generating an infinite lot of classes, from which all the usual luxuriance of further infinites can be generated.

One may object to thus identifying the world with the output of so arbitrarily chosen a system of coordinates. On the other hand, one may condone this on the ground that no numerically specific coordinates will appear in the laws of truly theoretical physics, thanks to the very arbitrariness of the coordinates. The specificity of the coordinates would make itself known only when one descends to coarser matters of astronomy, geography, geology, and history, and here it is perhaps appropriate.

We have now looked at three cases in which we interpret or reinterpret one domain of objects by identifying it with part of another domain. In the first example, numbers were identified with some of the classes in one way or another. In the second example, physical objects were identified with some of the place-times, namely, the full ones. In the third example, place-times were identified with some of the classes, namely, classes of quadruples of numbers. In each such case simplicity is gained, if to begin with we had been saddled with the two domains.

There is a fourth example of the same thing that is worth noting, for it concerns the long-debated dualism of mind and body. I hardly need say that the dualism is unattractive. If mind and body are to interact, we are at a loss for a plausible mechanism to the purpose. Also we are faced with the melancholy office of talking physicists out of their cherished conservation laws. On the other hand, an aseptic dualistic parallelism is monumentally redundant, a monument to everything multiplicacious that William of Ockham so rightly deplored. But now it is easily seen that dualism with or without interaction is reducible to physical monism, unless disembodied spirits are assumed. For the dualist who rejects disembodied spirits is bound to agree that for every state of mind there is an exactly concurrent and readily specifiable state of the accompanying body. Readily specifiable certainly; the bodily state is specifiable simply as the state of accompanying a mind that is in that mental state. But then we can settle for the bodily states outright, bypassing the mental states in terms of which I specified them. We can just reinterpret the mentalistic terms as denoting these correlated bodily states, and who is to know the difference?

This reinterpretation of mentalistic terms is reminiscent of the treatment of events that I suggested earlier, and it raises the same question of discrimination of concurrent events. But I would just propose again the answer that I gave then.

I take it as evident that there is no inverse option here, no hope of sustaining mental monism by assigning mental states to all states of physical objects.

These four cases of reductive reinterpretation are gratifying, enabling us as they do to dispense with one of two domains and make do with the other alone. But I find the other sort of reinterpretation equally instructive, the sort where we save nothing but merely change or seem to change our objects without disturbing either the structure or the empirical support of a scientific theory in the slightest. All that is needed in either case, clearly, is a rule whereby a unique object of the supposedly new sort is assigned to each of the old objects. I call such a rule a proxy function. Then, instead of predicating a general term 'P' of an old object x, saying that x is a P, we reinterpret x as a new object and say that it is the f of a P, where 'f' expresses the proxy function. Instead of saying that x is a dog, we say that x is the lifelong filament of space-time taken up by a dog. Or, really, we just adhere to the old term 'P,' 'dog,' and reinterpret it as 'f of a P,' 'place-time of a dog.' This is the strategy that we have seen in various examples.

The apparent change is twofold and sweeping. The original objects have been supplanted and the general terms reinterpreted. There has been a revision of ontology on the one hand and of ideology, so to say, on the other; they go together. Yet verbal behavior proceeds undisturbed, warranted by the same observations as before and elicited by the same observations. Nothing really has changed.

The conclusion I draw is the inscrutability of reference. To say what objects someone is talking about is to say no more than how we propose to translate his terms into ours; we are free to vary the decision with a proxy function. The translation adopted arrests the free-floating reference of the alien terms only relatively to the free-floating reference of our own terms, by linking the two.

The point is not that we ourselves are casting about in vain for a mooring. Staying aboard our own language and not rocking the boat, we are borne smoothly along on it and all is well; 'rabbit' denotes rabbits, and there is no sense in asking 'Rabbits in what sense of "rabbit"?' Reference goes inscrutable if, rocking the boat, we contemplate a permutational mapping of our language on itself, or if we undertake translation.

Structure is what matters to a theory, and not the choice of its objects. F. P. Ramsey urged this point fifty years ago, arguing along other lines, and in a vague way it had been a persistent theme also in Russell's *Analysis of Matter*. But Ramsey and Russell were talking only of what they called theoretical objects, as opposed to observable objects.

I extend the doctrine to objects generally, for I see all objects as theoretical. This is a consequence of taking seriously the insight that I traced from Bentham—namely, the semantic primacy of sentences. It is occasion sentences, not terms, that are to be seen as conditioned to stimulations. Even our primordial objects, bodies, are already theoretical—most conspicuously so when we look to their individuation over time. Whether we encounter the same apple the next time around, or only another one like it, is settled if at all by inference from a network of hypotheses that we have internalized little by little in the course of acquiring the nonobservational superstructure of our language.

It is occasion sentences that report the observations on which science rests. The scientific output is likewise sentential: true sentences, we hope, truths about nature. The objects, or values of variables, serve merely as indices along the way, and we may permute or supplant them as we please as long as the sentence-to-sentence structure is preserved. The scientific system, ontology and all, is a conceptual bridge of our own making, linking sensory stimulation to sensory stimulation. I am repeating what I said at the beginning.

But I also expressed, at the beginning, my unswerving belief in external things—people, nerve endings, sticks, stones. This I reaffirm. I believe also, if less firmly, in atoms and electrons and in classes. Now how is all this robust realism to be reconciled with the barren scene that I have just been depicting? The answer is naturalism: the recognition that it is within science itself, and not in some prior philosophy, that reality is to be identified and described.

The semantical considerations that seemed to undermine all this were concerned not with assessing reality but with analyzing method and evidence. They belong not to ontology but to the methodology of ontology, and thus to epistemology. Those considerations showed that I could indeed turn my back on my external things and classes and ride the proxy functions to something strange and different without doing violence to any evidence. But all ascription of reality must come rather from within one's theory of the world; it is incoherent otherwise.

My methodological talk of proxy functions and inscrutability of reference must be seen as naturalistic too; it likewise is no part of a first philosophy prior to science. The setting is still the physical world, seen in terms of the global science to which, with minor variations, we all subscribe. Amid all this there are our sensory receptors and the bodies near and far whose emanations impinge on our receptors. Epistemology, for me, or what comes nearest to it, is the study of how we animals can have contrived that very science, given just that sketchy neural input. It is this study that reveals that displacements of our ontology through proxy functions would have measured up to that neural input no less faithfully. To recognize this is not to repudiate the ontology in terms of which the recognition took place.

We *can* repudiate it. We are free to switch, without doing violence to any evidence. If we switch, then this epistemological remark itself undergoes appropriate reinterpretation too; nerve endings and other things give way to appropriate proxies, again without straining any evidence. But it is a confusion to suppose that we can stand aloof and recognize all the alternative ontologies as true in their several ways, all the envisaged worlds as real. It is a confusion of truth with evidential support. Truth is immanent, and there is no higher. We must speak from within a theory, albeit any of various.

Transcendental argument, or what purports to be first philosophy, tends generally to take on rather this status of immanent epistemology insofar as I succeed in making sense of it. What evaporates is the transcendental question of the reality of the external world—the question whether or in how far our science measures up to the *Ding an sich*.

Our scientific theory can indeed go wrong, and precisely in the familiar way: through failure of predicted observation. But what if, happily and unbeknownst, we have achieved a theory that is conformable to every possible observation, past and future? In what sense could the world then be said to deviate from what the theory claims? Clearly in none, even if we can somehow make sense of the phrase 'every possible observation.' Our overall scientific theory demands of the world only that it be so structured as to assure the sequences of stimulation that our theory gives us to expect. More concrete demands are empty, what with the freedom of proxy functions.

Radical skepticism stems from the sort of confusion I have alluded to, but is not of itself incoherent. Science is vulnerable to illusion on its own showing, what with seemingly bent sticks in water and the like, and the skeptic may be seen merely as overreacting when he repudiates science across the board. Experience might still take a turn that would justify his doubts about external objects. Our success in predicting observations might fall off sharply, and concomitantly with this we might begin to be somewhat successful in basing predictions upon dreams or reveries. At that point we might reasonably doubt our theory of nature in even fairly broad outlines. But our doubts would still be immanent, and of a piece with the scientific endeavor.

My attitude toward the project of a rational reconstruction of the world from sense data is similarly naturalistic. I do not regard the project as incoherent, though its motivation in some cases is confused. I see it as a project of positing a realm of entities intimately related to the stimulation of the sensory surfaces, and then, with the help perhaps of an auxiliary realm of entities in set theory, proceeding by contextual definition to construct a language adequate to natural science. It is an attractive idea, for it would bring scientific discourse into a much more explicit and systematic relation to its observational checkpoints. My only reservation is that I am convinced, regretfully, that it cannot be done.

Another notion that I would take pains to rescue from the abyss of the transcendental is the notion of a matter of fact. A place where the notion proves relevant is in connection with my doctrine of the indeterminacy of translation. I have argued that two conflicting manuals of translation can both do justice to all dispositions to behavior, and that, in such a case, there is no fact of the matter of which manual is right. The intended notion of matter of fact is not transcendental or yet epistemological, not even a question of evidence; it is ontological, a question of reality, and to be taken naturalistically within our scientific theory of the world. Thus suppose, to make things vivid, that we are settling still for a physics of elementary particles and recognizing a dozen or so basic states and relations in which they may stand. Then when I say there is no fact of the matter, as regards, say, the two rival manuals of translation, what I mean is that both manuals are compatible with all the same distributions of states and relations over elementary particles. In a word, they are physically equivalent. Needless to say, there is no presumption of our being able to sort out the pertinent distributions of microphysical states and relations. I speak of a physical condition and not an empirical criterion.

It is in the same sense that I say there is no fact of the matter of our interpreting any man's ontology in one way or, via proxy functions, in another. Any man's, that is to say, except ourselves. We can switch our own ontology too without doing violence to any evidence, but in so doing we switch from our elementary particles to some manner of proxies and thus reinterpret our standard of what counts as a fact of the matter. Factuality, like gravitation and electric charge, is internal to our theory of nature.

14

ON CARNAP'S VIEWS ON ONTOLOGY

Though no one has influenced my philosophical thought more than Carnap, an issue has persisted between us for years over questions of ontology and analyticity. These questions prove to be interrelated; their interrelations come out especially clearly in Carnap's paper "Empiricism, Semantics, and Ontology." I shall devote particular attention to that one paper in an effort to isolate and reduce our divergences.

When I inquire into the *ontological commitments* of a given doctrine or body of theory, I am merely asking what, according to that theory, there is. I might say in passing, though it is no substantial point of disagreement, that Carnap does not much like my terminology here. Now if he had a better use for this fine old word 'ontology,' I should be inclined to cast about for another word for my own meaning. But the fact is, I believe, that he disapproves of my giving meaning to a word which belongs to traditional metaphysics and should therefore be meaningless. Now my ethics of terminology demand, on occasion, the avoidance of a word for given purposes when the word has been preempted in a prior meaning; meaningless words, however, are precisely the words which I feel freest to specify meanings for. But actually my adoption of the word 'ontology' for the purpose described is not as arbitrary as I make it sound. Though no champion of traditional metaphysics, I suspect that the sense in which I use this crusty old word has been nuclear to its usage all along.

Let us agree, for the space of my remarks, on the word. The question of the ontological commitments of a theory, then, is the question what, according to that theory, there is. Carnap thinks—and here is a more than terminological issue—that the question what a theory presupposes that there is should be divided into *two* questions in a certain way; and I

249

disagree. What he thinks the division should be, and why I disagree, will appear soon; but first let us examine the undivided idea a bit.

It has not always been clear how to decide whether or not a given discourse involves commitment to a given alleged entity. When we say that all fish are aquatic, do we commit ourselves to the acceptance of two abstract entities, two classes or properties, named by the words 'fish' and 'aquatic'? When we use the word 'similar,' without defining it in any anterior terms, do we thereby commit ourselves to the acceptance of an abstract entity which is the relation of similarity? Russell has said that we do. But no nominalist would agree.

Every nominalist, every user of language, avails himself freely of general terms such as 'fish' and 'aquatic' and 'similar'; but only anti-nominalists imagine in such usage any allusion to abstract entities. The nominalist holds that the word 'fish' is *true of* each concrete fish, but that it does not, in addition, *name* an abstract fishhood or class of fish; and that the word 'similar' is true of each alligator with respect to each crocodile, and true of each Pontiac with respect to each Pontiac, but that it does not, in addition, name a relation of similarity. Why should 'fish' or 'aquatic' or 'similar' be put on a par with names such as 'Chicago' and 'Truman' and 'Parthenon'? Many words are admissible in significant sentences without claiming to name; witness 'the' and 'of' and 'sake' and 'kilter.' Why not 'fish' and 'aquatic' and 'similar'?

Perhaps we can convict a speaker of commitment to abstract entities not through his general terms, but only through his abstract terms such as 'fishhood,' 'aquaticity,' 'similarity'? But this is no feasible resting place. If you grant the nominalist his general terms, he can excuse his use of abstract terms as picturesque paraphrasing of what could be said in general terms.

All this tolerance of language and waiving of commitments is reasonable enough, but is there no end to it? The words 'Chicago' and 'Truman' and 'Parthenon' could themselves be excused in the same spirit, as admissible in sentences without claiming to name. There would appear to be no such thing as commitment to entities through discourse.

I think it is true that there is no commitment to entities through use of alleged *names* of them; other things being equal, we can always deny the allegation that the words in question are names. But still there is certainly commitment to entities through discourse; for we are quite capable of saying in so many words that *there are* black swans, that *there is* a mountain more than 8800 meters high, and that *there are* prime numbers above a hundred. Saying these things, we also say by implication that there are physical objects and abstract entities; for all the black swans are physical objects and all the prime numbers above a hundred are abstract entities.

Thus I consider that the essential commitment to entities of any sort comes through the variables of quantification and not through the use of alleged names. The entities to which a discourse commits us are the entities over which our variables of quantification have to range in order that the statements affirmed in that discourse be true.

Names are a red herring. The use of alleged names, we have seen, is no commitment to corresponding entities. Conversely, through our variables of quantification we are quite capable of committing ourselves to entities which cannot be named individually at all in the resources of our language; witness the real numbers, which, according to classical theory, constitute a larger infinity than does the totality of constructible names in any language. Names, in fact, can be dispensed with altogether in favor of *un*naming general terms, plus quantification and other logical devices; the trick of accomplishing this elimination is provided, in its main lines, by Russell's theory of descriptions. Thenceforward the variable of quantification becomes the sole channel of reference. For ontological commitment it is the variable that counts.

If I understand correctly, Carnap accepts my standard for judging whether a given theory accepts given alleged entities. The test is whether the variables of quantification have to include those entities in their range in order to make the theory true. Allow, of course, for a shudder between the word 'ontological' and the word 'commitment.'

Now to determine what entities a given theory presupposes is one thing, and to determine what entities a theory should be allowed to presuppose, what entities there really are, is another. It is especially in the latter connection that Carnap urges the dichotomy which I said I would talk about. On one side of his dichotomy he puts the question of there being black swans, or mountains more than 8800 meters, or prime numbers above a hundred; on the other side the question of there being physical objects or abstract entities. The distinction depends on what he calls a *framework*:

> If someone wishes to speak in his language about a new kind of entities, he has to introduce a system of new ways of speaking, subject to new rules; we shall call this procedure the construction of a *framework* for

the new entities in question. And now we must distinguish two kinds of questions of existence: first, questions of the existence of certain entities of the new kind *within the framework;* we call them *internal questions;* and second, questions concerning the existence or reality of *the framework itself,* called *external questions.* . . . Let us consider as an example the simplest framework dealt with in the everyday language: the spatio-temporally ordered system of observable things and events. Once we have accepted this thing language and thereby the framework of things, we can raise and answer internal questions, e.g., 'Is there a white piece of paper on my desk?,' 'Did King Arthur actually live?,' 'Are unicorns and centaurs real or merely imaginary?,' and the like. These questions are to be answered by empirical investigations.

. . . From these questions we must distinguish the external question of the reality of the thing world itself. In contrast to the former questions, this question is raised neither by the man in the street nor by scientists, but only by philosophers. . . . those who raise the question of the reality of the thing world itself have perhaps in mind not a theoretical question as their formulation seems to suggest, but rather a practical question, a matter of a practical decision concerning the structure of our language. We have to make the choice whether or not to accept and use the forms of expression for the framework in question.

. . . If someone decides to accept the thing language, there is no objection against saying that he has accepted the world of things. But this must not be interpreted as if it meant his acceptance of a *belief* in the reality of the thing world; there is no such belief or assertion or assumption, because it is not a theoretical question. To accept the thing world means nothing more than to accept a certain form of language.[1]

Let us recall now my account of wherein the countenancing of entities consists. It consists in the inclusion of them within the range or ranges of the variables of quantification. Accordingly Carnap describes the introduction of a framework as consisting essentially in these two steps:

First, the introduction of a general term, a predicate of higher level, for the new kind of entities, permitting us to say of any particular entity that it belongs to this kind (e.g., 'Red is a *property,*' 'Five is a *number*'). Second, the introduction of variables of the new type. The new entities

1. Rudolf Carnap, "Empiricism, Semantics, and Ontology," *Revue Internationale de Philosophie* 4 (1950).

are values of these variables; the constants (and the closed compound expressions, if any) are substitutable for the variables. With the help of the variables, general sentences concerning the new entities can be formulated.[2]

It begins to appear, then, that Carnap's dichotomy of questions of existence is a dichotomy between questions of the form "Are there so-and-so's?" where the so-and-so's purport to exhaust the range of a particular style of bound variables, and questions of the form "Are there so-and-so's?" where the so-and-so's do not purport to exhaust the range of a particular style of bound variables. Let me call the former questions *category* questions, and the latter ones *subclass* questions. I need this new terminology because Carnap's terms 'external' and 'internal' draw a somewhat different distinction which is derivative from the distinction between category questions and subclass questions. The external questions are the category questions conceived as propounded before the adoption of a given language; and they are, Carnap holds, properly to be construed as questions of the desirability of a given language form. The internal questions comprise the subclass questions and, in addition, the category questions when these are construed as treated within an adopted language as questions having trivially analytic or contradictory answers.[3]

But now I want to examine the dichotomy which, as we see, underlies Carnap's distinction of external and internal, and which I am phrasing as the distinction between category questions and subclass questions. It is evident that the question whether there are numbers will be a category question only with respect to languages which appropriate a separate style of variables for the exclusive purpose of referring to numbers. If our language refers to numbers through variables which also take classes other than numbers as values, then the question whether there are numbers becomes a subclass question, on a par with the question whether there are primes over a hundred. This will be the situation in the language of *Principia Mathematica* and in the languages of all the other familiar set theories.

Even the question whether there are classes, or whether there are physical objects, becomes a subclass question if our language uses a single style of variables to range over both sorts of entities. Whether the

2. Ibid., p. 30.
3. This is clearly intended; ibid., p. 24.

statement that there are physical objects and the statement that there are black swans should be put on the same side of the dichotomy, or on opposite sides, comes to depend on the rather trivial consideration of whether we use one style of variables or two for physical objects and classes.

I must now explain why I call this a rather trivial consideration. The use of different styles of variables for different ranges is common in mathematics, but can usually be explained as a casual and eliminable shorthand: instead of prefacing various of our statements with the words 'If x is a real number between 0 and 1, then,' we may find it convenient for the space of a chapter or a book of probability theory to reserve special letters 'p', 'q', 'r' to the real numbers between 0 and 1. The difference between using the explicit hypothesis 'x is a real number between 0 and 1' and introducing the restricted variables is so negligible that at the level of ordinary mathematical writing it cannot usually be detected; nor is there any reason why it should be detected.

But Carnap does not have just this trivial distinction in mind. He is thinking of languages which contain fundamentally segregated styles of variables before any definitional abbreviations; and he is thinking of styles of variables which are sealed off from one another so utterly that it is commonly ungrammatical to use a variable of one style where a variable of another style would be grammatical. A language which exploits this sort of basic compartmentalization of variables is that of Russell's theory of logical types. However, I think many of us overstress the theory of types to the neglect of its coeval alternative, Zermelo's set theory, and its descendants. In a notation of the latter tradition, carrying no distinctions in styles of variables, all questions regarding the acceptance not only of numbers in general but of abstract entities in general, or of physical objects in general, would become subclass questions—just as genuinely so as the question of there being black swans and prime numbers above a hundred. Thus Carnap's distinction between internal and external, based as it is upon a distinction between category questions and subclass questions, is of little concern to us apart from the adoption of something like the theory of types. I am one of those who have tended for many years not to adopt the theory of types.

Actually the case is a little worse than I have thus far represented it. Even if we adopt the theory of types we remain free to adopt the course which Russell himself adopted under the name of *typical ambiguity*—thus abandoning the use of a distinctive style of variables for every type. Russell uses his device in moderation, but we can go farther and use just a single style of variables for all types. The theory of types remains in force in this way: only those formulas are admitted as grammatical which *could,* by a one-to-one rewriting of variables, be turned into meaningful formulas of explicit type theory with distinctive styles of variables for all types.

This sort of indirect conformity to the theory of types, on the part of formulas written with a single style of variables, is a feature which I have called *stratification;* and it can be defined also directly, without any appeal to a supposedly more fundamental notation involving distinctive styles of variables. Stratification is simply freedom, on the part of the variables in a formula, from certain repetition patterns in connection with the symbol of class membership.

Next we can even abandon Russell's notion of a hierarchical universe of entities disposed into logical types; nothing remains of type theory except an ultimate grammatical restriction on the sorts of repetition patterns which variables are allowed to exhibit in formulas. Yet formally our logic, refurbished as described, is indistinguishable from Russell's theory of types plus Russell's convention of typical ambiguity. Now the point of this logical digression is that even under the theory of types the use of distinctive styles of variables, explicitly or even implicitly, is the most casual editorial detail.

I argued before that the distinction between category questions and subclass questions is of little concern apart from the adoption of something like the theory of types. But what I now think to have shown is that it is of little concern even under the theory of types. It is a distinction which is not invariant under logically irrelevant changes of typography.

I have doubly warranted hopes of persuading Carnap to abandon this particular distinction. First, as argued, I find it ill grounded. But second, also, I think it is a distinction which he can perfectly well discard compatibly with the philosophical purpose of the paper under discussion. No more than the distinction between *analytic* and *synthetic* is needed in support of Carnap's doctrine that the statements commonly thought of as ontological, viz., statements such as 'There are physical objects,' 'There are classes,' 'There are numbers,' are analytic or contradictory given the language. No more than the distinction between analytic and synthetic is needed in support of his doctrine that the statements commonly thought of as ontological are proper matters of contention only in the form of linguistic proposals. The contrast which he wants between those ontological statements and empirical existence statements such as 'There are black swans' is clinched by the distinction of analytic and synthetic. True, there is in these terms no contrast between analytic statements of an ontological kind and other analytic statements of existence such as 'There are prime numbers above a hundred'; but I don't see why he should care about this.

However, this is not an end of my dissent. On the contrary, the basic point of contention has just emerged: the distinction between analytic and synthetic itself. Carnap correctly states in a footnote:

> Quine does not acknowledge the distinction which I emphasize above [viz., the distinction between ontological questions and factual questions of existence], because according to his general conception there are no sharp boundary lines between logical and factual truth, between questions of meaning and questions of fact, between the acceptance of a language structure and the acceptance of an assertion formulated in the language.

I have set down my misgivings regarding the distinction between analytic and synthetic in a recent paper, "Two Dogmas of Empiricism," and will not retrace those steps here. Let me merely stress the consequence: if there is no proper distinction between analytic and synthetic, then no basis at all remains for the contrast which Carnap urges between ontological statements and empirical statements of existence. Ontological questions then end up on a par with questions of natural science.

Within natural science there is a continuum of gradations, from the statements which report observations to those which reflect basic features say of quantum theory or the theory of relativity. The view which I end up with, in the paper last cited, is that statements of ontology or even of mathematics and logic form a continuation of this continuum, a continuation which is perhaps yet more remote from observation than are the central principles of quantum theory or relativity. The differences here are in my view differences only in degree and not in kind. Science is a unified structure, and in principle it is the structure as a whole, and not its component statements one by one, that experience confirms or shows to be imperfect. Carnap maintains that ontological questions, and likewise questions of logical or mathematical principle, are questions not of fact but of choosing a convenient conceptual scheme or framework for science; and with this I agree only if the same be conceded for every scientific hypothesis.

IV

EPISTEMOLOGY AND PHILOSOPHY OF MIND

15

EPISTEMOLOGY NATURALIZED

Epistemology is concerned with the foundations of science. Conceived thus broadly, epistemology includes the study of the foundations of mathematics as one of its departments. Specialists at the turn of the century thought that their efforts in this particular department were achieving notable success: mathematics seemed to reduce altogether to logic. In a more recent perspective this reduction is seen to be better describable as a reduction to logic and set theory. This correction is a disappointment epistemologically, since the firmness and obviousness that we associate with logic cannot be claimed for set theory. But still the success achieved in the foundations of mathematics remains exemplary by comparative standards, and we can illuminate the rest of epistemology somewhat by drawing parallels to this department.

Studies in the foundations of mathematics divide symmetrically into two sorts, conceptual and doctrinal. The conceptual studies are concerned with meaning, the doctrinal with truth. The conceptual studies are concerned with clarifying concepts by defining them, some in terms of others. The doctrinal studies are concerned with establishing laws by proving them, some on the basis of others. Ideally the obscurer concepts would be defined in terms of the clearer ones so as to maximize clarity, and the less obvious laws would be proved from the more obvious ones so as to maximize certainty. Ideally the definitions would generate all the concepts from clear and distinct ideas, and the proofs would generate all the theorems from self-evident truths.

The two ideals are linked. For, if you define all the concepts by use of some favored subset of them, you thereby show how to translate all theorems into these favored terms. The clearer these terms are, the likelier it is that the truths couched in them will be obviously true, or derivable from obvious truths. If in particular the concepts of mathematics were all reducible to the clear terms of logic, then all the truths of mathematics would go over into truths of logic; and surely the truths of logic are all obvious or at least potentially obvious, i.e., derivable from obvious truths by individually obvious steps.

This particular outcome is in fact denied us, however, since mathematics reduces only to set theory and not to logic proper. Such reduction still enhances clarity, but only because of the interrelations that emerge and not because the end terms of the analysis are clearer than others. As for the end truths, the axioms of set theory, these have less obviousness and certainty to recommend them than do most of the mathematical theorems that we would derive from them. Moreover, we know from Gödel's work that no consistent axiom system can cover mathematics even when we renounce self-evidence. Reduction in the foundations of mathematics remains mathematically and philosophically fascinating, but it does not do what the epistemologist would like of it: it does not reveal the ground of mathematical knowledge, it does not show how mathematical certainty is possible.

Still there remains a helpful thought, regarding epistemology generally, in that duality of structure which was especially conspicuous in the foundations of mathematics. I refer to the bifurcation into a theory of concepts, or meaning, and a theory of doctrine, or truth; for this applies to the epistemology of natural knowledge no less than to the foundations of mathematics. The parallel is as follows. Just as mathematics is to be reduced to logic, or logic and set theory, so natural knowledge is to be based somehow on sense experience. This means explaining the notion of body in sensory terms; here is the conceptual side. And it means justifying our knowledge of truths of nature in sensory terms; here is the doctrinal side of the bifurcation.

Hume pondered the epistemology of natural knowledge on both sides of the bifurcation, the conceptual and the doctrinal. His handling of the conceptual side of the problem, the explanation of body in sensory terms, was bold and simple: he identified bodies outright with the sense impressions. If common sense distinguishes between the material apple and our sense impressions of it on the ground that the apple is one and enduring while the impressions are many and fleeting, then, Hume held, so much the worse for common sense; the notion of its being the same apple on one occasion and another is a vulgar confusion.

Nearly a century after Hume's *Treatise,* the same view of bodies was espoused by the early American philosopher Alexander Bryan Johnson.[1] "The word iron names an associated sight and feel," Johnson wrote.

What then of the doctrinal side, the justification of our knowledge of truths about nature? Here, Hume despaired. By his identification of bodies with impressions he did succeed in construing some singular statements about bodies as indubitable truths, yes; as truths about impressions, directly known. But general statements, also singular statements about the future, gained no increment of certainty by being construed as about impressions.

On the doctrinal side, I do not see that we are farther along today than where Hume left us. The Humean predicament is the human predicament. But on the conceptual side there has been progress. There the crucial step forward was made already before Alexander Bryan Johnson's day, although Johnson did not emulate it. It was made by Bentham in his theory of fictions. Bentham's step was the recognition of contextual definition, or what he called paraphrasis. He recognized that to explain a term we do not need to specify an object for it to refer to, nor even specify a synonymous word or phrase; we need only show, by whatever means, how to translate all the whole sentences in which the term is to be used. Hume's and Johnson's desperate measure of identifying bodies with impressions ceased to be the only conceivable way of making sense of talk of bodies, even granted that impressions were the only reality. One could undertake to explain talk of bodies in terms of talk of impressions by translating one's whole sentences about bodies into whole sentences about impressions, without equating the bodies themselves to anything at all.

This idea of contextual definition, or recognition of the sentence as the primary vehicle of meaning, was indispensable to the ensuing developments in the foundations of mathematics. It was explicit in Frege, and it attained its full flower in Russell's doctrine of singular descriptions as incomplete symbols.

Contextual definition was one of two resorts that could be expected to have a liberating effect upon the conceptual side of the epistemology of natural knowledge. The other is resort to the resources of set theory as auxiliary concepts. The epistemologist who is willing to eke out his austere ontology of sense impressions with these set-theoretic auxiliaries is suddenly rich: he has not just his impressions to play with, but sets of

1. A. B. Johnson, *A Treatise on Language* (New York, 1836; Berkeley, 1947).

them, and sets of sets, and so on up. Constructions in the foundations of mathematics have shown that such set-theoretic aids are a powerful addition; after all, the entire glossary of concepts of classical mathematics is constructible from them. Thus equipped, our epistemologist may not need either to identify bodies with impressions or to settle for contextual definition; he may hope to find in some subtle construction of sets upon sets of sense impressions a category of objects enjoying just the formula properties that he wants for bodies.

The two resorts are very unequal in epistemological status. Contextual definition is unassailable. Sentences that have been given meaning as wholes are undeniably meaningful, and the use they make of their component terms is therefore meaningful, regardless of whether any translations are offered for those terms in isolation. Surely Hume and A. B. Johnson would have used contextual definition with pleasure if they had thought of it. Recourse to sets, on the other hand, is a drastic ontological move, a retreat from the austere ontology of impressions. There are philosophers who would rather settle for bodies outright than accept all these sets, which amount, after all, to the whole abstract ontology of mathematics.

This issue has not always been clear, however, owing to deceptive hints of continuity between elementary logic and set theory. This is why mathematics was once believed to reduce to logic, that is, to an innocent and unquestionable logic, and to inherit these qualities. And this is probably why Russell was content to resort to sets as well as to contextual definition when in *Our Knowledge of the External World* and elsewhere he addressed himself to the epistemology of natural knowledge, on its conceptual side.

To account for the external world as a logical construct of sense data—such, in Russell's terms, was the program. It was Carnap, in his *Der logische Aufbau der Welt* of 1928, who came nearest to executing it.

This was the conceptual side of epistemology; what of the doctrinal? There the Humean predicament remained unaltered. Carnap's constructions, if carried successfully to completion, would have enabled us to translate all sentences about the world into terms of sense data, or observation, plus logic and set theory. But the mere fact that a sentence is *couched* in terms of observation, logic, and set theory does not mean that it can be *proved* from observation sentences by logic and set theory. The most modest of generalizations about observable traits will cover more cases than its utterer can have had occasion actually to observe.

The hopelessness of grounding natural science upon immediate experience in a firmly logical way was acknowledged. The Cartesian quest for certainty had been the remote motivation of epistemology, both on its conceptual and its doctrinal side; but that quest was seen as a lost cause. To endow the truths of nature with the full authority of immediate experience was as forlorn a hope as hoping to endow the truths of mathematics with the potential obviousness of elementary logic.

What then could have motivated Carnap's heroic efforts on the conceptual side of epistemology, when hope of certainty on the doctrinal side was abandoned? There were two good reasons still. One was that such constructions could be expected to elicit and clarify the sensory evidence for science, even if the inferential steps between sensory evidence and scientific doctrine must fall short of certainty. The other reason was that such constructions would deepen our understanding of our discourse about the world, even apart from questions of evidence; it would make all cognitive discourse as clear as observation terms and logic and, I must regretfully add, set theory.

It was sad for epistemologists, Hume and others, to have to acquiesce in the impossibility of strictly deriving the science of the external world from sensory evidence. Two cardinal tenets of empiricism remained unassailable, however, and so remain to this day. One is that whatever evidence there *is* for science *is* sensory evidence. The other, to which I shall recur, is that all inculcation of meanings of words must rest ultimately on sensory evidence. Hence the continuing attractiveness of the idea of a *logischer Aufbau* in which the sensory content of discourse would stand forth explicitly.

If Carnap had successfully carried such a construction through, how could he have told whether it was the right one? The question would have had no point. He was seeking what he called a *rational reconstruction*. Any construction of physicalistic discourse in terms of sense experience, logic, and set theory would have been seen as satisfactory if it made the physicalistic discourse come out right. If there is one way there are many, but any would be a great achievement.

But why all this creative reconstruction, all this make-believe? The stimulation of his sensory receptors is all the evidence anybody has had to go on, ultimately, in arriving at his picture of the world. Why not just see how this construction really proceeds? Why not settle for psychology? Such a surrender of the epistemological burden to psychology is a move that was disallowed in earlier times as circular reasoning. If the epistemologist's goal is validation of the grounds of empirical science, he defeats his purpose by using psychology or other empirical science in the validation. However, such scruples against circularity have little point once we have stopped dreaming of deducing science from observations. If we are out simply to understand the link between observation and science, we are well advised to use any available information, including that provided by the very science whose link with observation we are seeking to understand.

But there remains a different reason, unconnected with fears of circularity, for still favoring creative reconstruction. We should like to be able to *translate* science into logic and observation terms and set theory. This would be a great epistemological achievement, for it would show all the rest of the concepts of science to be theoretically superfluous. It would legitimize them—to whatever degree the concepts of set theory, logic, and observation are themselves legitimate—by showing that everything done with the one apparatus could in principle be done with the other. If psychology itself could deliver a truly translational reduction of this kind, we should welcome it; but certainly it cannot, for certainly we did not grow up learning definitions of physicalistic language in terms of a prior language of set theory, logic, and observation. Here, then, would be good reason for persisting in a rational reconstruction: we want to establish the essential innocence of physical concepts, by showing them to be theoretically dispensable.

The fact is, though, that the construction which Carnap outlined in *Der logische Aufbau der Welt* does not give translational reduction either. It would not even if the outline were filled in. The crucial point comes where Carnap is explaining how to assign sense qualities to positions in physical space and time. These assignments are to be made in such a way as to fulfill, as well as possible, certain desiderata which he states, and with growth of experience the assignments are to be revised to suit. This plan, however illuminating, does not offer any key to *translating* the sentences of science into terms of observation, logic, and set theory.

We must despair of any such reduction. Carnap had despaired of it by 1936, when, in "Testability and Meaning,"[2] he introduced so-called *reduction forms* of a type weaker than definition. Definitions had shown always how to translate sentences into equivalent sentences. Contextual

2. *Philosophy of Science* 3 (1936), pp. 419–471; 4 (1937), pp. 1–40.

definition of a term showed how to translate sentences containing the term into equivalent sentences lacking the term. Reduction forms of Carnap's liberalized kind, on the other hand, do not in general give equivalences; they give implications. They explain a new term, if only partially, by specifying some sentences which are implied by sentences containing the term, and other sentences which imply sentences containing the term.

It is tempting to suppose that the countenancing of reduction forms in this liberal sense is just one further step of liberalization comparable to the earlier one, taken by Bentham, of countenancing contextual definition. The former and sterner kind of rational reconstruction might have been represented as a fictitious history in which we imagined our ancestors introducing the terms of physicalistic discourse on a phenomenalistic and set-theoretic basis by a succession of contextual definitions. The new and more liberal kind of rational reconstruction is a fictitious history in which we imagine our ancestors introducing those terms by a succession rather of reduction forms of the weaker sort.

This, however, is a wrong comparison. The fact is rather that the former and sterner kind of rational reconstruction, where definition reigned, embodied no fictitious history at all. It was nothing more nor less than a set of directions—or would have been, if successful—for accomplishing everything in terms of phenomena and set theory that we now accomplish in terms of bodies. It would have been a true reduction by translation, a legitimation by elimination. *Definire est eliminare.* Rational reconstruction by Carnap's later and looser reduction forms does none of this.

To relax the demand for definition, and settle for a kind of reduction that does not eliminate, is to renounce the last remaining advantage that we supposed rational reconstruction to have over straight psychology; namely, the advantage of translational reduction. If all we hope for is a reconstruction that links science to experience in explicit ways short of translation, then it would seem more sensible to settle for psychology. Better to discover how science is in fact developed and learned than to fabricate a fictitious structure to a similar effect.

The empiricist made one major concession when he despaired of deducing the truths of nature from sensory evidence. In despairing now even of translating those truths into terms of observation and logico-mathematical auxiliaries, he makes another major concession. For suppose we hold, with the old empiricist Peirce, that the very meaning of a statement consists in the difference its truth would make to possible experience. Might we not formulate, in a chapter-length sentence in observational language, all the difference that the truth of a given statement might make to experience, and might we not then take all this as the translation? Even if the difference that the truth of the statement would make to experience ramifies indefinitely, we might still hope to embrace it all in the logical implications of our chapter-length formulation, just as we can axiomatize an infinity of theorems. In giving up hope of such translation, then, the empiricist is conceding that the empirical meanings of typical statements about the external world are inaccessible and ineffable.

How is this inaccessibility to be explained? Simply on the ground that the experiential implications of a typical statement about bodies are too complex for finite axiomatization, however lengthy? No; I have a different explanation. It is that the typical statement about bodies has no fund of experiential implications it can call its own. A substantial mass of theory, taken together, will commonly have experiential implications; this is how we make verifiable predictions. We may not be able to explain why we arrive at theories which make successful predictions, but we do arrive at such theories.

Sometimes also an experience implied by a theory fails to come off; and then, ideally, we declare the theory false. But the failure falsifies only a block of theory as a whole, a conjunction of many statements. The failure shows that one or more of those statements is false, but it does not show which. The predicted experiences, true and false, are not implied by any one of the component statements of the theory rather than another. The component statements simply do not have empirical meanings, by Peirce's standard; but a sufficiently inclusive portion of theory does. If we can aspire to a sort of *logischer Aufbau der Welt* at all, it must be to one in which the texts slated for translation into observational and logico-mathematical terms are mostly broad theories taken as wholes, rather than just terms or short sentences. The translation of a theory would be a ponderous axiomatization of all the experiential difference that the truth of the theory would make. It would be a queer translation, for it would translate the whole but none of the parts. We might better speak in such a case not of translation but simply of observational evidence for theories; and we may, following Peirce, still fairly call this the empirical meaning of the theories.

These considerations raise a philosophical question even about ordinary unphilosophical translation, such as from English into Arunta or

Chinese. For, if the English sentences of a theory have their meaning only together as a body, then we can justify their translation into Arunta only together as a body. There will be no justification for pairing off the component English sentences with component Arunta sentences, except as these correlations make the translation of the theory as a whole come out right. Any translations of the English sentences into Arunta sentences will be as correct as any other, so long as the net empirical implications of the theory as a whole are preserved in translation. But it is to be expected that many different ways of translating the component sentences, essentially different individually, would deliver the same empirical implications for the theory as a whole; deviations in the translation of one component sentence could be compensated for in the translation of another component sentence. Insofar, there can be no ground for saying which of two glaringly unlike translations of individual sentences is right.[3]

For an uncritical mentalist, no such indeterminacy threatens. Every term and every sentence is a label attached to an idea, simple or complex, which is stored in the mind. When on the other hand we take a verification theory of meaning seriously, the indeterminacy would appear to be inescapable. The Vienna Circle espoused a verification theory of meaning but did not take it seriously enough. If we recognize with Peirce that the meaning of a sentence turns purely on what would count as evidence for its truth, and if we recognize with Duhem that theoretical sentences have their evidence not as single sentences but only as larger blocks of theory, then the indeterminacy of translation of theoretical sentences is the natural conclusion. And most sentences, apart from observation sentences, are theoretical. This conclusion, conversely, once it is embraced, seals the fate of any general notion of propositional meaning or, for that matter, state of affairs.

Should the unwelcomeness of the conclusion persuade us to abandon the verification theory of meaning? Certainly not. The sort of meaning that is basic to translation, and to the learning of one's own language, is necessarily empirical meaning and nothing more. A child learns his first words and sentences by hearing and using them in the presence of appropriate stimuli. These must be external stimuli, for they must act both on the child and on the speaker from whom he is learning.[4] Language is so-

3. See above, pp. 2ff. [Chapter 5].
4. See above, p. 28 (W. V. Quine, "Ontological Relativity," in *Ontological Relativity and Other Essays* [New York: Columbia University Press, 1969]).

cially inculcated and controlled; the inculcation and control turn strictly on the keying of sentences to shared stimulation. Internal factors may vary *ad libitum* without prejudice to communication as long as the keying of language to external stimuli is undisturbed. Surely one has no choice but to be an empiricist so far as one's theory of linguistic meaning is concerned.

What I have said of infant learning applies equally to the linguist's learning of a new language in the field. If the linguist does not lean on related languages for which there are previously accepted translation practices, then obviously he has no data but the concomitances of native utterance and observable stimulus situation. No wonder there is indeterminacy of translation—for of course only a small fraction of our utterances report concurrent external stimulation. Granted, the linguist will end up with unequivocal translations of everything; but only by making many arbitrary choices—arbitrary even though unconscious—along the way. Arbitrary? By this I mean that different choices could still have made everything come out right that is susceptible in principle to any kind of check.

Let me link up, in a different order, some of the points I have made. The crucial consideration behind my argument for the indeterminacy of translation was that a statement about the world does not always or usually have a separable fund of empirical consequences that it can call its own. That consideration served also to account for the impossibility of an epistemological reduction of the sort where every sentence is equated to a sentence in observational and logico-mathematical terms. And the impossibility of that sort of epistemological reduction dissipated the last advantage that rational reconstruction seemed to have over psychology.

Philosophers have rightly despaired of translating everything into observational and logico-mathematical terms. They have despaired of this even when they have not recognized, as the reason for this irreducibility, that the statements largely do not have their private bundles of empirical consequences. And some philosophers have seen in this irreducibility the bankruptcy of epistemology. Carnap and the other logical positivists of the Vienna Circle had already pressed the term "metaphysics" into pejorative use, as connoting meaninglessness; and the term "epistemology" was next. Wittgenstein and his followers, mainly at Oxford, found a residual philosophical vocation in therapy: in curing philosophers of the delusion that there were epistemological problems.

But I think that at this point it may be more useful to say rather that epistemology still goes on, though in a new setting and a clarified status. Epistemology, or something like it, simply falls into place as a chapter of psychology and hence of natural science. It studies a natural phenomenon, viz., a physical human subject. This human subject is accorded a certain experimentally controlled input—certain patterns of irradiation in assorted frequencies, for instance—and in the fullness of time the subject delivers as output a description of the three-dimensional external world and its history. The relation between the meager input and the torrential output is a relation that we are prompted to study for somewhat the same reasons that always prompted epistemology; namely, in order to see how evidence relates to theory, and in what ways one's theory of nature transcends any available evidence.

Such a study could still include, even, something like the old rational reconstruction, to whatever degree such reconstruction is practicable; for imaginative constructions can afford hints of actual psychological processes, in much the way that mechanical simulations can. But a conspicuous difference between old epistemology and the epistemological enterprise in this new psychological setting is that we can now make free use of empirical psychology.

The old epistemology aspired to contain, in a sense, natural science; it would construct it somehow from sense data. Epistemology in its new setting, conversely, is contained in natural science, as a chapter of psychology. But the old containment remains valid too, in its way. We are studying how the human subject of our study posits bodies and projects his physics from his data, and we appreciate that our position in the world is just like his. Our very epistemological enterprise, therefore, and the psychology wherein it is a component chapter, and the whole of natural science wherein psychology is a component book—all this is our own construction or projection from stimulations like those we were meting out to our epistemological subject. There is thus reciprocal containment, though containment in different senses: epistemology in natural science and natural science in epistemology.

This interplay is reminiscent again of the old threat of circularity, but it is all right now that we have stopped dreaming of deducing science from sense data. We are after an understanding of science as an institution or process in the world, and we do not intend that understanding to be any better than the science which is its object. This attitude is indeed one that Neurath was already urging in Vienna Circle days, with his parable of the mariner who has to rebuild his boat while staying afloat in it.

One effect of seeing epistemology in a psychological setting is that it resolves a stubborn old enigma of epistemological priority. Our retinas are irradiated in two dimensions, yet we see things as three-dimensional without conscious inference. Which is to count as observation—the unconscious two-dimensional reception or the conscious three-dimensional apprehension? In the old epistemological context the conscious form had priority, for we were out to justify our knowledge of the external world by rational reconstruction, and that demands awareness. Awareness ceased to be demanded when we gave up trying to justify our knowledge of the external world by rational reconstruction. What to count as observation now can be settled in terms of the stimulation of sensory receptors, let consciousness fall where it may.

The Gestalt psychologists' challenge to sensory atomism, which seemed so relevant to epistemology forty years ago, is likewise deactivated. Regardless of whether sensory atoms or Gestalten are what favor the forefront of our consciousness, it is simply the stimulations of our sensory receptors that are best looked upon as the input to our cognitive mechanism. Old paradoxes about unconscious data and inference, old problems about chains of inference that would have to be completed too quickly—these no longer matter.

In the old anti-psychologistic days the question of epistemological priority was moot. What is epistemologically prior to what? Are Gestalten prior to sensory atoms because they are noticed, or should we favor sensory atoms on some more subtle ground? Now that we are permitted to appeal to physical stimulation, the problem dissolves; A is epistemologically prior to B if A is causally nearer than B to the sensory receptors. Or, what is in some ways better, just talk explicitly in terms of causal proximity to sensory receptors and drop the talk of epistemological priority.

Around 1932 there was debate in the Vienna Circle over what to count as observation sentences, or *Protokollsätze*.[5] One position was that they had the form of reports of sense impressions. Another was that they were statements of an elementary sort about the external world, e.g., "A red cube is standing on the table." Another, Neurath's, was that they had the form of reports of relations between percipients and external things: "Otto now sees a red cube on the table." The worst of it was that there seemed to be no objective way of settling the matter: no way of making real sense of the question.

5. Carnap and Neurath in *Erkenntnis* 3 (1932), pp. 204–228.

Let us now try to view the matter unreservedly in the context of the external world. Vaguely speaking, what we want of observation sentences is that they be the ones in closest causal proximity to the sensory receptors. But how is such proximity to be gauged? The idea may be rephrased this way: observation sentences are sentences which, as we learn language, are most strongly conditioned to concurrent sensory stimulation rather than to stored collateral information. Thus let us imagine a sentence queried for our verdict as to whether it is true or false; queried for our assent or dissent. Then the sentence is an observation sentence if our verdict depends only on the sensory stimulation present at the time.

But a verdict cannot depend on present stimulation to the exclusion of stored information. The very fact of our having learned the language evinces much storing of information, and of information without which we should be in no position to give verdicts on sentences however observational. Evidently then we must relax our definition of observation sentence to read thus: a sentence is an observation sentence if all verdicts on it depend on present sensory stimulation and on no stored information beyond what goes into understanding the sentence.

This formulation raises another problem: how are we to distinguish between information that goes into understanding a sentence and information that goes beyond? This is the problem of distinguishing between analytic truth, which issues from the mere meanings of words, and synthetic truth, which depends on more than meanings. Now I have long maintained that this distinction is illusory. There is one step toward such a distinction, however, which does make sense: a sentence that is true by mere meanings of words should be expected, at least if it is simple, to be subscribed to by all fluent speakers in the community. Perhaps the controversial notion of analyticity can be dispensed with, in our definition of observation sentence, in favor of this straightforward attribute of community-wide acceptance.

This attribute is of course no explication of analyticity. The community would agree that there have been black dogs, yet none who talk of analyticity would call this analytic. My rejection of the analyticity notion just means drawing no line between what goes into the mere understanding of the sentences of a language and what else the community sees eye-to-eye on. I doubt that an objective distinction can be made between meaning and such collateral information as is community-wide.

Turning back then to our task of defining observation sentences, we get this: an observation sentence is one on which all speakers of the language give the same verdict when given the same concurrent stimulation.

To put the point negatively, an observation sentence is one that is not sensitive to differences in past experience within the speech community.

This formulation accords perfectly with the traditional role of the observation sentence as the court of appeal of scientific theories. For by our definition the observation sentences are the sentences on which all members of the community will agree under uniform stimulation. And what is the criterion of membership in the same community? Simply general fluency of dialogue. This criterion admits of degrees, and indeed we may usefully take the community more narrowly for some studies than for others. What count as observation sentences for a community of specialists would not always so count for a larger community.

There is generally no subjectivity in the phrasing of observation sentences, as we are now conceiving them; they will usually be about bodies. Since the distinguishing trait of an observation sentence is intersubjective agreement under agreeing stimulation, a corporeal subject matter is likelier than not.

The old tendency to associate observation sentences with a subjective sensory subject matter is rather an irony when we reflect that observation sentences are also meant to be the intersubjective tribunal of scientific hypotheses. The old tendency was due to the drive to base science on something firmer and prior in the subject's experience; but we dropped that project.

The dislodging of epistemology from its old status of first philosophy loosed a wave, we saw, of epistemological nihilism. This mood is reflected somewhat in the tendency of Polányi, Kuhn, and the late Russell Hanson to belittle the role of evidence and to accentuate cultural relativism. Hanson ventured even to discredit the idea of observation, arguing that so-called observations vary from observer to observer with the amount of knowledge that the observers bring with them. The veteran physicist looks at some apparatus and sees an x-ray tube. The neophyte, looking at the same place, observes rather "a glass and metal instrument replete with wires, reflectors, screws, lamps, and pushbuttons."[6] One man's observation is another man's closed book or flight of fancy. The notion of observation as the impartial and objective source of evidence for science is bankrupt. Now my answer to the x-ray example was already hinted a little while back: what counts as an observation sentence

6. N. R. Hanson, "Observation and Interpretation," in S. Morgenbesser (ed.), *Philosophy of Science Today* (New York: Basic Books, 1966).

varies with the width of community considered. But we can also always get an absolute standard by taking in all speakers of the language, or most.[7] It is ironical that philosophers, finding the old epistemology untenable as a whole, should react by repudiating a part which has only now moved into clear focus.

Clarification of the notion of observation sentence is a good thing, for the notion is fundamental in two connections. These two correspond to the duality that I remarked upon early in this lecture: the duality between concept and doctrine, between knowing what a sentence means and knowing whether it is true. The observation sentence is basic to both enterprises. Its relation to doctrine, to our knowledge of what is true, is very much the traditional one: observation sentences are the repository of evidence for scientific hypotheses. Its relation to meaning is fundamental too, since observation sentences are the ones we are in a position to learn to understand first, both as children and as field linguists. For observation sentences are precisely the ones that we can correlate with observable circumstances of the occasion of utterance or assent, independently of variations in the past histories of individual informants. They afford the only entry to a language.

The observation sentence is the cornerstone of semantics. For it is, as we just saw, fundamental to the learning of meaning. Also, it is where meaning is firmest. Sentences higher up in theories have no empirical consequences they can call their own; they confront the tribunal of sensory evidence only in more or less inclusive aggregates. The observation sentence, situated at the sensory periphery of the body scientific, is the minimal verifiable aggregate; it has an empirical content all its own and wears it on its sleeve.

The predicament of the indeterminacy of translation has little bearing on observation sentences. The equating of an observation sentence of our language to an observation sentence of another language is mostly a matter of empirical generalization; it is a matter of identity between the range of stimulations that would prompt assent to the one sentence and the range of stimulations that would prompt assent to the other.[8]

7. This qualification allows for occasional deviants such as the insane or the blind. Alternatively, such cases might be excluded by adjusting the level of fluency of dialogue whereby we define sameness of language. (For prompting this note and influencing the development of this paper also in more substantial ways, I am indebted to Burton Dreben.)

8. See Quine, *Word and Object,* pp. 31–46, 68.

It is no shock to the preconceptions of old Vienna to say that epistemology now becomes semantics. For epistemology remains centered as always on evidence, and meaning remains centered as always on verification; and evidence is verification. What is likelier to shock preconceptions is that meaning, once we get beyond observation sentences, ceases in general to have any clear applicability to single sentences; also that epistemology merges with psychology, as well as with linguistics.

This rubbing out of boundaries could contribute to progress, it seems to me, in philosophically interesting inquiries of a scientific nature. One possible area is perceptual norms. Consider, to begin with, the linguistic phenomenon of phonemes. We form the habit, in hearing the myriad variations of spoken sounds, of treating each as an approximation to one or another of a limited number of norms—around thirty altogether—constituting so to speak a spoken alphabet. All speech in our language can be treated in practice as sequences of just those thirty elements, thus rectifying small deviations. Now outside the realm of language also there is probably only a rather limited alphabet of perceptual norms altogether, toward which we tend unconsciously to rectify all perceptions. These, if experimentally identified, could be taken as epistemological building blocks, the working elements of experience. They might prove in part to be culturally variable, as phonemes are, and in part universal.

Again there is the area that the psychologist Donald T. Campbell calls evolutionary epistemology.[9] In this area there is work by Hüseyin Yilmaz, who shows how some structural traits of color perception could have been predicted from survival value.[10] And a more emphatically epistemological topic that evolution helps to clarify is induction, now that we are allowing epistemology the resources of natural science.[11]

9. D. T. Campbell, "Methodological Suggestions from a Comparative Psychology of Knowledge Processes," *Inquiry* 2 (1959), pp. 152–182.

10. Hüseyin Yilmaz, "On Color Vision and a New Approach to General Perception," in E. E. Bernard and M. R. Kare (eds.), *Biological Prototypes and Synthetic Systems* (New York: Plenum, 1962); "Perceptual Invariance and the Psychophysical Law," *Perception and Psychophysics* 2 (1967), pp. 533–538.

11. See "Natural Kinds," in Quine, *Ontological Relativity*.

16

NATURALISM; OR, LIVING WITHIN ONE'S MEANS

Names of philosophical positions are a necessary evil. They are necessary because we need to refer to a stated position or doctrine from time to time, and it would be tiresome to keep restating it. They are evil in that they come to be conceived as designating schools of thought, objects of loyalty from within and objects of obloquy from without, and hence obstacles, within and without, to the pursuit of truth.

In identifying the philosophical position that I call naturalism, then, I shall just be describing my own position, without prejudice to possibly divergent uses of the term. In *Theories and Things* I wrote that naturalism is "the recognition that it is within science itself, and not in some prior philosophy, that reality is to be identified and described"; again that it is "abandonment of the goal of a first philosophy prior to natural science" (pp. 21, 67). These characterizations convey the right mood, but they would fare poorly in a debate. How much qualifies as "science itself" and not "some prior philosophy"?

In science itself I certainly want to include the farthest flights of physics and cosmology, as well as experimental psychology, history, and the social sciences. Also mathematics, insofar at least as it is applied, for it is indispensable to natural science. What then am I excluding as "some prior philosophy," and why? Descartes' dualism between mind and body is called metaphysics, but it could as well be reckoned as science, however false. He even had a causal theory of the interaction of mind and body through the pineal gland. If I saw indirect explanatory benefit in positing sensibilia, possibilia, spirits, a Creator, I would joyfully accord them scientific status too, on a par with such avowedly scientific posits as quarks and black holes. What then *have* I banned under the name of prior philosophy?

Demarcation is not my purpose. My point in the characterizations of naturalism that I quoted is just that the *most* we can reasonably seek in support of an inventory and description of reality is testability of its observable consequences in the time-honored hypothetico-deductive way—whereof more anon. Naturalism need not cast aspersions on irresponsible metaphysics, however deserved, much less on soft sciences or on the speculative reaches of the hard ones, except insofar as a firmer basis is claimed for them than the experimental method itself.

Where naturalistic renunciation shows itself most clearly and significantly is in naturalistic epistemology. Various epistemologists, from Descartes to Carnap, had sought a foundation for natural science in mental entities, the flux of raw sense data. It was as if we might first fashion a self-sufficient and infallible lore of sense data, innocent of reference to physical things, and then build our theory of the external world somehow on that finished foundation. The naturalistic epistemologist dismisses this dream of prior sense-datum language, arguing that the positing of physical things is itself our indispensable tool for organizing and remembering what is otherwise, in James' words, a "blooming, buzzing confusion."

To account for knowledge of an external thing or event, accordingly, the naturalistic epistemologist looks rather to the external thing or event itself and the causal chain of stimulation from it to one's brain. In a paradigm case, light rays are reflected from the object to one's retina, activating a patch of nerve endings, each of which initiates a neural impulse to one or another center of the brain. Through intricate processes within the brain, finally, and abetted by imitation of other people or by instruction, a child comes in time to utter or assent to some rudimentary sentence at the end of such a causal chain. I call it an observation sentence. Examples are "It's cold," "It's raining," "(That's) milk," "(That's a) dog."

Customarily the experimental psychologist chooses one or another object or event, from somewhere along such a causal chain, to represent the chain, and this he calls the stimulus. Usually it is an event of his own devising. In one experiment it will be a flash or a buzz in the subject's vicinity, and in another it will be an ice cube or a shock at the subject's surface. For our more general purposes, not linked to any particular experiment, an economical strategy in defining the stimulus is to intercept the causal chains just at the subject's surface. Nothing is lost, for it is only from that point inward that the chains contribute to the subject's knowledge of the external world.

Indeed, even what reaches the subject's surface is relevant only if it triggers neural receptors. So we might for our purposes simply identify the subject's stimulus, over a given brief moment, with the temporally ordered set of sensory receptors triggered in that moment.

Still further economy might be sought by intercepting the causal chains rather at a deeper level—somewhere within the brain; for even the surface receptors that are triggered on any given occasion are largely without relevant effect on the subject's behavior. However, our knowledge of these deeper levels is still too sketchy. Moreover, as research increasingly penetrates these depths, we become aware of complexity and heterogeneity radically at variance with the neat simplicity at the surface. Each receptor, after all, admits of just two clean-cut states: triggered or not.

Moreover, the behaviorally irrelevant triggerings in a global stimulus can be defined out anyway, in due course, by appeal to perceptual similarity of stimuli. The receptors whose firing is *salient* in a given stimulus are the ones that it shares with all perceptually similar stimuli. Perceptual similarity itself can be measured, for a given individual, by reinforcement and extinction of responses.

So it seems best for present purposes to construe the subject's stimulus on a given occasion simply as his global neural intake on that occasion. But I shall refer to it only as neural intake, not stimulus, for other notions of stimulus are wanted in other studies, particularly where different subjects are to get the same stimulus. Neural intake is private, for subjects do not share receptors.

Perceptual similarity, then, is a relation between a subject's neural intakes. Though testable, it is a private affair; the intakes are *his,* and are perceptually more or less similar for *him.* Perceptual similarity is the basis of all learning, all habit formation, all expectation by induction from past experience; for we are innately disposed to expect similar events to have sequels that are similar to each other.

The association of observation sentences with neural intakes is many-many. Any one of a range of perceptually fairly similar intakes may prompt the subject's assent to any one of a range of semantically kindred sentences. But in contrast to the privacy of neural intakes, and the privacy of their perceptual similarity, observation sentences and their semantics are a public matter, since the child has to learn these from her elders. Her learning then depends indeed both on the public currency of the observation sentences and on a preestablished harmony of people's private scales of perceptual similarity. The harmony is formal, in this sense: if a witness finds the first of three scenes less similar to the second than to the third, another witness is apt to do likewise. This approximate harmony is preestablished in a shared gene pool. Different people's feelings still might not match, whatever that might mean.

This much is a naturalistic analogue or counterpart of the traditional epistemologist's phenomenalistic foundation in sense data. However, it pretends to plausibility in psychology, in genetics, and even in prehistory. Observation sentences have their antecedents in birdcalls and in the signal cries of the apes.

Building on this naturalistic foundation, then, in parallel to the old epistemologist's proposed construction of science on a foundation of sense data, the naturalist would venture a psychologically and historically plausible sketch of the individual's acquisition of science and perhaps the evolution of science down the ages, with an eye primarily to the logic of evidence. I will spare you most of that, for I have gone into it in *Word and Object* and better in *The Roots of Reference, Pursuit of Truth,* and elsewhere. There are just a couple of aspects that I want to remind you of.

One is reification, or the positing of objects. Observation sentences commonly contain words that refer to objects when used in mature discourse, but the infant first acquires such a sentence only as a seamless whole, conditioned—like the signal cry of the ape—to an appropriate range of global neural intakes. But there is a harbinger of reification already in our innate propensity, and that of other animals, to confer salience on those components of a neural intake that transmit corporeal patches of the visual field. It is what Donald Campbell calls our innate reification of bodies, but I construe reification rather in degrees. Special ways of compounding observation sentences mark further steps in the reification of bodies, and the job is complete only when the speaker has mastered past and future tense and knows about the unseen but continuous translation of an identical body through space between observations. It is only then that she makes sense of a body's being the same body from one observation to another despite intervening changes in appearance.

At that point the reification of bodies is full fledged. Reification of less conspicuous objects, notably abstract ones such as numbers and classes, takes further explaining, and admits of it. A crucial step there, as I see it, is mastery of relative clauses and pronouns.

This burgeoning language of science is a direct extension of the faltering language of observation. Segments of observation sentences carry over and become—some of them—terms for objects. Conversely, sentences learned only later by grammatical synthesis from a sophisticated vocabulary can come to qualify as observation sentences as well. For, what I take as definitive of observation sentences is just this pair of conditions: first, the speaker must be disposed to assent to the sentence or dissent from it outright on making the appropriate observation, irrespective of his interrupted line of thought if any, and second, the verdict must command the agreement of any witnesses from the appropriate language community. This second requirement, intersubjectivity, is needed in order that the child be able to learn observation sentences from his elders; and those sentences, some of them, are his indispensable entering wedge in acquiring cognitive language. Intersubjectivity of observation sentences is likewise essential at the other end, to assure objectivity of science.

The sharing of vocabulary by observation sentences and sentences of science was necessary not only for the emergence of scientific language; it is necessary also as a channel for the empirical testing of scientific hypotheses. The primordial hypotheses are what I call observation categoricals, compounded of pairs of observation sentences: thus "When it snows, it's cold." To check such a hypothesis experimentally, we contrive to put ourselves in a situation where the first component, "It's snowing," is observably fulfilled, and then we check for fulfillment of the second component. If it is fulfilled, the categorical remains standing until further notice. If it is not fulfilled, the categorical is refuted once for all.

I see this as the key to the empirical testing also of more sophisticated hypotheses. We conjoin the hypothesis in question to a set of already previously accepted statements, sufficient together to imply some observation categorical that was not implied by the previous set alone. Then we check the observation categorical.

The appeal to logical implication here presents no problem. The basic laws of logic are internalized in learning the use of the logical particles. For instance, the child learns by observation and parental correction that it is misuse of the conjunction "and" to affirm an "and" compound and then deny one of the components. The child has thus internalized one simple logical implication, namely that an "and" compound implies its components, on pain of simply getting a word wrong. Correspondingly for other basic implications, up to and including the laws of quantifiers and identity. Insofar I am with Lauener in recognizing analyticity.

Scientists of course do not trace all these links of implication from hypothesis to observation categorical. It would mean filling in all the logically requisite supporting statements, most of which are so familiar to him or so trivial as to go without saying. In practice, moreover, many tacit premises often express mere statistical trends or probabilities, which he will take in stride unless unexpected results prompt him to reconsider.

Still the deduction and checking of observation categoricals is the essence, surely, of the experimental method, the hypothetico-deductive method, the method, in Popper's words, of conjecture and refutation. It brings out that prediction of observable events is the ultimate test of scientific theory.

I speak of test, not purpose. The purpose of science is to be sought rather in intellectual curiosity and technology. In our prehistoric beginnings, however, the purpose of the first glimmerings of scientific theory *was* presumably prediction, insofar as purpose can be despiritualized into natural selection and survival value. This takes us back to our innate sense or standard of perceptual similarity, and the innate expectation that similars will have mutually similar sequels. In short, primitive induction.

Prediction is verbalized expectation. Conditional expectation, when correct, has survival value. Natural selection has accordingly favored innate standards of perceptual similarity that have harmonized with trends in our environment. Natural science, finally, is conditional expectation hypertrophied.

I said that prediction is not the main purpose of science, but only the test. It is a negative test at that, a test by refutation. As a further disavowal let me add, contrary to positivism, that a sentence does not even need to be testable in order to qualify as a respectable sentence of science. A sentence is testable, in my liberal or holistic sense, if adding it to previously accepted sentences clinches an observation categorical that was not implied by those previous sentences alone; but much good science is untestable even in this liberal sense. We believe many things because they fit in smoothly by analogy, or they symmetrize and simplify the overall design. Surely much history and social science is of this sort, and some hard science. Moreover, such acceptations are not idle fancy; their proliferation generates, every here and there, a hypothesis that can indeed be tested. Surely this is the major source of testable hypotheses and the growth of science.

The naturalization of epistemology, as I have been sketching it, is both a limitation and a liberation. The old quest for a foundation for natural science, firmer than science itself, is abandoned: that much is the limitation. The liberation is free access to the resources of natural science, without fear of circularity. The naturalistic epistemologist settles for what he can learn about the strategy, logic, and mechanics by which our elaborate theory of the physical world is in fact projected, or might be, or should be, from just that amorphous neural intake.

Is this sort of thing still philosophy? Naturalism brings a salutary blurring of such boundaries. Naturalistic philosophy is continuous with natural science. It undertakes to clarify, organize, and simplify the broadest and most basic concepts, and to analyze scientific method and evidence within the framework of science itself. The boundary between naturalistic philosophy and the rest of science is just a vague matter of degree.

Naturalism is naturally associated with physicalism, or materialism. I do not equate them, as witness my earlier remark on Cartesian dualism. I do embrace physicalism as a scientific position, but I could be dissuaded of it on future scientific grounds without being dissuaded of naturalism. Quantum mechanics today, indeed, in its neoclassical or Copenhagen interpretation, has a distinctly mentalistic ring.

My naturalism has evidently been boiling down to the claim that in our pursuit of truth about the world we cannot do better than our traditional scientific procedure, the hypothetico-deductive method. A rebuttal suggests itself here: surely mathematicians. The obvious defense against that rebuttal is to say that mathematical truths are not about the world. But this is not a defense of my choosing. In my view applied mathematics *is* about the world.

Thus consider again a case where we are testing a scientific hypothesis by conjoining it to some already accepted statements and deducing an observation categorical. Likely as not, some of those already accepted statements are purely mathematical. This is how pure mathematics gets applied. Whatever empirical content those already accepted statements can claim, then, from being needed in implying the observation categorical, is imbibed in particular by the mathematical ones.

Thus it is that I am inclined to blur the boundary between mathematics and natural science, no less than the boundary between philosophy and natural science. If it is protested that proved mathematical truths are not subject to subsequent refutation, my answer is that we safeguard them by choosing to revoke non-mathematical statements instead, in cases where a set of statements has been found conjointly to imply a false observation categorical. Reasons can be adduced for doing so; but enough.

That leaves open the vast proliferations of mathematics that there is no thought or prospect of applying. I see these domains as integral to our overall theory of reality only on sufferance: they are expressed in the same syntax and lexicon as applicable mathematics, and to exclude them as meaningless by *ad hoc* gerrymandering of our syntax would be thankless at best. So it is left to us to try to assess these sentences also as true or false, if we care to. Many are settled by the same laws that settle applicable mathematics. For the rest, I would settle them as far as practicable by considerations of economy, on a par with the decisions we make in natural science when trying to frame empirical hypotheses worthy of experimental testing.

Traditional epistemology was in part normative in intent. Naturalistic epistemology, in contrast, is viewed by Henri Lauener and others as purely descriptive. I disagree. Just as traditional epistemology on its speculative side gets naturalized into science, or next of kin, so on its normative side it gets naturalized into technology, the technology of scientizing.

What might be offered first of all as a norm of naturalized epistemology is *prediction of observation* as a test of a hypothesis. I think of this as more than a norm: as the name of the game. Science cannot all be tested, and the softer the science the sparser the tests; but when it *is* tested, the test is prediction of observation. Moreover, naturalism has no special claims on the principle, which is rather the crux of empiricism.

What are more distinctively naturalistic and technological are norms based on scientific findings. Thus science has pretty well established— subject to future disestablishment, as always—that our information about distant events and other people reaches us only through impact of rays and particles on our sensory receptors. A normative corollary is that we should be wary of astrologers, palmists, and other soothsayers. Think twice about E.S.P.

For a richer array of norms, vague in various degrees, we may look to the heuristics of hypothesis: how to think up a hypothesis worth testing. This is where considerations of conservatism and simplicity come in, and, at a more technical level, probability theory and statistics. In practice those technical matters spill over also, as I remarked, to complicate the hypothetico-deductive method itself.

I said at the beginning of this paper that according to naturalism is it within science itself and not some prior philosophy that reality is to be identified. Farther along in a more narrowly scientific spirit, I speculated on how we round out our recognition of objects *as* objects, bit by bit, with our acquisition of language and science. These matters call now for some more broadly philosophical reflections.

Let us recall, to begin with, that the association of observation sentences with neural intake is holophrastic. What objects the component words may designate in other contexts is irrelevant to the association. This is obviously so if the observation sentence is to be acquired as a first step in language learning; but the association is equally direct and holophrastic in its operation even if the sentence was acquired through synthesis of its words, and gained its immediacy only through subsequent familiarization.

Moreover, the specifics of designation and denotation are not only indifferent to the association of observation sentences to neural intake; they are indifferent also to the implication of observation categoricals by scientific theory. It is logical implication; and logic, unlike set theory and the rest of mathematics, responds to no traits of objects beyond sameness and difference. So we must conclude that objects of any sort figure only as neutral nodes in the structure of scientific theory, so far as empirical evidence is concerned. We can arbitrarily change the values of our variables, the designata of our names, and the denotata of our predicates without disturbing the evidence, so long anyway as the new objects are explicitly correlated one to one with the old. Such is the indeterminacy of reference, as I have come to call it.

At first it is perhaps alarming. We are left with no basis, it would seem, for judging whether we are talking about familiar things or some arbitrary proxies. The shock subsides, however, when we reflect on a homely example or two. Thus think of a body in the scientific framework of space and time. Insofar as you specify the precise sinuous filament of four-dimensional space-time that the body takes up in the course of its career, you have fixed the object uniquely. We could go farther and *identify* the object, a chipmunk perhaps, with its portion of space-time, thus saying that it is tiny at its early end and bigger at its late end. The move is artificial, but actually it confers a bit of economy, if we are going to have the space-time anyway. Subjective connotations of brownness, softness, swift and erratic movement, and the rest simply carry over. Surely all matters of evidence remain undisturbed. We are even prepared to say that it was what a body was all along, an appropriately filled-in portion of space-time as over against empty ones.

Next we might identify space-time regions in turn with the sets of quadruples of numbers that determine them in some arbitrarily adopted frame of coordinates. We can transfer sensory connotations now to this abstract mathematical object, and still there is no violence to scientific evidence. To speak intuitively, nothing really happened.

Thus we can come to terms somewhat with the indeterminacy of reference, as applied to bodies and other sensible substances, by just letting the sensory connotations of the observation sentences carry over from the old objects to their proxies.

In the case of abstract objects such as numbers, devoid of sensory connotations, the indeterminacy of reference is already familiar. It is seen in Frege's so-called Caesar problem: the number five may be Julius Caesar. We happily use numbers without caring whether they be taken according to the Frege-Russell constructions or Ackermann's or von Neumann's. The point was dramatized long ago by F.P. Ramsey with his expedient of Ramsey sentences, as they have come to be called. Instead of invoking the abstract objects specifically, when certain of their properties are needed in an argument, the Ramsey sentence just says that there *are* objects with the properties, and then invokes the objects by variables without further identification. This expedient only works for abstract objects, however, used as auxiliaries here and there without regard to whether they remain the same objects from one context to another.

The indeterminacy of reference can be seen again in its full generality, as Davidson once remarked, by an examination of Tarski's classical truth definition. If a sentence comes out true under that definition, it continues to do so when objects are reassigned to its predicates in any one-to-one way.

These reflections on ontology are a salutary reminder that the ultimate data of science are limited to our neural intake, and that the very notion of object, concrete or abstract, is of our own making, along with the rest of natural science and mathematics. It is our overwhelmingly ingenious apparatus for systematizing, predicting, and partially controlling our intake, and we may take pride.

This conventionalist view of ontology appeals, I expect, to Henri Lauener. He in his pragmatism even settles for a plurality of scientific specialties, each with its working ontology, and no dream of an overarching, unifying fact of the matter.

Naturalism itself is noncommittal on this question of unity of science. Naturalism just sees it as a question within science itself, albeit a question more remote from observational checkpoints than the most speculative questions of the hard and soft sciences ordinarily so called.

Naturalism can still respect the drive, on the part of some of us, for a unified, all-purpose ontology. The drive is typical of the scientific temper, and of a piece with the drive for simplicity that shapes scientific hypotheses generally. Physicalism is its familiar manifestation, and physicalism is bound to have had important side effects in the framing of more special hypotheses in various branches of science; for physicalism puts a premium on hypotheses favorable to closer integration with physics itself. We have here a conspicuous case of what I touched on earlier: scientific hypotheses which, though not themselves testable, help to elicit others that are.

In any event, we are now seeing ontology as more utterly a human option than we used to. We are drawn to Lauener's pragmatism. Must we then conclude that true reality is beyond our ken? No, that would be to forsake naturalism. Rather, the notion of reality is itself part of the apparatus; and sticks, stones, atoms, quarks, numbers, and classes all are utterly real denizens of an ultimate real world, except insofar as our present science may prove false on further testing.

What then is naturalism's line on truth and falsity themselves? The truth predicate raises no problem in its normal daily use as an instrument of what I have called semantic ascent. Tarski's disquotational account accommodates it, so long as what are called true are sentences in our own language; and we then extend the predicate to sentences of other languages that we accept as translations of truths of our own. However, paradoxes arise when the truth predicate is applied to sentences that contain that very predicate or related ones; so we are called upon to recognize rather a hierarchy of truth predicates, each of which behaves properly only in application to sentences that do not contain that predicate itself or higher ones. It is a hierarchy of better and better truth predicates but no best. In practice, except in contexts such as these philosophical ones, occasions seldom arise for venturing above the first rung of the ladder. Truth *off* the hierarchy, absolute truth, would indeed be transcendent; bringing it down into scientific theory of the world engenders paradox. So naturalism has no place for that.

Still, our concept of truth strains at its naturalistic moorings in another way. We naturalists say that science is the highest path to truth, but still we do not say that everything on which scientists agree is true. Nor do we say that something that was true became false when scientists changed their minds. What we say is that they and we *thought* it was true, but it wasn't. We have scientists pursuing truth, not decreeing it. Truth thus stands forth as an ideal of pure reason, in Kant's apt phrase, and transcendent indeed. On this score I am again with Lauener.

C.S. Peirce tried to naturalize truth by identifying it with the limit that scientific progress approaches. This depends on optimistic assumptions, but if we reconstrue it as mere metaphor it does epitomize the scientists' persistent give and take of conjecture and refutation. Truth as goal remains the established usage of the term, and I acquiesce in it as just a vivid metaphor for our continued adjustment of our world picture to our neural intake. Metaphor is perhaps a handy category in which to accommodate transcendental concepts from a naturalist point of view.

17

THE NATURE OF NATURAL KNOWLEDGE

Doubt has oft been said to be the mother of philosophy. This has a true ring for those of us who look upon philosophy primarily as the theory of knowledge. For the theory of knowledge has its origin in doubt, in scepticism. Doubt is what prompts us to try to develop a theory of knowledge. Furthermore, doubt is also the first step to take in developing a theory of knowledge, if we adopt the line of Descartes.

But this is only half of a curious interplay between doubt and knowledge. Doubt prompts the theory of knowledge, yes; but knowledge, also, was what prompted the doubt. Scepticism is an offshoot of science. The basis for scepticism is the awareness of illusion, the discovery that we must not always believe our eyes. Scepticism battens on mirages, on seemingly bent sticks in water, on rainbows, after-images, double images, dreams. But in what sense are these illusions? In the sense that they seem to be material objects which they in fact are not. Illusions are illusions only relative to a prior acceptance of genuine bodies with which to contrast them. In a world of immediate sense data with no bodies posited and no questions asked, a distinction between reality and illusion would have no place. The positing of bodies is already rudimentary physical science; and it is only after that stage that the sceptic's invidious distinctions can make sense. Bodies have to be posited before there can be a motive, however tenuous, for acquiescing in a non-committal world of the immediate given.

Rudimentary physical science, that is, common sense about bodies, is

This paper is meant as a summary statement of my attitude towards our knowledge of nature. Consequently I must warn the more omnivorous of my readers (dear souls) that they are apt to experience a certain indefinable sense of *déjà lu*. The main traces of novelty come towards the end.

thus needed as a springboard for scepticism. It contributes the needed notion of a distinction between reality and illusion, and that is not all. It also discerns regularities of bodily behaviour which are indispensable to that distinction. The sceptic's example of the seemingly bent stick owes its force to our knowledge that sticks do not bend by immersion; and his examples of mirages, after-images, dreams, and the rest are similarly parasitic upon positive science, however primitive.

I am not accusing the sceptic of begging the question. He is quite within his rights in assuming science in order to refute science; this, if carried out, would be a straightforward argument by *reductio ad absurdum*. I am only making the point that sceptical doubts are scientific doubts.

Epistemologists have coped with their sceptical doubts by trying to reconstruct our knowledge of the external world from sensations. A characteristic effort was Berkeley's theory of vision, in which he sought our clues for a third dimension, depth, in our two-dimensional visual field. The very posing of this epistemological problem depends in a striking way upon acceptations of physical science. The goal of the construction, namely the depth dimension, is of course deliberately taken from the science of the external world; but what particularly wants noticing is that also the accepted basis of the construction, the two-dimensional visual field, was itself dictated by the science of the external world as well. The light that informs us of the external world impinges on the two-dimensional surface of the eye, and it was Berkeley's awareness of this that set his problem.

Epistemology is best looked upon, then, as an enterprise within natural science. Cartesian doubt is not the way to begin. Retaining our present beliefs about nature, we can still ask how we can have arrived at them. Science tells us that our only source of information about the external world is through the impact of light rays and molecules upon our sensory surfaces. Stimulated in these ways, we somehow evolve an elaborate and useful science. How do we do this, and why does the resulting science work so well? These are genuine questions, and no feigning of doubt is needed to appreciate them. They are scientific questions about a species of primates, and they are open to investigation in natural science, the very science whose acquisition is being investigated.

The utility of science, from a practical point of view, lies in fulfilled expectation: true prediction. This is true not only of sophisticated science, but of its primitive progenitor as well; and it may be good strategy on

our part to think first of the most primitive case. This case is simple induction. It is the expectation, when some past event recurs, that the sequel of that past event will recur too. People are prone to this, and so are
other animals.

It may be felt that I am unduly intellectualizing the dumb animals in
attributing expectation and induction to them. Still the net resultant behaviour of dumb animals is much on a par with our own, at the level of
simple induction. In a dog's experience, a clatter of pans in the kitchen
has been followed by something to eat. So now, hearing the clatter again,
he goes to the kitchen in expectation of dinner. His going to the kitchen
is our evidence of his expectation, if we care to speak of expectation.
Or we can skip this intervening variable, as Skinner calls it, and speak
merely of reinforced response, conditioned reflex, habit formation.

When we talk easily of repetition of events, repetition of stimuli, we
cover over a certain significant factor. It is the *similarity* factor. It can be
brought into the open by speaking of events rather as unique, dated,
unrepeated particulars, and then speaking of similarities between them.
Each of the noisy episodes of the pans is a distinct event, however similar, and so is each of the ensuing dinners. What we can say of the dog in
those terms is that he hears something similar to the old clatter and proceeds to expect something similar to the old dinner. Or, if we want to
eliminate the intervening variable, we can still say this: when the dog
hears something similar to the old clatter and, going to the kitchen, gets
something similar to the old dinner, he is reinforced in his disposition to
go to the kitchen after each further event similar to the old clatter.

What is significant about this similarity factor is its subjectivity. Is similarity the mere sharing of many attributes? But any two things share
countless attributes—or anyway any two objects share membership in
countless classes. The similarity that matters, in the clatter of the pans, is
similarity for the dog. Again I seem to appeal to the dog's mental life, but
again I can eliminate this intervening variable. We can analyse similarity,
for the dog, in terms of his dispositions to behaviour: his patterns of
habit formation. His habit of going to the kitchen after a clatter of pans
is itself our basis for saying that the clatter events are similar for the dog,
and that the dinner events are similar for the dog. It is by experimental
reinforcement and extinction along these lines that we can assess similarities for the dog, determining whether event a is more similar to b than to
c for him. Meanwhile his mental life is as may be.

Now our question 'Why is science so successful?' makes some rudimentary sense already at this level, as applied to the dog. For the dog's habit formation, his primitive induction, involved extrapolation along similarity lines: episodes similar to the old clattering episode engendered expectation of episodes similar to the old dinner episode. And now the crux of the problem is the subjectivity of similarity. Why should nature, however lawful, match up at all with the dog's subjective similarity ratings? Here, at its most primitive, is the question 'Why is science so successful?'

We are taking this as a scientific question, remember, open to investigation by natural science itself. Why should the dog's implicit similarity ratings tend to fit world trends, in such a way as to favour the dog's implicit expectations? An answer is offered by Darwin's theory of natural selection. Individuals whose similarity groupings conduce largely to true expectations have a good chance of finding food and avoiding predators, and so a good chance of living to reproduce their kind.

What I have said of the dog holds equally of us, at least in our pursuit of the rudimentary science of common sense. We predict in the light of observed uniformities, and these are uniformities by our subjective similarity standards. These standards are innate ones, overlaid and modified by experience; and natural selection has endowed us, like the dog, with a head start in the way of helpful, innate similarity standards.

I am not appealing to Darwinian biology to justify induction. This would be circular, since biological knowledge depends on induction. Rather I am granting the efficacy of induction, and then observing that Darwinian biology, if true, helps explain why induction is as efficacious as it is.

We must notice, still, a further limitation. Natural selection may be expected only to have encouraged similarity standards conducive to rough and ready anticipations of experience in a state of nature. Such standards are not necessarily conducive to deep science. Colour is a case in point. Colour dominates our scene; similarity in colour is similarity at its most conspicuous. Yet, as J. J. C. Smart points out, colour plays little role in natural science. Things can be alike in colour even though one of them is reflecting green light of uniform wave length while the other is reflecting mixed waves of yellow and blue. Properties that are most germane to sophisticated science are camouflaged by colour more than revealed by it. Over-sensitivity to colour may have been all to the good when we were bent on quickly distinguishing predator from prey or good plants from bad. But true science cuts through all this and sorts things out differently, leaving colour largely irrelevant.

Colour is not the only such case. Taxonomy is rich in examples to show that visual resemblance is a poor index of kinship. Natural selection has even abetted the deception; thus some owls have grown to resemble cats, for their own good, and others resemble monkeys. Natural selection works both to improve a creature's similarity standards and to help him abuse his enemies' similarity standards.

For all their fallibility, our innate similarity standards are indispensable to science as an entering wedge. They continue to be indispensable, moreover, even as science advances. For the advance of science depends on continued observation, continued checking of predictions. And there, at the observational level, the unsophisticated similarity standards of common sense remain in force.

An individual's innate similarity standards undergo some revision, of course, even at the common-sense level, indeed even at the subhuman level, through learning. An animal may learn to tell a cat from an owl. The ability to learn is itself a product of natural selection, with evident survival value. An animal's innate similarity standards are a rudimentary instrument for prediction, and then learning is a progressive refinement of that instrument, making for more dependable prediction. In man, and most conspicuously in recent centuries, this refinement has consisted in the development of a vast and bewildering growth of conceptual or linguistic apparatus, the whole of natural science. Biologically, still, it is like the animal's learning about cats and owls; it is a learned improvement over simple induction by innate similarity standards. It makes for more and better prediction.

Science revises our similarity standards, we saw; thus we discount colour, for some purposes, and we liken whales to cows rather than to fish. But this is not the sole or principal way in which science fosters prediction. Mere improvement of similarity standards would increase our success at simple induction, but this is the least of it. Science departs from simple induction. Science is a ponderous linguistic structure, fabricated of theoretical terms linked by fabricated hypotheses, and keyed to observable events here and there. Indirectly, via this labyrinthine superstructure, the scientist predicts future observations on the basis of past ones; and he may revise the superstructure when the predictions fail. It is no longer simple induction. It is the hypothetico-deductive method. But, like the animal's simple induction over innate similarities, it is still a biological device for anticipating experience. It owes its elements still to natural selection—notably, the similarity standards that continue to operate at the observational level. The biological survival value of the resulting scientific structure, however, is as may be. Traits that were developed by natural selection have been known to prove lethal, through overdevelopment or remote effects or changing environment. In any event, and for whatever good it may do us, the hypothetico-deductive method is delivering knowledge hand over fist. It is facilitating prediction.

I said that science is a linguistic structure that is keyed to observation at some points. Some sentences are keyed directly to observation: the observation sentences. Let us examine this connection. First I must explain what I mean by an observation sentence. One distinctive trait of such a sentence is that its truth value varies with the circumstances prevailing at the time of the utterance. It is a sentence like 'This is red' or 'It is raining,' which is true on one occasion and false on another; unlike 'Sugar is sweet,' whose truth value endures regardless of occasion of utterance. In a word, observation sentences are occasion sentences, not standing sentences.

But their being occasion sentences is not the only distinctive trait of observation sentences. Not only must the truth value of an observation sentence depend on the circumstances of its utterance; it must depend on intersubjectively observable circumstances. Certainly the fisherman's sentence 'I just felt a nibble' is true or false depending on the circumstances of its utterance; but the relevant circumstances are privy to the speaker rather than being out in the open for all present witnesses to share. The sentence 'I just felt a nibble' is an occasion sentence but not an observation sentence, in my sense of the term.

An observation sentence, then, is an occasion sentence whose occasion is intersubjectively observable. But this is still not enough. After all, the sentence 'There goes John's old tutor' meets these requirements; it is an occasion sentence, and all present witnesses can see the old tutor plodding by. But the sentence fails of a third requirement: the witnesses must in general be able to appreciate that the observation which they are sharing is one that verifies the sentence. They must have been in a position, equally with the speaker, to have assented to the sentence on their own in the circumstances. They are in that position in the case of 'This is red' and 'It is raining' and 'There goes an old man,' but not in the case of 'There goes John's old tutor.'

Such, then, is an observation sentence: it is an occasion sentence whose occasion is not only intersubjectively observable but is generally adequate, moreover, to elicit assent to the sentence from any present witness conversant with the language. It is not a report of private sense data; typically, rather, it contains references to physical objects.

These sentences, I say, are keyed directly to observation. But how *keyed,* now—what is the nature of the connection? It is a case of conditioned response. It is not quite the simplest kind; we do not say 'red' or 'This is red' whenever we see something red. But we do assent if asked. Mastery of the term 'red' is acquisition of the habit of assenting when the term is queried in the presence of red, and only in the presence of red.

At the primitive level, an observation sentence is apt to take the form of a single word, thus 'ball,' or 'red.' What makes it easy to learn is the intersubjective observability of the relevant circumstances at the time of utterance. The parent can verify that the child is seeing red at the time, and so can reward the child's assent to the query. Also the child can verify that the parent is seeing red when the parent assents to such a query.

In this habit formation the child is in effect determining, by induction, the range of situations in which the adult will assent to the query 'red,' or approve the child's utterance of 'red.' He is extrapolating along similarity lines; this red episode is similar to that red episode by his lights. His success depends, therefore, on substantial agreement between his similarity standards and those of the adult. Happily the agreement holds; and no wonder, since our similarity standards are a matter partly of natural selection and partly of subsequent experience in a shared environment. If substantial agreement in similarity standards were not there, this first step in language acquisition would be blocked.

We have been seeing that observation sentences are the starting-points in the learning of language. Also, they are the starting-points and the check points of scientific theory. They serve both purposes for one and the same reason: the intersubjective observability of the relevant circumstances at the time of utterance. It is this, intersubjective observability at the time, that enables the child to learn when to assent to the observation sentence. And it is this also, intersubjective observability at the time, that qualifies observation sentences as check points for scientific theory. Observation sentences state the evidence, to which all witnesses must accede.

I had characterized science as a linguistic structure that is keyed to observation at some points. Now we have seen how it is keyed to observation: some of the sentences, the observation sentences, are conditioned to observable events in combination with a routine of query and assent. There is the beginning, here, of a partnership between the theory of language learning and the theory of scientific evidence. It is clear, when you think about it, that this partnership must continue. For when a child learns his language from his elders, what has he to go on? He can learn observation sentences by consideration of their observable circumstances, as we saw. But how can he learn the rest of the language, including the theoretical sentences of science? Somehow he learns to carry his observation terms over into theoretical contexts, variously embedded. Somehow he learns to connect his observation sentences with standing sentences, sentences whose truth values do not depend on the occasion of utterance. It is only by such moves, however ill understood, that anyone masters the non-observational part of his mother tongue. He can learn the observational part in firm and well-understood ways, and then he must build out somehow, imitating what he hears and linking it tenuously and conjecturally to what he knows, until by dint of trial and social correction he achieves fluent dialogue with his community. This discourse depends, for whatever empirical content it has, on its devious and tenuous connections with the observation sentences; and those are the same connections, nearly enough, through which one has achieved one's fluent part in that discourse. The channels by which, having learned observation sentences, we acquire theoretical language, are the very channels by which observation lends evidence to scientific theory. It all stands to reason; for language is man-made and the locutions of scientific theory have no meaning but what they acquired by our learning to use them.

We see, then, a strategy for investigating the relation of evidential support, between observation and scientific theory. We can adopt a genetic approach, studying how theoretical language is learned. For the evidential relation is virtually enacted, it would seem, in the learning. This genetic strategy is attractive because the learning of language goes on in the world and is open to scientific study. It is a strategy for the scientific study of scientific method and evidence. We have here a good reason to regard the theory of language as vital to the theory of knowledge.

When we try to understand the relation between scientific theory and the observation sentences, we are brought up short by the break between occasion sentences and standing sentences; for observation sentences are of the one kind while theoretical sentences are of the other. The scientific system cannot digest occasion sentences; their substance must first be converted into standing sentences. The observation sentence 'Rain' or 'It is raining' will not do; we must put the information into a standing sentence: 'Rain at Heathrow 1600 G.M.T. 23 February 1974.' This report is ready for filing in the archives of science. It still reports an observation, but it is a standing report rather than an occasion sentence. How do we get from the passing observation of rain to the standing report?

This can be explained by a cluster of observations and observation sentences, having to do with other matters besides the rain. Thus take the term 'Heathrow.' Proper names of persons, buildings, and localities are best treated as observation terms, on a par with 'red' and 'rain.' All such terms can be learned by ostension, repeated sufficiently to suggest the intended scope and limits of application. 'Here is Heathrow,' then, is an observation sentence on a par with 'It is raining'; and their conjunction, 'Raining at Heathrow,' is an observation sentence as well. It is an occasion sentence still, of course, and not a standing report of observation. But now the two further needed ingredients, hour and date, can be added as pointer readings: 'The clock reads 1600' and 'The calendar reads 23 February 1974' are further observation sentences. Taking the conjunction of all four, we still have an observation sentence: 'Rain at Heathrow with clock at 1600 and calendar at 23 February 1974.' But it is an observation sentence with this curious trait: it gives lasting information, dependent no longer on the vicissitudes of tense or of indicator words like 'here' and 'now.' It is suitable for filing.

True, the clock and calendar may have been wrong. As an observation sentence our report must be viewed as stating the temporal readings and not the temporal facts. The question of the temporal facts belongs to scientific theory, somewhat above the observational level. Theoretical repercussions of this and other observations could eventually even prompt a modest scientific hypothesis to the effect that the clock or the calendar had been wrong.

I think this example serves pretty well as a paradigm case, to show how we can get from the occasion sentences of observation to the standing reports of observation that are needed for scientific theory. But this connection is by no means the only connection between observation sentences and standing sentences. Thus consider the universal categorical, 'A dog is an animal.' This is a standing sentence, but it is not, like the example of rain at Heathrow, a standing report of observation. Let us resume our genetic strategy: how might a child have mastered such a universal categorical?

I shall venture one hypothesis, hoping that it may be improved upon. The child has learned to assent to the observation term 'a dog' when it is queried in the conspicuous presence of dogs, and he has learned to assent to 'an animal' likewise when it is queried in the conspicuous presence of dogs (though not only dogs). Because of his close association of the word 'dog' with dogs, the mere sound of the word 'dog' disposes him to respond to the subsequent query 'an animal' as he would have done if a dog had been there; so he assents when he hears 'a dog' followed by the query, 'an animal?.' Being rewarded for so doing, he ever after assents to the query 'A dog is an animal?' In the same way he learns a few other examples of the universal categorical. Next he rises to a mastery of the universal categorical construction 'An S is a P' in general: he learns to apply it to new cases on his own. This important step of abstraction can perhaps be explained in parallel fashion to the early learning of observation sentences, namely, by simple induction along similarity lines; but the similarity now is a language-dependent similarity.

Much the same account can be offered for the learning of the seemingly simpler construction, mere predication: 'Fido is a dog,' 'Sugar is sweet.'

The child has now made creditable progress from observation sentences towards theoretical language, by mastering predication and the universal categorical construction. Another important step will be mastery of the relative clause; and I think I can give a convincing hypothesis of how this comes about. What is conspicuous about the relative clause is its role in predication. Thus take a relative clause, 'something that chases its tail,' and predicate it of Dinah: 'Dinah is something that chases its tail.' This is equivalent to the simple sentence 'Dinah chases its tail' (or 'her tail'). When we predicate the relative clause, the effect is the same as substituting the subject of the predication for the pronoun of the relative clause. Now my suggestion regarding the learning of the relative clause is that the child learns this substitution transformation. He discovers that the adult is prepared to assent to a predication of a relative clause in just the circumstances where he is prepared to assent to the simpler sentence obtained by the substitution.

This explains how the child could learn relative clauses in one standard position: predicative position. He learns how to eliminate them, in that position, by the substitution transformation—and how to introduce them into that position by the converse transformation, superstition. But then, having learned this much, he is struck by an analogy between relative clauses and ordinary simple predicates or general terms; for these also appear in predicative position. So, pursuing the analogy, he presses relative clauses into other positions where general terms have been appearing—notably into the universal categorical construction. Or, if the child does not press this analogy on his own, he is at any rate well prepared to grasp adult usage and follow it in the light of the analogy. In this way the relative clause gets into the universal categorical construction, from which it cannot be eliminated by the substitution transformation. It is there to stay.

We can easily imagine how the child might learn the truth functions—negation, conjunction, alternation. Take conjunction: the child notices, by degrees, that the adult affirms '*p* and *q*' in only those circumstances where he is disposed, if queried, to assent to '*p*' and also to '*q*'.

We have now seen, in outline and crude conjecture, how one might start at the observational edge of language and work one's way into the discursive interior where scientific theory can begin to be expressed. Predication is at hand, and the universal categorical, the relative clause, and the truth functions. Once this stage is reached, it is easy to see that the whole strength of logical quantification is available. I shall not pause over the details of this, except to remark that the pronouns of relative clauses take on the role of the bound variable of quantification. By further conjectures in the same spirit, some of them more convincing and some less, we can outline the learner's further progress, to where he is bandying abstract terms and quantifying over properties, numbers, functions, and hypothetical physical particles and forces. This progress is not a continuous derivation, which, followed backward, would enable us to reduce scientific theory to sheer observation. It is a progress rather by short leaps of analogy. One such was the pressing of relative clauses into universal categoricals, where they cease to be eliminable. There are further such psychological speculations that I could report, but time does not allow.

Such speculations would gain, certainly, from experimental investigation of the child's actual learning of language. Experimental findings already available in the literature could perhaps be used to sustain or correct these conjectures at points, and further empirical investigations could be devised. But a speculative approach of the present sort seems required to begin with, in order to isolate just the factual questions that bear on our purposes. For our objective here is still philosophical—a better understanding of the relations between evidence and scientific theory. Moreover, the way to this objective requires consideration of linguistics and logic along with psychology. This is why the speculative phase has to precede, for the most part, the formulation of relevant questions to be posed to the experimental psychologist.

In any event the present speculations, however inaccurate, are presumably true to the general nature of language acquisition. And already they help us to understand how the logical links are forged that connect theoretical sentences with the reports of observation. We learn the grammatical construction '*p* and *q*' by learning, among other things, to assent to the compound only in circumstances where we are disposed to assent to each component. Thus it is that the logical law of inference which leads from '*p* and *q*' to '*p*' is built into our habits by the very learning of 'and.' Similarly for the other laws of conjunction, and correspondingly for the laws of alternation and other truth functions. Correspondingly, again, for laws of quantification. The law of inference that leads form '$(x)Fx$' to 'Fa' should be traceable back, through the derivation of quantification that I have passed over, until it is found finally to hinge upon the substitution transformation by which we learn to use the relative clause. Thus, in general, the acquisition of our basic logical habits is to be accounted for in our acquisition of grammatical constructions.

Related remarks hold true of inferential habits that exceed pure logic. We learn when to assent to 'dog,' and to 'animal,' only by becoming disposed to assent to 'animal' in all circumstances where we will assent to 'dog.' Connections more accidental and casual in aspect can also come about through the learning of words; thus a child may have begun to learn the term 'good' in application to chocolate.

I characterized science as a linguistic structure that is keyed to observation here and there. I said also that it is an instrument for predicting observations on the basis of earlier observations. It is keyed to observations, earlier and later, forming a labyrinthine connection between them; and it is through this labyrinth that the prediction takes place. A powerful improvement, this, over simple induction from past observations to future ones; powerful and costly. I have now sketched the nature of the connection between the observations and the labyrinthine interior of scientific theory. I have sketched it in terms of the learning of language. This seemed reasonable, since the scientist himself can make no sense of the language of scientific theory beyond what goes into his learning of it. The paths of language learning, which lead from observation sentences to theoretical sentences, are the only connection there is between observation and theory. This has been a sketch, but a fuller understanding may be sought along the same line: by a more painstaking investigation of how we learn theoretical language.

One important point that already stands forth, regarding the relation of theory to observation, is the vast freedom that the form of the theory must enjoy, relative even to all possible observation. Theory is empirically under-determined. Surely even if we had an observational oracle, capable of assigning a truth value to every standing observational report expressible in our language, still this would not suffice to adjudicate between a host of possible physical theories, each of them completely in accord with the oracle. This seems clear in view of the tenuousness of the connections that we have noted between observation sentences and theoretical ones. At the level of observation sentences, even the general form of the eventual theoretical language remained indeterminate, to say nothing of the ontology. The observation sentences were associated, as wholes, with the stimulatory situations that warranted assent to them; but there was in this no hint of what aspects of the stimulatory situations to single out somehow as objects, if indeed any. The question of ontology simply makes no sense until we get to something recognizable as quantification, or perhaps as a relative clause, with pronouns as potential variables. At the level of observation sentences there was no foreseeing even that the superimposed theoretical language would contain anything recognizable as quantification or relative clauses. The steps by which the child was seen to progress from observational language to relative clauses and categoricals and quantification had the arbitrary character of historical accident and cultural heritage; there was no hint of inevitability.

It was a tremendous achievement, on the part of our long-term culture and our latter-day scientists, to develop a theory that leads from observation to predicted observation as successfully as ours. It is a near miracle. If our theory were in full conformity with the observational oracle that we just now imagined, which surely it is not, that would be yet a nearer miracle. But if, even granted that nearer miracle, our theory were not still just one of many equally perfect possible theories to the same observational effect, that would be too miraculous to make sense.

But it must be said that the issue of under-determination proves slippery when we try to grasp it more firmly. If two theories conform to the same totality of possible observations, in what sense are they two? Perhaps they are both stated in English, and they are alike, word for word, except that one of them calls molecules electrons and electrons molecules. Literally the two theories are in contradiction, saying incompatible things about so-called molecules. But of course we would not want to count this case; we would call it terminological. Or again, following Poincaré, suppose the two theories are alike except that one of them assumes an infinite space while the other has a finite space in which bodies shrink in proportion to their distance from centre. Even here we want to say that the difference is rather terminological than real; and our reason is that we see how to bring the theories into agreement by translation: by reconstruing the English of one of the theories.

At this point it may be protested that after all there can never be two complete theories agreeing on the total output of the observational oracle. It may be protested that since such theories would be empirically equivalent, would have the same empirical meaning, their difference is purely verbal. For surely there is no meaning but empirical meaning, and theories with the same meaning must be seen as translations one of the other. This argument simply rules out, by definition, the doctrine that physical theory is under-determined by all possible observation.

The best reaction at this point is to back away from terminology and sort things out on their merits. Where the significant difference comes is perhaps where we no longer see how to state rules of translation that would bring the two empirically equivalent theories together. Terminology aside, what wants recognizing is that a physical theory of radically different form from ours, with nothing even recognizably similar to our quantification or objective reference, might still be empirically equivalent to ours, in the sense of predicting the same episodes of sensory bombardment on the strength of the same past episodes. Once this is recognized, the scientific achievement of our culture becomes in a way more impressive than ever. For, in the midst of all this formless freedom for variation, our science has developed in such a way as to maintain always a manageably narrow spectrum of visible alternatives among which to choose when need arises to revise a theory. It is this narrowing of sights, or tunnel vision, that has made for the continuity of science, through the vicissitudes of refutation and correction. And it is this also that has fostered the illusion of there being only one solution to the riddle of the universe.

18

FIVE MILESTONES OF EMPIRICISM

In the past two centuries there have been five points where empiricism has taken a turn for the better. The first is the shift from ideas to words. The second is the shift of semantic focus from terms to sentences. The third is the shift of semantic focus from sentences to systems of sentences. The fourth is, in Morton White's phrase, methodological monism: abandonment of the analytic-synthetic dualism. The fifth is naturalism: abandonment of the goal of a first philosophy prior to natural science. I shall proceed to elaborate on each of the five.

The first was the shift of attention from ideas to words. This was the adoption of the policy, in epistemology, of talking about linguistic expressions where possible instead of ideas. This policy was of course pursued by the medieval nominalists, but I think of it as entering modern empiricism only in 1786, when the philologist John Horne Tooke wrote as follows: "The greatest part of Mr. Locke's essay, that is, all which relates to what he calls the abstraction, complexity, generalization, relation, etc., of ideas, does indeed merely concern language."[1]

British empiricism was dedicated to the proposition that only sense makes sense. Ideas were acceptable only if based on sense impressions. But Tooke appreciated that the *idea* idea itself measures up poorly to empiricist standards. Translated into Tooke's terms, then, the basic proposition of British empiricism would seem to say that words make sense only insofar as they are definable in sensory terms.

At this point, trouble arises over grammatical particles: what of our prepositions, our conjunctions, our copula? These are indispensable to

---

1. John Horne Tooke, *The Diversions of Purley,* vol. 1 (London, 1786; Boston, 1806), p. 32.

coherent discourse, yet how are they definable in sensory terms? John Horne Tooke adopted a heroic line here, arguing that the particles were really ordinary concrete terms in degenerate form. He advanced ingenious etymologies: 'if' was 'give,' 'but' was 'be out.' However, this line was needless and hopeless. If we could make concrete terms do all the work of the grammatical particles, we could make them do so without awaiting justification from etymologists. But surely we cannot, and there is no valid reason to want to; for there is another approach to the problem of defining the grammatical particles in sensory terms. We have only to recognize that they are *syncategorematic*. They are definable not in isolation but in context.

This brings us to the second of the five turning points, the shift from terms to sentences. The medievals had the notion of syncategorematic words, but it was a contemporary of John Horne Tooke who developed it into an explicit theory of contextual definition; namely, Jeremy Bentham. He applied contextual definition not just to grammatical particles and the like, but even to some genuine terms, categorematic ones. If he found some term convenient but ontologically embarrassing, contextual definition enabled him in some cases to continue to enjoy the services of the term while disclaiming its denotation. He could declare the term syncategorematic, despite grammatical appearances, and then could justify his continued use of it if he could show systematically how to paraphrase as wholes all sentences in which he chose to imbed it. Such was his theory of fictions:[2] what he called paraphrasis, and what we now call contextual definition. The term, like the grammatical particles, is meaningful as a part of meaningful wholes. If every sentence in which we use a term can be paraphrased into a sentence that makes good sense, no more can be asked.

Comfort could be derived from Bentham's doctrine of paraphrasis by all who may have inherited Berkeley's and Hume's misgivings over abstract ideas. Reconsidered in the spirit of John Horne Tooke, these misgivings become misgivings over abstract terms; and then Bentham's approach offers hope of accommodating such terms, in some contexts anyway, without conceding an ontology of abstract objects. I am persuaded that one cannot thus make a clean sweep of all abstract objects without sacrificing much of science, including classical mathematics. But certainly one can pursue those nominalistic aims much further

2. See C. K. Ogden, *Bentham's Theory of Fictions* (London: Routledge, 1932).

than could have been clearly conceived in the days before Bentham and Tooke.

Contextual definition precipitated a revolution in semantics: less sudden perhaps than the Copernican revolution in astronomy, but like it in being a shift of center. The primary vehicle of meaning is seen no longer as the word, but as the sentence. Terms, like grammatical particles, mean by contributing to the meaning of the sentences that contain them. The heliocentrism propounded by Copernicus was not obvious, and neither is this. It is not obvious because, for the most part, we understand sentences only by construction from understood words. This is necessarily so, since sentences are potentially infinite in variety. We learn some words in isolation, in effect as one-word sentences; we learn further words in context, by learning various short sentences that contain them; and we understand further sentences by construction from the words thus learned. If the language that we thus learn is afterward compiled, the manual will necessarily consist for the most part of a word-by-word dictionary, thus obscuring the fact that the meanings of words are abstractions from the truth conditions of sentences that contain them.

It was the recognition of this semantic primacy of sentences that gave us contextual definition, and vice versa. I attributed this to Bentham. Generations later we find Frege celebrating the semantic primacy of sentences, and Russell giving contextual definition its fullest exploitation in technical logic. But Bentham's contribution had not been lying ineffective all that while. In the course of the nineteenth century a practice emerged in the differential calculus of using differential operators as simulated coefficients while recognizing that the operators were really intelligible only as fragments of larger terms. It was this usage, indeed, rather than Bentham's writings, that directly inspired Russell's contextual definitions.[3]

In consequence of the shift of attention from term to sentence, epistemology came in the twentieth century to be a critique not primarily of concepts but of truths and beliefs. The verification theory of meaning, which dominated the Vienna Circle, was concerned with the meaning and meaningfulness of sentences rather than of words. The English philosophers of ordinary language have likewise directed their analyses to sentences rather than to words, in keeping with the example that was set

3. See Alfred North Whitehead and Bertrand Russell, *Principia Mathematica*, vol. 1, 2d ed. (Cambridge, 1925), p. 24.

by both the earlier and the later work of their mentor Wittgenstein. Bentham's lesson penetrated and permeated epistemology in the fullness of time.

The next move, number three in my five, shifts the focus from sentences to systems of sentences. We come to recognize that in a scientific theory even a whole sentence is ordinarily too short a text to serve as an independent vehicle of empirical meaning. It will not have its separable bundle of observable or testable consequences. A reasonably inclusive body of scientific theory, taken as a whole, will indeed have such consequences. The theory will imply a lot of observation conditionals, as I call them,[4] each of which says that if certain observable conditions are met then a certain observable event will occur. But, as Duhem has emphasized, these observation conditionals are implied only by the theory as a whole. If any of them proves false, then the theory is false, but on the face of it there is no saying which of the component sentences of the theory to blame. The observation conditionals cannot be distributed as consequences of the several sentences of the theory. A single sentence of the theory is apt not to imply any of the observation conditionals.

The scientist does indeed test a single sentence of his theory by observation conditionals, but only through having chosen to treat that sentence as vulnerable and the rest, for the time being, as firm. This is the situation when he is testing a new hypothesis with a view to adding it, if he may, to his growing system of beliefs.

When we look thus to a whole theory or system of sentences as the vehicle of empirical meaning, how inclusive should we take this system to be? Should it be the whole of science? or the whole of *a* science, a branch of science? This should be seen as a matter of degree, and of diminishing returns. All sciences interlock to some extent; they share a common logic and generally some common part of mathematics, even when nothing else. It is an uninteresting legalism, however, to think of our scientific system of the world as involved *en bloc* in every prediction. More modest chunks suffice, and so may be ascribed their independent empirical meaning, nearly enough, since some vagueness in meaning must be allowed for in any event.

It would also be wrong to suppose that *no* single sentence of a theory has its separable empirical meaning. Theoretical sentences grade off to observation sentences; observationality is a matter of degree, namely, the

4. See Quine, *Theories and Things,* Essay 2 ("Empirical Content").

degree of spontaneous agreement that the sentence would command from present witnesses. And while it may be argued that even an observation sentence may be recanted in the light of the rest of one's theory, this is an extreme case and happily not characteristic. And in any event there will be single sentences at the other extreme—long theoretical ones—that surely have their separable empirical meaning, for we can make a conjunctive sentence of a whole theory.

Thus the holism that the third move brings should be seen only as a moderate or relative holism. What is important is that we cease to demand or expect of a scientific sentence that it have its own separable empirical meaning.

The fourth move, to methodological monism, follows closely on this holism. Holism blurs the supposed contrast between the synthetic sentence, with its empirical content, and the analytic sentence, with its null content. The organizing role that was supposedly the role of analytic sentences is now seen as shared by sentences generally, and the empirical content that was supposedly peculiar to synthetic sentences is now seen as diffused through the system.

The fifth move, finally, brings naturalism: abandonment of the goal of a first philosophy. It sees natural science as an inquiry into reality, fallible and corrigible but not answerable to any supra-scientific tribunal, and not in need of any justification beyond observation and the hypothetico-deductive method. Naturalism has two sources, both negative. One of them is despair of being able to define theoretical terms generally in terms of phenomena, even by contextual definition. A holistic or system-centered attitude should suffice to induce this despair. The other negative source of naturalism is unregenerate realism, the robust state of mind of the natural scientist who has never felt any qualms beyond the negotiable uncertainties internal to science. Naturalism had a representative already in 1830 in the antimetaphysician Auguste Comte, who declared that "positive philosophy" does not differ in method from the special sciences.

Naturalism does not repudiate epistemology, but assimilates it to empirical psychology. Science itself tells us that our information about the world is limited to irritations of our surfaces, and then the epistemological question is in turn a question within science: the question how we human animals can have managed to arrive at science from such limited information. Our scientific epistemologist pursues this inquiry and comes out with an account that has a good deal to do with the learning of language and with the neurology of perception. He talks of how men posit bodies and hypothetical particles, but he does not mean to suggest that the things thus posited do not exist. Evolution and natural selection will doubtless figure in this account, and he will feel free to apply physics if he sees a way.

The naturalistic philosopher begins his reasoning within the inherited world theory as a going concern. He tentatively believes all of it, but believes also that some unidentified portions are wrong. He tries to improve, clarify, and understand the system from within. He is the busy sailor adrift on Neurath's boat.

19

ON MENTAL ENTITIES

A question which is very much in the air is whether we should affirm or deny that there are such things as *sensations*, these being conceived as immediate, subjective experiences. I shall touch on this question, but not just yet. For a while it will be convenient to talk as if there are.

Falling in thus uncritically with the usage of old-fashioned epistemology and introspective psychology, let us consider, to begin with, the process of language. It has been the fashion in recent philosophy, both that of some of the English analysts and that of some of the logical positivists, to think of the terms of science and ordinary language as having some sort of hidden or implicit definitions which carry each such term back finally to terms relating to immediate experience. Now this view is clearly unrealistic. A better description, though countenancing the notion of immediate experience still, is as follows. On the one hand we have language, as an infinite totality of said or appropriately sayable phrases and sentences. On the other hand we have our sense experience, which, by a process of psychological association or conditioned response, is keyed in with the linguistic material at numerous and varied places. The linguistic material is an interlocked system which is tied here and there to experience; it is not a society of separately established terms and statements, each with its separate empirical definition. There is no separate meaning, in terms of direct experience, for the statement that there is a table here, or that there is a planet somewhere in outer space. The statement that there is the planet may be keyed with our sense experience by our seeing the planet, or by our merely noting perturbations in the orbits of other planets. And even the statement that there is a table right here may be keyed with our sense experience through touch *or* sight *or* hearsay. Again the statement that I have cut my finger may be tied with experience either by sight or by pain or both. I have often argued that it is mistaken to try to distinguish even between those scientific statements which are true by virtue of the meanings of our terms and those which are true or probable by inductive evidence. As Pierre Duhem urged, it is the system as a whole that is keyed to experience. It is taught by exploitation of its heterogeneous and sporadic links with experience, and it stands or falls, is retained or modified, according as it continues to serve us well or ill in the face of continuing experience.

We get the system, in its main lines, from our forebears. As children learning the language, we get on to various simple terms and key phrases by direct association with appropriate experiences. When we have progressed a bit with this kind of learning, we learn further usages contextually. Eventually we are in a position to receive traditional doctrine a whole chapter at a time. Finally some men venture to revise the tradition here and there, for the sake of greater simplicity or better experiential links; and these are scientists.

So much for the individual's mastery of language and lore; but what of the origins of all this in the race? It would be irrational to suppose that those origins were rational. The prehistory of science was probably a composite of primitive unconscious symbolism of the Freudian kind, confusions of sign and object, word magic, wishful thinking, and a lazy acquiescence in forms whose motivation had been long forgotten. Biases in our conceptual schemes may have great utility in the systematizing of science, and therewith high survival value, despite humble origins in the random workings of unreason—just as chance mutations in the chromosome may launch a sturdy and efficient new race. Natural selection through the ages tends to favor the happy accidents at the expense of the unpropitious ones, in the evolution of ideas as in the evolution of living species.

As scientists we accept provisionally our heritage from the dim past, with intermediate revisions by our more recent forebears; and then we continue to warp and revise. As Neurath has said, we are in the position of a mariner who must rebuild his ship plank by plank while continuing to stay afloat on the open sea.

How do we decide on such retentions and revisions? To be more specific: how do we decide, apropos of the real world, what things there *are*? Ultimately, I think, by considerations of simplicity plus a pragmatic guess as to how the overall system will continue to work in connection with experience. We posit molecules, and eventually electrons, even though these are not given to direct experience, merely because they contribute to an overall system which is simpler as a whole than its known alternatives; the empirical relevance of the notion of molecules and electrons is indirect, and exists only by virtue of the links with experience which exist at *other* points of the system. Actually I expect that tables and sheep are, in the last analysis, on much the same footing as molecules and electrons. Even these have a continuing right to a place in our conceptual scheme only by virtue of their indirect contribution to the overall simplicity of our linguistic or conceptual organization of experience; for note that even tables and sheep are not direct sensations.

The notion of macroscopic objects, tables and sheep, differs from that of molecules and electrons mainly, from an epistemological point of view, in point of degree of antiquity. Molecules were posited consciously in historic times, whereas the positing of the external objects of common sense is an original trait of human nature. Men have believed in something very like our common-sense world of external objects as long, surely, as anything properly describable as language has existed; for the teaching of language and the use of it for communication depend on investing linguistic forms with intersubjectively fixed references. It would be senseless to speak of a motive for this archaic and unconscious posit, but we can significantly speak of its function and its survival value; and in these respects the hypothesis of common-sense external objects is quite like that of molecules and electrons.

Because the notion of external macroscopic objects is so fundamental both to the origins of language and to the continued learning of language, we may be pretty sure that it is here to stay, though electrons and other more hypothetical entities may, with the continued revisions of science, come and go. Experience is continually reminding us that it is over the external macroscopic objects that there is least semantical misunderstanding between speakers; it is naturally to tables and sheep and the like that we keep returning when there is trouble about new concepts.

Epistemologists, put off by the fact that macroscopic objects are epistemologically on the same footing as molecules and electrons, have looked to sense data—the raw content of sensation itself—as a more ultimate realm of entities. The ensuing difficulties are notorious. They may be seen most vividly if to begin with we think about memory. Our present data of our own past experiences are, on this theory, some sort of faint present replicas of past sense impressions; faint echoes of past sensation accompanying the blare of present sensation. Now it takes little soul-searching to persuade oneself that such double impressions, dim against bright, are rather the exception than the rule. Ordinarily we do not remember the trapezoidal sensory surface of a desk, as a color patch extending across the lower half of the visual field; what we remember is *that* there was a desk meeting such-and-such approximate specifications of form and size in three-dimensional space. Memory is just as much a product of the past positing of extra-sensory objects as it is a datum for the positing of past sense data.

What has been said just now of memory applies in some degree to the stream of sensory experience generally. It would be increasingly apparent from the findings of the Gestalt psychologists, if it were not quite apparent from everyday experience, that our selective awareness of present sensory surfaces is a function of present purposes and past conceptualizations. The contribution of reason cannot be viewed as limited merely to conceptualizing a presented pageant of experience and positing objects behind it; for this activity reacts, by selection and emphasis, on the qualitative make-up of the pageant itself in its succeeding portions. It is not an instructive oversimplification, but a basic falsification, to represent cognition as a discernment of regularities in an unadulterated stream of experience. Better to conceive of the stream itself as polluted, at each succeeding point of its course, by every prior cognition.

So the notion of pure sense datum is a pretty tenuous abstraction, a good deal more conjectural than the notion of an external object, a table or a sheep. It is significant that when we try to talk of the subjective we borrow our terminology from the objective: I feel as if I were falling, I have a sinking sensation, I feel on top of the world, I see pink elephants (better: I feel as if I were really seeing real pink elephants), etc. Even the terms which we have come to regard as strictly and immediately sensory, like 'red,' are obviously objective in reference in the first instance: we learn the word 'red' by being confronted with an external object which our parent calls red, just as we learn the word 'sheep' by being confronted with an external object which our parent calls a sheep. When, at a certain stage of epistemological sophistication, we transfer the word 'red' to an alleged datum of immediate subjective sense experience, we are doing just what we do when we say we have a sinking sensation: I feel *as if* I were really, externally falling, and I feel *as if* I were really confronted by an external red object.

I suggest that it is a mistake to seek an immediately evident reality, somehow more immediately evident than the realm of external objects.

Unbemused by philosophy, we would all go along with Dr. Johnson, whose toe was his touchstone of reality. Sheep are real, unicorns not. Clouds are real, the sky (as a solid canopy) not. Odd numbers are perhaps real, but prime even numbers other than 2 not. Everything, of course, is real; but there are sheep and there are no unicorns, there are clouds and there is (in the specified sense of the term) no sky, there are odd numbers and there are no even primes other than 2. Such is the ordinary usage of the word 'real,' a separation of the sheep from the unicorns. Failing some aberrant definition which is certainly not before us, this is the only usage we have to go on.

The crucial insight of empiricism is that any evidence for science has its end points in the senses. This insight remains valid, but it is an insight which comes after physics, physiology, and psychology, not before. Epistemologists have wanted to posit a realm of sense data, situated somehow just me-ward of the physical stimulus, for fear of circularity: to view the physical stimulation rather than the sense datum as the end point of scientific evidence would be to make physical science rest for its evidence on physical science. But if with Neurath we accept this circularity, simply recognizing that the science of science is a science, then we dispose of the epistemological motive for assuming a realm of sense data. May we then make a clean sweep of mental entities?

I urged earlier that we decide what things there are, or what things to treat as there being, by considerations of simplicity of the overall system and its utility in connection with experience, so to speak. I say "so to speak" because I do not want to force the issue of recognizing experience as an entity or composite of entities. I have talked up to now as if there were such entities; I had to talk some language, and I uncritically talked this one. But the history of the mind–body problem bears witness to the awkwardness of the practice. We are virtually bound, as remarked earlier, to hold to an ontology of external objects; but it is moot indeed whether the positing of additional objects of a mental kind is a help or a hindrance to science. Or perhaps not so moot. At any rate it is moot or else it is clear that they are a hindrance.

To repudiate mental entities is not to deny that we sense or even that we are conscious; it is merely to report and try to describe these facts without assuming entities of a mental kind. What is spoken of in terms of the residual posited objects of science and common sense as my cut finger is keyed into our nervous responses in various ways; nerves from my eye and other eyes are involved, and nerves from my finger. Some persons are so situated as to be accessible to the stimuli which are most closely relevant to the phrase 'Quine's cut finger' and some are not. A dozen of us are in a position for the appropriate stimulation of the eye, and one of us for the appropriate stimulation of the finger.

None of us is oriented to external objects quite like anyone else, for we occupy different positions, and while we exchange positions the objects age. None of us learned his words quite like anyone else. But we use them in sufficient systematic agreement for fair communication—which is no accident, since language is subject to the law of survival of the fittest. We manage to talk effectively about other people's cut fingers because of a pattern of habits connecting with present and past stimulation of the eye together with past stimulation, under optically similar circumstances, of our own fingers. The same is true of pain—but no argument against construing pain as a state of the physical organism. If we repudiate mental entities as entities, there ceases to be an iron curtain between the private and the public; there remains only a smoke screen, a matter of varying degrees of privacy of events in the physical world. Consciousness still retains a place, as a state of a physical object, if—following the suggestion made by Professor Deutsch in addressing this institute last year—we construe consciousness as a faculty of responding to one's own responses. The responses here are, or can be construed as, physical behavior. It is not the purpose of this view to leave any aspect of life out of account. The issue is merely whether, in an ideal last accounting of everything or a present practical accounting of everything we can, it is efficacious so to frame our conceptual scheme as to mark out a range of entities or units of a so-called mental kind in addition to the physical ones. My hypothesis, put forward in the spirit of a hypothesis of natural science, is that it is not efficacious.

20

MIND AND VERBAL DISPOSITIONS

Descartes supposed that man is the only animal endowed with mind; the others are automata. It is held further, and more widely and on better evidence, that man is the only animal endowed with language. Now if man is unique in enjoying these two gifts, it is no coincidence. One may argue that no mindless creature could cope with so intricate a device as language. Or one may argue conversely that no appreciable mental activity is conceivable without linguistic aids.

Most thought simply *is* speech, according to the pioneer behaviourist John B. Watson: silent, repressed, incipient speech. Not all thought is that. A geometer or an engineer may think by means also of little incipient tugs of the muscles that are used in drawing curves or twirling cogwheels. Still, the muscles that play by far the major role, according to Watson's muscular theory of meditation, are the muscles used in making speeches.

Conversely, there is an age-old and persistent tendency to try to explain and analyse the physical phenomenon of speech by appealing to mind, mental activity, and mental entities: by appealing to thoughts, ideas, meanings. Language, we are told, serves to convey ideas. We learn language from our elders by learning to associate the words with the same ideas with which our elders have learned to associate them. Thus it is, we may be told, that approximate uniformity of association of words with ideas is achieved and maintained throughout the community.

Such an account would of course be extravagantly perverse. Thus consider the case where we teach the infant a word by reinforcing his random babbling on some appropriate occasion. His chance utterance bears a chance resemblance to a word appropriate to the occasion, and we reward him. The occasion must be some object or some stimulus source that we as well as the child are in a position to notice. Furthermore, we must be in a position to observe that the child is in a position to notice it. Only thus would there be any purpose in our rewarding his chance utterance. In so doing we encourage the child to repeat the word on future similar occasions. But are we causing him to associate the word with the same *idea* that we adults associate it with? Do we adults all associate it with the same idea ourselves, for that matter? And what would that mean?

The moral of this is that the fixed points are just the shared stimulus and the word; the ideas in between are as may be and may vary as they please, so long as the external stimulus in question stays paired up with the word in question for all concerned. The point is well dramatized by the familiar fantasy of complementary colour perception. Who knows but that I see things in colours opposite to those in which you see the things? For communication it is a matter of indifference.

I believe in the affinity of mind and language, but I want to keep the relation right side up. Watson's theory of thought, however inadequate, has matters right side up. A theory of mind can gain clarity and substance, I think, from a better understanding of the workings of language, whereas little understanding of the workings of language is to be hoped for in mentalistic terms.

I shall say a little about how it is that people feel drawn to a mentalistic account of language, despite the conspicuous fact that language is a social enterprise which is keyed to intersubjectively observable objects in the external world. Also I shall speculate on how we might hope to get on with a properly physicalistic account of language. First I must talk a little more about learning.

I mentioned one primitive way of learning a word: through reinforcement of random babbling. Another way, somewhat the reverse, is imitation. In the case of babbling it was the adult that witnessed what was confronting the child when the child chanced to babble the appropriate word. In the case of imitation it is the child, conversely, that witnesses what is confronting the adult when the adult volunteers the word. The child then volunteers the word when similarly confronted, and thereupon the adult proceeds to reinforce the child's behaviour just as in the case of babbling. The imitation method is more sophisticated than the babbling method. It can still be explained, indirectly, in terms of stimulus and reinforced response; but I won't pause over it.

What we do need to notice is that all language learning at this primitive level is directed only to the learning of what may be called observation terms, or, more properly, observation sentences. The child learns to assent to the query 'red?' in the conspicuous presence of red things. Also he masters the trick of getting the object by uttering the word; 'red' is a poor example here, but 'ball' and 'milk' and 'Mama' are clear cases. Also he masters the word in a passive way, responding in some distinctive fashion on hearing it. He may respond by turning to face the object, or by fetching it.

Now the observation term, or observation sentence, is a ground on which John the rational animal and Fido the automaton can meet and to some degree communicate. The dog learns observation sentences in his passive way. He learns to respond to them by salivating, by running to the kitchen, by turning to face the object, or by fetching it.

Already at this lowly level of observation sentences the small child differs from the dog, it may seem, in that he learns the sentences also actively: he utters them. This still is not a clear contrast. Dogs learn to ask for things, in their inarticulate way. Let us not arrogate to rationality what may be merely superior agility of lips and tongue and larynx. Premack and his chimpanzee have circumvented these muscular obstacles by resorting to plastic symbols, which they push around on a board. Premack succeeds in teaching his chimpanzee to volunteer observation sentences appropriately and to play a passable game of query and assent.

A contrast that has long been remarked, between human language and animal signals, is the combinatorial productivity of language: man's ability to compose new and unprecedented sentences from old materials, and to respond appropriately to such new creations. But Premack reports that his chimpanzee even passes this test, within modest limits. It would thus appear that combinatorial productivity in language affords no sharp line between man and beast. Man may plume himself on having been the first to develop a combinatorially productive language, but the ability to learn it may be more widespread.

Combinatorial productivity, however, is not the only trait that has seemed to distinguish mind-governed discourse from the performance of trained animals. A major factor is the unpredictable spontaneity of speech. Animal drives are still at work behind the torrent of human speech, but they are seldom clearly to be traced. Even if in our verbal output we differ from Premack's chimpanzee only in degree and not in kind, still it is this overwhelming difference of degree that invites the mentalistic accounts of verbal behaviour. The torrent of words is seen as a manifestation of the speaker's inner life beyond animal drives. Nowadays one is apt to resort thus to a mentalistic semantics not so much because one sees an ontological gulf between man and the apes, as because one despairs of adhering to the standards of natural science in coping with the complexities of intelligent discourse.

The central notion in mentalistic semantics is an unanalysed notion of meaning. It figures mainly in two contexts: where we speak of knowing the meaning of an expression, and where we speak of sameness of meaning. We say we know the meaning of an expression when we are able to produce a clearer or more familiar expression having the same meaning. We ask the meaning of an expression when what we want is a clearer or more familiar expression having the same meaning.

I said to my small son, 'Eighty-two. You know what I mean?' He said, 'No.' Then I said to my small daughter, 'Ottantadue. You know what I mean?' She said, 'Yes. Eighty-two.' I said, 'See, Margaret understands Italian better than Douglas understands English.'

Our ways of talking of meaning are thus misleading. To understand an expression is, one would say, to know the meaning; and to know the meaning is, one would say, to be able to give the meaning. Yet Douglas could rightly claim to *understand* the expression 'eighty-two,' despite answering 'No' to 'You know what I mean?' He answered 'No' because he was unable to *give* the meaning; and he was unable to give the meaning because what we call giving the meaning consists really in the asymmetrical operation of producing an equivalent expression that is clearer. Margaret was ready with a clearer equivalent of 'ottantadue,' but Douglas was at a loss for a *still* clearer equivalent of 'eighty-two.' In another context he might have ventured, 'Yes, you mean the temperature is eighty-two.'

People persist in talking thus of knowing the meaning, and of giving the meaning, and of sameness of meaning, where they could omit mention of meaning and merely talk of understanding an expression, or talk of the equivalence of expressions and the paraphrasing of expressions. They do so because the notion of meaning is felt somehow to *explain* the understanding and equivalence of expressions. We understand expressions by knowing or grasping their meanings; and one expression serves as a translation or paraphrase of another because they mean the same. It is of course spurious explanation, mentalistic explanation at its worst. The paradoxical little confusion between understanding 'eighty-two' and knowing or giving its meaning is always symptomatic of awkward concept-building; but where the real threat lies, in talking of meaning, is in the illusion of explanation.

In all we may distinguish three levels of purported explanation, three degrees of depth: the mental, the behavioural, and the physiological. The mental is the most superficial of these, scarcely deserving the name of explanation. The physiological is the deepest and most ambitious, and it is the place for causal explanations. The behavioural level, in between, is what we must settle for in our descriptions of language, in our formulations of language rules, and in our explications of semantical terms. It is here, if anywhere, that we must give our account of the understanding of an expression, and our account of the equivalence that holds between an expression and its translation or paraphrase. These things need to be explained, if at all, in behavioural terms: in terms of dispositions to overt gross behaviour.

Take understanding. Part of the understanding of a word consists in the ability to use it properly in all manner of admissible contexts. Part consists in reacting properly to all such uses. So there is a good deal here to sort out and organize. We must divide and define. To begin with we can set aside the complication of the myriad sentential contexts of a word, by beginning rather with sentences as wholes: with complete little isolated speeches, consisting perhaps of a single word and perhaps of more.

Bewildering variety confronts us even so. One and the same little sentence may be uttered for various purposes: to warn, to remind, to obtain possession, to gain confirmation, to gain admiration, or to give pleasure by pointing something out. The occasions for uttering one and the same sentence are so various that we can seldom predict when a sentence will be uttered or which one it will be. An unpromising setting, this, in which to explore and exploit verbal dispositions. Somehow we must further divide; we must find some significant central strand to extract from the tangle.

Truth will do nicely. Some sentences, of course, do not have truth values: thus questions and imperatives. Those that do may still be uttered for a variety of reasons unconnected with instruction; I just now enumerated some. But, among these sentences, truth is a great leveller, enabling us to postpone consideration of all those troublesome excrescences. Here, then, is an adjusted standard of understanding: a man understands a sentence in so far as he knows its truth conditions. This kind of understanding stops short of humour, irony, innuendo, and other literary values, but it goes a long way. In particular it is all we can ask of an understanding of the language of science.

We are interested not only in explaining what it is for someone else to understand a sentence, but also in setting a standard for ourselves, as when we try to penetrate a new language and to understand its sentences, or try to teach the language. Our standard, still, is this: give the truth conditions. Hence Davidson's plan for a semantics in the style of Tarski's truth definition.

But when I define the understanding of a sentence as knowledge of its truth conditions I am certainly not offering a definition to rest with; my term 'knowledge' is as poor a resting-point as the term 'understanding' itself.

We were supposed to be getting things down to terms of dispositions to behaviour. In what behavioural disposition then does a man's knowledge of the truth conditions of the sentence 'This is red' consist? Not, certainly, in a disposition to affirm the sentence on every occasion of observing a red object, and to deny it on all other occasions; it is the disposition to assent or dissent when asked in the presence or absence of red. Query and assent, query and dissent—here is the solvent that reduces understanding to verbal disposition. Without this device there would be no hope of handing language down the generations, nor any hope of breaking into newly discovered languages. It is primarily by querying sentences for assent and dissent that we tap the reservoirs of verbal disposition.

This approach applies primarily to terms, or occasion sentences, rather than to standing sentences. For the disposition to assent to or dissent from the sentence 'This is red' is marked by a correlation between assent and the presence of red, and between dissent and the absence of red, on occasions where the sentence is queried. A standing sentence, whose truth value remains fixed over long periods, offers no significant correlation of the kind. Where the method of queried assent and dissent is at its best, indeed, is in application to occasion sentences of the special sort that I have called observation sentences; for the occasions that make the sentence true are going to have to be intersubjectively recognizable if we are to be able to *tell* whether the speaker has the disposition in question. Even in these cases, of course, we remain at the mercy of the speaker's veracity: we assume when querying him that his assents and dissents are sincere. Happily we live in a moral climate where this assumption generally holds up; language could not flourish otherwise.

Standing sentences can be queried too, but the stimulating situation at the time of querying them will usually have no bearing on the verdict; and for this reason we cannot identify the understanding of a standing sentence, even approximately, with a disposition to assent or dissent when queried on particular occasions. I do not know how, in general, in terms of behavioural dispositions, to approximate to the notion of understanding at all, when the sentences understood are standing sentences. Perhaps it cannot be done, taking standing sentences one by one.

Once in a while we get a hint of a specifically relevant disposition, still, when we find someone reversing his verdict on a standing sentence in the face of some observation. But with all conceivable luck we cannot hope to correlate standing sentences generally with observations, because the sentences one by one simply do not have their own separable empirical implications. A multiplicity of standing sentences will interlock, rather, as a theory; and an observation in conflict with that theory may be accommodated by revoking one or other of the sentences—no one sentence in particular.

One sees how a semanticist might despair and seek shelter in the jungle of mentalistic semantics. But there are other courses. Perhaps the very notion of understanding, as applied to single standing sentences, simply cannot be explicated in terms of behavioural dispositions. Perhaps therefore it is simply an untenable notion, notwithstanding our intuitive predilections. It stands to reason that a proper semantical analysis of standing sentences, in terms of behavioural dispositions, will be primarily occupied with the interrelations of sentences rather than with standing sentences one by one.

I mentioned two central semantical notions which, in mentalistic semantics, are obscured by talk of meaning. One was the notion of understanding an expression, and the other was the relation of equivalence between an expression and its paraphrase. Afterwards I considered what might be done about understanding. Now what about the other notion, the equivalence relation? Much of what I have said about understanding applies in parallel fashion to equivalence. Here, as there, we can conveniently organize our work by looking first to sentences as wholes, seeking an equivalence concept for them. Here, as there, we can usefully narrow our problem by focusing on truth conditions and so exploiting a method of query and assent. And here, of course, as there, the sentences that prove reasonably amenable are the occasion sentences, especially the observation sentences. What relates such a sentence to its equivalent is simply a coinciding of dispositions: we are disposed to assent to both sentences in the same circumstances.

Moreover, in a behavioural account of equivalence, just as in a behavioural account of understanding, we encounter difficulty when we move to standing sentences. Since a man is apt to assent to a standing sentence, if asked, in all sorts of circumstances or in none, the coinciding of dispositions to assent to two standing sentences gives no basis for equating them.

I am persuaded, indeed, that a satisfactory equivalence concept is impossible for standing sentences. My view of this matter can be conveyed most clearly if we consider translation between two languages. I am persuaded that alternative manuals of translation can exist, incompatible with each other, and both of them conforming fully to the dispositions to behaviour on the part of the speakers of the two languages. The two manuals would agree on observation sentences but conflict in some of the standing sentences. Each manual, being a manual of translation, purports to specify the equivalence relation between sentences and their translations, and neither manual is right to the exclusion of the other.

This indeterminacy of translation is unsuspected in mentalistic semantics, because of the facile talk of meaning. Sentences have meanings, and a translation is right if it has the same meaning. Mentalistic semantics requires that one of two conflicting manuals of translation be wrong, though it conforms to every speaker's dispositions. Mentalistic semantics thus sets a false goal, which, even though vague and ill defined, tends to obstruct other lines of thought.

Of course, translation must go on. Indeterminacy means that there is more than one way; we can still proceed to develop one of them, as good as any. And, in a more theoretical mood, we must still consider what counts as evidence for *an* acceptable translation relation, even if the relation is not unique. The evidence will be behavioural still, of course, even though the relation is no simple coinciding of behavioural dispositions, as it was in the case of the equivalence of observation sentences. We have to examine relations of interdependence between verbal dispositions: systematic interdependences between dispositions to assent to standing sentences and dispositions to assent in certain circumstances to observation sentences. Here again, in the problem of equivalence as in the problem of understanding, it would seem that genetic semantics offers a likely approach. But we must expect no simple picture, no easy answers. For it is a question again of the relations of standing sentences to observation sentences, and hence nothing less than the relation of scientific theory to scientific evidence.

Let us then recognize that the semantical study of language is worth pursuing with all the scruples of the natural scientist. We must study language as a system of dispositions to verbal behaviour, and not just surface listlessly to the Sargasso Sea of mentalism.

It has been objected that when I talk of query and assent I am not really escaping mentalism after all, because assent itself has a mental component. It is objected that assent is no mere mindless parroting of an arbitrary syllable; utterance of the syllable counts as assent only if there is the appropriate mental act behind it. Very well, let us adopt the term *surface assent* for the utterance or gesture itself. My behavioural approach does indeed permit me, then, only to appeal to surface assent; assent as I talk of it must be understood as surface assent. This behavioural notion has its powers, however, and must not be underrated. For the syllable or gesture of assent in a community is not identified at random, after all; it is itself singled out, in turn, by behavioural criteria. One partial criterion of what to count as a sign of assent is that a speaker is disposed to produce that sign whenever a sentence is queried in circumstances in which he would be disposed to volunteer the sentence himself. Even surface assent, thus, is not just the parroting of any arbitrary syllable. Granted, some cases of surface assent are insincere, but happily they are rare enough, as I have already remarked, to permit the field linguist still to find laws and translations on the strength of statistical trends.

I have been inveighing against mentalistic semantics and urging in its place the study of dispositions to behaviour. This move could be represented alternatively and more picturesquely as a matter not so much of substitution as of identification: let us *construe* mind as a system of disposition to behaviour. This version somewhat recalls Gilbert Ryle and Wilfrid Sellars, who have urged a generally dispositional philosophy of mind. Some small further encouragement for it may be seen in the fact that even our most ordinary and characteristic mentalistic idioms already take almost the form of attributions of verbal dispositions. These are the idioms of propositional attitude: 'x believes that p,' 'x wishes that p,' 'x expects that p,' and so on. They all follow the broad pattern of indirect quotation, 'x says that p,' as if to attribute to x the disposition to utter the sentence 'p' in some mood. Thus x believes that p if, approximately, he will affirm p; he wishes or regrets that p if, approximately, he will exclaim 'Oh that p!' or 'Alas, p!'

I am offering no proper analysis of the propositional attitudes. People do not volunteer all their beliefs in affirmations. A better criterion of belief is the disposition to assent if asked; and this still leaves no room for questioning sincerity. Also there is the problem of allowable latitude of translation or paraphrase, when the '*p*' clause in '*x* believes that *p*' contains words alien to *x*'s actual vocabulary. This question of allowable latitude of course arises acutely in indirect discourse itself, '*x* said that *p*,' and it plagues all the idioms of propositional attitude. And finally there are quandaries over the referential opacity of the idioms of propositional attitude: quandaries having to do with the substitutivity of identity, and with quantifying into opaque contexts. All in all, the propositional attitudes are in a bad way. These are the idioms most stubbornly at variance with scientific patterns. Consequently I find it particularly striking that these, of all idioms, already describe mental states in a way that hints at dispositions to verbal behaviour. A philosophy of mind as verbal disposition is after all not so very alien to deep-rooted popular attitudes.

I spoke of three levels of purported explanation: the mental, the behavioural, and the physiological. We have just now been contemplating the second, the behavioural. Now the relation of this level to the third and deepest, the physiological, begins to be evident when we examine the notion of a *disposition* to behaviour and consider what we mean by a disposition.

A disposition is in my view simply a physical trait, a configuration or mechanism. It can be a disjunctive physical trait, since like effects can come of unlike mechanisms. What makes it a disposition is no significant character of its own, but only the style in which we happen to specify it. Thus take the classical example, solubility in water. This is a physical trait that can be specified, with varying degrees of thoroughness, in various ways. It can be described quite fully, I gather, in terms of the relative positions of small particles. It can also be described, less fully, by citing a simple test: put an object in water and see if it dissolves. Instructions for this convenient test are compactly encoded, as it happens, in the adjective 'soluble' itself, with its verb stem 'solu-' and its dispositional ending '-ble.' The adjective 'soluble' is a disposition word, and this is an important classification of words; but the physical traits themselves do not divide into dispositions and others, any more significantly than mankind divides into passers-by and others. The term 'disposition' has its significant application rather as a preface, each time, to an actual singling out of some physical trait; thus we may significantly specify some physical trait as the disposition to behave thus and so in such-and-such circumstances. It is this that is accomplished also, and more laconically, by dispositional adjectives such as 'soluble,' 'fragile,' 'docile,' 'portable.' The dispositional way of specifying physical traits is as frequent and as useful as it is because we are so often not prepared, as we now happen to be in the case of solubility, to specify the intended physical trait in other than the dispositional style.

The dispositional way of specifying physical states and traits is indeed pretty generally *the* way of specifying them, except at high levels of scientific theory. The explicit dispositional idiom does not always appear, either as the word 'disposition' or as a suffix '-ble' or '-ile'; commonly the dispositional force is only implicit. Hardness, for instance, is the disposition to resist if pressed, or to scratch. Redness, said of a body, is the disposition to blush in white light. Hardness and redness come finally, like solubility, to be explained in terms of minute structure, but our first access to these physical traits is dispositional. In fact the same may be said of the very notion of body itself; for a body comes to be known, as Kant remarked, by its disposition to present a repeatable sequence of views as we walk around it or revisit it. True to form, even this disposition qualifies as a physical mechanism: *body.* Like the other physical mechanisms, this one also comes in the fullness of time to be explained in terms of small particles.

John Stuart Mill's characterization of a body as 'a permanent possibility of sensation' was meant in an idealistic spirit, as a reduction of matter to sensory disposition. Thanks to symmetry, however, the identity admits also of a materialistic inversion: corporeality, like solubility, is an objective physical arrangement of particles, but known first in dispositional terms.

Dispositions to behaviour, then, are physiological states or traits or mechanisms. In citing them dispositionally we are singling them out by behavioural symptoms, behavioural tests. Usually we are in no position to detail them in physiological terms, but in this there is no anomaly; we also commonly specify ailments *per accidens,* citing gross signs and symptoms and knowing no physiological details.

We now see the relation of the second level of explanation, the behavioural, to the third and deepest level, the physiological. At the second level we treat of dispositions to behaviour, and these dispositions are indeed physiological states, but we identify them only by their behavioural manifestations. The deepest explanation, the physiological, would ana-

lyse these dispositions in explicit terms of nerve impulses and other ana-
tomically and chemically identified organic processes.

Our three levels thus are levels of reduction: mind consists in dispositions to behaviour, and these are physiological states. We recall that John
B. Watson did not claim that quite *all* thought was incipient speech; it
was all incipient twitching of muscles, and *mostly* of speech muscles.
Just so, I would not identify mind quite wholly with verbal disposition;
with Ryle and Sellars I would identify it with behavioural disposition,
and *mostly* verbal. And then, having construed behavioural dispositions
in turn as physiological states, I end up with the so-called identity theory
of mind: mental states are states of the body.

However, a word of caution is in order regarding the so-called identity
theory. How does it differ from a repudiation theory? Let us think for a
moment about an analogous question elsewhere, concerning the definitions of natural number in set theory. We may say that numbers are defined as sets in Frege's way, or in Zermelo's way, or in von Neumann's
way, these ways all being good but incompatible. Or we may say that
numbers may be repudiated, dispensed with; that we can get along with
just sets instead, in any of various ways—Frege's way, Zermelo's way,
von Neumann's way. This repudiation version has the advantage that we
no longer seem called upon to adjudicate between three identifications of
the natural numbers, the three being incompatible and yet all somehow
correct.

Correspondingly, instead of saying that mental states are identical
with physiological ones, we could repudiate them; we could claim that
they can be dispensed with, in all our theorizing, in favour of physiological states, these being specified usually not in actual physiological terms
but in the idiom of behavioural dispositions. This repudiation version
has a certain advantage, though a different one from what we noted in
the case of number. Its advantage here is that it discourages a possible
abuse of the identity theory. For, product though the identity theory is of
hard-headed materialism, we must beware of its sedative use to relieve
intellectual discomfort. We can imagine someone appealing to the identity theory to excuse his own free and uncritical recourse to mentalistic
semantics. We can imagine him pleading that it is after all just a matter
of physiology, even if no one knows quite how. This would be a sat irony
indeed, and the repudiation theory has the virtue, over the identity theory, of precluding it.

Until we can aspire to actual physiological explanation of linguistic activity in physiological terms, the level at which to work is the middle one; that of dispositions to overt behaviour. Its virtue is not that it affords causal explanations but that it is less likely than the mentalistic level to engender an illusion of being more explanatory than it is. The easy familiarity of mentalistic talk is not to be trusted.

Still, among the dispositions to behaviour, some are more explanatory than others. The ones that we should favour, in explanations, are the ones whose physiological mechanisms seem likeliest to be detected in the foreseeable future. To cite a behavioural disposition is to posit an unexplained neural mechanism, and such posits should be made in the hope of their submitting some day to a physical explanation.

V

EXTENSIONALISM

21

CONFESSIONS OF A CONFIRMED EXTENSIONALIST

I am neither an essentialist nor, so far as I know, an existentialist. But I am a confirmed extensionalist. Extensionalism is a policy I have clung to through thick, thin, and nearly seven decades of logicizing and philosophizing. I shall now define it, though I was heeding it before knowing the word or having the concept clearly in mind.

I shall call two closed sentences *coextensive* if they are both true or both false. Two predicates or general terms or open sentences are coextensive, of course, if they are true of just the same objects or sequences of objects. Two singular terms are coextensive if they designate the same object. And finally to the point: an expression is *extensional* if replacement of its component expressions by coextensive expressions always yields a coextensive whole. *Extensionalism* is a predilection for extensional theories.

In defining coextensiveness I lumped predicates, general terms, and open sentences together. They are what can be predicated of objects or sequences of objects, and in that capacity they all three come to the same thing. They are what the schematic predicate letters in quantification theory stand for. Open sentences are the most graphic of the three renderings. Two open sentences are coextensive if they have the same free variables and agree with each other in truth-value for all values of those variables.

The clarity and convenience conferred by extensionality are evident: free interchangeability of coextensive components *salva veritate*. When in particular those components are singular terms, indeed, their interchangeability would seem mandatory from any point of view; for this is simply the substitutivity of identity. Still, "Tom believes that Cicero denounced Catiline" and "Tom believes that Tully denounced Catiline"

329

might be respectively true and false despite the identity of Cicero and Tully. We must come to terms with such cases either by compromising extensionalism or in some happier way, whereof more anon.

Meanwhile extensionalism faces a challenge from another quarter. Karel Lambert has argued[1] that an irreferential singular term such as "Pegasus" can disrupt extensionality. The predicates "flies if existent" and "flies and exists" are coextensive, since everything exists. But the sentence, "Pegasus flies if existent" is vacuously true, since Pegasus is not existent, whereas "Pegasus flies and exists" is false. So these two sentences are not extensional; their truth values are switched by switching coextensive predicates.

Happily this threat is thwarted by my practice, for lo these many decades, of treating all singular terms as singular descriptions—thus "Pegasus" as "$(\iota x)(x$ pegasizes$)$." We may think of the descriptions as defined contextually, following Russell. Under his definition, where "F" stands for any predicate, "$F(\iota x)(x$ pegasizes$)$" becomes

$$\exists x(x \text{ and only } x \text{ pegasizes } . \; Fx),$$

and this is false regardless of "F." So both of Lambert's predicates, both "flies if existent" and "flies and exists," must issue in falsehood when the subject is "Pegasus." Then there is no breach of extensionality.

To reckon "Pegasus flies if existent" true, as Lambert does, we would have to analyze "Pegasus flies if existent" into "If Pegasus exists then Pegasus flies," using two predicates. Then, treating "Pegasus flies and exists" correspondingly, we do find the sentences respectively true and false, as he claims. But our predicates are no longer the coextensive pair "flies if existent" and "flies and exists" that raised the problem. When singular description is evaporated into primitive notation, all is in order.

Lambert already recognized this, writing that my way with singular terms bypasses his challenge to extensionalism. This would indeed have been a good reason for that early move on my part, but actually my motive for it back then was just simplicity of foundations.

The elimination of singular terms bears also, it might seem, on our question regarding the singular terms "Tully" and "Cicero." But that is another story, and I shall continue to postpone it.

I have discussed extensionality thus far without mentioning classes. I

---

1. Karel Lambert, "Predication and Extensionality," *Journal of Philosophical Logic* 3 (1974), pp. 255–264.

hasten to do so, for classes are deemed the very paradigms of extensionality. Thus far I only defined extensionality of an *expression:* "Replacement of its parts by coextensives always yields a coextensive whole." But classes are not expressions. They are objects, abstract objects. To bring them into the act I turn rather to the familiar expression for specifying a class: the class abstract "$\{x: Fx\}$." Being a singular term, "$\{x: Fx\}$" may be thought of as defined as a singular description in the obvious way, namely as "$(\iota y)((\forall x)(x \; \varepsilon \; y . \equiv . Fx))$," and then dissolved into Russell's contextual definition of descriptions.

The expression "$\{x: Fx\}$" is indeed extensional by my definition. For, if "Fx" and "Gx" stand for coextensive open sentences, then the singular terms "$\{x: Fx\}$" and "$\{x: Gx\}$" designate the same class, the same abstract thing, and such was my definition of coextensiveness of singular terms. If now we transfer the epithet "extensional" from the class abstract to the class itself, saying that classes are extensional just means that they are determined by their members.

The one difference between classes and properties, apart from metaphor and free association, is extensionality: a class is determined by its members. A property is not in general determined by its instances. I am told that among normal animals the property of having a heart and the property of having kidneys are coextensive, but we would never call them the same property. Classes are extensional, properties not.

We have no clear basis in general for saying what coextensive properties qualify as identical and what ones do not. In a word, properties lack a clear principle of *individuation*. Groping for such as basis, one settles for obscure talk of essence and necessity. Anything that can be described in terms of properties and not equally directly in terms of classes is unclear to my mind. I doubt that I have ever fully understood anything that I could not explain in extensional language.

Now that I have slipped back into the first person, I shall continue in that mode for a while; for the pertinent definitions are now explicitly before us. Afterward I shall resume the selfless business of making the world safe for extensionalism.

My first inarticulate hint of extensionalism may date from boyhood, when my liking for some Jewish schoolmates collided with someone's occasional derogatory remark about Jews. I reasoned in effect that a class is to be evaluated, if at all, by evaluating its members individually.

By my senior year in Oberlin College, 1929–1930, my extensionalism was full blown. I was majoring in mathematics with honors reading in mathematical logic. There was little mathematical logic in America, and none at Oberlin. But my professor, W. D. Cairns, had got me a reading list, culminating in Whitehead and Russell's *Principia Mathematica*.

My admiration for the three volumes, mostly in logical symbols, was almost unbounded. There was the spectacular analysis, the reduction of classical mathematics to a few basic notions of so-called logic, really logic and set theory. Further there was the rigor, explicitness, and clarity of the definitions, theorems, and proofs.

My admiration was not quite unbounded. It was bounded by the explanations in prose that were preposed and interposed as explanatory chapters and in briefer bits among the expanses of symbols.

Doubtful of the reality of classes, our authors undertook to accommodate them as fictions, eliminable by contextual definition in terms of purportedly more substantial things called propositional functions. These were functions which, when applied to objects, yielded propositions, which were the meanings of sentences. Thus the propositional functions of one variable were evidently identifiable with properties, and those of two or more variables were identifiable with relations "in intension."

Extensionality was seen by our authors as having to be worked for by devious contextual definition. The *in*tentional, for all its failure of individuation, was the given. I suppose the reasoning was that, since the propositions and propositional functions are the *meanings* of sentences, adjective phrases, and verb phrases, surely they are clear to us insofar as we understand the expressions whose meanings they are.

If so, the authors' fallacy lay in tacitly taking in stride the giant step of reifying those meanings. Reification incurs the responsibility to individuate the reified entities, for there is no entity without identity. I suspect that our authors thus put undue weight on the adjective phrases that express the properties; for the phrases could differ conspicuously even if the properties did not.

Along with this regrettably intentional orientation, but independent of it, there was a detail that calls for notice only because of its disproportionate consequences in subsequent literature. The truth-functional conditional "$p \supset q$" or "not p or q" was called material implication in *Principia* and read indifferently as "if p then q" and "p implies q." On the face of it this was a grammatical aberration, independently of logical considerations. The grammar of "if p then q" requires "p" and "q" to stand for sentences, whereas that of "p implies q" requires them to stand for nouns, in this case names of sentences.

C. I. Lewis lashed out against material implication,[2] but his objection was not to the grammar. He was protesting, and rightly, that the truth function "not-or" was a hollow mockery of implication, demanding as it does no semantic relevance of the one component sentence to the other. He supplanted the weak "⊃" by a stronger connective "⊰" for what he called strict implication. He explained "$p ⊰ q$" as meaning "necessarily if p then q," and offered no further reduction. It was an emphatic departure from extensionalism, and it pioneered modal logic. Succeeding modal logicians have not all persisted in the grammatical confusion between "if-then" and "implies," but they still sacrifice extensionality to their "necessarily if-then."

I find the truth-functional conditional "$p ⊃ q$" a satisfactory rendering of "if-then" in the indicative mood. Implication is quite another thing, in strength as well as in grammar. It is a relation between sentences, expressed by putting the verb "implies" between names of the sentences, and it is established by steps of deduction.

Whitehead and Russell's regrettable use of "implies" virtually spoiled the word, prompting subsequent logicians to cast about for synonyms such as "entails" for the real thing. But I have been stubborn on that point.

Unlike the enduring intentionality of modal logic, the intentionality of propositional functions in *Principia* was mercifully just a flash in the pan. The propositional functions carry over only briefly into the formulas as values of quantified variables: only long enough to introduce classes as fictions by contextual definition. From there on the constructions proceed on greased wheels, greased by extensionality.

I was quite aware of these matters when I graduated from Oberlin in 1930, but my admiration for *Principia* was still almost unbounded. I proceeded to Harvard for graduate work in philosophy because Whitehead was in philosophy there. My doctoral dissertation was in mathematical logic still, under Whitehead's sponsorship, and was devoted to improving *Principia*. He seemed tickled by my little shortcuts and clarifications, except that I cannot have swayed him in my extensionalism. Anyway I imposed it in my dissertation. Individuals, classes, and sequences of them were all there was.

Mathematical logic, scarce in America, was sketchy even at Harvard.

---

2. C. I. Lewis, *A Survey of Symbolic Logic* (Berkeley: University of California Press, 1918), pp. 222–239.

Principia was still the last word, and little was done even with it. I did not know that in Poland, Germany, and Austria the subject had been proceeding apace and that classes were the unquestioned staple from scratch. In 1931, while I wrote my dissertation, logicians in Europe were freely pursuing logic and set theory on the frugal conceptual basis of just truth functions, quantification, and membership.

This startling economy came of Kazimierz Kuratowski's discovery in 1921 that the ordered pair of *x* and *y* can be construed as the class whose two members are the class of *x* alone and the class of *x* and *y*. Kuratowski's definition had been anticipated by a slightly less elegant one in 1914 by a young American, Norbert Wiener, but his three-page paper in the *Proceedings of the Cambridge* [England] *Philosophical Society* escaped notice everywhere.[3] Both contributions, Wiener's and Kuratowski's, escaped notice in America.

The economies over *Principia* that I achieved in my dissertation had thus been long surpassed, as I learned only after getting to Europe the following year, 1932, complete with doctorate. But in 1937 I published a more extreme reduction, assuming just class inclusion and class abstraction.[4]

The reduction of classical mathematics to one or another so meager a conceptual basis was amazing and illuminating, but calling it a reduction of mathematics to logic—*logicism,* in a word—gave the wrong message. Logic was proverbially slight and trivial. Mathematics proverbially ranged from the profound to the impenetrable, and reduction of mathematics to logic challenged belief, as indeed it well might. The reduction was to the unbridled theory of classes, or set theory, which, far from being slight and trivial, is so strong as to tangle itself in paradox until bridled in one way or another. This is no fault of extensionalism, be it noted; properties are enmeshed in those paradoxes too. But what it shows is that the startling reduction of mathematics is to something far richer than traditional logic. I prefer to limit the term "logic" to the logic of truth functions, quantification, and identity, drawing the line at the reification of classes. Above that line we have set theory, the mathematics of classes.

3. Norbert Wiener, "A Simplification of the Logic of Relations," *Proceedings of the Cambridge Philosophical Society* 17 (1914), pp. 387–390.

4. "Logic Based on Inclusion and Abstraction," *Journal of Symbolic Logic* 2 (1937), pp. 145–152. Reprinted in Quine, *Selected Logic Papers,* enlarged ed. (Cambridge, Mass.: Harvard University Press, 1995).

I think of logic in this narrow sense as the grammar of strictly scientific theory. When a bit of science is thus regimented, the one place where extralogical vocabulary enters the picture is as interpretation of the schematic predicate letters. Within this grammar, extensionality prevails.

But extensionality had no evident charm for the Harvard philosophers during my two years of graduate study. Whitehead, Lewis, and Sheffer all swore by properties and propositions. It was with Carnap in Prague and Tarski. Lesniewski, and Łukasiewicz in Warsaw the following year that my extensionalism went without saying as a matter of course.

So much for reminiscence. But I have more to say of extensionalism, for properties and necessity are not its only hurdles. The domain of meanings of expressions is hopelessly intensional and in trouble over individuation. Propositions, seen as meanings of sentences, are conspicuous here. Properties themselves might be seen correspondingly as meanings of adjective phrases.

Properties, meanings, and necessity were violations of extensionality that I repudiated without regret. But the breach of extensionality that I cited early in this essay is of another sort: "Tom believes that Cicero denounced Catiline." Those idioms of propositional attitude—belief, hope, regret, and the rest—are not to be lightly dismissed. It is not clear how to do without them. But there is a strategy by which, in the majority of cases, they can be rendered extensional.

I call it *semantic ascent*. It is the strategy of talking about expressions instead of using those expressions to talk about something more dubious. It already did us routine service in correcting Whitehead and Russell's confused treatment of "implies" as a connective to be written between sentences. We lifted it to its rightful place as a transitive verb between names of sentences. Now the strategy can be used also on ascriptions of belief, artificially this time, by reconstruing belief as a relation between believers and sentences: thus

Tom believes "Cicero denounced Catiline"

or perhaps, for usage sticklers,

Tom believes true "Cicero denounced Catiline."

This reinterpretation of the propositional attitudes, as relating the person to the sentence, does not require him to know the language. The quoted sentence is the ascriber's expression of what he would be prompted to assert if he were in the state of mind in which he takes the subject to be. The effect of semantic ascent here is to seal the belief off from the context in which it is ascribed, so that Tom's disbelief of "Tully denounced Catiline" will not violate extensionality of the combined ascriptions of belief and disbelief.

Some ascriptions of propositional attitudes resist semantic ascent. For example,

> There was an orator whom Tom believes to have denounced Catiline.

This example switches us from what are called propositional attitudes *de dicto* to attitudes *de re*. In ascribing a belief *de re* the ascriber ventures to assign a role within the ascribed belief to a denizen of the ascriber's real world. Such identifications can depend in varying degrees upon collateral information or conjecture about the subject's past behavior.[5] Semantically these idioms *de re* of belief and other attitudes are comparable to the contrary-to-fact conditional, which depends so utterly for its truth upon tacit factual knowledge or assumptions that the interlocutors are assumed to share. The particles "you," "I," "here," "there," "now," and "then" are simpler examples of such dependence on circumstances of utterance. So the propositional attitudes *de re* belong with these extraneous idioms, ancillary to the self-contained language of scientific record.

Finally I turn to some further thoughts about our extensionalizing strategy of semantic ascent from use to mention. To the extensionalist eye, the ascent could seem paradoxically to be rather a descent from bad to worse, from frying pan to fire. We mention expressions by quoting them, and nothing could be less extensional on the face of it than quotation. Within a quotation you cannot supplant a word by even the strictest synonym without changing the designatum of the quotation, namely the quoted expression itself. Nothing could be farther from extensionality than quotation.

This quandary is dispelled by recognizing the quotation as merely a graphic abbreviation, analyzable into spelling. We possess or coin a name for each of the simple signs of our language, and one for the space, and one for the operation of juxtaposition. Then we spell out the quoted expression. The spelling leaves no word of the quoted expression intact

5. See Robert Sleigh, "On a Proposed System of Epistemic Logic," *Noûs* 2 (1968), pp. 391–398.

for replacement by a synonym. It thus blocks this latest little debacle before it begins.

Spelling is similar to polynomials and multi-digit numerals. It reduces similarly to truth functions, quantification, and predicates, with the help of contextual definition of singular description.

We have been seeing semantic ascent at work in achieving extensionality, but it has other uses. Someone's revolutionary scientific idea may prove difficult to promote because it undercuts one of the principles on which his colleagues' very thought and judgment depend. Holding that principle at bay for impartial assessment leaves the judge himself at a loss for a basis for judging. Semantic ascent, then, to the rescue. The innovator ascends from his subject matter to the formulas and laws themselves, dwells on their simplicity, and shows that they logically imply his strange new hypothesis together with essentials of the antecedent theory. The change of subject matter, from waves or quarks or fields to the formulas themselves, has bridged the gaps in his colleagues' intuition. Something like this perhaps went on at crucial points in the advance of science, though with no awareness of an ascent from use to mention.

22

QUANTIFIERS AND PROPOSITIONAL ATTITUDES

I

The incorrectness of rendering 'Ctesias is hunting unicorns' in the fashion:

$$(\exists x)(x \text{ is a unicorn . Ctesias is hunting } x)$$

is conveniently attested by the non-existence of unicorns, but is not due simply to that zoological lacuna. It would be equally incorrect to render 'Ernest is hunting lions' as:

(1) $(\exists x)(x \text{ is a lion . Ernest is hunting } x)$,

where Ernest is a sportsman in Africa. The force of (1) is rather that there is some individual lion (or several) which Ernest is hunting; stray circus property, for example.

The contrast recurs in 'I want a sloop.' The version:

(2) $(\exists x)(x \text{ is a sloop . I want } x)$

is suitable insofar only as there may be said to be a certain sloop that I want. If what I seek is mere relief from slooplessness, then (2) gives the wrong idea.

The contrast is that between what may be called the *relational* sense of lion-hunting or sloop-wanting, viz., (1)–(2), and the likelier or *notional* sense. Appreciation of the difference is evinced in Latin and Romance languages by a distinction of mood in subordinate clauses; thus '*Procuro un perro que habla*' has the relational sense:

$$(\exists x)(x \text{ is a dog . } x \text{ talks . I seek } x)$$

as against the notional '*Procuro un perro que hable*':

I strive that $(\exists x)(x$ is a dog . x talks . I find $x)$.

Pending considerations to the contrary in later pages, we may represent the contrast strikingly in terms of permutations of components. Thus (1) and (2) may be expanded (with some violence to both logic and grammar) as follows:

(3) $(\exists x)(x$ is a lion . Ernest strives that Ernest finds $x)$,

(4) $(\exists x)(x$ is a sloop . I wish that I have $x)$,

whereas 'Ernest is hunting lions' and 'I want a sloop' in their notional senses may be rendered rather thus:

(5)   Ernest strives that $(\exists x)(x$ is a lion . Ernest finds $x)$,

(6)   I wish that $(\exists x)(x$ is a sloop . I have $x)$.

The contrasting versions (3)–(6) have been wrought by so paraphrasing 'hunt' and 'want' as to uncover the locutions 'strive that' and 'wish that,' expressive of what Russell has called *propositional attitudes*. Now of all examples of propositional attitudes, the first and foremost is *belief*; and, true to form, this example can be used to point up the contrast between relational and notional senses still better than (3)–(6) do. Consider the relational and notional senses of believing in spies:

(7) $(\exists x)($Ralph believes that x is a spy$)$,

(8)   Ralph believes that $(\exists x)(x$ is a spy$)$.

Both may perhaps be ambiguously phrased as 'Ralph believes that someone is a spy,' but they may be unambiguously phrased respectively as 'There is someone whom Ralph believes to be a spy' and 'Ralph believes there are spies.' The difference is vast; indeed, if Ralph is like most of us, (8) is true and (7) false.

In moving over to propositional attitudes, as we did in (3)–(6), we gain not only the graphic structural contrast between (3)–(4) and (5)–(6) but also a certain generality. For we can now multiply examples of striving and wishing, unrelated to hunting and wanting. Thus we get the relational and notional senses of wishing for a president:

(9) $(\exists x)($Witold wishes that x is president$)$,

(10)   Witold wishes that $(\exists x)(x$ is president).

According to (9), Witold has his candidate; according to (10) he merely wishes the appropriate form of government were in force. Also we open other propositional attitudes to similar consideration—as witness (7)–(8).

However, the suggested formulations of the relational senses—viz., (3), (4), (7), and (9)—all involve quantifying into a propositional-attitude idiom from outside. This is a dubious business, as may be seen from the following example.

There is a certain man in a brown hat whom Ralph has glimpsed several times under questionable circumstances on which we need not enter here; suffice it to say that Ralph suspects he is a spy. Also there is a gray-haired man, vaguely known to Ralph as rather a pillar of the community, whom Ralph is not aware of having seen except once at the beach. Now Ralph does not know it, but the men are one and the same. Can we say of this *man* (Bernard J. Ortcutt, to give him a name) that Ralph believes him to be a spy? If so, we find ourselves accepting a conjunction of the type:

(11)   *w* sincerely denies '. . .' . *w* believes that . . .

as true, with one and the same sentence in both blanks. For, Ralph is ready enough to say, in all sincerity, 'Bernard J. Ortcutt is no spy.' If, on the other hand, with a view to disallowing situations of the type (11), we rule simultaneously that

(12)   Ralph believes that the man in the brown hat is a spy,

(13)   Ralph does not believe that the man seen at the beach is a spy,

then we cease to affirm any relationship between Ralph and any man at all. Both of the component 'that'-clauses are indeed about the man Ortcutt; but the 'that' must be viewed in (12) and (13) as sealing those clauses off, thereby rendering (12) and (13) compatible because not, as wholes, about Ortcutt at all. It then becomes improper to quantify as in (7); 'believes that' becomes, in a word, referentially opaque.[1]

No question arises over (8); it exhibits only a quantification *within* the 'believes that' context, not a quantification *into* it. What goes by the

---

1. See *From a Logical Point of View,* pp. 142–149 [Chapter 24]; also "Three Grades of Modal Involvement," Essay 15 above [Chapter 25].

board, when we rule (12) and (13) both true, is just (7). Yet we are scarcely prepared to sacrifice the relational construction 'There is someone whom Ralph believes to be a spy,' which (7) as against (8) was supposed to reproduce.

The obvious next move is to try to make the best of our dilemma by distinguishing two senses of belief: $belief_1$, which disallows (11), and $belief_2$, which tolerates (11) but makes sense of (7). For $belief_1$, accordingly, we sustain (12)–(13) and ban (7) as nonsense. For $belief_2$, on the other hand, we sustain (7); and for *this* sense of belief we must reject (13) and acquiesce in the conclusion that Ralph $believes_2$ that the man at the beach is a spy even though he *also* $believes_2$ (and $believes_1$) that the man at the beach is not a spy.

II

But there is a more suggestive treatment. Beginning with a single sense of belief, viz., $belief_1$ above, let us think of this at first as a relation between the believer and a certain *intension*, named by the 'that'-clause. Intensions are creatures of darkness, and I shall rejoice with the reader when they are exorcised, but first I want to make certain points with the help of them. Now intensions named thus by 'that'-clauses, without free variables, I shall speak of more specifically as intensions of degree 0, or propositions. In addition I shall (for the moment) recognize intensions of degree 1, or attributes. These are to be named by prefixing a variable to a sentence in which it occurs free; thus z (z is a spy) is spyhood. Similarly we may specify intensions of higher degrees by prefixing multiple variables.

Now just as we have recognized a dyadic relation of belief between a believer and a proposition, thus:

(14)   Ralph believes that Ortcutt is a spy,

so we may recognize also a triadic relation of belief among a believer, an object, and an attribute, thus:

(15)   Ralph believes $z(z$ is a spy$)$ of Ortcutt.

For reasons which will appear, this is to be viewed not as dyadic belief between Ralph and the proposition *that* Ortcutt has $z(z$ is a spy$)$, but rather as an irreducibly triadic relation among the three things Ralph, $z(z$ is a spy$)$, and Ortcutt. Similarly there is tetradic belief:

(16)   Tom believes $yz(y$ denounced $z)$ of Cicero and Catiline,

and so on.

Now we can clap on a hard and fast rule against quantifying into propositional-attitude idioms; but we give it the form now of a rule against quantifying into names of intensions. Thus, though (7) as it stands becomes unallowable, we can meet the needs which prompted (7) by quantifying rather into the triadic belief construction, thus:

(17) $(\exists x)$(Ralph believes $z(z$ is a spy) of x).

Here then, in place of (7), is our new way of saying that there is someone whom Ralph believes to be a spy.

Belief$_1$ was belief so construed that a proposition might be believed when an object was specified in it in one way, and yet not believed when the same object was specified in another way; witness (12)–(13). Hereafter we can adhere uniformly to this narrow sense of belief, both for the dyadic case and for triadic and higher; in each case the term which names the intension (whether proposition or attribute or intension of higher degree) is to be looked on as referentially opaque.

The situation (11) is thus excluded. At the same time the effect of belief$_2$ can be gained, simply by ascending from dyadic to triadic belief as in (15). For (15) does relate the men Ralph and Ortcutt precisely as belief$_2$ was intended to do. (15) does remain true of Ortcutt under any designation; and hence the legitimacy of (17).

Similarly, whereas from:

Tom believes that Cicero denounced Catiline

we cannot conclude:

Tom believes that Tully denounced Catiline,

on the other hand we can conclude from:

Tom believes $y(y$ denounced Catiline) of Cicero

that

Tom believes $y(y$ denounced Catiline) of Tully,

and also that

(18) $(\exists x)$(Tom believes $y(y$ denounced Catiline) of x).

From (16), similarly, we may infer that

(19) $(\exists w)(\exists x)$(Tom believes yz(y denounced z) of w and x).

Such quantifications as:

$(\exists x)$(Tom believes that x denounced Catiline),

$(\exists x)$(Tom believes y(y denounced x) of Cicero)

still count as nonsense, along with (7); but such legitimate purposes as these might have served are served by (17)–(19) and the like. Our names of intensions, and these only, are what count as referentially opaque.

Let us sum up our findings concerning the seven numbered statements about Ralph. (7) is now counted as nonsense, (8) as true, (12)–(13) as true, (14) as false, and (15) and (17) as true. Another that is true is:

(20)   Ralph believes that the man seen at the beach is not a spy,

which of course must not be confused with (13).

The kind of exportation which leads from (14) to (15) should doubtless be viewed in general as implicative. [Correction: see Sleigh, p. 397.] Under the terms of our illustrative story, (14) happens to be false; but (20) is true, and it leads by exportation to:

(21)   Ralph believes z(z is not a spy) of the man seen at the beach.

The man at the beach, hence Ortcutt, does not receive reference in (20), because of referential opacity; but he does in (21), so we may conclude from (21) that

(22)   Ralph believes z(z is not a spy) of Ortcutt.

Thus (15) and (22) both count as true. This is not, however, to charge Ralph with contradictory beliefs. Such a charge might reasonably be read into:

(23)   Ralph believes z(z is a spy . z is not a spy) of Ortcutt,

but this merely goes to show that it is undesirable to look upon (15) and (22) as implying (23).

It hardly needs be said that the barbarous usage illustrated in (15)–(19) and (21)–(23) is not urged as a practical reform. It is put forward by way of straightening out a theoretical difficulty, which, summed up, was as follows: Belief contexts are referentially opaque; therefore it is *prima facie* meaningless to quantify into them; how then to provide for those indispensable relational statements of belief, like 'There is someone whom Ralph believes to be a spy'?

Let it not be supposed that the theory which we have been examining is just a matter of allowing unbridled quantification into belief contexts after all, with a legalistic change of notation. On the contrary, the crucial choice recurs at each point: quantify if you will, but pay the price of accepting near-contraries like (15) and (22) at each point at which you choose to quantify. In other words: distinguish as you please between referential and non-referential positions, but keep track, so as to treat each kind appropriately. The notation of intensions, of degree one and higher, is in effect a device for inking in a boundary between referential and non-referential occurrences of terms.

III

Striving and wishing, like believing, are propositional attitudes and referentially opaque. (3) and (4) are objectionable in the same way as (7), and our recent treatment of belief can be repeated for these propositional attitudes. Thus, just as (7) gave way to (17), so (3) and (4) give way to:

(24) $(\exists x)(x$ is a lion . Ernest strives z(Ernest finds z) of $x)$,

(25) $(\exists x(x$ is a sloop . I wish z(I have z) of $x)$,

a certain breach of idiom being allowed for the sake of analogy in the case of 'strives.'

These examples came from a study of hunting and wanting. Observing in (3)–(4) the quantification into opaque contexts, then, we might have retreated to (1)–(2) and forborne to paraphrase them into terms of striving and wishing. For (1)–(2) were quite straightforward renderings of lion-hunting and sloop-wanting in their relational senses; it was only the notional senses that really needed the breakdown into terms of striving and wishing, (5)–(6).

Actually, though, it would be myopic to leave the relational senses of lion-hunting and sloop-wanting at the unanalyzed stage (1)–(2). For, whether or not we choose to put these over into terms of wishing and striving, there are other relational cases of wishing and striving which require our consideration anyway—as witness (9). The untenable formulations (3)–(4) may indeed be either corrected as (24)–(25) or condensed back into (1)–(2); on the other hand we have no choice but to correct the untenable (9) on the pattern of (24)–(25), viz., as:

$(\exists x)$(Witold wishes $y(y$ is president) of x).

The untenable versions (3)–(4) and (9) all had to do with wishing and striving in the relational sense. We see in contrast that (5)–(6) and (10), on the notional side of wishing and striving, are innocent of any illicit quantification into opaque contexts from outside. But now notice that exactly the same trouble begins also on the notional side, as soon as we try to say not just that Ernest hunts lions and I want a sloop, but that *someone* hunts lions or wants a sloop. This move carries us, ostensibly, from (5)–(6) to:

(26) $(\exists w)(w$ strives that $(\exists x)(x$ is a lion . w finds $x))$,

(27) $(\exists w)(w$ wishes that $(\exists x)(x$ is a sloop . w has $x))$,

and these do quantify unallowably into opaque contexts.

We know how, with help of the attribute apparatus, to put (26)–(27) in order; the pattern, indeed, is substantially before us in (24)–(25). Admissible versions are:

$(\exists w)(w$ strives $y(\exists x)(x$ is a lion . y finds $x)$ of $w)$,

$(\exists w)(w$ wishes $y(\exists x)(x$ is a sloop . y has $x)$ of $w)$,

or briefly:

(28) $(\exists w)(w$ strives $y(y$ finds a lion) of $w)$,

(29) $(\exists w)(w$ wishes $y(y$ has a sloop) of $w)$.

Such quantification of the subject of the propositional attitude can of course occur in belief as well; and, if the subject is mentioned in the belief itself, the above pattern is the one to use. Thus 'Someone believes he is Napoleon' must be rendered:

$(\exists w)(w$ believes $y(y = \text{Napoleon})$ of $w)$.

For concreteness I have been discussing belief primarily, and two other propositional attitudes secondarily: striving and wishing. The treatment is, we see, closely parallel for the three; and it will pretty evidently carry over to other propositional attitudes as well—e.g., hope, fear, surprise.

In all cases my concern is, of course, with a special technical aspect of the propositional attitudes: the problem of quantifying in.

IV

There are good reasons for being discontent with an analysis that leaves us with propositions, attributes, and the rest of the intensions. Intensions are less economical than extensions (truth values, classes, relations), in that they are more narrowly individuated. The principle of their individuation, moreover, is obscure.

Commonly logical equivalence is adopted as the principle of individuation of intensions. More explicitly: if S and S' are any two sentences with n ($\geqq 0$) free variables, the same in each, then the respective intensions which we name by putting the n variables (or 'that,' if $n = 0$) before S and S' shall be one and the same intension if and only if S and S' are logically equivalent. But the relevant concept of logical equivalence raises serious questions in turn.[2] The intensions are at best a pretty obscure lot.

Yet it is evident enough that we cannot, in the foregoing treatment of propositional attitudes, drop the intensions in favor of the corresponding extensions. Thus, to take a trivial example, consider 'w is hunting unicorns.' On the analogy of (28), it becomes:

w strives y (y finds a unicorn) of w.

Correspondingly for the hunting of griffins. Hence, if anyone w is to hunt unicorns without hunting griffins, the attributes

$y(y$ finds a unicorn$)$,
$y(y$ finds a griffin$)$

must be distinct. But the corresponding classes are identical, being empty. So it is indeed the attributes, and not the classes, that were needed in our formulation. The same moral could be drawn, though less briefly, without appeal to empty cases.

But there is a way of dodging the intensions which merits serious consideration. Instead of speaking of intensions we can speak of sentences, naming these by quotation. Instead of:

w believes that . . .

2. See my "Two Dogmas" [Chapter 2]; also "Carnap and Logical Truth" [Chapter 4].

we may say:

> w believes-true '. . .'.

Instead of:

(30) w believes $y(. . . y . . .)$ of x

we may say:

(31) w believes '. . . y . . .' satisfied by x.

The words 'believes satisfied by' here, like 'believes of' before, would be viewed as an irreducibly triadic predicate. A similar shift can be made in the case of the other propositional attitudes, of course, and in the tetradic and higher cases.

This semantical reformulation is not, of course, intended to suggest that the subject of the propositional attitude speaks the language of the quotation, or any language. We may treat a mouse's fear of a cat as his fearing true a certain English sentence. This is unnatural without being therefore wrong. It is a little like describing a prehistoric ocean current as clockwise.

How, where, and on what grounds to draw a boundary between those who believe or wish or strive that p, and those who do not quite believe or wish or strive that p, is undeniably a vague and obscure affair. However, if anyone does approve of speaking of belief of a proposition at all and of speaking of a proposition in turn as meant by a sentence, then certainly he cannot object to our semantical reformulation 'w believes-true S' on any special grounds of obscurity; for, 'w believes-true S' is explicitly definable in *his* terms as 'w believes the proposition meant by S.' Similarly for the semantical reformulation (31) of (30); similarly for the tetradic and higher cases; and similarly for wishing, striving, and other propositional attitudes.

Our semantical versions do involve a relativity to language, however, which must be made explicit. When we say that w believes-true S, we need to be able to say what language the sentence S is thought of as belonging to; not because w needs to understand S, but because S might by coincidence exist (as a linguistic form) with very different meanings in two languages.[3] Strictly, therefore, we should think of the dyadic 'be-

3. This point is made by Church, "On Carnap's Analysis of Statements of Assertion and Belief," *Analysis* 10 (1950), pp. 97–99.

lieves-true *S*' as expanded to a triadic '*w* believes-true *S* in *L*'; and correspondingly for (31) and its suite.

As noted two paragraphs back, the semantical form of expression:

(32)   *w* believes-true '. . .' in *L*

can be explained in intensional terms, for persons who favor them, as:

(33)   *w* believes the proposition meant by '. . .' in *L*,

thus leaving no cause for protest on the score of relative clarity. Protest may still be heard, however, on a different score: (32) and (33), though equivalent to each other, are not strictly equivalent to the '*w* believes that . . .' which is our real concern. For, it is argued, in order to infer (33) we need not only the information about *w* which '*w* believes that . . .' provides, but also some extraneous information about the language *L*. Church[4] brings the point out by appeal to translations, substantially as follows. The respective statements:

> *w* believes that there are unicorns,

> *w* believes the proposition meant by 'There are unicorns' in English

go into German as:

(34)   *w glaubt, dass es Einhörne gibt,*

(35)   *w glaubt diejenige Aussage, die* „There are unicorns" *auf Englisch bedeutet,*

and clearly (34) does not provide enough information to enable a German ignorant of English to infer (35).

The same reasoning can be used to show that 'There are unicorns' is not strictly or analytically equivalent to:

> 'There are unicorns' is true in English.

Nor, indeed, was Tarski's truth paradigm intended to assert analytic equivalence. Similarly, then, for (32) in relation to '*w* believes that . . .'; a systematic agreement in truth value can be claimed, and no more. This limitation will prove of little moment to persons who share my skepticism about analyticity.

4. Ibid., with an acknowledgment to Langford.

What I find more disturbing about the semantical versions, such as (32), is the need of dragging in the language concept at all. What is a language? What degree of fixity is supposed? When do we have one language and not two? The propositional attitudes are dim affairs to begin with, and it is a pity to have to add obscurity to obscurity by bringing in language variables too. Only let it not be supposed that any clarity is gained by restituting the intensions.

23

INTENSIONS REVISITED

For the necessity predicate, as distinct from the necessity functor '$\Box$', I shall write 'Nec.' I affirm it of a sentence, to mean that the sentence is a necessary truth, or, if one like, analytic. Whatever its shortcomings in respect of clear criteria, the predicate is more comfortable than the sentence functor, for it occasions no departure from extensional logic. Hence there would be comfort in being able to regard '$\Box$' as mere shorthand for 'Nec' and a pair of quotation marks—thus '$\Box$(9 is odd)' for 'Nec '9 is odd'.' But it will not do. In modal logic one wants to quantify into necessity contexts, and we cannot quantify into quotations.

We can adjust matters by giving 'Nec' *multigrade* status:[1] letting it figure as an n-place predicate for each n. As a two-place predicate it amounts to the words 'is necessarily true of'; thus Nec ('odd,' 9). As a three-place predicate it amounts to those same words said of a two-place predicate and two objects; thus Nec ('<', 5, 9). And so on up. In terms now of multigrade 'Nec' we can explain the use of '$\Box$' on open sentences. We can explain '$\Box$(x is odd),' '$\Box$($x < y$),' etc., as short for 'Nec ('odd,' x),' 'Nec ('<', x, y),' etc.[2] There is no longer an obstacle to quantifying into '$\Box$(x is odd),' '$\Box$($x < y$),' etc. since the definientia do not quote the variables.

This multigrade use of 'Nec' is much like my multigrade treatment in 1956 of the verbs of propositional attitude.[3] Critics of that paper reveal that I have to explain—what I thought went without saying—that the

1. The word was first used by Nelson Goodman, at my suggestion.

2. David Kaplan anticipated this procedure in the third footnote of his "Quantifying in," which appeared in D. Davidson and J. Hintikka (eds.), *Words and Objections* (Dordrecht: D. Reidel, 1969).

3. "Quantifiers and Propositional Attitudes," reprinted in *Ways of Paradox* [Chapter 22].

adoption of a multigrade predicate involves no logical anomaly or any infinite lexicon. It can be viewed as a one-place predicate whose arguments are sequences. As for the use of quotation, it of course is reducible by inductive definition to the concatenation functor and names of signs.

Perhaps also a caution is in order regarding two ways of taking 'necessarily true.' The sentence '9 is odd' is a necessary truth; still, that the form of words '9 is odd' means what it does, and is thus true at all, is only a contingent fact of social usage. Of course I intend 'Nec' in the former way. Similarly for its polyadic use, applied to predicates.

Commonly the predicate wanted as argument of 'Nec' will not be available in the language as a separate word or consecutive phrase. At that point the 'such that' functor serves. For example, the definiens of '$\Box((x + y)(x - y) = x^2 - y^2)$' is:

$$\text{Nec}('zw \; 3 \; ((z + w)(z - w) = z^2 - w^2),' \; x, y).$$

The 'such that' functor, '$zw \; 3$' in this example, connotes no abstraction of classes or relations or attributes. It is only a device for forming complex predicates, tantamount to relative clauses.[4]

When predication in the mode of necessity is directed upon a variable, the necessity is *de re:* the predicate is meant to be true of the value of the variable by whatever name, there being indeed no name at hand. 'Nec('odd,' x)' says of the unspecified object x that oddity is of its essence. Thus it is true not only that Nec('odd,' 9), but equally that Nec('odd,' number of planets), since this very object 9, essence and all, happens to *be* the number of the planets. The 'Nec' notation accommodates *de dicto* necessity too, but differently: the term concerned *de dicto* is within the quoted sentence or predicate. Thus 'Nec '9 is odd'', unlike 'Nec('odd,' 9),' is *de dicto,* and 'Nec 'number of planets is odd'', unlike 'Nec ('odd,' number of planets),' is false.

De re and *de dicto* can be distinguished also in terms of '$\Box$', but along other lines. When the term concerned is a variable, there is nothing to distinguish; *de re* is *de rigueur.* When it is not a variable, we keep it in the scope of '$\Box$' for *de dicto:*

$$\Box(\text{number of planets is odd}) \qquad (\text{false})$$

and bring it out thus for *de re:*

(1) $(\exists x)(x = \text{number of planets}. \Box(x \text{ is odd})).$ (true)

4. See Essay 1 above, §1 [Chapter 13].

In the system of definitions of '□' in terms of 'Nec' we observe a radical twist: '□(x is odd)' and '□(number of planets is odd)' look alike in form, as do 'Nec ('odd,' x)' and 'Nec('odd,' number of planets),' but the translations do not run true to form. '□(x is odd)' and '□(number of planets is odd)' stand rather for the dissimilar formulas 'Nec('odd,' x)' and 'Nec 'number of planets is odd'', whereas what stands for 'Nec('odd,' number of planets)' is (1).

Definitional expansion of '□' thus goes awry under substitution of constants for variables. This is legitimate; unique eliminability is the only formal demand on definition. What the irregularity does portend is a drastic difference in form between the modal logic of '□' and such laws as govern its defining predicate 'Nec.' Drastic difference there is indeed. In particular the distinction between *de re* and *de dicto* is drawn with a simpler uniformity in terms of 'Nec' than in terms of '□'.

Some simplification of theory can be gained by dispensing with singular terms other than variables in familiar fashion: primitive names can be dropped in favor of uniquely fulfilled predicates and then restored as singular descriptions, which finally can be defined away in essentially Russell's way. That done, we can explain '□' fully in terms of 'Nec' and vice versa by this schematic biconditional:

$$(2) \qquad \Box Fx_1x_2 \ldots x_n \equiv \mathrm{Nec}(\text{`}F\text{'}, x_1, x_2, \ldots, x_n).$$

Here *n* may be 0. A certain liberty has been taken in quoting a schematic letter.

It may be noted in passing that '□' on the left of (2) could alternatively be viewed not as a sentence functor but as a predicate functor, governing just the '*F*' and forming a modal predicate '□*F*'.[5]

The reconstruction of '□' in terms of 'Nec' has lent some clarity to the foundations of modal logic by embedding it in extensional logic, quotation, and a special predicate. Incidentally the contrast between *de re* and *de dicto* has thereby been heightened. But the special predicate takes some swallowing. In its monadic use it is at best the controversial semantic predicate of analyticity, and in its polyadic use it imposes an essentialist metaphysics. Let me be read, then, as expounding rather than propounding. I am in the position of a Jewish chef preparing ham for a gentile clientele. Analyticity, essence, and modality are not my meat.

---

5. For the truth theory of a functor to this effect see Christopher Peacocke, "An Appendix to David Wiggins' 'Note,'" in Gareth Evans and John McDowell (eds.), *Truth and Meaning* (Oxford: Oxford University Press, 1976).

If these somber reflections make one wonder whether 'Nec' may be more than we need for '□', a negative answer is visible in (2): they are interdefinable.[6]

A project that I shall not undertake is that of codifying laws of 'Nec' from which those of modal logic can be derived through the definitions. The laws of 'Nec' would involve continual interplay between quotations and their contents. Obviously we would want:

> Nec '. . .' ⊃ . . .,

where the dots stand for any closed sentence. Also, where '——' and '. . .' stand for any closed sentences, we would want 'Nec '—— ≡ . . .'' to assure the interchangeability of '——' with '. . .' inside any quotation preceded by 'Nec.' This is needed for the substitutivity of '□(—— ≡ . . .)' in the modal logic. Also we would need corresponding laws governing the polyadic use of 'Nec' in application to predicates; and here complexities mount. No doubt modal logic is better codified in its own terms; such is the very utility of defining '□' instead of staying with 'Nec.' The latter is merely of conceptual interest in distilling the net import of modal logic over and above extensional logic.

Necessity *de dicto* is notoriously resistant to the substitutivity of identity. When only variables are concerned, the question does not arise; for they figure only *de re*, or, as I have often put it, only in referential position. Moreover, we have decided that only variables *are* concerned, definitions aside. Still, let us consider how singular terms fare when restored definitionally as descriptions. Expanded by those definitions, an identity joining two descriptions or a description and a variable obviously implies the corresponding universally quantified biconditional. We may be sure therefore that even in *de dicto* positions, where substitutivity of simple identity fails, we can depend on substitutivity of necessary identity, $\Box(\zeta = \eta)$; this is assured by the substitutivity of '□(—— ≡ . . .)' noted above.

The substitutivity of $\ulcorner \Box(\zeta = \eta) \urcorner$ is gospel in modal logic. Still, some readers are perhaps brought up short by my appeal to $\ulcorner \Box(\zeta = \eta) \urcorner$, as if I did not know that

(3) $(x)(y)(x = y . \supset \Box (x = y))$.

The point is that I am not free to put ζ and η for 'x' and 'y' in (3).

6. But see P. A. Schilpp and L. E. Hahn (eds.), *The Philosophy of W. V. Quine* (La Salle, Ill.: Open Court, 1986; expanded edition, 1998), pp. 269, 279 (n. 27), 293.

Instantiation of quantification by singular terms is under the same wraps as the substitutivity of identity.

Let instantiation then be our next topic. From the true universal quantification:

$$(x)(x \text{ is a number} . \supset . \Box(5 < x) \lor \Box(5 \geqq x))$$

we cannot, one hopes, infer the falsehood:

$$\Box(5 < \text{number of planets}) \lor \Box(5 \geqq \text{number of planets}).$$

From the truth:

$$5 < \text{number of planets} . - \Box(5 < \text{number of planets}),$$

again, we cannot, one hopes, infer the falsehood:

$$(\exists x)(5 < x . - \Box(5 < x)).$$

When *can* we trust the instantial laws of quantification? The answer is implicit in the substitutivity of $\ulcorner\Box(\zeta = \eta)\urcorner$. For, instantiation is unquestioned when the instantial term is a mere variable 'x'; and we can supplant 'x' here by any desired term η, thanks to the substitutivity of $\ulcorner\Box(x = \eta)\urcorner$, if we can establish $\ulcorner(\exists x)\Box(x = \eta)\urcorner$. This last, then, is the condition that qualifies a term η for the instantial role in steps of universal instantiation and existential generalization in modal contexts. A term thus qualified is what Føllesdal called a genuine name and Kripke has called a rigid designator.[7] It is a term such that $(\exists x)\Box(x = a)$, that is, something is necessarily a, where 'a' stands for the term.

Such a term enjoys *de re* privileges even in a *de dicto* setting. Besides acquitting themselves in instantiation, such terms lend themselves in pairs to the substitutivity of simple identity. For, where ζ and η are rigid designators, we are free to put them for 'x' and 'y' in (3) and thus derive necessary identity.

A rigid designator differs from others in that it picks out its object by essential traits. It designates the object in all possible worlds in which it exists. Talk of possible worlds is a graphic way of waging the essentialist philosophy, but it is only that; it is not an explication. Essence is needed to identify an object from one possible world to another.

Let us turn now to the propositional attitudes. As remarked above, my

---

7. Saul Kripke, "A Completeness Theorem in Modal Logic," *Journal of Symbolic Logic* 24 (1959), pp. 1–11; Quine, *Theories and Things,* p. 173.

treatment of them in 1956 resembled my present use of 'Nec.' At that time I provisionally invoked attributes and propositions, however reluctantly, for the roles here played by mere predicates and sentences. Switching now to the latter style, I would write:

(4)   Tom believes 'Cicero denounced Catiline,'

(5)   Tom believes 'x з (x denounced Catiline)' of Cicero,

(6)   Tom believes 'x з (Cicero denounced x)' of Catiline,

(7)   Tom believes 'xy з (x denounced y)' of Cicero, Catiline,

depending on which terms I want in referential position—that is, with respect to which terms I want the belief to be *de re*. The multigrade predicate 'believes' in these examples is dyadic, triadic, triadic, and tetradic.

Whatever the obscurities of the notion of belief, the underlying logic thus far is extensional—as in the case of 'Nec.' But we can immediately convert the whole to an intensional logic of belief, analogous to that of '□', Where 'B_t' is a sentence functor ascribing belief to Tom, the analogue of the sketchy translation schema (2) is this:

$$B_t F x_1 x_2 \ldots x_n \equiv. \text{ Tom believes '}F\text{' of } x_1, x_2, \ldots, x_n.$$

Parallel to (1) we get:

$$(\exists x)(x = \text{Cicero} . B_t(x \text{ denounced Catiline})),$$

$$(\exists x)(x = \text{Catiline} . B_t(\text{Cicero denounced } x)),$$

$$(\exists x)(\exists y)(x = \text{Cicero} . y = \text{Catiline} . B_t(x \text{ denounced } y))$$

as our transcriptions of the *de re* constructions (5)–(7).

In the 1956 paper I dwelt on the practical difference between the *de dicto* statement:

(8)   Ralph believes '$(\exists x)(x$ is a spy)'

and the *de re* statement 'There is someone whom Ralph believes to be a spy,' that is:

(9) $(\exists y)$(Ralph believes 'spy' of y).

I noted also the more narrowly logical difference between the *de dicto* statement:

(10)   Ralph believes 'Ortcutt is a spy'

and the *de re* statement:

(11)   Ralph believes 'spy' of Ortcutt,

and conjectured that the step of 'exportation' leading from (10) to (11) is generally valid. However, if we transcribe (10) and (11) into terms of 'B$_r$,' according to the foregoing patterns, we get:

(12)   B$_r$(Ortcutt is a spy),

(13) $(\exists x)(x = $ Ortcutt . B$_r(x$ is a spy$))$,

and here the existential force of (13) would seem to belie the validity of the exportation. Sleigh, moreover, has challenged this step on other grounds. Surely, he observes (nearly enough), Ralph believes there are spies. If he believes further, as he reasonably may, that

(14)   No two spies are of exactly the same height,

then he will believe that the shortest spy is a spy. If exportation were valid, it would follow that

   Ralph believes 'spy' of the shortest spy,

and this, having the term 'the shortest spy' out in referential position, implies (9). Thus the portentous belief (9) would follow from trivial ones, (8) and belief of (14).

Let us consult incidentally the analogues of (10) and (11) in modal logic. Looking to the transcriptions (12) and (13), we see that the analogous modal structures are '$\Box Fa$' and '$(\exists x)(x = a . \Box Fx)$.' Does the one imply the other? Again the existential force of the latter would suggest not. And again we can dispute the implication also apart from that existential consideration, as follows [abbreviating (14) and 'there are spies' in conjunction as '14']:

(15) $\Box(14 \supset $. the shortest spy is a spy$)$,

(16) $(\exists x)(x = $ the shortest spy . $\Box(14 \supset . x$ is a spy$))$.

Surely (15) is true. On the other hand, granted (14), presumably (16) is false; for it would require someone to be a spy *de re,* or in essence.

Evidently we must find against exportation. Kaplan's judgment, which he credits to Montgomery Furth, is that the step is sound only in the case of what he calls a *vivid* designator, which is the analogue, in the logic of belief, of a rigid designator. And what might this analogue be? We saw that in modal logic a term is a rigid designator if $(\exists x)\Box(x = a)$, where 'a' stands for the term; so the parallel condition for the logic of belief is that $(\exists x)B_t(x = a)$, if Tom is our man. Thus a term is a vivid designator, for Tom, when there is a specific thing that he believes it designates. Vivid designators, analogues of the rigid designators in modal logic, are the terms that can be freely used to instantiate quantifications in belief contexts, and that are subject to the substitutivity of identity—and, now, to exportation.

Hintikka's criterion for this superior type of term was that Tom *know* who or what the person or thing is; whom or what the term designates.[8] The difference is accountable to the fact that Hintikka's was a logic of both belief and knowledge.

The notion of knowing or believing who or what someone or something is, is utterly dependent on context. Sometimes, when we ask who someone is, we see the face and want the name; sometimes the reverse. Sometimes we want to know his role in the community.[9] Of itself the notion is empty.

It and the notion of essence are on a par. Both make sense in context. Relative to a particular inquiry, some predicates may play a more basic role than others, or may apply more fixedly; and these may be treated as essential. The respective derivative notions, then, of vivid designator and rigid designator, are similarly dependent on context and empty otherwise. The same is true of the whole quantified modal logic of necessity; for it collapses if essence is withdrawn. For that matter, the very notion of necessity makes sense to me only relative to context. Typically it is applied to what is assumed in an inquiry, as against what has yet to transpire.

In thus writing off modal logic I find little to regret. Regarding the propositional attitudes, however, I cannot be so cavalier. Where does the passing of the vivid designator leave us with respect to belief? It leaves us with no distinction between admissible and inadmissible cases of the exportation that leads from (10) to (11), except that those cases remain in-

8. Jaakko Hintikka, *Knowledge and Belief* (Ithaca, N.Y.: Cornell University Press, 1962).

9. Such variation is recognized by Hintikka, *Knowledge and Belief*, p. 149n. For a study of it in depth see S. E. Boër and W. G. Lycan, "Knowing Who," *Philosophical Studies* 28 (1975), pp. 299–344.

admissible in which the exported term fails to name anything. It leaves us defenseless against Sleigh's deduction of the strong (9) from (8) and belief of (14). Thus it virtually annuls the seemingly vital contrast between (8) and (9): between merely believing there are spies and suspecting a specific person. At first this seems intolerable, but it grows on one. I now think the distinction is every bit as empty, apart from context, as that of vivid designator: that of knowing or believing who someone is. In context it can still be important. In one case we can be of service by pointing out the suspect; in another, by naming him; in others, by giving his address or specifying his ostensible employment.

Renunciation does not stop here. The condition for being a vivid designator is that $(\exists x)B_t(x = a)$, or, in the other notation, that

$$(\exists x)(\text{Tom believes ‘} y \, 3 \, (y = a)\text{’ of } x).$$

Surely this makes every bit as good sense as the idiom 'believes of'; there can be no trouble over '$y \, 3 \, (y = a)$.' So our renunciation must extend to all *de re* belief, and similarly, no doubt, for the other propositional attitudes. We end up rejecting *de re* or quantified propositional attitudes generally, on a par with *de re* or quantified modal logic. Rejecting them, that is, except as idioms relativized to the context or situation at hand. We remain less cavalier toward propositional attitudes than toward modal logic only in the unquantified or *de dicto* case, where the attitudes are taken as dyadic relations between people or other animals and closed sentences.

Even these relations present difficulties in respect of criterion. Belief is not to be recognized simply by assent, for this leaves no place for insincerity or sanctimonious self-deception. Belief can be nicely tested and even measured by the betting odds that the subject will accept, allowance being made for the positive or negative value for him of risk as such. This allowance can be measured by testing him on even chances. However, bets work only for sentences for which there is a verification or falsification procedure acceptable to both parties as settling the bet. I see the verb 'believe' even in its *de dicto* use as varying in meaningfulness from sentence to sentence.

Ascribed to the dumb and illiterate animal, belief *de dicto* seems a *contradictio in adjecto*. The betting test is never available. I have suggested elsewhere that some propositional attitudes—desire, fear—might be construed as a relation of the animal to a set of sets of his sensory receptors; but this works only for what I called egocentric desire and fear.[10] I see no way of extending this to belief. Certainly the ascription of a specific simple belief to a dumb animal often can be supported by citing its observable behavior; but a general definition to the purpose is not evident.

Raymond Nelson has ascribed beliefs to machines. He has done so in support of a mechanist philosophy, and I share his attitude. The objects of belief with which he deals are discrete, observable alternatives, and the machine's belief or expectation with respect to them lends itself to a straightforward definition. But this is of no evident help in the kind of problem that is exercising me here. For my problem is not one of reconciling mind and matter, but only a quest for general criteria suitable for unprefabricated cases.

10. "Propositional Objects," reprinted in *Ontological Relativity*.

24

REFERENCE AND MODALITY

1

One of the fundamental principles governing identity is that of *substitutivity*—or, as it might well be called, that of *indiscernibility of identicals*. It provides that, *given a true statement of identity, one of its two terms may be substituted for the other in any true statement and the result will be true.* It is easy to find cases contrary to this principle. For example, the statements:

(1)   Giorgione = Barbarelli,

(2)   Giorgione was so-called because of his size

are true; however, replacement of the name 'Giorgione' by the name 'Barbarelli' turns (2) into the falsehood:

> Barbarelli was so-called because of his size.

Furthermore, the statements:

(3)   Cicero = Tully,

(4)   'Cicero' contains six letters

are true, but replacement of the first name by the second turns (4) false. Yet the basis of the principle of substitutivity appears quite solid; whatever can be said about the person Cicero (or Giorgione) should be equally true of the person Tully (or Barbarelli), this being the same person.

In the case of (4), this paradox resolves itself immediately. The fact is that (4) is not a statement about the person Cicero, but simply about the word 'Cicero.' The principle of substitutivity should not be extended to contexts in which the name to be supplanted occurs without referring simply to the object. Failure of substitutivity reveals merely that the occurrence to be supplanted is not *purely referential*,[1] that is, that the statement depends not only on the object but on the form of the name. For it is clear that whatever can be affirmed about the object remains true when we refer to the object by any other name.

An expression which consists of another expression between single quotes constitutes a name of that other expression; and it is clear that the occurrence of that other expression or a part of it, within the context of quotes, is not in general referential. In particular, the occurrence of the personal name within the context of quotes in (4) is not referential, not subject to the substitutivity principle. The personal name occurs there merely as a fragment of a longer name which contains, beside this fragment, the two quotation marks. To make a substitution upon a personal name, within such a context, would be no more justifiable than to make a substitution upon the term 'cat' within the context 'cattle.'

The example (2) is a little more subtle, for it is a statement about a man and not merely about his name. It was the man, not his name, that was called so and so because of his size. Nevertheless, the failure of substitutivity shows that the occurrence of the personal name in (2) is not *purely* referential. It is easy in fact to translate (2) into another statement which contains two occurrences of the name, one purely referential and the other not:

(5)   Giorgione was called 'Giorgione' because of his size.

The first occurrence is purely referential. Substitution on the basis of (1) converts (5) into another statement equally true:

Barbarelli was called 'Giorgione' because of his size.

The second occurrence of the personal name is no more referential than any other occurrence within a context of quotes.

It would not be quite accurate to conclude that an occurrence of a name within single quotes is *never* referential. Consider the statements:

1. Gottlob Frege, in his "On Sense and Nominatum," which appeared in Herbert Feigl and Wilfrid Sellars (eds.), *Readings in Philosophical Analysis* (New York: Appleton-Century-Crofts, 1949), spoke of *direct (gerade)* and *oblique (ungerade)* occurrences, and used substitutivity of identity as a criterion just as here.

(6)   'Giorgione played chess' is true,

(7)   'Giorgione' named a chess player,

each of which is true or false according as the quotationless statement:

(8)   Giorgione played chess

is true or false. Our criterion of referential occurrence makes the occurrence of the name 'Giorgione' in (8) referential, and must make the occurrences of 'Giorgione' in (6) and (7) referential by the same token, despite the presence of single quotes in (6) and (7). The point about quotation is not that it must destroy referential occurrence, but that it can (and ordinarily does) destroy referential occurrence. The examples (6) and (7) are exceptional in that the special predicates 'is true' and 'named' have the effect of undoing the single quotes—as is evident on comparison of (6) and (7) with (8).

To get an example of another common type of statement in which names do not occur referentially, consider any person who is called Philip and satisfies the condition:

(9)   Philip is unaware that Tully denounced Catiline,

or perhaps the condition:

(10)   Philip believes that Tegucigalpa is in Nicaragua.

Substitution on the basis of (3) transforms (9) into the statement:

(11)   Philip is unaware that Cicero denounced Catiline,

no doubt false. Substitution on the basis of the true identity:

Tegucigalpa = capital of Honduras

transforms the truth (10) likewise into the falsehood:

(12)   Philip believes that the capital of Honduras is in Nicaragua.

We see therefore that the occurrences of the names 'Tully' and 'Tegucigalpa' in (9)–(10) are not purely referential.

In this there is a fundamental contrast between (9), or (10), and:

Crassus heard Tully denounce Catiline.

This statement affirms a relation between three persons, and the persons remain so related independently of the names applied to them. But (9) cannot be considered simply as affirming a relation between three persons, nor (10) a relation between person, city, and country—at least not so long as we interpret our words in such a way as to admit (9) and (10) as true and (11) and (12) as false.

Some readers may wish to construe unawareness and belief as relations between persons and statements, thus writing (9) and (10) in the manner:

(13)   Philip is unaware of 'Tully denounced Catiline,'

(14)   Philip believes 'Tegucigalpa is in Nicaragua,'

in order to put within a context of single quotes every not purely referential occurrence of a name. Church argues against this. In so doing he exploits the concept of analyticity, concerning which we have felt misgivings (pp. 23–37 above); still his argument cannot be set lightly aside, nor are we required here to take a stand on the matter. Suffice it to say that there is certainly no *need* to reconstrue (9)–(10) in the manner (13)–(14). What *is* imperative is to observe merely that the contexts 'is unaware that . . .' and 'believes that . . .' *resemble* the context of the single quotes in this respect: a name may occur referentially in a statement S and yet not occur referentially in a longer statement which is formed by embedding S in the context 'is unaware that . . .' or 'believes that . . . .' To sum up the situation in a word, we may speak of the contexts 'is unaware that . . .' and 'believes that . . .' as *referentially opaque.*[2] The same is true of the contexts 'knows that . . . ,' 'says that . . . ,' 'doubts that . . . ,' 'is surprised that . . . ,' etc. It would be tidy but unnecessary to force all referentially opaque contexts into the quotational mold; alternatively we can recognize quotation as one referentially opaque context among many.

It will next be shown that referential opacity afflicts also the so-called *modal* contexts 'Necessarily . . .' and 'Possibly . . . ,' at least when those are given the sense of *strict* necessity and possibility as in Lewis's modal logic.[3] According to the strict sense of 'necessarily' and 'possibly,' these statements would be regarded as true:

(15)   9 is necessarily greater than 7,

2. This term is roughly the opposite of Russell's 'transparent' as he uses it in his Appendix C to *Principia,* 2d ed., vol. 1.

3. Lewis, *Survey of Symbolic Logic,* Ch. 5; C. I. Lewis and C. H. Langford, *Symbolic Logic* (New York, 1932; reprinted, New York: Dover, 1951), pp. 78–89, 120–166.

(16) Necessarily if there is life on the Evening Star then there is life on the Evening Star,

(17) The number of planets is possibly less than 7,

and these are false:

(18) The number of planets is necessarily greater than 7,

(19) Necessarily if there is life on the Evening Star then there is life on the Morning Star,

(20) 9 is possibly less than 7.

The general idea of strict modalities is based on the putative notion of *analyticity* as follows: a statement of the form 'Necessarily . . .' is true if and only if the component statement which 'necessarily' governs is analytic, and a statement of the form 'Possibly . . .' is false if and only if the negation of the component statement which 'possibly' governs is analytic. Thus (15)–(17) could be paraphrased as follows:

(21) '9 > 7' is analytic,

(22) 'If there is life on the Evening Star then there is life on the Evening Star' is analytic,

(23) 'The number of planets is not less than 7' is not analytic,

and correspondingly for (18)–(20).

That the contexts 'Necessarily . . .' and 'Possibly . . .' are referentially opaque can now be quickly seen; for substitution on the basis of the true identities:

(24) The number of planets = 9,

(25) The Evening Star = the Morning Star

turns the truths (15)–(17) into the falsehoods (18)–(20).

Note that the fact that (15)–(17) are equivalent to (21)–(23), and the fact that '9' and 'Evening Star' and 'the number of planets' occur within quotations in (21)–(23), would not of themselves have justified us in concluding that '9' and 'Evening Star' and 'the number of planets' occur irreferentially in (15)–(17). To argue thus would be like citing the equivalence of (8) to (6) and (7) as evidence that 'Giorgione' occurs irreferentially in (8). What shows the occurrences of '9,' 'Evening Star,' and 'the number of planets' to be irreferential in (15)–(17) (and in (18)–(20))

is the fact that substitution by (24)–(25) turns the truths (15)–(17) into falsehoods (and the falsehoods (18)–(20) into truths).

Some, it was remarked, may like to think of (9) and (10) as receiving their more fundamental expression in (13) and (14). In the same spirit, many will like to think of (15)–(17) as receiving their more fundamental expression in (21)–(23).[4] But this again is unnecessary. We would certainly not think of (6) and (7) as somehow more basic than (8), and we need not view (21)–(23) as more basic than (15)–(17). What is important is to appreciate that the contexts 'Necessarily . . .' and 'Possibly . . .' are, like quotation and 'is unaware that . . .' and 'believes that . . . ,' referentially opaque.

2

The phenomenon of referential opacity has just now been explained by appeal to the behavior of singular terms. But singular terms are eliminable, we know, by paraphrase. Ultimately the objects referred to in a theory are to be accounted not as the things named by the singular terms, but as the values of the variables of quantification. So, if referential opacity is an infirmity worth worrying about, it must show symptoms in connection with quantification as well as in connection with singular terms.[5] Let us then turn our attention to quantification.

The connection between naming and quantification is implicit in the operation whereby, from 'Socrates is mortal,' we infer '$(\exists x)(x$ is mortal),' that is, 'Something is mortal.' This is the operation which was spoken of earlier as *existential generalization,* except that we now have a singular term 'Socrates' where we then had a free variable. The idea behind such inference is that whatever is true of the object named by a given singular term is true of something; and clearly the inference loses its justification when the singular term in question does not happen to name. From:

> There is no such thing as Pegasus,

for example, we do not infer:

> $(\exists x)$(there is no such thing as x),

4. See Carnap, *The Logical Syntax of Language,* pp. 245–259.

5. Substantially this point was made by Alonzo Church, in review of Quine, *Journal of Symbolic Logic* 7 (1942), pp. 100f.

that is, 'There is something which there is no such thing as,' or 'There is something which there is not.'

Such inference is of course equally unwarranted in the case of an irreferential occurrence of any substantive. From (2), existential generalization would lead to:

$$(\exists x)(x \text{ was so-called because of its size}),$$

that is, 'Something was so-called because of its size.' This is clearly meaningless, there being no longer any suitable antecedent for 'so-called.' Note, in contrast, that existential generalization with respect to the purely referential occurrence in (5) yields the sound conclusion:

$$(\exists x)(x \text{ was called 'Giorgione' because of its size}),$$

that is, 'Something was called 'Giorgione' because of its size.'

The logical operation of *universal instantiation* is that whereby we infer from 'Everything is itself,' for example, or in symbols '$(x)(x = x)$,' the conclusion that Socrates = Socrates. This and existential generalization are two aspects of a single principle; for instead of saying that '$(x)(x = x)$' implies 'Socrates = Socrates,' we could as well say that the denial 'Socrates $\neq$ Socrates' implies '$(\exists x)(x \neq x)$.' The principle embodied in these two operations is the link between quantifications and the singular statements that are related to them as instances. Yet it is a principle only by courtesy. It holds only in the case where a term names and, furthermore, occurs referentially. It is simply the logical content of the idea that a given occurrence is referential. The principle is, for this reason, anomalous as an adjunct to the purely logical theory of quantification. Hence the logical importance of the fact that all singular terms, aside from the variables that serve as pronouns in connection with quantifiers, are dispensable and eliminable by paraphrase.[6]

We saw just now how the referentially opaque context (2) fared under existential generalization. Let us see what happens to our other referentially opaque contexts. Applied to the occurrence of the personal name in (4), existential generalization would lead us to:

6. See above, pp. 7–8, 13 [Chapter 13], and *From a Logical Point of View*, pp. 166–167. Note that existential generalization as of p. 120 does belong to pure quantification theory, for it has to do with free variables rather than singular terms. The same is true of a correlative use of universal instantiation, such as is embodied in R2 of Essay 5 (Quine, "New Foundations for Mathematical Logic," *From a Logical Point of View* [Cambridge, Mass.: Harvard University Press, 1980], pp. 80–101).

(26) $(\exists x)($ 'x' contains six letters$)$,

that is:

(27) There is something such that 'it' contains six letters,

or perhaps:

(28) 'Something' contains six letters.

Now the expression:

'x' contains six letters

means simply:

The 24th letter of the alphabet contains six letters.

In (26) the occurrence of the letter within the context of quotes is as irrelevant to the quantifier that precedes it as is the occurrence of the same letter in the context 'six.' (26) consists merely of a falsehood preceded by an irrelevant quantifier. (27) is similar; its part:

'it' contains six letters

is false, and the prefix 'there is something such that' is irrelevant. (28), again, is false—if by 'contains six' we mean 'contains exactly six.'

It is less obvious, and correspondingly more important to recognize, that existential generalization is unwarranted likewise in the case of (9) and (10). Applied to (9), it leads to:

$(\exists x)($Philip is unaware that x denounced Catiline$)$,

that is:

(29) Something is such that Philip is unaware that it denounced Catiline.

What is this object, that denounced Catiline without Philip's having become aware of the fact? Tully, that is, Cicero? But to suppose this would conflict with the fact that (11) is false.

Note that (29) is not to be confused with:

Philip is unaware that $(\exists x)($ x denounced Catiline$)$,

which, though it happens to be false, is quite straightforward and in no danger of being inferred by existential generalization from (9).

Now the difficulty involved in the apparent consequence (29) of (9) recurs when we try to apply existential generalization to modal statements. The apparent consequences:

(30) $(\exists x)(x$ is necessarily greater than 7),

(31) $(\exists x)$(necessarily if there is life on the Evening Star then there is life on x)

of (15) and (16) raise the same questions as did (29). What is this number which, according to (30), is necessarily greater than 7? According to (15), from which (30) was inferred, it was 9, that is, the number of planets; but to suppose this would conflict with the fact that (18) is false. In a word, to be necessarily greater than 7 is not a trait of a number, but depends on the manner of referring to the number. Again, what is the thing x whose existence is affirmed in (31)? According to (16), from which (31) was inferred, it was the Evening Star, that is, the Morning Star; but to suppose this would conflict with the fact that (19) is false. Being necessarily or possibly thus and so is in general not a trait of the object concerned, but depends on the manner of referring to the object.

Note that (30) and (31) are not to be confused with:

Necessarily $(\exists x)(x > 7)$,

Necessarily $(\exists x)$(if there is life on the Evening Star then there is life on x),

which present no problem of interpretation comparable to that presented by (30) and (31). The difference may be accentuated by a change of example: in a game of a type admitting of no tie it is necessary that some one of the players will win, but there is no one player of whom it may be said to be necessary that he win.

We had seen, in the preceding section, how referential opacity manifests itself in connection with singular terms; and the task which we then set ourselves at the beginning of this section was to see how referential opacity manifests itself in connection rather with variables of quantification. The answer is now apparent: if to a referentially opaque context of a variable we apply a quantifier, with the intention that it govern that variable from outside the referentially opaque context, then what we commonly end up with is unintended sense or nonsense of the type (26)–(31). In a word, we cannot in general properly *quantify into* referentially opaque contexts.

The context of quotation and the further contexts '. . . was so called,' 'is unaware that . . . ,' 'believes that . . . ,' 'Necessarily . . . ,' and 'Possibly . . .' were found referentially opaque in the preceding section by consideration of the failure of substitutivity of identity as applied to singular terms. In the present section these contexts have been found referentially opaque by a criterion having to do no longer with singular terms, but with the miscarriage of quantification. The reader may feel, indeed, that in this second criterion we have not really got away from singular terms after all; for the discrediting of the quantifications (29)–(31) turned still on an expository interplay between the singular terms 'Tully' and 'Cicero,' '9' and 'the number of planets,' 'Evening Star' and 'Morning Star.' Actually, though, this expository reversion to our old singular terms is avoidable, as may now be illustrated by re-arguing the meaninglessness of (30) in another way. Whatever is greater than 7 is a number, and any given number x greater than 7 can be uniquely determined by any of various conditions, some of which have '$x > 7$' as a *necessary* consequence and some of which do not. One and the same number x is uniquely determined by the condition:

(32) $x = \sqrt{x} + \sqrt{x} + \sqrt{x} \neq \sqrt{x}$

and by the condition:

(33)   There are exactly x planets,

but (32) has '$x > 7$' as a necessary consequence while (33) does not. *Necessary* greaterness than 7 makes no sense as applied to a *number x*; necessity attaches only to the connection between '$x > 7$' and the particular method (32), as opposed to (33), of specifying x.

Similarly, (31) was meaningless because the sort of thing x which fulfills the condition:

(34)   If there is life on the Evening Star then there is life on x,

namely, a physical object, can be uniquely determined by any of various conditions, not all of which have (34) as a necessary consequence. *Necessary* fulfillment of (34) makes no sense as applied to a physical object x; necessity attaches, at best, only to the connection between (34) and one or another particular means of specifying x.

The importance of recognizing referential opacity is not easily overstressed. We saw in §1 that referential opacity can obstruct substitutivity of identity. We now see that it also can interrupt quantification: quantifiers outside a referentially opaque construction need have no bearing on variables inside it. This again is obvious in the case of quotation, as witness the grotesque example:

$(\exists x)(\text{'}six\text{' contains '}x\text{'}).$

3

We see from (30)–(31) how a quantifier applied to a modal sentence may lead simply to nonsense. Nonsense is indeed mere absence of sense, and can always be remedied by arbitrarily assigning some sense. But the important point to observe is that granted an understanding of the modalities (through uncritical acceptance, for the sake of argument, of the underlying notion of analyticity), and given an understanding of quantification ordinarily so called, we do not come out automatically with any meaning for quantified modal sentences such as (30)–(31). This point must be taken into account by anyone who undertakes to work out laws for a quantified modal logic.

The root of the trouble was the referential opacity of modal contexts. But referential opacity depends in part on the ontology accepted, that is, on what objects are admitted as possible objects of reference. This may be seen most readily by reverting for a while to the point of view of §1, where referential opacity was explained in terms of failure of interchangeability of names which name the same object. Suppose now we were to repudiate all objects which, like 9 and the planet Venus, or Evening Star, are nameable by names which fail of interchangeability in modal contexts. To do so would be to sweep away all examples indicative of the opacity of modal contexts.

But what objects would remain in a thus purified universe? An object x must, to survive, meet this condition: if S is a statement containing a referential occurrence of a name of x, and S' is formed from S by substituting any different name of x, then S and S' not only must be alike in truth value as they stand, but must stay alike in truth value even when 'necessarily' or 'possibly' is prefixed. Equivalently: putting one name of x for another in any analytic statement must yield an analytic statement. Equivalently: any two names of x must be synonymous.[7]

Thus the planet Venus as a material object is ruled out by the posses-

---

7. See above, p. 32 [Chapter 2]. Synonymy of names does not mean merely naming the same thing; it means that the statement of identity formed of the two names is analytic.

sion of heteronymous names 'Venus,' 'Evening Star,' 'Morning Star.' Corresponding to these three names we must, if modal contexts are not to be referentially opaque, recognize three objects rather than one—perhaps the Venus-concept, the Evening-Star-concept, and the Morning-Star-concept.

Similarly 9, as a unique whole number between 8 and 10, is ruled out by the possession of heteronymous names '9' and 'the number of the planets.' Corresponding to these two names we must, if modal contexts are not to be referentially opaque, recognize two objects rather than one; perhaps the 9-concept and the number-of-planets-concept. These concepts are not numbers, for the one is neither identical with nor less than nor greater than the other.

The requirement that any two names of x be synonymous might be seen as a restriction not on the admissible objects x, but on the admissible vocabulary of singular terms. So much the worse, then, for this way of phrasing the requirement; we have here simply one more manifestation of the superficiality of treating ontological questions from the vantage point of singular terms. The real insight, in danger now of being obscured, was rather this: necessity does not properly apply to the fulfillment of conditions by *objects* (such as the ball of rock which is Venus, or the number which numbers the planets), apart from special ways of specifying them. This point was most conveniently brought out by consideration of singular terms, but it is not abrogated by their elimination. Let us now review the matter from the point of view of quantification rather than singular terms.

From the point of view of quantification, the referential opacity of modal contexts was reflected in the meaninglessness of such quantifications as (30)–(31). The crux of the trouble with (30) is that a number x may be uniquely determined by each of two conditions, for example, (32) and (33), which are not necessarily, that is, analytically, equivalent to each other. But suppose now we were to repudiate all such objects and retain only objects x such that *any two conditions uniquely determining x are analytically equivalent*. All examples such as (30)–(31), illustrative of the referential opacity of modal contexts, would then be swept away. It would come to make sense in general to say that there is an object which, independently of any particular means of specifying it, is necessarily thus and so. It would become legitimate, in short, to quantify into modal contexts.

Our examples suggest no objection to quantifying into modal contexts as long as the values of any variables thus quantified are limited to *intensional objects*. This limitation would mean allowing, for purposes of such quantification anyway, not classes but only class-concepts or attributes, it being understood that two open sentences which determine the same class still determine distinct attributes unless they are analytically equivalent. It would mean allowing, for purposes of such quantification, not numbers but only some sort of concepts which are related to the numbers in a many-one way. Further it would mean allowing, for purposes of such quantification, no concrete objects but only what Frege called senses of names, and Carnap and Church have called individual concepts. It is a drawback of such an ontology that the principle of individuation of its entities rests invariably on the putative notion of synonymy, or analyticity.

Actually, even granted these dubious entities, we can quickly see that the expedient of limiting the values of variables to them is after all a mistaken one. It does not relieve the original difficulty over quantifying into modal contexts; on the contrary, examples quite as disturbing as the old ones can be adduced within the realm of intensional objects. For, where A is any intensional object, say an attribute, and 'p' stands for an arbitrary true sentence, clearly

$$(35) \quad A = (\imath x)[p \cdot (x = A)].$$

Yet, if the true sentence represented by 'p' is not analytic, then neither is (35), and its sides are no more interchangeable in modal contexts than are 'Evening Star' and 'Morning Star,' or '9' and 'the number of the planets.'

Or, to state the point without recourse to singular terms, it is that the requirement lately italicized—"any two conditions uniquely determining x are analytically equivalent"—is not assured merely by taking x as an intensional object. For, think of 'Fx' as any condition uniquely determining x, and think of 'p' as any nonanalytic truth. Then '$p \cdot Fx$' uniquely determines x but is not analytically equivalent to 'Fx', even though x be an intensional object.

It was in my 1943 paper that I first objected to quantifying into modal contexts, and it was in his review of it that Church proposed the remedy of limiting the variables thus quantified to intensional values. This remedy, which I have just now represented as mistaken, seemed all right at the time. Carnap adopted it in an extreme form, limiting the range of his variables to intensional objects throughout his system. He did not indeed describe his procedure thus; he complicated the picture by propounding a curious double interpretation of variables. But I have argued[8] that this complicating device has no essential bearing and is better put aside.

By the time Church came to propound an intensional logic of his own, he perhaps appreciated that quantification into modal contexts could not after all be legitimized simply by limiting the thus quantified variables to intensional values. Anyway his departures are more radical. Instead of a necessity operator attachable to sentences, he has a necessity predicate attachable to complex names of certain intensional objects called propositions. What makes this departure more serious than it sounds is that the constants and variables occurring in a sentence do not, without special provision, recur in the name of the corresponding proposition. Church makes such provision by introducing a primitive function that applies to intensional objects and yields their extensions as values. The interplay, usual in modal logic, between occurrences of expressions outside modal contexts and recurrences of them inside modal contexts, is mediated in Church's system by this function. Perhaps we should not call it a system of modal logic; Church generally did not. Anyway let my continuing discussion be understood as relating to modal logics only in the narrower sense, where the modal operator attaches to sentences.

Church and Carnap tried—unsuccessfully, I have just argued—to meet my criticism of quantified modal logic by restricting the values of their variables. Arthur Smullyan took the alternative course of challenging my criticism itself. His argument depends on positing a fundamental division of names into proper names and (overt or covert) descriptions, such that proper names which name the same object are always synonymous. (Cf. (38) below.) He observes, quite rightly on these assumptions, that any examples which, like (15)–(20) and (24)–(25), show failure of substitutivity of identity in modal contexts, must exploit some descriptions rather than just proper names. Then, taking a leaf from Russell, he explains the failure of substitutivity by differences in the structure of the contexts, in respect of what Russell called the scopes of the descriptions.[9] As stressed in the preceding section, however, referential opacity remains

8. In a criticism which Carnap generously included in his *Meaning and Necessity*, pp. 196–197.

9. Unless a description fails to name, its scope is indifferent to extensional contexts. But it can still matter to intensional ones.

to be reckoned with even when descriptions and other singular terms are eliminated altogether.

Nevertheless, the only hope of sustaining quantified modal logic lies in adopting a course that resembles Smullyan's, rather than Church and Carnap, in this way: it must overrule my objection. It must consist in arguing or deciding that quantification into modal contexts makes sense even though any value of the variable of such a quantification be determinable by conditions that are not analytically equivalent to each other. The only hope lies in accepting the situation illustrated by (32) and (33) and insisting, despite it, that the object x in question is necessarily greater than 7. This means adopting an invidious attitude toward certain ways of uniquely specifying x, for example (33), and favoring other ways, for example (32), as somehow better revealing the "essence" of the object. Consequences of (32) can, from such a point of view, be looked upon as necessarily true of the object which is 9 (and is the number of the planets), while some consequences of (33) are rated still as only contingently true of that object.

Evidently this reversion to Aristotelian essentialism (cf. p. 22) is required if quantification into modal contexts is to be insisted on. An object, of itself and by whatever name or none, must be seen as having some of its traits necessarily and others contingently, despite the fact that the latter traits follow just as analytically from some ways of specifying the object as the former traits do from other ways of specifying it. In fact, we can see pretty directly that any quantified modal logic is bound to show such favoritism among the traits of an object; for surely it will be held, for each thing x, on the one hand that

(36)   necessarily $(x = x)$

and on the other hand that

(37) $\sim$ necessarily $[p \,.\, (x = x)]$,

where 'p' stands for an arbitrary contingent truth.

Essentialism is abruptly at variance with the idea, favored by Carnap, Lewis, and others, of explaining necessity by analyticity. For the appeal to analyticity can pretend to distinguish essential and accidental traits of an object only relative to how the object is specified, not absolutely. Yet the champion of quantified modal logic must settle for essentialism.

Limiting the values of his variables is neither necessary nor sufficient to justify quantifying the variables into modal contexts. Limiting their values can, however, still have this purpose in conjunction with his essentialism: if he wants to limit his essentialism to special sorts of objects, he must correspondingly limit the values of the variables which he quantifies into modal contexts.

The system presented in Miss Barcan's pioneer papers on quantified modal logic differed from the systems of Carnap and Church in imposing no special limitations on the values of variables. That she was prepared, moreover, to accept the essentialist presuppositions seems rather hinted in her theorem:

(38) $(x)(y)\{(x = y) \supset [\text{necessarily } (x = y)]\}$,

for this is as if to say that some at least (and in fact at most; cf. '$p \cdot Fx$') of the traits that determine an object do so necessarily. The modal logic in Fitch [1] follows Miss Barcan on both points. Note incidentally that (38) follows directly from (36) and a law of substitutivity of identity for variables:

$(x)(y)[(x = y \cdot Fx) \supset Fy]$.

The upshot of these reflections is meant to be that the way to do quantified modal logic, if at all, is to accept Aristotelian essentialism. To defend Aristotelian essentialism, however, is not part of my plan. Such a philosophy is as unreasonable by my lights as it is by Carnap's or Lewis's. And in conclusion I say, as Carnap and Lewis have not: so much the worse for quantified modal logic. By implication, so much the worse for unquantified modal logic as well; for, if we do not propose to quantify across the necessity operator, the use of that operator ceases to have any clear advantage over merely quoting a sentence and saying that it is analytic.

4

The worries introduced by the logical modalities are introduced also by the admission of attributes (as opposed to classes). The idiom 'the attribute of being thus and so' is referentially opaque, as may be seen, for example, from the fact that the true statement:

(39)   The attribute of exceeding 9 = the attribute of exceeding 9

goes over into the falsehood:

> The attribute of exceeding the number of the planets = the
> attribute of exceeding 9

under substitution according to the true identity (24). Moreover, existential generalization of (39) would lead to:

(40) $(\exists x)$(the attribute of exceeding x = the attribute of exceeding 9)

which resists coherent interpretation just as did the existential generalizations (29)–(31) of (9), (15), and (16). Quantification of a sentence which contains the variable of quantification within a context of the form 'the attribute of . . .' is exactly on a par with quantification of a modal sentence.

Attributes, as remarked earlier, are individuated by this principle: two open sentences which determine the same class do not determine the same attribute unless they are analytically equivalent. Now another popular sort of intensional entity is the *proposition*. Propositions are conceived in relation to statements as attributes are conceived in relation to open sentences: two statements determine the same proposition just in case they are analytically equivalent. The foregoing strictures on attributes obviously apply equally to propositions. The truth:

(41)   The proposition that 9 > 7 = the proposition that 9 > 7

goes over into the falsehood:

> The proposition that the number of the planets > 7 = the
> proposition that 9 > 7.

under substitution according to (24). Existential generalization of (41) yields a result comparable to (29)–(31) and (40).

Most of the logicians, semanticists, and analytical philosophers who discourse freely of attributes, propositions, or logical modalities betray failure to appreciate that they thereby imply a metaphysical position which they themselves would scarcely condone. It is noteworthy that in *Principia Mathematica,* where attributes were nominally admitted as entities, all actual contexts occurring in the course of formal work are such as could be fulfilled as well by classes as by attributes. All actual contexts are *extensional.* The authors of *Principia Mathematica* thus adhered in practice to a principle of extensionality which they did not espouse in theory. If their practice had been otherwise, we might have been brought sooner to an appreciation of the urgency of the principle.

We have seen how modal sentences, attribute terms, and proposition terms conflict with the nonessentialist view of the universe. It must be kept in mind that those expressions create such conflict only when they are quantified into, that is, when they are put under a quantifier and themselves contain the variable of quantification. We are familiar with the fact (illustrated by (26) above) that a quotation cannot contain an effectively free variable, reachable by an outside quantifier. If we preserve a similar attitude toward modalities, attribute terms, and proposition terms, we may then make free use of them without any misgivings of the present urgent kind.

What has been said of modality in these pages relates only to strict modality. For other sorts, for example, physical necessity and possibility, the first problem would be to formulate the notions clearly and exactly. Afterward we could investigate whether such modalities, like the strict ones, cannot be quantified into without precipitating an ontological crisis. The question concerns intimately the practical use of language. It concerns, for example, the use of the contrary-to-fact conditional within a quantification; for it is reasonable to suppose that the contrary-to-fact conditional reduces to the form 'Necessarily, if p then q' in some sense of necessity. Upon the contrary-to-fact conditional depends in turn, for example, this definition of solubility in water: To say that an object is soluble in water is to say that it would dissolve if it were in water. In discussions of physics, naturally, we need quantifications containing the clause 'x is soluble in water,' or the equivalent in words; but, according to the definition suggested, we should then have to admit within quantifications the expression 'if x were in water then x would dissolve,' that is, 'necessarily if x is in water then x dissolves.' Yet we do not know whether there is a suitable sense of 'necessarily' into which we can so quantify.[10]

Any way of imbedding statements within statements, whether based on some notion of "necessity" or, for example, on a notion of "probability" as in Reichenbach, must be carefully examined in relation to its susceptibility to quantification. Perhaps the only useful modes of statement

10. For a theory of disposition terms, like 'soluble,' see Rudolf Carnap, "Testability and Meaning," *Philosophy and Science* 3 (1936), pp. 419–471; 4 (1937), pp. 1–40 (reprinted, New Haven: Graduate Philosophy Club, Yale University, 1950).

composition susceptible to unrestricted quantification are the truth functions. Happily, no other mode of statement composition is needed, at any rate, in mathematics; and mathematics, significantly, is the branch of science whose needs are most clearly understood.

Let us return, for a final sweeping observation, to our first test of referential opacity, namely, failure of substitutivity of identity; and let us suppose that we are dealing with a theory in which (a) *logically* equivalent formulas are interchangeable in all contexts *salva veritate* and (b) the logic of classes is at hand.[11] For such a theory it can be shown that *any* mode of statement composition, other than the truth functions, is referentially opaque. For, let ϕ and ψ be any statements alike in truth value, and let $\Phi(\phi)$ be any true statement containing ϕ as a part. What is to be shown is that $\Phi(\psi)$ will also be true, unless the context represented by 'Φ' is referentially opaque. Now the class named by $\hat{\alpha}\phi$ is either V or Λ, according as ϕ is true or false; for remember that ϕ is a statement, devoid of free α. (If the notation $\hat{\alpha}\phi$ without recurrence of α seems puzzling, read it as $\hat{\alpha}(\alpha = \alpha . \phi)$.) Moreover ϕ is logically equivalent to $\hat{\alpha}\phi = $ V. Hence, by (a), since $\Phi(\phi)$ is true, so is $\Phi(\hat{\alpha}\phi = $ V). But $\hat{\alpha}\phi$ and $\hat{\alpha}\psi$ name one and the same class, since ϕ and ψ are alike in truth value. Then, since $\Phi(\hat{\alpha}\phi = $ V) is true, so is $\Phi(\hat{\alpha}\psi = $ V) unless the context represented by 'Φ' is referentially opaque. But if $\Phi(\hat{\alpha}\psi = $ V) is true, then so in turn is $\Phi(\psi)$, by (a).

11. See above, p. 27 [Chapter 2], and *From a Logical Point of View*, p. 87.

25

THREE GRADES OF MODAL INVOLVEMENT

There are several closely interrelated operators, called *modal* operators, which are characteristic of modal logic. There are the operators of *necessity, possibility, impossibility, non-necessity.* Also there are the binary operators, or connectives, of *strict implication* and *strict equivalence.* These various operators are easily definable in terms of one another. Thus impossibility is necessity of the negation; possibility and non-necessity are the negations of impossibility and necessity; and strict implication and strict equivalence are necessity of the material conditional and biconditional. In a philosophical examination of modal logic we may therefore conveniently limit ourselves for the most part to a single modal operator, that of *necessity.* Whatever may be said about necessity may be said also, with easy and obvious adjustments, about the other modes.

There are three different degrees to which we may allow our logic, or semantics, to embrace the idea of necessity. The first or least degree of acceptance is this: necessity is expressed by a *semantical predicate* attributable to statements as notational forms—hence attachable to names of statements. We write, e.g.:

(1)   Nec '9 > 5',

(2)   Nec (Sturm's theorem),

(3)   Nec 'Napoleon escaped from Elba,'

in each case attaching the predicate 'Nec' to a noun, a singular term, which is a *name of* the statement which is affirmed to be necessary (or necessarily true). Of the above examples, (1) and (2) would presumably be regarded as true and (3) as false; for the necessity concerned in modal logic is generally conceived to be of a logical or a priori sort.

A second and more drastic degree in which the notion of necessity may be adopted is in the form of a *statement operator.* Here we have no longer a predicate, attaching to names of statements as in (1)–(3), but a logical operator 'nec,' which attaches to statements themselves, in the manner of the negation sign. Under this usage, (1) and (3) would be rendered rather as:

(4)   nec $(9 > 5)$,

(5)   nec (Napoleon escaped from Elba),

and (2) would be rendered by prefixing 'nec' to Sturm's actual theorem rather than to its name. Thus whereas 'Nec' is a predicate or verb, 'is necessary,' which attaches to a noun to form a statement, 'nec' is rather an adverb, 'necessarily,' which attaches to a statement to form a statement.

Finally the third and gravest degree is expression of necessity by a sentence operator. This is an extension of the second degree, and goes beyond it in allowing the attachment of 'nec' not only to statements but also to open sentences, such as '$x > 5$,' preparatory to the ultimate attachment of quantifiers:

(6) (x) nec $(x > 5)$,

(7) $(\exists x)$ nec $(x > 5)$,

(8) $(x)[x = 9 . \supset$ nec $(x > 5)]$.

The example (6) would doubtless be rated as false, and perhaps (7) and (8) as true.

I shall be concerned in this paper to bring out the logical and philosophical significance of these three degrees of acceptance of a necessity device.

I

I call an occurrence of a singular term in a statement *purely referential*[1] (Frege: *gerade*),[2] if, roughly speaking, the term serves in that particular

1. Quine, *From a Logical Point of View:* pp. 75–76 ["Identity, Ostension, and Hypostasis"], 139ff., 145 [Chapter 24].

2. Gottlob Frege, "Über Sinn und Bedeutung," *Zeitschrift fur Philosophie und philosophische Kritik* 100 (1892), pp. 22–50. Translated in *Translations from the Philosophical Writings of Gottlob Frege* (Oxford: Blackwell, 1952).

context simply to refer to its object. Occurrences within quotation are not in general referential; e.g., the statements:

(9)   'Cicero' contains six letters,

(10)   '9 > 5' contains just three characters

say nothing about the statesman Cicero or the number 9. Frege's criterion for referential occurrence is substitutivity of identity. Since

(11)   Tully = Cicero,

(12)   the number of planets = 9,

whatever is true of Cicero is true *ipso facto* of Tully (these being one and the same) and whatever is true of 9 is true of the number of planets. If by putting 'Tully' for 'Cicero' or 'the number of planets' for '9' in a truth, e.g., (9) or (10), we come out with a falsehood:

(13)   'Tully' contains six letters,

(14)   'the number of planets > 5' contains just three characters,

we may be sure that the position on which the substitution was made was not purely referential.

(9) must not be confused with:

(15)   Cicero has a six-letter name,

which *does* say something about the man Cicero, and—unlike (9)—remains true when the name 'Cicero' is supplanted by 'Tully.'

Taking a hint from Russell,[3] we may speak of a context as *referentially opaque* when, by putting a statement ϕ into that context, we can cause a purely referential occurrence in ϕ to be not purely referential in the whole context. E.g., the context:

'. . .' contains just three characters

is referentially opaque; for, the occurrence of '9' in '9 > 5' is purely referential, but the occurrence of '9' in (10) is not. Briefly, a context is referentially opaque if it can render a referential occurrence non-referential.

Quotation is the referentially opaque context par excellence. Intuitively, what occurs inside a referentially opaque context may be looked upon as an orthographic accident, without logical status, like the occur-

3. Whitehead and Russell, *Principia Mathematica*, 2d ed., vol. 1, Appendix C.

rence of 'cat' in 'cattle.' The quotational context "9 > 5" of the statement '9 > 5' has, perhaps, unlike the context 'cattle' of 'cat,' a deceptively systematic air which tempts us to think of its parts as somehow logically germane. Insofar as this temptation exists, it is salutary to paraphrase quotations by the following expedient. We may adopt names for each of our letters and other characters, and Tarski's '⌢' to express concatenation. Then, instead of naming a notational form by putting that notational form itself bodily between quotation marks, we can name it by spelling it. E.g., since 'μ' is mu, 'ε' is epsilon, and 'ν' is nu, the word '$\mu\varepsilon\nu$' is mu⌢epsilon⌢nu. Similarly the statement '9 > 5' is n⌢g⌢f, if we adopt the letters 'n,' 'g,' and 'f' as names of the characters '9,' '>', and '5.' The example (10) can thus be transcribed as:

(16)   n⌢g⌢f contains just three characters.

Here there is no non-referential occurrence of the numeral '9,' for there is no occurrence of it all; and here there is no referentially opaque containment of one statement by another, because there is no contained statement at all. Paraphrasing (10) into (16), so as to get rid altogether of the opaquely contained statement '9 > 5,' is like paraphrasing 'cattle' into 'kine' so as to rid it of the merely orthographic occurrence of the term 'cat.' Neither paraphrase is mandatory, but both are helpful when the irreferential occurrences draw undue attention.

An occurrence of a statement as a part of a longer statement is called *truth-functional* if, whenever we supplant the contained statement by another statement having the same truth value, the containing statement remains unchanged in truth value. Naturally one would not expect occurrences of statements within referentially opaque contexts, such as quotations, to be truth-functional. E.g., the truth (10) becomes false when the contained statement '9 > 5' is supplanted by another, 'Napoleon escaped from Elba,' which has the same truth value as '9 > 5.' Again the truth (1) is carried, by that same substitution, into the falsehood (3). One might not expect occurrences of statements within statements to be truth-functional, in general, even when the contexts are not referentially opaque; certainly not when the contexts are referentially opaque.

In mathematical logic, however, a policy of *extensionality* is widely espoused: a policy of admitting statements within statements truth-functionally only (apart of course from such contexts as quotation, which are referentially opaque). Note that the semantical predicate 'Nec' as of (1)–(3) is reconcilable with this policy of extensionality, since whatever breach of extensionality it *prima facie* involves is shared by examples like (10) and attributable to the referential opacity of quotation. We can always switch to the spelling expedient, thus rewriting (1) as:

(17)   Nec (n⌢g⌢f).

(17), like (16) and indeed (2) and unlike (1) and (3), contains no component statement but only a name of a statement.

The statement operator 'nec,' on the other hand, is a premeditated departure from extensionality. The occurrence of the truth '9 > 5' in (4) is non-truth-functional, since by supplanting it by a different truth we can turn the true context (4) into a falsehood such as (5). Such occurrences, moreover, are not looked upon as somehow spurious or irrelevant to logical structure, like occurrences in quotation or like 'cat' in 'cattle.' On the contrary, the modal logic typified in (4) is usually put forward as a corrective of extensionality, a needed supplementation of an otherwise impoverished logic. Truth-functional occurrence is by no means the rule in ordinary language, as witness occurrences of statements governed by 'because,' 'thinks that,' 'wishes that,' etc., as well as 'necessarily.' Modal logicians, adopting 'nec,' have seen no reason to suppose that an adequate logic might adhere to a policy of extensionality.

But, for all the willingness of modal logicians to flout the policy of extensionality, is there really any difference—on the score of extensionality—between their statement operator 'nec' and the extensionally quite admissible semantical predicate 'Nec'? The latter was excusable, within a policy of extensionality, by citing the referential opacity of quotation. But the statement operator 'nec' is likewise excusable, within a policy of extensionality, by citing the referential opacity of 'nec' itself! To see the referential opacity of 'nec' we have only to note that (4) and (12) are true and yet this is false:

(18)   nec (the number of planets > 5).

The statement operator 'nec' is, in short, on a part with quotation. (1) happens to be written with quotation marks and (4) without, but from the point of view of a policy of extensionality one is no worse than the other. (1) might be preferable to (4) only on the score of a possible ancillary policy of trying to reduce referentially opaque contexts to uniformly quotational form.

Genuine violation of the extensionality policy, by admitting non-truth-functional occurrences of statements within statements *without* referential opacity, is less easy than one at first supposes. Extensionality does not merely recommend itself on the score of simplicity and convenience; it rests on somewhat more compelling grounds, as the following argument will reveal. Think of 'p' as short for some statement, and think of '$F(p)$' as short for some containing true statement, such that the context represented by 'F' is not referentially opaque. Suppose further that the context represented by 'F' is such that logical equivalents are interchangeable, within it, *salvâ veritate*. (This is true in particular of 'nec.') What I shall show is that the occurrence of 'p' in '$F(p)$' is then truth-functional. I.e., think of 'q' as short for some statement having the same truth value as 'p'; I shall show that '$F(q)$' is, like '$F(p)$', true.

What 'p' represents is a statement, hence true or false (and devoid of free 'x'). If 'p' is true, then the conjunction '$x = \Lambda \,.\, p$' is true if one and only one object x, viz., the empty class Λ; whereas if 'p' is false the conjunction '$x = \Lambda \,.\, p$' is true of no object x whatever. The class $\hat{x}(x = \Lambda \,.\, p)$, therefore, is the unit class $\iota\Lambda$ or Λ itself according as 'p' is true or false. Moreover, the equation:

$$\hat{x}(x = \Lambda \,.\, p) = \iota\Lambda$$

is, by the above considerations, *logically* equivalent to 'p'. Then, since '$F(p)$' is true and logical equivalents are interchangeable within it, this will be true:

(19) $F[\hat{x}(x = \Lambda \,.\, p) = \iota\Lambda]$.

Since 'p' and 'q' are alike in truth value, the classes $\hat{x}(x = \Lambda \,.\, p)$ and $\hat{x}(x = \Lambda \,.\, q)$ are both $\iota\Lambda$ or both Λ; so

(20) $\hat{x}(x = \Lambda \,.\, p) = \hat{x}(x = \Lambda \,.\, q)$.

Since the context represented by 'F' is not referentially opaque, the occurrence of '$\hat{x}(x = \Lambda \,.\, p)$' in (19) is a purely referential occurrence and hence subject to the substitutivity of identity; so from (19) by (20) we can conclude that

$F[\hat{x}(x = \Lambda \,.\, q) = \iota\Lambda]$.

Thence in turn, by the logical equivalence of '$\hat{x}(x = \Lambda \,.\, q) = \iota\Lambda$' to '$q$', we conclude that $F(q)$.

The above argument cannot be evaded by denying (20), as long as the notation in (20) is construed, as usual, as referring to classes. For classes, properly so-called, are one and the same if their members are the same—regardless of whether that sameness be a matter of logical proof or of historical accident. But the argument could be contested by one who does not admit class names '$\hat{x}(\ldots)$.' It could also be contested by one who, though admitting such class names, does not see a final criterion of referential occurrence in the substitutivity of identity, as applied to constant singular terms. These points will come up, perforce, when we turn to 'nec' as a sentence operator under quantification. Meanwhile the above argument does serve to show that the policy of extensionality has more behind it than its obvious simplicity and convenience, and that any real departure from the policy (at least where logical equivalents remain interchangeable) must involve revisions of the logic of singular terms.

The simpler earlier argument for the referential opacity of the statement operator 'nec,' viz., observation of the truths (4) and (12) and the falsehood (18), could likewise be contested by one who either repudiates constant singular terms or questions the criterion of referential opacity which involves them. Short of adopting 'nec' as a full-fledged *sentence* operator, however, no such searching revisions of classical mathematical logic are required. We can keep to a classical theory of classes and singular terms, and even to a policy of extensionality. We have only to recognize, in the *statement* operator 'nec,' a referentially opaque context comparable to the thoroughly legitimate and very convenient context of quotation. We can even look upon (4) and (5) as elliptical renderings of (1) and (3).

II

Something very much to the purpose of the semantical predicate 'Nec' is regularly needed in the theory of proof. When, e.g., we speak of the completeness of a deductive system of quantification theory, we have in mind some concept of *validity* as norm with which to compare the class of obtainable theorems. The notion of validity in such contexts is not identifiable with truth. A true statement is not a valid statement of quantification theory unless not only it but all other statements similar to it in quantificational structure are true. Definition of such a notion of validity presents no problem, and the importance of the notion for proof theory is incontestable.

A conspicuous derivative of the notion of quantificational validity is that of quantificational implication. One statement quantificationally implies another if the material conditional composed of the two statements is valid for quantification theory.

This reference to quantification theory is only illustrative. There are parallels for truth-function theory: a statement is valid for truth-function theory if it and all statements like it in truth-functional structure are true, and one statement truth-functionally implies another if the material conditional formed of the two statements is valid for truth-function theory.

And there are parallels, again, for logic taken as a whole: a statement is logically valid if it and all statements like it in logical structure are true, and one statement logically implies another if the material conditional formed of the two statements is logically valid.

Modal logic received special impetus years ago from a confused reading of '⊃', the material 'if–then,' as 'implies': a confusion of the material conditional with the relation of implication.[4] Properly, whereas '⊃' or 'if–then' connects statements, 'implies' is a verb which connects names *of* statements and thus expresses a relation of the named statements. Carelessness over the distinction of use and mention having allowed this intrusion of 'implies' as a reading of '⊃', the protest thereupon arose that '⊃' in its material sense was too weak to do justice to 'implies,' which connotes something like logical implication. Accordingly an effort was made to repair the discrepancy by introducing an improved substitute for '⊃', written '⥽' and called strict implication.[5] The initial failure to distinguish use from mention persisted; so '⥽', though read 'implies' and motivated by the connotations of the word 'implies,' functioned actually not as a verb but as a statement connective, a much strengthened 'if–then.' Finally, in recognition of the fact that logical implication is validity of the material conditional, a validity operator 'nec' was adopted to implement the definition of '$p \dashv 3\, q$' as 'nec $(p \supset q)$.' Since '⥽' had been left at the level of a statement connective, 'nec' in turn was of course rendered as an operator directly attachable to statements—whereas 'is valid,' properly, is a verb attachable to a name of a statement and expressing an attribute of the statement named.[6]

In any event, the use of 'nec' as statement operator is easily converted

---

4. Notably in Whitehead and Russell, *Principia Mathematica*.

5. Lewis, *A Survey of Symbolic Logic*, Chapter 5.

6. On the concerns of this paragraph and the next, see also §69 of Carnap, *Logical Syntax*, and §5 of my *Mathematical Logic*.

into use of 'Nec' as semantical predicate. We have merely to supply quotation marks, thus rewriting (4) and (5) as (1) and (3). The strong 'if–then,' '$\dashv$' can correspondingly be rectified to a relation of implication properly so-called. What had been:

(21)   the witness lied $\dashv$. the witness lied $\lor$ the owner is liable,

explained as:

(22)   nec (the witness lied $\supset$. the witness lied $\lor$ the owner is liable),

becomes:

(23)   'the witness lied' implies 'the witness lied $\lor$ the owner is liable,'

explained as:

(24)   Nec 'the witness lied $\supset$. the witness lied $\lor$ the owner is liable.'

Typically, in modal logic, laws are expressed with help of schematic letters 'p', 'q', etc., thus:

(25) $p \dashv. p \lor q$,

(26)   nec $(p \supset. p \lor q)$.

The schematic letters are to be thought of as supplanted by any specific statements so as to yield actual cases like (21) and (22). Now just as (21) and (22) are translatable into (23) and (24), so the schemata (25) and (26) themselves might be supposed translatable as:

(27)   'p' implies '$p \lor q$',

(28)   Nec '$p \supset. p \lor q$'.

Here, however, we must beware of a subtle confusion. A quotation names precisely the expression inside it; a quoted 'p' names the sixteenth letter of the alphabet and nothing else. Thus whereas (25) and (26) are schemata or diagrams which depict the forms of actual statements, such as (21) and (22), on the other hand (27) and (28) are *not* schemata depicting the forms of actual statements such as (23) and (24). On the contrary, (27) and (28) are not schemata at all, but actual statements: statements *about* the specific schemata 'p', '$p \lor q$,' and '$p \supset. p \lor q$' (with just those letters). Moreover, the predicates 'implies' and 'Nec' have thus far been looked upon as true only of statements, not of schemata; so in

(27) and (28) they are misapplied (pending some deliberate extension of usage).

The letters 'p' and 'q' in (25) and (26) stand in place of statements. For translation of (25) and (26) into semantical form, on the other hand, we need some special variables which refer *to* statements and thus stand in place of names of statements. Let us use 'ϕ', 'ψ', etc., for that purpose. Then the analogues of (25) and (26) in semantical form can be rendered:

(29) ϕ implies the alternation of ϕ and ψ,

(30)   Nec (the conditional of ϕ with the alternation of ϕ and ψ).

We can condense (29) and (30) by use of a conventional notation which I have elsewhere[7] called *quasi-quotation*, thus:

(31) ϕ implies $\ulcorner \phi \vee \psi \urcorner$,

(32)   Nec $\ulcorner \phi \supset . \phi \vee \psi \urcorner$.

The relationship between the modal logic of statement operators and the semantical approach, which was pretty simple and obvious when we compared (21)–(22) with (23)–(24), is thus seen to take on some slight measure of subtlety at the stage of (25)–(26); these correspond not to (27)–(28) but to (31)–(32). It is schemata like (25)–(26), moreover, and not actual statements like (21)–(22), that fill the pages of works on modal logic. However, be that as it may, it is in actual statements such as (21)–(24) that the point of modal logic lies, and it is the comparison of (21)–(22) with (23)–(24) that reflects the true relationship between the use of statement operators and that of semantical predicates. Schemata such as (25)–(26) are mere heuristic devices, useful in expounding the theory of (21)–(22) and their like; and the heuristic devices which bear similarly on (23)–(24) are (31)–(32).

Seeing how modal statement operators can be converted into semantical predicates, one may of course just note the conversion as a principle and leave it undone in practice. But there are five reasons why it is important to note it in principle. One is that the inclination to condemn '$\supset$' unduly, through a wrong association of 'if-then' with 'implies,' is thereby removed. A second reason is that it is at the semantical or proof-theoretic level, where we talk *about* expressions and their truth values under various substitutions, that we make clear and useful sense of logi-

7. *Mathematical Logic*, §6.

cal validity; and it is logical validity that comes nearest to being a clear explication of 'Nec,' taken as a semantical predicate. A third reason is that in using 'Nec' as a semantical predicate we flaunt a familiar reminder of referential opacity, in the form of quotation marks. A fourth reason is that the adoption of 'nec' as a statement operator tempts one to go a step further and use it as a sentence operator subject to quantification. The momentousness of this further step—whereof more anon—tends to be overlooked save as one expressly conceives of the 'nec,' in its use as statement operator, as shorthand for the semantical usage.

A fifth reason has to do with iteration. Since 'nec' attaches to a statement and produces a statement, 'nec' can then be applied again. On the other hand 'Nec' attaches to a name and yields a statement, to which, therefore, it cannot be applied again. An iterated 'nec,' e.g.:

(33)   nec nec$(x)(x$ is red $\supset x$ is red),

can of course be translated by our regular procedure into semantical form thus:

(34)   Nec 'Nec '$(x)(x$ is red $\supset x$ is red)' ',

and we are thereby reminded that 'Nec' can indeed be iterated if we insert new quotation marks as needed. But the fact remains that (34) is, in contrast with (33), an unlikely move. For, suppose we have made fair sense of 'Nec' as logical validity, relative say to the logic of truth functions, quantification, and perhaps classes. The statement:

(35) $(x)(x$ is red $\supset x$ is red),

then, is typical of the statements to which we would attribute such validity; so

(36)   Nec '$(x)(x$ is red $\supset x$ is red)'.

The validity of (35) resides in the fact that (35) is true and so are all other statements with the same quantificational and truth-functional structure as (35). Thus it is that (36) is *true*. But if (36) in turn is also *valid*, it is valid only in an extended sense with which we are not likely to have been previously concerned: a sense involving not only quantificational and truth-functional structure but also the semantical structure, somehow, of quotation and 'Nec' itself.

Ordinarily we work in a metalanguage, as in (36), treating of an object language, exemplified by (35). We would not rise to (34) except in the rare case where we want to treat the metalanguage by means of itself, and want furthermore to extend the notion of validity beyond the semantics of logic to the semantics of semantics. When on the other hand the statement operator 'nec' is used, iteration as in (33) is the most natural of steps; and it is significant that in modal logic there has been some question as to just what might most suitably be postulated regarding such iteration.[8]

The iterations need not of course be consecutive. In the use of modal statement operators we are led also into complex iterations such as:

(37) $p \dashv q . \dashv . \sim q \dashv \sim p$,

short for:

(38) nec [nec $(p \supset q) \supset$ nec $(\sim q \supset \sim p)$].

Or, to take an actual example:

(39) $(x)(x$ has mass$) \dashv (\exists x)(x$ has mass$) . \dashv .$
  $\sim (\exists x)(x$ has mass$) \dashv \sim (x)(x$ has mass$)$,

(40) nec {nec $[(x)(x$ has mass$) \supset (\exists x)(x$ has mass$)] \supset$
  nec $[\sim(\exists x)(x$ has mass$) \supset \sim (x)(x$ has mass$)]$}.

In terms of semantical predicates the correspondents of (39) and (40) are:

(41) "'$(x)(x$ has mass)' implies '$(\exists x)(x$ has mass)'" implies
  "'$\sim(\exists x)(x$ has mass)' implies '$\sim(x)(x$ has mass)'",

(42) Nec 'Nec '$(x)(x$ has mass$) \supset (\exists x)(x$ has mass$)$' $\supset$
  Nec '$\sim(\exists x)(x$ has mass$) \supset \sim (x)(x$ has mass$)$'".

But (41)–(42), like (34), have singularly little interest or motivation when we think of necessity semantically.

It is important to note that we must not translate the schemata (37)–(38) into semantical form in the manner:

  "'p' implies 'q'" implies, etc.

To do so would be to compound, to an altogether horrifying degree, the

8. See Lewis and Langford, *Symbolic Logic,* pp. 497ff.

error noted earlier of equating (25)–(26) to (27)–(28). The analogues of (37)–(38) in semantical application should be rendered rather:

(43) $\ulcorner\phi$ implies $\psi\urcorner$ implies $\ulcorner\ulcorner{\sim}\psi\urcorner$ implies $\ulcorner{\sim}\phi\urcorner\urcorner$,

(44)   Nec $\ulcorner$Nec $\ulcorner\phi \supset \psi\urcorner \supset$ Nec $\ulcorner{\sim}\psi \supset {\sim}\phi\urcorner\urcorner$,

subject to some special conventions governing the nesting of quasi-quotations. Such conventions would turn on certain subtle consider-ations which will not be entered upon here. Suffice it to recall that the sort of thing formulated in (33)–(34) and (37)–(44) is precisely the sort of thing we are likely to see least point in formulating when we think of necessity strictly as a semantical predicate rather than a statement opera-tor. It is impressive and significant that *most* of modal logic (short of quantified modal logic, to which we shall soon turn) is taken up with it-erated cases like (33) and (37)–(40) which would simply not recommend themselves to our attention if necessity were held to the status of a se-mantical predicate and not depressed to the level of a statement op-erator.

Our reflections have favored the semantical side immensely, but they must not be allowed to obscure the fact that even as a semantical predi-cate necessity can raise grave questions. There is no difficulty as long as necessity is construed as validity relative say to the logic of truth func-tions and quantification and perhaps classes. If we think of arithmetic as reduced to class theory, then such validity covers also the truths of arith-metic. But one tends to include further territory still; cases such as 'No bachelor is married,' whose truth is supposed to depend on "meanings of terms" or on "synonymy" (e.g., the synonymy of 'bachelor' and 'man not married'). The synonymy relation on which such cases depend is supposedly a narrower relation than that of the mere coextensiveness of terms, and it is not known to be amenable to any satisfactory analy-sis. In short, necessity in semantical application tends to be identified with what philosophers call analyticity; and analyticity, I have argued elsewhere,[9] is a pseudo-concept which philosophy would be better off without.

As long as necessity in semantical application is construed simply as explicit truth-functional validity, on the other hand, or quantificational validity, or set-theoretic validity, or validity of any other well-determined kind, the logic of the semantical necessity predicate is a significant and

9. "Two Dogmas of Empiricism" [Chapter 2].

very central strand of proof theory. But it is not modal logic, even un-quantified modal logic, as the latter ordinarily presents itself; for it is a remarkably meager thing, bereft of all the complexities which are en-couraged by the use of 'nec' as a statement operator. It is unquantified modal logic minus all principles which, explicitly or implicitly (via '⤳', etc.), involve iteration of necessity; and plus, if we are literal-minded, a pair of quotation marks after each 'Nec.'

III

Having adopted the operator '~' of negation as applicable to state-ments, one applies it without second thought to open sentences as well: sentences containing free variables ripe for quantification. Thus we can write not only '~(Socrates is mortal)' but also '~(x is mortal),' from which, by quantification and further negation, we have '~(x) ~(x is mortal)' or briefly '($\exists x$)(x is mortal).' With negation this is as it should be. As long as 'nec' is used as a statement operator, on a par with nega-tion, the analogous course suggests itself again: we write not only 'nec $(9 > 5)$' but also 'nec $(x > 5)$,' from which by quantification we can form (6)–(8) and the like.

This step brings us to 'nec' as sentence operator. Given 'nec' as state-ment operator, the step is natural. Yet it is a drastic one, for it suddenly obstructs the earlier expedient of translation into terms of 'Nec' as se-mantical predicate. We can reconstrue (4) and (5) at will as (1) and (3), but we cannot reconstrue:

(45)   nec $(x > 5)$

correspondingly as:

(46)   Nec '$x > 5$'.

'Nec' has been understood up to now as a predicate true only of state-ments, whereas (46) attributes it rather to an open sentence and is thus trivially false, at least pending some deliberate extension of usage. More important, whereas (45) is an open sentence with free 'x', (46) has no corresponding generality; (46) is simply a statement *about* a specific open sentence. For, it must be remembered that '$x > 5$' in quotation marks is a name of the specific quoted expression, with fixed letter 'x'. The 'x' in (46) cannot be reached by a quantifier. To write:

(47) $(x)(\text{Nec } 'x > 5')$, $(\exists x)(\text{Nec } 'x > 5')$

is like writing:

(48) $(x)(\text{Socrates is mortal})$, $(\exists x)(\text{Socrates is mortal})$;

the quantifier is followed by no germane occurrence of its variable. In a word, necessity as sentence operator does not go over into terms of necessity as semantical predicate.

Moreover, acceptance of necessity as a sentence operator implies an attitude quite opposite to our earlier one (in §§I–II above), which was that 'nec' as statement operator is referentially opaque. For, one would clearly have no business quantifying into a referentially opaque context; witness (47) above. We can reasonably infer '$(\exists x)$ nec $(x > 5)$' from 'nec $(9 > 5)$' only if we regard the latter as telling us something about the *object* 9, a number, viz. that it necessarily exceeds 5. If 'nec $(\ldots > 5)$' can turn out true or false "of" the number 9 depending merely on how that number is referred to (as the falsity of (18) suggests), then evidently 'nec $(x > 5)$' expresses no genuine condition on objects of any kind. If the occurrence of '9' in 'nec $(9 > 5)$' is not purely referential, then putting 'x' for '9' in 'nec $(9 > 5)$' makes no more sense than putting 'x' for 'nine' within the context 'canine.'

But isn't it settled by the truth of (4) and (12) and the falsity of (18) that the occurrence of '9' in question is irreferential, and more generally that 'nec' is referentially opaque, and hence that 'nec' as a sentence operator under quantifiers is a mistake? No, not if one is prepared to accede to certain pretty drastic departures, as we shall see.

Thus far we have tentatively condemned necessity as general sentence operator on the ground that 'nec' is referentially opaque. Its referential opacity has been shown by a breakdown in the operation of putting one constant singular term for another which names the same object. But it may justly be protested that constant singular terms are a notational accident, not needed at the level of primitive notation.

For it is well known that primitively nothing in the way of singular terms is needed except the variables of quantification themselves. Derivatively all manner of singular terms may be introduced by contextual definition in conformity with Russell's theory of singular descriptions. Class names, in particular, which figured in the general argument for extensionality in §I above, may be got either by explaining '$\hat{x}(\ldots)$' as short for the contextually defined description '$(\imath y)(x)(x \; \varepsilon \; y \; . \; \equiv \; \dots \;)$' or by adopting a separate set of contextual definitions for the purpose.[10]

Now the modal logician intent on quantifying into 'nec' sentences may say that 'nec' is not referentially opaque, but that it merely interferes somewhat with the contextual definition of singular terms. He may argue that '$(\exists x)$ nec $(x > 5)$' is not meaningless but true, and in particular that the number 9 is one of the things of which 'nec $(x > 5)$' is true. He may blame the real or apparent discrepancy in truth value between (4) and (18) simply on a queer behavior of contextually defined singular terms. Specifically he may hold that (18) is true if construed as:

(49) $(\exists x)$[there are exactly x planets . nec $(x > 5)$]

and false if construed as:

(50)   nec $(\exists x)$(there are exactly x planets . $x > 5$),

and that (18) as it stands is ambiguous for lack of a distinguishing mark favoring (49) or (50).[11] No such ambiguity arises in the contextual definition of a singular term in extensional logic (as long as the named object exists), and our modal logician may well deplore the complications which thus issue from the presence of 'nec' in his primitive notation. Still he can fairly protest that the erratic behavior of contextually defined singular terms is no reflection on the meaningfulness of his primitive notation, including his open 'nec' sentences and his quantification of them.

Looking upon quantification as fundamental, and constant singular terms as contextually defined, one must indeed concede the inconclusiveness of a criterion of referential opacity that rests on interchanges of constant singular terms. The objects of a theory are not properly describable as the things named by the singular terms; they are the values, rather, of the variables of quantification.[12] Fundamentally the proper criterion of referential opacity turns on quantification rather than naming, and is this: a referentially opaque context is one that cannot properly be *quantified into* (with quantifier outside the context and variable inside). Quo-

10. See my *Methods of Logic* (New York: Holt, 1950; rev. eds., 1959, 1972), §§36–38 (3rd ed., §§41–43); *Mathematical Logic*, §§24, 26.

11. Thus A. F. Smullyan, "Modality and Description," *Journal of Symbolic Logic* 13 (1948), pp. 31–37.

12. See *From a Logical Point of View*, pp. 12ff. [Chapter 2], 75–76, 102–110, 113ff., 148ff. [Chapter 33].

tation, again, is the referentially opaque context par excellence; cf. (47). However, to object to necessity as sentence operator on the grounds of referential opacity so defined would be simply the beg the question.

Frege's criterion of referential occurrence, viz., substitutivity of identity, underlay the notion of referential opacity as developed in §I above. The statements of identity there concerned were formed of constant singular terms; cf. (11), (12). But there is a more fundamental form of the law of substitutivity of identity, which involves no constant singular terms, but only variables of quantification; viz.:

$$(51) \quad (x)(y)(x = y \mathbin{.} \supset. Fx \equiv Fy).$$

This law is independent of any theory of singular terms, and cannot properly be challenged. For, to challenge it were simply to use the sign '=' in some unaccustomed way irrelevant to our inquiry. In any theory, whatever the shapes of its symbols, an open sentence whose free variables are 'x' and 'y' is an expression of identity only in case it fulfills (51) in the role of '$x = y$.' The generality of 'F' in (51) is this: 'Fx' is to be interpretable as any open sentence of the system in question, having 'x' as free (quantifiable) variable; and 'Fy', of course, is to be a corresponding context of 'y'.

If 'nec' is not referentially opaque, 'Fx' and 'Fy' in (51) can in particular be taken respectively as 'nec $(x = x)$' and 'nec $(x = y)$.' From (51), therefore, since surely 'nec $(x = x)$' is true for all x, we have:

$$(52) \quad (x)(y)[x = y \mathbin{.} \supset \text{nec } (x = y)].$$

I.e., identity holds necessarily if it holds at all.

Let us not jump to the conclusion, just because (12) is true, that

$$(53) \quad \text{nec (the number of planets} = 9).$$

This does not follow from (12) and (52) except with help of a law of universal instantiation, allowing us to put singular terms 'the number of planets' and '9' for the universally quantified 'x' and 'y' of (52). Such instantiation is allowable, certainly, in extensional logic; but it is a question of good behavior of constant singular terms, and we have lately observed that such behavior is not to be counted on when there is a 'nec' in the woodpile.

So our observations on necessity in quantificational application are, up to now, as follows. Necessity in such application is not *prima facie* absurd if we accept some interference in the contextual definition of singular terms. The effect of this interference is that constant singular terms cannot be manipulated with the customary freedom, even when their objects exist. In particular they cannot be used to instantiate universal quantifications, unless special supporting lemmas are at hand. A further effect of necessity in quantificational application is that objects come to be necessarily identical if identical at all.

There is yet a further consequence, and a particularly striking one: Aristotelian essentialism. This is the doctrine that some of the attributes of a thing (quite independently of the language in which the thing is referred to, if at all) may be essential to the thing, and others accidental. E.g., a man, or talking animal, or featherless biped (for they are in fact all the same *things*), is essentially rational and accidentally two-legged and talkative, not merely qua man but qua itself. More formally, what Aristotelian essentialism says is that you can have open sentences—which I shall represent here as 'Fx' and 'Gx'—such that

(54) $(\exists x)(\text{nec } Fx \,.\, Gx \,.\, \sim \text{nec } Gx).$

An example of (54) related to the falsity of (53) might be:

$(\exists x)[\text{nec}(x > 5) \,.\, \text{there are just } x \text{ planets} \,.$
$\sim \text{nec (there are just } x \text{ planets)}],$

such an object x being the number (by whatever name) which is variously known as 9 and the number of planets.

How Aristotelian essentialism as above formulated is required by quantified modal logic can be quickly shown. Actually something yet stronger can be shown: that there are open sentences 'Fx' and 'Gx' fulfilling not merely (54) but:

$(x)(\text{nec } Fx \,.\, Gx \,.\, \sim \text{nec } Gx),$

i.e.:

$(x) \text{ nec } Fx \,.\, (x) \, Gx \,.\, (x) \sim \text{nec } Gx.$

An appropriate choice of 'Fx' is easy: '$x = x$.' And an appropriate choice of 'Gx' is '$x = x \,.\, p$,' where in place of 'p' any statement is chosen which is true but not necessarily true. Surely there *is* such a statement, for otherwise 'nec' would be a vacuous operator and there would be no point in modal logic.

Necessity as semantical predicate reflects a non-Aristotelian view of necessity: necessity resides in the way in which we say things, and not in the things we talk about. Necessity as statement operator is capable, we saw, of being reconstrued in terms of necessity as a semantical predicate, but has, nevertheless, its special dangers; it makes for an excessive and idle elaboration of laws of iterated modality, and it tempts one to a final plunge into quantified modality. This last complicates the logic of singular terms; worse, it leads us back into the metaphysical jungle of Aristotelian essentialism.

CREDITS

Chapter 1

First published in O. H. Lee, ed., *Philosophical Essays for A. N. Whitehead* (New York: Longmans, 1936), 90–124. It appears in H. Feigl and W. Sellars, eds., *Readings in Philosophical Analysis* (New York: Appleton, 1949), and in P. Benacerraf and H. Putnam, eds., *Readings in the Philosophy of Mathematics* (Englewood, N.J.: Prentice-Hall, 1964). The revised version of the essay that has been reproduced here first appeared in W. V. Quine, *The Ways of Paradox* (New York: Random House, 1966; and Cambridge, Mass.: Harvard University Press, 1976), 77–106. Reprinted by permission of Harvard University Press.

Chapter 2

Originally published in the *Philosophical Review* (January 1951). Reprinted in revised form in W. V. Quine, *From a Logical Point of View* (Cambridge, Mass.: Harvard University Press, 1953), 20–46. Reprinted by permission of Harvard University Press.

Chapter 3

Originally published in *The Canadian Journal of Philosophy* (1991), 21. Copyright ©1991 by The Canadian Journal of Philosophy. Reprinted by permission of The Canadian Journal of Philosophy.

Chapter 4

Written early in 1954 for P. A. Schilpp, ed., *The Philosophy of Rudolf Carnap* (La Salle, Ill.: Open Court, 1963) at the request of the editor. It appeared in Italian translation in *Rivista di Filosofia*, 1957, and selected portions amounting to somewhat less than half appeared also in Sidney Hook, ed., *American Philosophers at Work* (New York: Criterion, 1956). Its first appearance whole in English was in the Carnap jubilee issue of *Synthèse* (vol. 12, 1960), which was subsequently reissued as a book: B. H. Kazemier and D. Vuysje, eds., *Logic and Language* (Dordrecht: D. Reidel, 1962). Reprinted with the permission of D. Reidel Publishing Company for its inclusion in W. V. Quine, *The Ways of Paradox* (New York: Random House, 1966; and Cambridge, Mass.: Harvard University Press, 1976), 107–132. Reprinted with the permission of Harvard University Press.

Chapter 5
Originally published in 1958 in the *Proceedings and Addresses of The American Philosophical Association,* 31 (1958), 5–22. Reprinted with the permission of the American Philosophical Association.

Chapter 6
Originally published in W. V. Quine, *Pursuit of Truth* (Cambridge, Mass.: Harvard University Press, 1990), 23–36. Reprinted with the permission of Harvard University Press.

Chapter 7
Originally published in W. V. Quine, *Word and Object* (Cambridge, Mass.: MIT Press, 1960), 26–79. © 1960 by MIT Press. Reprinted with the permission of MIT Press.

Chapter 8
Originally published in *The Journal of Philosophy,* XCIII, 4 (April 1996), 159–163. © 1996 by *The Journal of Philosophy.* Reprinted with the permission of The Journal of Philosophy.

Chapter 9
Originally published in the *Review of Metaphysics* in 1948, earlier versions having been presented as lectures at Princeton and Yale in March and May of that year. The paper lent its title to a symposium at the joint session of the Aristotelian Society and the Mind Association at Edinburgh, July 1951, and was reprinted, along with the animadversions of the symposiasts, in the Aristotelian Society's supplementary volume *Freedom, Language, and Reality* (London: Harrison, 1951). It is reprinted also in Linsky's anthology. The revised version reproduced here first appeared in W. V. Quine, *From a Logical Point of View* (Cambridge, Mass.: Harvard University Press, 1953), 1–19. Reprinted with the permission of Harvard University Press.

Chapter 10
Originally presented as an invited address in one of the Bicentennial Conferences at Columbia University, October 1954, and published with the editor's revisions in Lewis Leary, ed., *The Unity of Knowledge* (New York: Doubleday, 1955). The original text appeared afterward in the *British Journal for the Phi-*

losophy of Science, 1957. Reprinted in W. V. Quine, *The Ways of Paradox* (New York: Random House, 1966; and Cambridge, Mass.: Harvard University Press, 1976), 228–245, with negligible emendations, with the permission of the Columbia University trustees and with the approval of the editor of the *British Journal*.

Chapter 11
Written in 1960 for J. H. Woodger's seventieth birthday. In company with other such papers, it appeared in *Synthèse* (vol. 15, 1963), and afterward in J. R. Gregg and F. T. C. Harris, eds., *Form and Strategy in Science* (Dordrecht: D. Reidel, 1964). Reprinted in an enlarged and revised form with the permission of D. Reidel Publishing Company for its inclusion in W. V. Quine, *The Ways of Paradox* (New York: Random House, 1966; and Cambridge, Mass.: Harvard University Press, 1976), 255–258. Reprinted with the permission of Harvard University Press.

Chapter 12
Originally published in W. V. Quine, *Word and Object* (Cambridge, Mass.: MIT Press, 1960), 233–248. © 1960 by MIT Press. Reprinted with the permission of MIT Press.

Chapter 13
This originally took shape from several papers and lectures. It was published for the first time in W. V. Quine, *Theories and Things* (Cambridge, Mass.: Harvard University Press, 1981), 1–23. Reprinted with the permission of Harvard University Press.

Chapter 14
Part of a paper presented at a colloquium with Rudolf Carnap at the University of Chicago, February 1, 1951. This portion went to *Philosophical Studies* at the editors' request and was published later that year (vol. 2, 1951). Reprinted in W. V. Quine, *The Ways of Paradox* (New York: Random House, 1966; and Cambridge, Mass.: Harvard University Press, 1976), 203–211. Reprinted with the permission of Harvard University Press.

Chapter 15
Originally published in W. V. Quine, *Ontological Relativity and Other Essays* (New York: Columbia University Press, 1969), 69–90. © 1969 by Columbia University Press. Reprinted with the permission of Columbia University Press.

Chapter 16
Originally published in *Dialectica* 49 (1990), 251–261. © 1990 by *Dialectica*. Reprinted with the permission of *Dialectica* and its editor.

Chapter 17
Originally published in Samuel Guttenplan, ed., *Mind and Language* (Oxford: Oxford University Press, 1975), 67–82. © 1975 by Oxford University Press. Reprinted with the permission of Oxford University Press.

Chapter 18
This essay is part of a paper that Quine presented under the title "The Pragmatists' Place in Empiricism" at a symposium at the University of South Carolina in 1975. The paper was published in Robert J. Mulvaney and Philip M. Zeltner, eds., *Pragmatism, Its Sources and Prospects* (Columbia: University of South Carolina Press, 1981); and in W. V. Quine, *Theories and Things* (Cambridge, Mass.: Harvard University Press, 1981), 67–72. Reprinted with the permission of Harvard University Press.

Chapter 19
Presented at Cambridge, Mass., November 18, 1952, in a colloquium of the Institute for the Unity of Science, and published in 1953 in *Contributions to the Analysis and Synthesis of Knowledge,* which was vol. 80 of the *Proceedings* of the American Academy of Arts and Sciences. Reprinted with the permission of the American Academy of Arts and Sciences in W. V. Quine, *The Ways of Paradox* (New York: Random House, 1966; and Cambridge, Mass.: Harvard University Press, 1976), 221–227.

Chapter 20
Originally published in Samuel Guttenplan, ed., *Mind and Language* (Oxford: Oxford University Press, 1975), 83–95. © 1975 by Oxford University Press. Reprinted with the permission of Oxford University Press.

Chapter 21
Originally published in J. Floyd and S. Shieh, eds., *Future Pasts* (New York: Oxford University Press, 2001), 215–221. © 2001 by Oxford University Press. Reprinted with the permission of Oxford University Press.

Chapter 22
This paper appeared in the *Journal of Philosophy* (vol. 53, 1956), summing up some points made in lectures at Harvard and Oxford from 1952 onward. Reprinted in W. V. Quine, *The Ways of Paradox* (New York: Random House, 1966; and Cambridge, Mass.: Harvard University Press, 1976), 185–196. Reprinted with the permission of Harvard University Press.

Chapter 23
Originally published in *Midwest Studies in Philosophy* 2 (1977). Reprinted with the permission of *Midwest Studies in Philosophy* in W. V. Quine, *Theories and*

Things (Cambridge, Mass.: Harvard University Press, 1981), 113–123. Reprinted with the permission of Harvard University Press.

Chapter 24
This essay grew out of a fusion of "Notes on Existence and Necessity," *Journal of Philosophy*, 1943, with "The Problem of Interpreting Modal Logic," *Journal of Symbolic Logic*, 1947. Sundry omissions, revisions, and insertions have been made. The parent article, "Notes on Existence and Necessity," is reproduced in Linsky. It was in the main a translation in turn of portions of W. V. Quine, *O Sentido da nova lógica* (São Paolo, Brazil: Livraria Martins, 1944), which embodied a course of lectures delivered at São Paulo in 1942. Reprinted with the permission of both the *Journal of Philosophy* and the *Journal of Symbolic Logic* in W. V. Quine, *From a Logical Point of View* (Cambridge, Mass.: Harvard University Press, 1953), 139–159.

Chapter 25
Originally published in the *Proceedings of the XIth International Congress of Philosophy*, Brussels, 1953, vol. 14 (Amsterdam: North-Holland). Reprinted with the permission of the North-Holland Publishing Company in W. V. Quine, *The Ways of Paradox* (New York: Random House, 1966; and Cambridge, Mass.: Harvard University Press, 1976), 158–176. Reprinted with the permission of Harvard University Press.

INDEX